MARKETING
REAL
ESTATE

MARKETING REAL ESTATE

William M. Shenkel
University of Georgia

Prentice-Hall, Inc., Englewood Cliffs, N.J. 07632

Library of Congress Cataloging in Publication Data

SHENKEL, WILLIAM MONROE, (date)
  Marketing real estate.

  Includes bibliographical references and index.
  1.–Real estate business. 2.–House selling.
I.–Title.
HD1375.S35789   658.8109133333   79-14770
ISBN 0-13-557488-9

Editorial/production supervision and interior design by Kim Gueterman
Cover design by Saiki & Sprung Design
Manufacturing buyer: Anthony Caruso

©1980 by Prentice-Hall, Inc., Englewood Cliffs, N.J. 07632

Printed in the United States of America

10 9 8 7 6 5 4 3 2 1

PRENTICE-HALL INTERNATIONAL, INC., *London*
PRENTICE-HALL OF AUSTRALIA PTY. LIMITED, *Sydney*
PRENTICE-HALL OF CANADA, LTD., *Toronto*
PRENTICE-HALL OF INDIA PRIVATE LIMITED, *New Delhi*
PRENTICE-HALL OF JAPAN, INC., *Tokyo*
PRENTICE-HALL OF SOUTHEAST ASIA PTE. LTD., *Singapore*
WHITEHALL BOOKS LIMITED, *Wellington, New Zealand*

Contents

Preface

This book fills a void among books available to real estate brokers and their sales associates. Over my 25 years in teaching and practicing real estate, I have found the void to be growing and increasingly serious. Largely because today, the technical demands placed on real estate salespersons are much greater. Consider further the added regulations and complex financial arrangements common to real estate transactions. The competition among salespersons for listings and buyer-prospects, moreover, justifies the highest development of real estate marketing skills.

Accordingly the text divides into four parts, starting with **Part 1 Developing Marketing Skills.** Here the reader is first introduced to *communication* and *listening* skills. The next chapter follows with suggestions on how to *motivate salespersons* and *improve interviewing* skills. Practical aspects are covered in separate chapters on *meeting buyer objections, presenting houses,* and *understanding the sales process.*

Part 2 The Selling Operation begins with a chapter on securing *new listings.* Other chapters focus on the best *advertising practices* (especially for classified ads). *Qualifying the prospect, knowing the product,* and *negotiating and closing.* Attention is especially invited to the chapter on negotiating which explains recommended negotiation practices for real estate salespersons.

The three chapters added in **Part 3** deal with the **sales organization:** *selecting qualified salespersons, incentive plans,* and *sales meetings* are the main topics of these chapters.

Part 4, the last section, covers the **technical aspects of selling** and provides relevant information for the advanced sales associates. Chapter 15 briefly reviews the main *federal regulations affecting real estate brokers.* In Chapter 16, *Understanding Home Ownership,* examples are provided to help deal with renters and others who hope to gain the maximum housing utility. A separate chapter on *condominium sales and residential land* apply marketing techniques to these more specialized properties.

Because the sale frequently depends on the financing plan, a separate chapter develops this important topic. The growing popularity of *home warranties* and *trade-in housing plans* are offered in a separate chapter to help in the more efficient listing and sale of houses, both new and existing. The last chapter on *rental housing* deals mostly with the financial analysis and income tax factors that affect the value of houses bought and sold for strictly investment purposes.

In this undertaking I have benefited from dozens of persons who have submitted comments and materials. For the most part their contribution is acknowledged within the text. However, I am especially indebted to many individuals who reviewed chapters in their area of specialization. For their helpful assistance the author gratefully acknowledges the assistance of *Dr. Richard C. Huseman,* Professor and Head, Department of Management, College of Business Administration, University of Georgia; *Dr. James M. Lahiff,* Assistant Professor, Department of Management, College of Business Administration, University of Georgia; *John R. Clements,* Clements Realty, Phoenix, Arizona; *Gordon French,* Real Estate Marketing Consultant, The Atlanta Journal and Constitution; *Lloyd D. Werner,* Director of Training, E. G. Stassens, Inc., Portland, Oregon; *Edward M. Klein,* Vice President, Morton G. Thalhimer, Inc., Richmond, Virginia; *Elaine Schiff,* Realtor,® of Louisville, Kentucky; *Dr. Cecilia A. Hopkins,* Director, Division of Business, College of San Mateo, San Mateo, California; *Roger J. Karvel,* McLennan Company, Chicago, Illinois; *Lloyd A. Hanford, Jr.,* MAI, San Francisco, California; *Maggie S. Lassetter,* Realtor® of Tallahassee, Florida and Chairman, Florida Real Estate Commission; *John Levinson,* Hill and Company, San Francisco, California; and *Percy E. Wagner,* Chicago, Illinois. Their many contributions materially improved the text and its practical value.

Add to this list others who reviewed selected chapters and made many useful suggestions: *Betty I. McDonald,* Associate Broker, Northside Realty Associates, Atlanta, Georgia and *Dale J. Kreuscher,* Thom and Kreuscher Realty, Union Grove, Wisconsin. The author must also thank two reviewers who read the manuscript in full—*Ginny McCanna* of McCanna Realty, Inc. (Edina, Minnesota) and *Dr. Donald Nielson* of the University of Nebraska. Their comprehensive review helped in completing the final draft.

The conscientious work of my editorial assistant and typist, *Ms. Janice Clark,* deserves special attention. Her attention to detail minimized any possible errors and omissions for which the author assumes final responsibility.

WILLIAM M. SHENKEL

ATHENS, GEORGIA

A Special Note
to the Reader

Your study of real estate marketing and selling should be personally satisfying and financially rewarding. The satisfaction is gained in knowing that an orderly housing market depends on work of the salesperson. Salespersons serve sellers, who want the best price, and buyers, who turn to real estate brokers to find houses meeting their specifications. Your personal effort on behalf of clients and prospects is usually the key to a sale, satisfactory to both buyer and seller.

You will find the study of real estate marketing financially rewarding for several reasons. First, you will not prevail with knowledge of real estate license laws, housing features, and real estate finance alone. Even the salesperson knowledgeable in all of these areas, will increase commissions if selling rules are closely followed. Skilled selling techniques can be learned and practiced by the average person. The chapters in this book have been carefully selected and presented in an order that allows you to progress in each state of the selling process. The successful careers of the many persons who have contributed to this book show the effectiveness of techniques suggested in these chapters.

As you read each chapter turn to the review questions as a study aid. Reread those sections where your answers seem weak. You will find that the questions treat the main topics in each chapter. Note also the illustrations that are taken from numerous sources. Illustrations supplement the text showing that the point raised in the text has practical application. Finally as you develop skills in selling, your increased income, in itself, will show that you have become more efficient in serving the public in buying and selling real estate.

MARKETING
REAL
ESTATE

Part 1

DEVELOPING MARKETING SKILLS

1

Communicating with Prospects

Salespersons are judged by the way they communicate with their buyer-prospects. Communication refers to *verbal* and *nonverbal* communication. It is not only what you say but how you say it, that is, your nonverbal communication which includes your listening skills and questioning techniques. Each of these aspects of communication deserves your close attention.

It is true that you must have a knowledge of real estate license law and the real estate market. It is also true that your communication skills are more important than other factors in successful selling. I recall a real estate broker who showed me an "income property." I had just moved to a new community and wanted to invest in a rental property having a good occupancy rate in a stable neighborhood. The first property shown was a former three-story wood frame house converted to 10 one-bedroom apartments. The property was in a poor state of repair, probably in violation of building and housing codes, and in a declining district. It was almost the opposite of what I wanted. The broker failed to learn my wants with the result that I ended the interview and never returned. Failure to communicate lost a prospect.

THE COMMUNICATION PROCESS

The prospect who telephones in response to one of your classified ads communicates a housing need. But before the communication may be effective, it must satisfy four requirements: (1) It must be heard or received. This requirement emphasizes skills in listening. (2) It must be understood. This aspect covers the act of perceiving, in itself a source of misunderstanding. (3) It must be accepted. That is, the house listed must satisfy qualified prospects. (4) It must be acted upon.

In this process, your ability to fulfill these requirements must be verified through feedback, and listening is the main method of obtaining feedback. Critical listening enables you to achieve your objectives.

Developing Listening Techniques

Consider the common view of the successful salesperson: the stereotype of the glib, persuasive salesperson who can sell an icebox to an eskimo. This view of the well-dressed, high-pressure salesperson has no basis in fact. On the contrary, the most valuable attribute is not the ability to verbalize; it is the ability to center attention on prospects by listening more than by talking.

In this regard, salespersons master effective listening techniques as they master real estate license law. They listen for the purpose of modifying human behavior. They avoid the poor listening habits practiced in our nonprofessional life. Even the most naive recognize that certain listening habits adapt to different roles.

Your listening habits when you watch the television news broadcast are different from those when you talk informally with attractive members of the opposite sex. Each listening role demands various degrees and kinds of involvement. To maximize listening for the present purpose, trained listeners must avoid bad habits acquired from nonselling roles.

Bad Listening Habits. Listening calls for intellectual skills. It is a mistaken idea that the mere determination to listen provides an infallible way to ensure good communication. Favorable results are unattainable unless listening is deliberately developed as a means of communication.

At some time or another we are all guilty of *faking attention.* The boring sermon, the dry lecture, and the dull conversationalist give us much practice in faking attention. If you merely look like a listener, you fail to communicate. This is one certain way of cheating yourself out of a commission since you will not determine your prospect's needs and how he or she reacts to your listings. You will not learn your client's objections if you do not listen. And even though your client digresses, the digression itself will indicate objectives that you will not learn if you do not listen and try to interpret. In other words, your ability to listen can be far more persuasive than your sales presentation but only if you listen sincerely and are not condescending.

Some persons *listen only to memorize facts,* a second bad habit. If you are a "getting at the facts" listener you may not understand a prospect's attitudes and ideas. Your listening should concentrate on remembering facts only long enough to understand your prospect's preferences. By grasping ideas and thoughts, the good listener remembers more effectively than the person who concentrates only on listening for stated facts.

Some persons *avoid difficult listening.* Suppose that after a day of several prospect interviews your remaining task is to qualify a new prospect. During the initial interview you find that it becomes more difficult to listen, your concentration lags, and you avoid listening concentration which guides prospect qualification. You find it increasingly difficult to understand your prospect's needs and you start a downward spiral of listening effectiveness. The end result is a poorly qualified prospect, time wasted in showing the wrong house and worse yet, a prospect lost to another broker.

The best solution is to make a special effort to listen attentively to the more difficult prospect. Some of these interviews will require mental effort to understand the real communication being expressed.

Some persons *fail to listen to "uninteresting" conversation.* It is a mistake not to listen carefully because you have labeled the discussion uninteresting. The danger is that you stop listening prematurely and go into your sales presentation prematurely. This is a habit that can be easily broken by deliberately planning to listen to a number of prospects with all their varying attitudes and needs. Even the most boring prospects will convey critical information about their neighborhoods and housing preferences. You must learn to accept, and quite selfishly, all the boring information so that you can focus on the points that contribute to understanding your customers.

Some persons *fail to listen because of the prospect's delivery and appearance.* The active real estate salesperson encounters prospects who have a broad range of occupations, religions, education, and cultural backgrounds. Because we all have our personal preferences, there is the danger of allowing our prejudices to affect our listening habits. While you may not embrace a prospect's attitudes, background, and culture—and looks—these differences should not serve as alibis for not listening. Focus instead on the content of the message and not on the prospect's delivery or appearance.

Some persons *fail to listen because of unavoidable distractions.* After showing a house, you would be unlikely to listen effectively if a barking dog were to distract your attention or if in driving from the house the prospect were to comment on his or her impressions. Traffic distractions limit your listening ability. If you are faced with distractions like these, suggest to your prospect that you stop at the local restaurant for coffee and discussion. Or suggest that you leave the house to avoid the barking dog. If it is not possible to avoid distractions, and you must listen to a speaker who cannot be interrupted, make every effort to give the speaker your full attention.

Rules for Good Listening. It is probably true that successful salespersons spend most of their time listening and not talking. Ideally, the salesperson listens and then responds meaningfully to the buyer who also listens carefully about the listed house. Effective listening that leads to effective communication saves time for the salesperson since he or she learns more during the interview. A good listener learns not only what the person is saying but also learns something about the person who is talking. Furthermore, good listening demonstrates good manners. The prospect appreciates an attentive listener. By listening you encourage your prospect to return the listening courtesy.

There are eight commonly accepted rules for good listening practice. A brief discussion of these rules shows their importance in the sales process.[1]

1. *Stop talking.* Salespersons are in danger of becoming overstimulated which leads to inefficient listening. The salesperson may respond too quickly to the prospect's inquiries. That is, the salesperson is overstimulated to the point that he or she is unable to control the immediate desire to answer the prospect. Overstimulation to the prospect's comments may result in interruptions without fully comprehending the buyer's attitudes, needs, and problems. Therefore, you should not respond until you are sure that you understand your prospect's inquiries.

2. *Place your prospect at ease.* Your first concern is to let the prospect know that he or she is free to talk. Create a permissive environment by finding an area of interest with the buyer and searching for worthwhile ideas. It has been said that there is no such thing as an uninteresting subject, that there are only uninterested people.

3. *Act interested.* Do not read your listing cards while the prospect is talking. Listen in order to understand; do not feign interest. Give your speaker your complete attention. Establish eye contact and indicate your interest by an appropriate posture and by appropriate facial expressions. Show that you want to understand what the buyer is saying by reacting favorably to his or her comments.

4. *Resist distractions.* Make certain that your colleagues and office staff do not interrupt. Postpone answering incoming telephone calls. It is best that you have a separate room, close the door, and move closer to your speaker and concentrate on what is said. Never tap your fingers, shuffle papers, or doodle.

5. *Be patient with your speaker.* Listen for key words that reveal the buyer's motives. Try to discriminate between what the buyer says he or she wants and what he or she really requires. Listen for key ideas that reveal true motives.

6. *Ask revealing questions.* The importance of asking the right questions is treated separately at the end of this chapter. Skillful questioning shows

---

[1]Adapted from Keith Davis, *The Dynamics of Organizational Behavior,* 3rd ed. (New York: McGraw-Hill Book Company, 1967), p. 333.

buyers that you are listening and that you are interested in their immediate problems. Since you will not understand everything that the speaker is saying, you can raise your level of understanding by asking appropriate questions.

7. *Avoid argument and criticism.* Guard against putting the speaker on the defensive. Criticizing the prospect's expressed desires may cause the prospect to adopt defenses. Prospects may be wrong in wanting unreasonable financing, but it may not be the time to discuss these issues. First listen to what the prospect is saying and later plan your presentation so that the prospect's demands will be overcome.

8. *Learn to be a flexible listener.* In some situations you may want to take notes. In other situations note taking may be distracting. It is probably better to work at listening. Your speaker is probably talking at more than 100–150 words a minute. In listening you must try to sift out the more important concerns of the buyer. This calls for careful listening. The buyer may not state everything that is important; consequently, you must learn to interpret voice tones and nonverbal communication. Be patient in listening to the buyer even though he or she appears to be making slow progress in communicating his or her needs.

Listening Attitudes. The successful salesperson who practices effective listening as a sales tool removes a factor that causes the buyer to be on the defensive. A climate must be created which to the buyer is neither critical, evaluative, nor moralizing. In truth, the salesperson works toward creating an atmosphere of equality, acceptance, and sympathetic understanding. It is only in this climate that the prospect can communicate needs and work toward receiving and accepting your presentation.

Try to be consistent in showing that you are interested in prospects as persons. Show that you respect their thoughts and that what they require in a house is important. Develop behavior that shows you believe that they are worth listening to, that you are familiar with their needs, and that you are the kind of person they can talk to about a new home.

Though you will not state your position in this way, you must make sure that these messages are conveyed. To do this, you must work toward creating an atmosphere of helpfulness. You must actually demonstrate respect for your prospects, and one of the best ways to show respect is to listen effectively.

The Act of Perceiving

Next to listening, the act of perceiving critically affects the communication process. Suppose you show a house that seems to meet your prospect's requirements and you suggest that the prospect make an offer and assume an existing mortgage. After receiving the communication, the buyer goes through a process of perceiving. That is, the buyer may indicate a certain insight or apprehension about your suggestion. Conversely, the buyer's perception may represent full comprehension over your suggestion.

FIGURE 1-1. Problems in Perception

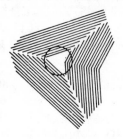

Is the circle round or lopsided?

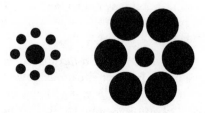

Are the center circles the same size?

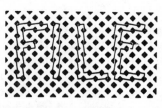

Are the letters parallel?

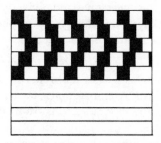

Are the checkers parallel?

Source: William V. Haney, *Communication and Organizational Behavior,* rev. ed. (Homewood, Ill.: © Richard D. Irwin, Inc., 1967), p. 78.

Judging prospect perceptions requires skill. You must be sure that what the prospect actually perceives is what you intended. Figure 1–1 illustrates the possibilities of erroneous perceptions. In each of the four illustrations what appears to be at first glance a distorted figure is not a distorted figure: The circle is round; the center circles are the same size; the letters and the checkers are parallel. The client's act of perceiving could be also subject to misinterpretation.

Your ability to perceive is often tested in selling homes. Consider, for example, my broker friend who showed a home listed for $105,000. As he took the prospect through the home, my friend came to the kitchen and noted, "The dishwasher is new and a greenhouse adjoins the kitchen." The Realtor® did not know that the prospect had a real interest in growing flowers and was very taken with the greenhouse.

As they were ready to leave the house, the prospect returned to the

TABLE 1-1. Controllable and Uncontrollable Communication Elements

Means of Communication	Uncontrollable	Controllable Factors		
		Preliminary	Active	Very Active
Visual	Personal physical features: age, sex, race, height	Clothing: style, neatness Physical appearance: hair style, facial hair	Posture Distance Orientation to prospect	Body movements Facial expressions Eye movements Gestures Head movements
Sound	Voice	Accent	Voice quality Speech patterns	Verbal expressions Vocalizations
Touch and smell		Personal odor	Touching	

Source: Adapted from James Hulbert and Noel Capon, "Interpersonal Communication in Marketing: An Overview," *Journal of Marketing Research* (February, 1972), p. 29.

greenhouse. Later that day the broker closed the sale. That night the Realtor® explained to friends how he sold a $105,000 home. He never realized that the prospect had really purchased a $105,000 greenhouse.

Especially note that perception depends on personal values, knowledge, motives, and attitudes. For example, the prospect may not wish to pay more than $10,000 down which is not enough for the sale. Or the prospect—unknown to you—may be conditioned by previous experience to reject a split-level house because of its numerous stairways. These values and attitudes held by your prospect may lead to a habitual response. A habitual response is made automatically without conscious thought. If not, then a decision must be made on the merits of your suggestion. Typically, if no habitual response is present, the decision will be postponed until it is consciously deliberated.

Controllable Communication

Most aspects of communication are controllable. Table 1–1 lists the four senses used in communicating with others. The visual means of communication that are uncontrollable are largely inherited personal characteristics or the result of life history. Similarly, we must take as given inherited voice characteristics which are largely beyond our control.

Preliminary Factors. In other respects, the elements that are available to you as a communicator and salesperson are largely controllable. Certain preliminary factors, for example, the style and neatness of your clothing and your personal appearance, convey impressions that are under your control. Similarly, your accent can be adapted to your purpose. Even the sense of smell affects your ability to communicate with others. Odors should be neither offensive nor overbearing.

Active Factors.   Note further that the more active controllable factors bear on sight, sound, and the sense of touch. Your posture, your distance from your prospect, and even the orientation to your prospect, i.e., whether you are behind a desk or sitting beside the prospect, make considerable difference. Your speech pattern and grammar, the use of slang or obscene words, and the tone of your voice convey meaning to prospects. Touching (handshaking) is another means under your control that affects the communication process.

Very Active Factors.   The very active controllable factors are more subtle. The movement of your body in response to what your prospect is communicating, your facial expressions, your eye movements, and your gestures have a bearing on how the prospect perceives your communication. Verbal expressions involve the kind of questions you ask and how you deliver your statements. Vocalizations refer to laughs, exclamations, and other means of voicing approval or disapproval.

VERBAL COMMUNICATION

Salespersons may be technically competent; they may know the appeal of the houses listed for sale; they may be very aware of the housing needs of their prospect, and they may know details about the community. But not all salespersons know the importance of verbal communication.

Barriers to Communication

Knowing the facts does not necessarily mean that you are communicating effectively. There may be certain communication barriers that prevent the buyer from receiving your intended message. For example, your speech pattern or the tone of your voice may have an effect on the final impression. For instance, take the following simple sentence: *"I am going to show the house this morning."* This sentence has at least three separate meanings. If you stress the *I,* you may be saying that you are the one who will show the house and not Mrs. Jones, another salesperson. If you are talking to the prospect and stress the word *the,* a different meaning is conveyed. Here you are emphasizing that you have a very special house suited to the prospect's needs. By stressing *this morning* you are conveying the importance of immediately preparing the house for your prospect.

The major communication barriers include *inferences* made by prospects, certain *defenses,* sometimes adopted unconsciously by prospective buyers, and the use of jargon.

Inferences. In your work it is possible to make two kinds of statements: a statement of observation and a statement of inference. I can say, "The Johnson house was constructed last year at a cost of $75,000." This is a statement of fact that can be verified from the construction contract. But I cannot say that the house will sell for $75,000. The house may be worth more or less depending on the local market. The latter statement is an *inference.*

The distinction between statements of observation and statements of inference may be critical to the sale. You may wrongly infer that you have sold the house to a prospect when in fact the prospect favors a house shown by another office. The point is that both you and your prospect are making inferences that may be incorrect. In order to see the difference between observation and inference, read the following paragraph and complete the self-test by circling "T," "F," or "?" indicating a "true," "false," or an "unknown" answer.

A real estate broker stated that a three-bedroom house sold for $55,000. The house being appraised has three bedrooms and a brick veneer exterior. An adjoining house with three bedrooms and a brick veneer exterior was listed for $58,000. The owner of the house under appraisal said his house was worth $57,000.

T F ? 1. The house under appraisal has a market value of $57,000.

T F ? 2. The house listed for sale has an indicated value of $58,000.

T F ? 3. In this case, a three-bedroom, brick veneer house is worth $55,000.

T F ? 4. In the opinion of a qualified real estate broker, three-bedroom brick veneer houses have a market value of $55,000.

T F ? 5. Property owners know the true value of houses.

T F ? 6. A three-bedroom house sold for $55,000.

T F ? 7. Three-bedroom, brick veneer houses are worth $55,000.

T F ? 8. The broker stated that the house under valuation was worth $55,000.

T F ? 9. According to an informed owner, three-bedroom brick houses are worth $57,000.

T F ? 10. Houses recently sold by willing sellers to informed buyers indicate a value of $55,000.

T F ? 11. A three-bedroom, brick veneer house sold at the current market value.

T F ? 12. A three-bedroom, brick veneer house sold for less than its market value.

T F ? 13. Appraised values are less than the listing prices of property offered for sale.

T F ? 14. The house listed for sale has a value of $55,000.

T F ? 15. A competent real estate expert said the house was worth $55,000.

To guard against making unrealistic inferences, ask yourself the following questions:

1. Did I observe what I am talking about?
2. Did my statements go beyond my observations?
3. When I make inferences, do I consider their probabilities?
4. When I talk to prospects, do I identify my inferences?

You cannot avoid making inferences. Some events are so probable that we feel safe in making an inference: The sun will rise tomorrow morning. But in real estate you make numerous inferences about prospects and their responses to your communications. In short, you take a calculated risk when you infer that your prospect will give a favorable or an unfavorable response to your listings.

The recommended answers to the inference test demonstrate these points.

?	1.	T	6.	?	11.
?	2.	F	7.	?	12.
?	3.	F	8.	F	13.
F	4.	F	9.	?	14.
F	5.	F	10.	?	15.

The first answer is "unknown" because the statement does not report a market value for the house under appraisal. In question 2 there is no statement saying that the house listed for sale has an indicated value of $58,000, which is the listing price. To illustrate further, question 8 is false because it is not clear that the house under valuation is the same house considered by the real estate broker. In other words, if you make an inference, there is the danger that it will not be recognized as an inference. If the risks in making an inference are not considered and if a party acts on the assumption that the inference is fact, the results may be costly.

Defenses.   Buyers who are unconsciously threatened by salespersons or who are inherently suspicious react defensively. If you recognize these perceived threats—which act as critical obstacles to the sale—you can use certain threat-reducing techniques. The six main ways of reacting defensively to threats of change or threats of imagined harm are summarized below:[2]

1. *Defenses that protect personal standards and values.* These defenses protect a person from others who make unfavorable personal judgments. As a person becomes more defensive he or she is less able to interpret the motives or communications of the salesperson. The best reaction to this behavior would be to

[2]Adapted from the work of Jack Gibb. See William V. Haney, *Communication and Organizational Behavior,* rev. ed. (Homewood, Ill.: Richard D. Irwin, Inc.,© 1967), pp. 73–75.

be nonregimental in all matters. Ask questions for information; present personal impressions so that the buyer must change his or her behavior or attitudes.

The recommended response to this defense builds prospect confidence. The object is to reduce defenses so that the buyer concentrates on his or her housing needs and your suggestions.

2. *Defenses against control by others.* This buyer is inherently suspicious. He or she thinks that the salesperson is trying to unload a property or otherwise restrict his or her opportunity to consider other dwellings. The best way to combat this attitude is to

collaborate with the buyer in defining problems and ways to solve buyer needs. Impress on the buyer that you have no preconceived solutions, attitudes, or methods to impose on the buyer. Help buyers see their needs; help buyers make their own decisions and share their concerns.

Here it is advised to be direct and spontaneous and help the buyer reach a decision. In contrast, if you prematurely "force the sale" or try to lead negotiations to a premature closing, you may stimulate buyer defenses. Remember that buyer suspicions of your hidden motives increase buyer resistance.

3. *Defenses against being manipulated or tricked.* The new home buyer may be placed in this position. The buyer has a distorted view of real estate salespersons. To help this prospect

create a feeling of straightforwardness and honesty. Approach the prospect naturally. Be completely free of any form of hidden complicated motives.

Your supportive role builds confidence. Remove these fears so that the buyer responds to your presentation. Keeping this buyer on the defensive will lead to a lost prospect.

4. *Buyer defenses against the clinical, coldly detached salesperson.* This buyer is defensive against salespersons who he or she thinks has no concern for his or her welfare. The best way to overcome this attitude is to

express a personal respect for the buyer's position. Identify closely with the buyer's problem. Show a mutual interest in sharing the buyer's feeling and accept the buyer's concerns at face value.

5. *Defenses against salespersons who create an attitude of superiority.* The buyer feels that salespersons can give little help in solving his or her housing problem. The buyer believes that the salesperson does not want to hear buyer objections and, unconsciously, he or she feels that the relationship with the salesperson reduces his or her status or individual worth. The best way to counteract this attitude is to

show a willingness to plan the housing purchase with the buyer. Try to create an attitude of mutual, constant respect. The salesperson tries to minimize personal differences in wealth, talent, ability, status, or other matters.

Probably the buyer's behavior will be the product of his or her feelings in the role that the salesperson plays in his or her life. The buyer who has this attitude remains defensive unless steps are taken to minimize defensive reactions.

6. *Defenses against dogmatic persons.* These buyers have a need to be right; they try to win arguments and then solve a problem. Note that this is a perceived behavior on the part of the salesperson. To counteract this defense,

do not take sides on issues but rather encourage their investigation. Show an intent to solve problems rather than debate issues. Get the buyer to partly control the investigation of controversial issues.

The salesperson who tries to overly control the buyer encourages defensiveness on the part of his or her prospect. Even the suspicion of being manipulated heightens buyer resistance. Preferably the salesperson not only assumes a nondefensive role but assumes a supportive attitude, an attitude showing the willingness to explore the buyer's needs and to solve the housing problem. The supportive role is partly aided by avoiding jargon.

Jargon.   In order to gain admittance to the industry, real estate people must acquire a technical vocabulary. State license examinations require familiarity with a long list of real estate terms, financing terms, legal definitions, and the like. Moreover, active salespersons attend numerous meetings, educational conferences, and programs to learn the more technical aspects of their job. Much of their time is spent talking to other salespersons on real estate matters. As a result technical terms that are unfamiliar to the layperson become part of the common vocabulary of salespersons.

Especially for the first-time home buyer, your use of real estate terms may create suspicions and raise buyer defenses. To be sure, if your prospect is an attorney, an architect, or an experienced real estate buyer, you can communicate effectively with technical terms. But ordinarily you would take care that the buyer understands your vocabulary. Common words that are familiar to most real estate salespersons but that would be avoided in dealing with the general public, especially your prospect, would include the following:

Abstracts	Conveyance instrument
Acceleration clause	Deficiency judgment
Acknowledgment	Deposit receipt
Agreement	Discount points
Amortization	Earnest money
Construction bond	Easement
Constructive notice	Economic depreciation

Economic value	Metes and bounds
Equity	Mortgage constant
Equity of redemption	Mortgagee
Escrow	Objective value
Exclusive agency	Obsolescence
Fee simple	Open listing
Functional depreciation	Points
Grantee	Prorates
Grantor	Purchase money mortgage
Header	Quitclaim deed
Intrinsic value	Restrictive covenant
Joist	Special warranty deed
Junior mortgage	Wall studs
Loan to value ratio	Warranted value
	Warranty deed

If you suggest financing the purchase with a new type of mortgage, for example, a flexible payment mortgage, a variable rate mortgage, or a second mortgage, be sure that the buyer understands these terms. Almost all of the terms listed above could be avoided in favor of simpler language or synonyms.

Voice Patterns

Here we are concerned with *how* you speak to the prospect. Your buyer is listening for verbal cues that reveal much meaning beyond the words that you use. Voice patterns that affect meaning include:

Voice pitch, resonance, volume, rate, and rhythm
Laughing, coughing, throat clearing, and sighing
Momentary variations in voice pitch and volume.
Silent pauses and sounds such as "ahs," "ers," and "ums"

It is the combination of what you say and your vocal cues that determine your meaning. For example, the change in the rate at which you speak may be interpreted as impatience, anger, or anxiety. A slowing of your presentation may indicate boredom or contemplation.

A salesperson must be aware of *paralanguage cues* and must learn to interpret the buyer's voice patterns. The trained salesperson improves communication by cultivating voice characteristics that sound pleasant, confident, and competent, for it is well known that the stresses placed on certain words change their intended meanings. Even the "ahs," "ers," and "ums" may reveal a lack of confidence, hesitation, and doubt. Although it would be easy to overgeneralize on voice characteristics, it is recognized that voice patterns may act as additional barriers.

To emphasize the importance of overcoming barriers to communication,

FIGURE 1-2.   Checklist for Barriers to Effective Communication

It is helpful to anticipate communication problems. In your contacts with prospects have you encountered the communication problems listed below? Ideally, you should be able to anticipate barriers to communications that might arise in your sales interview.

1. Do you and the prospective buyer see the communication problem in the same way?
2. What is your real purpose in communicating to the prospect?
3. Does the prospect think you are trying to fool him or her?
4. Does the potential buyer believe that real estate salespersons are out to sell the property at the highest price regardless of the needs of the buyer?
5. Does the buyer think you are unfair or uninformed?
6. Does your picture of the buyer agree with the buyer's personal view of himself or herself?
7. Have I shown the prospect that I am sympathetic to his or her needs?
8. Have I engaged in a two-way communication with the prospect?
9. Has the buyer viewed me as a talker? Or a listener? Have I shown that I have really cared about what he or she has to say?
10. Have I shown a true understanding of the buyer's thoughts by restating what was unclear?
11. Have I listened without interrupting even though the prospect is highly critical or stating an untruth?
12. Have I communicated with the prospect in a common language?
13. Am I certain that the owner understands technical real estate terms or legal terms? Have I used terms like FHA points, loan assumptions, comparable sales, fixtures, prorates, and the like?
14. Have I stated my main points in an organized fashion?
15. Have I carefully distinguished facts from mere inferences?
16. Have I understood that people interpret words differently, that words stand for things?
17. Have I used examples to communicate and to clarify the communication problem?
18. Have I presented too much or too little information during the interview?
19. Have I avoided faulty grammar?
20. Has the buyer felt at ease with me?
21. Do I convey an attitude of understanding toward others?
22. Have I made a favorable first impression and have I maintained this impression by being personable, warm, friendly, interested, and enthusiastic? Am I neatly groomed?
23. Do I use a sales approach that develops from that which is acceptable to the buyer to that which is controversial? In other words, have my appeals been based on points that the owner can accept?
24. Have I avoided talking down to a buyer?
25. Have I used facts and specific examples? And have they been accurate and void of unreasonable exaggeration?
26. Has my presentation been verbally communicative? Has my voice been forceful and devoid of distracting speech habits?

on your next presentation test yourself by using the checklist in Figure 1–2. The checklist is not complete (it does not cover the questioning techniques, interviewing procedures, and body language) but it does provide a review of your ability to avoid the main barriers to effective communication.

NONVERBAL COMMUNICATION

In the final analysis, your ability to communicate effectively turns on a wide range of nonverbal communications. They include the environment in which you are talking to your prospect. Moreover, your appearance and certain body movements affect your ability to communicate with your receiver, the buyer.

To cite major examples, consider the traffic policeman who communicates almost entirely by body movements. Similarly, relatives and friends who wave to departing airplanes often display considerable emotion with goodbye gestures; the speaker who raises a finger as he says, "This is my first point" supplements the spoken word with body movement and effectively emphasizes his or her message. Because of the importance of these nonverbal aspects of communication, it is necessary to adapt your environment, your appearance, and your body language to communication goals.

The Influence of Environment

The layout of the office can create an environment that promotes sales. For example, status is often conveyed by how the office is arranged. For example, an office that has an outer wall and a window is usually reserved for persons of higher status; offices on the top floors are reserved for executives. Partitions indicate status: permanent walls suggest more status than temporary partitions. An office having a door conveys more importance than an office not having a door.

Studies have shown that furniture arrangements may be adapted to improve communications. Persons sitting behind a desk have more difficulty communicating with prospects than do persons who have seating arrangements more adapted to counseling and interviewing. The preferred practice for interviewing purposes is to have two chairs at a 45-degree angle or two chairs placed around an intervening table corner.

If a desk must be used, it should be moved to a less conspicuous location. The front part of the desk should be against the wall so that the prospect is given immediate access to salespersons. This arrangement gives the prospect equal status with the salesperson. Furnishings such as carpets, paneling, and name plates are other items that telegraph meaning to the prospect. In other words, furnishings indicate the degree of responsibility, competence, and success of the occupant.

Personal Appearance

We have been conditioned to interpret occupations by dress. While the more obvious nurses and policemen's uniforms are familiar, the clothes worn by a stranger, i.e., the salesperson, influence the prospect's judgments about the salesperson. The attire of the salesperson selling a dwelling would not be the same as that of the salesperson selling a farm or a multimillion dollar income property. Even before you say a word it is likely the prospect has already formed a judgment about you on the basis of your dress, hair arrangement, and appearance.

Body Movement

Facial expressions probably give us the most information about the sender. At the first meeting, prospects learn much more about you by your facial cues than by your vocal cues. In this respect, salespersons are cautioned not to mislead prospects by personal mannerisms and facial cues.

The evidence shows that certain emotions are accurately perceived by facial expressions. Among these are annoyance, disgust, quiet pleasure, joy, and worry, emotions that are vitally important in communicating with a prospective buyer. Probably the eyes provide most of the information. Professor Ray L. Birdwhistell, a leader in the study of body language (which he called *kinesics*) identified 23 eye positions that have different meanings. For this reason an interviewer is advised to maintain eye contact. Looking another person in the eye imparts a feeling of confidence.

Next in importance are facial expressions of the mouth that show either the warmth and friendliness of a smile or disapproval. Also of importance are body gestures. Although you ordinarily would not pound on the desk to emphasize a point, you should be aware of the nonverbal gestures that reinforce verbal communications—the movement of the arms, fingers, and the like.

By the same token, gestures can be distracting. The tapping of a foot or fingers, nodding of the head, swaying of the body, or a rigid posture send communications which the skillful salesperson learns to interpret and avoid.

Posture, including the relaxed posture of the interviewer and the more rigid posture of the nervous prospect, are other ways in which nonverbal communications convey information. Add to this the tactile means of communication more familiarly expressed in the handshake. For instance, does your handshake convey friendliness and sincerity? Does it demonstrate a helpful attitude?

QUESTIONING TECHNIQUES

There are some accepted rules guiding questioning techniques helpful to salespersons. First, questions stimulate the buyer. Second, they help you obtain needed facts and, third, they stimulate the discussion with the prospects so that you can have control over the interview. Questions must meet certain minimum requirements. Although you will not follow hard and fast rules in phrasing questions, the MACK principles discussed below will be of help to you.

MACK Principles

MACK is an acronym that stands for the four questioning principles listed below:

M	ake questions brief.
A	void yes or no answers.
C	onfine questions to a single topic.
K	eep to simple words.

The importance of these rules deserves added comment.

Make Questions Brief. Do not confuse the prospect by long drawn out questions that only confuse your listener. Every question should be a one-sentence question and that sentence should be short.

Avoid Yes or No Answers. Questions that require a yes or no answer do not allow discussion. If the answer to your question is yes, the discussion is ended and you need a second question to further the interview. For instance, do not ask, "Do you want a three-bedroom house?" Rephrase the question by asking, "How many bedrooms do you prefer?"

Confine Questions to a Single Topic. Avoid double questions such as, "Can you finance a house with $5,000 dollars down with a 10 percent mortgage or $2,000 down with a $10\frac{1}{2}$ percent mortgage?" You place the prospect in a difficult position by asking a question that requires a double response.

Keep to Simple Words. Remember that your prospect knows little about the technical aspects of housing construction, land development, real estate finance, appraisal terms, and legal terminology. Your questions should avoid the jargon that you would use with the mortgage banker, tax assessor, or colleagues.

In addition to these initial rules, you should learn the following kinds of questions:

1. Open questions
2. Probing questions

3. Mirror questions
4. Leading questions

Open Questions

An open question is a direct question that requires more than a few words to answer your inquiry. The question gives the prospect an opportunity to decide what information he or she will provide. For example:

Do you need to sell your present house?
What do you like about your present home?
What type of neighborhood do you prefer?

The open question is preferred to the direct question that elicits limited information and frequently calls only for a yes or no response. Open questions will provide you with information on attitudes, feelings, opinions, and the prospect's perception of the preferred home.

Probing Questions

A probing question focuses attention on specific information. For example:

What advantages do you appreciate in your present location?
What features do you appreciate most in a new home?
Do you have hobbies that affect the type of home you need?

The probing question continues the inquiry elicited by an earlier question. It gives you more information on the prospect's attitudes and preferences.

Mirror Questions

A mirror question evokes further response from your prospect and it gives you further information from your prospective buyer. It is especially effective in gaining additional information if you think your prospect's answer is incomplete. A mirror question consists of a carefully worded phrase or repetition of a key word used by the buyer. For example:

Prospect: We are primarily interested in a three-bedroom brick house.
Salesperson: A brick house? (This is a mirror question. You have a new subdivision of three-bedroom, split-level houses of frame construction with brick trim and you want to know why your prospect prefers brick veneer.)
Prospect: Yes, a brick house. Our present house is a frame house which we have had to paint every four years and we like the looks of a brick house.
Salesperson: That is certainly true. How would you feel about a cedar shake house finished with good quality stain and with brick veneer trim on the front part of the house? By cutting down on the amount of brick veneer, the builder gives you more floor space at a lower cost.

Prospect: Well, we might consider this type of house with some brick veneer if it's a good buy.

Salesperson: Suppose we look at a three-bedroom house with brick trim that meets your other requirements.

Mirror questions can be used to follow up other portions of the interview. The mirror question causes the prospect to expand on reasons for his or her preferences.

Leading Questions

Leading questions are directive. That is, they guide the buyer to a specific response. For example, "Isn't it true that you are interested in lowering your monthly payments to the smallest amount?" The words "Isn't it true" clue the listener to the preferred answer.

Leading questions are helpful in validating additional information. Examples would be: "Isn't it true that you are anticipating a pay raise over the next six months?" "You and your wife have talked about the advantages of shade trees in the backyard, haven't you?"

These questions serve the purpose if they do not give the buyer a chance to offer a biased response. In the second question if the response is likely to be no, the question should be restructured to lead the buyer to another response.

POINTS TO REMEMBER

Clearly, success in real estate sales calls for skillful communication. Communication must be heard, understood, accepted, and acted upon. Effective listening techniques are an important part of this process. The salesperson should avoid bad listening habits such as faking attention or listening only to memorized facts. Moreover, the salesperson should avoid difficult listening and should learn to listen even to uninteresting conversation. The salesperson should avoid the bad habit of allowing his or her listening to be affected by the prospect's delivery and appearance The salesperson should also listen more effectively by avoiding distractions that interfere with the listening technique. In addition to avoiding these bad listening habits, the salesperson should concentrate on the eight accepted rules for good listening.

A second part of the communication process deals with perceptions. The salesperson must be sure that the prospect perceives what is intended.

Moreover, most elements of communication are directly *controllable.* Preliminary factors bearing on communication relate to clothing, physical appearance, accent, and even personal odors. The more active factors (nonverbal communication), the salesperson's posture, orientation to the prospect, voice pattern, and the many possible body movements, largely determine the salesperson's communication effectiveness.

Barriers to communication relate to the danger of making risky *inferences* and coping with the *defensive buyer.* The salesperson should avoid technical terms unknown to the buyer (jargon) which may elicit unwanted defenses. Finally, even voice inflections have an effect on communication.

The salesperson should learn to recognize the forms of *nonverbal communication,* starting with the environment such as an office arrangement that facilitates successful interviews and sales closing. The salesperson should study how personal appearance relates to communication efforts and should study how his or her mannerisms and body movements influence communication. Equally important is the salesperson's interpretation of the prospect's nonverbal communication.

More significant, the salesperson should practice *questioning techniques.* These techniques involve the use of *open, probing, mirror,* and *leading* questions. Almost all salespersons would benefit materially by refining their skillful use of recommended questioning techniques.

REVIEW QUESTIONS

1. Explain what is meant by the communication process.

2. In what way are statements of observation and inference critical to a sale?

3. Suppose a prospect is reluctant to disclose how much available cash he or she has and how much his or her annual income is. How would you react to this behavior?

4. Assume that a prospect-buyer thinks he or she is being "tricked" into buying an overpriced house. Explain how you would respond to this prospect.

5. Make a list of jargon terms that you would avoid using in communicating with clients and prospects.

6. Give an example of nonverbal communication that you regularly use.

7. Discuss the importance of the eight rules for good listening.

8. What are the recommended general principles of asking questions?

9. Give examples of open, probing, mirror, and leading questions that would be asked in real estate sales.

2

Sales Motivation: Interviewing Techniques

Sales motivation refers to the personal drive that starts the selling process. Why is sales motivation important? Because sales motivation guides the salesperson's work. It helps to allocate his or her time and it helps the salesperson learn new skills, including self-analysis and his or her rating on a motivation chart.

Why are interviewing techniques important? Because the salesperson's interviewing techniques determine how successful he or she is with prospects, sellers, and others. Again, a knowledge of technical matters is very essential, but the salesperson will not prevail without the expert use of communication skills.

SELF-ANALYSIS

Preferably self-analysis is undertaken in a group setting. To stimulate discussion, the group should consist of approximately five persons. If you are in a large class, it would be better to divide into small groups. If you are not part of a class, form a small group among your associates. Or you can perform the analysis individually, but you will not have the advantage of group discussion and feedback.

Preliminary Self-Analysis

The preliminary analysis helps the group to interact. Start by asking the leader to present the preliminary analysis questions to the group. Although it would not be as effective, the analysis could even be conducted by an informal group of your colleagues during a coffee break. In a more formal setting the preliminary self-analysis leads to more in-depth discussion.

When you meet strangers for the first time, they form an immediate impression of you as a person. The preliminary analysis reveals this first impression you make on others. In making this analysis, encourage others to be honest and forthright. Best results are obtained in a training session that is meeting for the first time.

The group leader starts by asking each member of the group to answer the following questions:

1. How old am I?
2. What is my educational background?
3. What kind of house or apartment do I live in?
4. What kind of husband (or wife) do I have?
5. Write a brief description of your impression of me?

The questions are introduced with the following comment: "Each of you has gained an impression of me as I started to talk. By answering these questions you can determine the accuracy of your impressions by writing down your perception of me."

Do not have members sign the answers to these questions. Read the answers to the group. After group members have compared their answers with your actual circumstances, they will tend to be more open and forthright in completing the self-analysis.

Self-Analysis Questions

At least two one-hour sessions should be allowed for discussing the questions for the self-analysis. Since these are discussion questions, members should be divided into small groups. One member should play the role of a leader and each person should set limits on how much to tell about himself or herself. Each group leader should act as as group stimulator in discussing the following eight questions.

1. *What is your concept of communication?*

The group leader asks each member to read his or her definition and then the group discusses various interpretations, stressing similarities and differences. The group leader encourages discussion by asking more direct questions such as:

How do you know when you have communicated?
How can communication be made more effective?
Does communication refer to transferring a message or meaning?
Do words give meaning or do people give meaning?
What are the different kinds of communication?

Before ending discussion of this question, the group leader makes certain that there is an understanding of the verbal, nonverbal, and *intended* or *unintended* communications.

2. *How effective am I as a communicator with prospects?*

In answering this question, personal communication *strengths* and communication *weaknesses* and the steps that should be taken to overcome weaknesses should be listed.

Each member reads his or her list of personal communication strengths. Such lists would usually include good appearance, favorable voice characteristics, attitudes toward the prospect, good eye contact, or effective use of body gestures—and superior knowledge of houses and their value.

After participants have talked about themselves, the group leader then asks group members to comment on communication strengths they see in other members that were not mentioned. Next the members' weaknesses are discussed. Such weaknesses would probably include lack of knowledge about real estate, construction, real estate financing, inaccurate pronunciation, limited real estate vocabulary, nervousness before prospects, or the inability to explain technical matters. By sharing individual experiences, group members help themselves overcome nervousness, a common weakness.

Now that both strengths and weaknesses have been covered, the group leader asks members to list methods of overcoming weaknesses. Suggestions would probably range from taking more formal real estate courses to deliberately practicing new questioning techniques, developing better interviewing practices, working toward better eye contact, controlling personal mannerisms and body gestures, and improving grammar. The leader should be sure that the group discusses ways of improving their listening habits.

The group leader closes the discussion by asking the members of the group to volunteer ways of overcoming weaknesses.

3. *In what situations do I have the greatest difficulty in communicating with prospects? Why?*

Each member should be given time to list situations in which he or she has the greatest difficulty in communicating with prospects. Typically, the answers will include communication problems in first meeting the prospect, difficulty in communicating, in closing the sale, or in communicating with prospects who ask about the quality of construction or about financing or who ask legal questions. Some members may mention difficulties in communicating with members of the same sex, the opposite sex, older persons, or younger prospects.

It would be unusual if someone did not express difficulty in communicating with persons who call in response to an advertisement. If this communication problem is not mentioned, the group leader should ask if everyone communicates well with callers who try to control the interview and withhold personal information. It takes the highest level of skill to overcome this common communication gap.

By sharing experiences, the group members explore common ways of overcoming these communication problems. Frequently the group members find ways of improving communication in the roles they assume as salespersons. In other cases, individuals may discover common prejudices that limit their effectiveness.

4. *Am I satisfied with my progress in (a) my real estate education, (b) my choice in pursuing a real estate specialty, (c) my social life, and (d) my other goals?*

There are so many educational programs available to the real estate community that at least some members will express satisfaction or dissatisfaction over their education. Similarly, real estate provides virtually unlimited opportunities for specialization. Members of the group should be encouraged to discuss their success in sales, job satisfaction, and long-term career goals.

Under social goals, the group should discuss participation in community organizations, personal exercise, hobbies, and other personal interests.

5. *What are my main attitudes, prejudices, and values that affect my ability to communicate?* Explain in terms of ones with which I am *satisfied* (give reasons) and ones with which I am *dissatisfied* (give reasons).

Members should freely examine their problems, including psychological barriers or personal habits of stereotyping that limit their ability to communicate. Their ability to work with prospects may include personal prejudices about beards, hair style, clothing, race, nationality, and sex. Discuss psychological barriers created by socioeconomic differences between agents and prospects. Normally, the group would include members who are prejudiced against elderly people, younger people, or individuals whose education, occupation, and income are different from theirs.

6. *How do these prejudices affect my ability to communicate with prospects?*

Responses to this question are natural extensions of question five. Ideally, members should admit communication difficulties with prospects they dislike. Members should be asked to relate experiences showing how they failed to communicate because of their personal attitudes. The main purpose is to help members discuss their individual barriers to specific communication situations. Making members aware of these barriers helps them to turn to methods that would minimize these difficulties.

7. *What initial impression do I make on others? Why do I think I make this impression?*

Although group members may be willing to talk about how other members impress them, probably very few persons have tested the kind of impression they think they make on others. After each member is allowed to express his or her personal feelings on how he or she thinks he or she impresses others, the members should be asked to express their initial impressions of each other. The group leader creates an attitude of openness by helping members give and receive feedback on matters of self-disclosure.

8. *How would I describe myself? How does my perception of myself compare with others' perception of me?*

The group leader asks each member in turn to describe the personality of each group member. After this the discussion members read their prepared descriptions of their own personalities; then they compare their own perceptions of themselves with the *group's* perception of themselves.

After finishing the eighth question, members will have learned how to establish better relations with others; they will have learned to give and receive interpersonal feedback. Each person will have a more accurate concept of his or her interpersonal feelings. Self-analysis teaches salespersons to accept feedback without feeling threatened. Group members acquire a greater mutual trust and an increased awareness of communication.

The main advantages of the self-analysis may be summarized as follows:

1. Members learn to think about their own communication behavior.
2. They learn how they are perceived by others.
3. They learn to give and receive criticisms.
4. They learn that they share common problems and that they can share solutions.
5. They learn that communication problems may be reduced by cooperating in constructive group criticism.

In short, the self-analysis teaches members to work with others; it develops greater openness and a better ability to communicate with buyers and sellers.

SALES ORIENTATION

When you train as a real estate salesperson, you are confronted with two kinds of information. One deals with the product and requires that you learn about real estate laws, financing, construction, valuation, housing characteristics, and the like. The other concerns the sales technique. Consequently, depending on personal background and training, some salespersons tend to be "sale" oriented while others tend to be "people" oriented. In the latter case, the sales presentation depends on building a personal relationship (and probably neglecting the technical job of selling) and the other bears heavily on selling techniques without dealing with buyers as people.

In preparing for the many types of interviews taken in making a sale, you must realize that you are not selling houses but that you are *selling benefits*. The benefits lie in not only supplying your prospect needed housing but also in giving the prospect and his or her family certain amenities associated with your listing. As a consequence, you first identify the needs of the prospect and then you show how a particular listing fills those needs. You are successful if the prospect believes that his or her needs are met by your listing. In this case, you would probably be ranked among salespeople who show an extreme concern for the sale or an unusual concern for persons. The various salesperson orientations are shown in Figure 2-1.

Note that in Figure 2-1 persons oriented toward the sale rank between positions (1) and (2) on the graph. The first position describes the salesperson who assumes an attitude of take it or leave it. This person casually shows the house and assumes that the house sells itself. Or such a salesperson is likely to show a prospect numerous houses without gaining an impression of how the house satisfies prospect needs. The sales process is confined to showing the maximum number of houses until the prospect buys. This position is given the lowest point value of Figure 2-1: *1 point.*

The second position describes the salesperson who uses pressure selling techniques even to the point of harassing prospects. Covert threats that another buyer is ready to make the down payment tomorrow are examples of the hard sell. This salesperson pushes the product without considering the prospect's needs. Point value: *5 points.*

The opposite position is taken by the salesperson who is highly concerned for people (position 3 in Figure 2-1). The main emphasis here is the attempt to establish the prospect as a friend. It is hoped that by understanding the prospect and responding to the prospect's feelings and interests the prospect will select a house solely on the basis of their personal relationship. Point value: *10 points.*

Point 4 includes some of the features of position 3. This person sells by formula, by personality, and, hopefully, by emphasizing housing features, the sale is made. Point value: *25 points.*

The preferred position, which has a *point value of 100,* covers salespersons who are oriented toward solving a problem. The sale begins with a careful interview with the prospect. The salesperson associates the problem with respect to the prospect's family; the salesperson engages in sufficient conversation to learn the prospect's needs, likes, and living preferences. The house and neighborhood are selected to maximize the prospect's benefits.

In this case, the sales effort solves the problem. In the end the buyer is

FIGURE 2-1 The Salesperson Orientation Chart

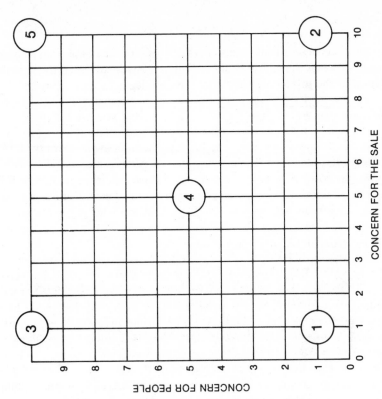

1. Points: 1
TAKE IT OR LEAVE IT

   I place the house before the prospect; the house sells itself.

2. Points: 10
PUSH THE PRODUCT ORIENTED

   I hard sell the prospect, using the maximum pressure to make the prospect buy.

3. Points: 10
PEOPLE ORIENTED

   I'm the prospect's friend. I hope to understand him or her and respond to his or her feelings and interests. I want to establish a personal relationship that leads the buyer to buy from me.

4. Points: 25
SALES TECHNIQUES ORIENTED

   I have a tested routine for making prospects buy. I motivate prospects by my personality and by emphasizing housing features.

5. Points: 100
PROBLEM SOLVING ORIENTED

   I carefully interview prospects so that I know all their needs, selecting the listing that most satisfies the prospect.

   We work toward making the best housing decision on the part of the prospect which gives the most satisfaction to the prospect and his or her family.

Source: Adapted from John. D. Hatfield, "Communication in Retail Salesmanship: A Balanced Approach," in Richard C. Huseman et al., *Readings in Interpersonal and Organizational Communication,* 2nd ed. (Boston: Holbrook Press, Inc., 1969), p. 398.

counseled to the best housing decision; the buyer gains maximum satisfaction. A *problem-solving* orientation creates a satisfied buyer, advances the personal reputation of the salesperson and the firm, and leads to repeat business.

INTERVIEWING TECHNIQUES

The sales interview is more than a casual response to an inquiry into the listing you have on 430 Westview Drive. Every interview assumes a formal structure. If you know how an interview develops, you can improve your interview techniques whether they are undertaken with the prospect or with a potential seller who might list with you.

The Structure of the Interview

The interview is a *goal-directed* communication. That is, it is not like social conversation at a cocktail party. When your prospect inquires about your advertisement, he or she is making a predetermined, explicit, and formal request. Similarly, the prospect who visits your office in response to an advertisement has a purpose. It is this goal-directed nature of the interview that gives each interview a definite structure.

In most instances, the interview is a two-party interaction. The real estate interview may involve more than one person. The interview may be complicated by interaction between a husband and wife who are acting as receivers of your communications.

Thus, your participation in the sales interview involves a formal setting in which you consciously structure the interview into five parts: (1) the preplanning, (2) the opening, (3) the body, (4) the ending, and (5) the follow-up. Before studying the ways of developing the five parts of an interview, first identify the main purposes of real estate sales interviews.

Purposes of Sale Interviews

In dealing with prospective buyers and sellers, your interviews may take one of four forms. Under special circumstances, a single interview could incorporate all four purposes, but the interview generally focuses on a single purpose. Each type of interview requires a different preparation. With careful preparation, even the less experienced salesperson can successfully complete the first type of interview: *to receive or give prospects information.*

For instance, in your initial interview with the prospect, the prospect provides you with information on his or her housing preferences. Or in soliciting a listing from a seller who has the house advertised "for sale by owner," you provide information on the listing and on the selling services of your company. In either case, the interview requires careful structuring if it is to serve its main purpose: to give or receive information for later decision making.

A second type of interview is aimed at *discovering new information.* In listing a new house, for example, you want to know what sale terms are acceptable to the seller. Or in inspecting a listed house for the first time, you want new information from the seller that is not on the listing form. Because this interview focuses on obtaining new information, it is frequently used by real estate appraisers and others engaged in data research. Additionally, salespersons use this technique in making the competitive market survey described in later chapters or in working a neighborhood for new listings.

The third type of interview is the *interview for decision making.* Typically, this is the interview you have with the seller in which you present an offer below the listed price. Salespersons use this type of interview frequently in negotiating with buyers and sellers.

The last type of interview, regarded as the most difficult, seeks to *change attitudes or behavior.* In attempting to list a house "for sale by owner," you try to overcome the owner's prejudices against real estate agents. The trained salesperson structures this interview with special care and uses proven presentations to make a point. Similarly, in dealing with a buyer-prospect, you may arrange a special interview with a husband and wife to overcome their objections to a particular neighborhood on grounds that it is too far to commute.

Advance Planning

Knowing that the interview will include five parts will help you control the interview. To be sure, not all interviews are subject to advance planning, but with experience, you will find that impromptu interviews tend to follow the same general plan. Knowing the following five parts of an interview will give you more confidence in interviewing prospective buyers and sellers.

Preplanning the Interview. Suppose a prospect telephones after reading your classified ad and wants to know the address of the house advertised. You withhold the address and try to convince the prospect to visit your office. Probably the prospect wants only the address and minimum information about the house advertised. During this interview you want to qualify the prospect, determine housing preferences, and select a house that suits the prospect's needs, a house that might not necessarily be the advertised house.

Preplanning for this and other interviews requires that you:

1. Review your information on the advertised and similar houses.
2. Prepare questions that help you qualify the buyer and learn buyer preferences.

Go over a buyer qualification form so that you are prepared to ask the right questions as the interview progresses. Indeed, the importance of the buyer qualification interview justifies a separate chapter. Your personal preparation not only includes a study of available financing terms and neighborhood characteristics, but it also includes preparing the office for the best interview environment. Let the seller know of the possible showing of the house after the interview.

Preplanning may require agreement with a seller or buyer on a time and place for the interview, the probable time to be set aside for the interview, and other details. Preplanning leads to a more professional presentation, makes your interview more efficient, and helps you accomplish your interviewing goals.

The Opening of the Interview.   The opening starts with the first face-to-face contact with a prospect who visits your office for the first time or at the house where you try to obtain a new listing. It is assumed that your opening remarks establish a *rapport* that creates a favorable climate for later interaction.

After discussing social amenities or other topics to establish rapport, you will probably explain the *interview purpose,* the second part of opening the interview. Your object here is to provide a statement of purpose which may take the form of several introductory comments. Huseman, Lahiff, and Hatfield review eight attention-getting statements which they call *starters.*[1] To review how to explain the interview purpose, assume that you are trying to negotiate a new listing.

1. *Summarize the problem.* "Because we have families wanting to buy houses in this neighborhood, we need new houses listed for sale."

2. *Explain how you knew about the problem.* "I noticed that you advertised your house for sale in last night's paper. Have you had any good prospects?"

3. *Mention a reward for participating in the interview.* "We are making a marketing survey in this neighborhood. We will be pleased to share our survey with you for your help." Offer some form of service since real estate license laws usually prohibit giving gifts for new business.

4. *Request advice or assistance.* "We are making a market survey in this neighborhood. Do you know if any of your neighbors have recently sold or are planning to sell their house?"

5. *Refer to a person's position on an issue.* "I know you want the highest price. May I show you how our firm is prepared to get the best qualified buyer for your house?"

6. *Refer to the person who suggested the interview.* "Your neighbor, Mrs. Jones, suggested that you might want to sell your house."

7. *Refer to the organization one represents.* "I'm with Ajax Realty. You may recall that we sold your neighbor's house last week."

8. *Request a specific period of time.* "May I take five minutes of your time to explain our services?"

[1]Richard C. Huseman, James M. Lahiff, and John D. Hatfield, *Interpersonal Communication and Organizations* (Boston: Holbrook Press, Inc., 1976), pp. 180–81.

The above represent opening statements which probably would require additional explanation. Explaining the purpose of the interview is best undertaken after establishing rapport. When you are sure that the person being interviewed understands the interview, move to the body of the interview.

The Body of the Interview.   At this point you demonstrate your personal skills in communicating with buyers and sellers. Following the communication process, you depend heavily on questions and comments that support the buyer and seller, and you constantly engage in feedback. The body of the interview follows the preplanning in which you communicate relevant information, listen effectively, and motivate the person interviewed with new or additional information as the interview progresses. By using properly worded questions, you control the interview and determine the best time to close.

The Closing of the Interview.   There is no hard and fast rule for determining the best time to close the interview. If you are helping the buyer reach a final decision, closing would probably include a review of the main points you consider important. Some closings are brief, but if the interviews are long, you must avoid showing impatience or making abrupt statements that reveal your irritation. Prolonged closings are often advised for interviews directed to a decision. Skilled closers use this portion of the interview to make a summary, to arrange follow-up meetings, and to express appreciation.

The Interview Follow-Up.   The follow-up may take many forms. Even if the sale is completed, a later follow-up with your satisfied prospect provides additional listings and future sales. Consider also the unsatisfied prospect who inspects your listings. Here a follow-up letter may reestablish communications. Whether the follow-up takes the form of a telephone call, a personal visit, or a letter, it confirms the fact that interviews have a definite structure; that is, the sales interview is not a random, isolated event. It should be viewed as a process that eventually accomplishes its purpose and builds sales volume.

The Format of the Interview

Interviews may be further classified as *scheduled interviews* or *nonscheduled interviews.* If you have been selling homes for five years and have been a member of the Million Dollar Club in each of those years, you probably follow the nonscheduled format and use a minimum of forms or questionnaires. If you are less experienced, you probably use a buyer qualification form that lists recommended questions for qualifying a buyer. By referring to a prepared form during the interview, you are more likely to ask open and probing questions.

Scheduled Interviews.   Interviews tend to be more formal and highly scheduled if the information you need is critical. Scheduled interviews are favored if the information gained will be repeatedly used, your interviewing time is short, or you are relatively inexperienced. Hence, in listing a house for sale, you are advised to use a form because the information gained will be reproduced and relied upon by other salespersons and buyer-prospects. The information must be precise and it will be used over the next several weeks. If, however, you are qualifying a buyer during an unscheduled, informal interview, the preciseness of the information is not nearly so critical. However, buyer qualification without a guiding form is not advised for the inexperienced.

If the form is used, the interview tends to be more highly preplanned and concentrates on factual information. This form of interview lacks the flexibility exercised by more experienced persons who gain the same information with the skillful use of open and probing questions.

Nonscheduled Interview.   In the nonscheduled interview you depend on spontaneous interaction with the buyer. Here you create a friendly atmosphere and conduct the interview to solve the buyer's problems. In this case, the buyer does most of the talking, but you ask open questions in order to clarify and gain additional information from the prospective buyer.

It is recognized that this format requires a high level of skill. An incorrect interpretation of buyer attitudes and needs or failure to ask the right probing and open questions may lose the prospect. Moreover, probably more time is spent with the prospect under the nonscheduled format.

Interviewing Procedures

Your skill in conducting the interview must overcome the lack of skill of the person being interviewed. Your buyer will not know the questions that should be asked and probably has little understanding of real estate financing and property values. Some will prolong the interview with irrelevant discussion and others will try to terminate the interview before either party has accomplished its purpose.

Your interviewing technique will improve if you concentrate on procedures recommended by authorities in communication.[2] The more common suggestions overcome the possible lack of motivation by the buyer or seller.

Establish Rapport.   Experts in establishing rapport avoid such trite openings as "May I help you" as the prospect enters the office for the first time. You should avoid being overfriendly. Being overfriendly focuses the interview on cultivating a friendship instead of eliciting information. An overfriendly

[2]See Huseman, Lahiff, and Hatfield, *Interpersonal Communication and Organizations,* pp. 183–93.

attitude may adversely affect the prospect's perception. At the same time, too little rapport makes the prospect uneasy and also adversely affects how he or she receives your communications. In the end, there are no broadly accepted rules for establishing rapport.

However, it is equally clear that you draw on your *own personality* to establish rapport effectively. Your personality controls the amount of courtesy, interest, sincerity, and attention you give your interviewee. Your demeanor may show undesirable qualities such as personal deference, impersonality, and pretentiousness.

Some salespersons use *common ground remarks* (small talk about mutual interests). This is really a matter of making conversation unrelated to the topic at hand. Conversation that eventually leads to common mutual interest breeds a friendly atmosphere. Other salespersons concentrate on *simple courtesies* to develop rapport. This is more than extending a cigarette or offering coffee; it includes such acts as thanking the prospect for inquiring about the advertisement or making sure that the prospect and family are comfortable in the office setting.

Finally, extra care should be taken in *demonstrating respect and admiration;* you complement the prospect or agree with his or her beliefs or interests in order to create the right atmosphere. After you have created the correct degree of rapport, you must maintain rapport throughout your relations with the prospect. Above all, make the prospect feel important.

Ask Questions.   The interview progresses by effectively using direct, open, probing, mirror, and leading questions. Select a few examples of each type of question that seem to fit the main parts of your scheduled and non-scheduled interviews in dealing with prospects and sellers.

Listen Effectively.   In this context listening requires that you observe behavior by noting both nonverbal and verbal communication. You soon learn to recognize a buyer-prospect's common defense mechanisms. You learn what measures effectively cope with common defenses and you soon learn the housing aspirations, family goals, and personal values that are important to your prospect.

Recall the nonverbal communication clues to a prospect's attitudes: (1) body motion, (2) touching behavior, and (3) voice characteristics that help in interpreting statements. Effective communication depends partly on personal appearance (clothes, eyeglasses, perfume, and hair style) and certain spatial factors such as the placement of the furniture, lighting, and room noises. You are aware that you will unconsciously judge your buyer on his or her appearance, the sound of his or her voice, and his or her body movements during the interview. You will place special meaning on body movements that show approval, nervousness, irritation, or disapproval.

Provide Support for Prospects.   Be sure to show an awareness of the prospect's problems. Support the prospect's desire to improve housing and sympathize with his or her beliefs, interests, and goals. Support tends to reduce the prospect's defenses so that he or she is more likely to concentrate on your message.

Provide Periodic Summaries.   In focusing on a particular house that seems to meet your prospect's needs, summarize the main reasons why you think the house is suited to the prospect. Periodically remind your prospect of the important points: for example, the house has an attractive family room, there is basement space for the husband's hobby shop, and there is an unusually large two-car carport with storage space for bicycles.

Or, alternatively, at the appropriate time summarize by reminding the prospect that the property can be financed with second mortgage financing which will allow the prospect to buy this particular house with the cash available while temporarily increasing monthly payments until the second mortgage is paid. Summarizing enables you to communicate the situation to the prospect and move from one critical point to another.

Respond to Questions.   Your presentation should encourage the prospect to ask questions. Questions about your services, the house shown, the neighborhood, or other related topics deserve clear, specific, and direct answers. If your response involves a negative point, reply directly and honestly and turn to factors that compensate for the negative point. If you do not know the answer, get additional information from the best source in the shortest time. Do not try to minimize or avoid negative factors since there are always many compensating positive factors in favor of the house you are showing.

POINTS TO REMEMBER

Recall the critical orientation you give to the selling process. You determine this orientation by beginning with the self-analysis which (preferably in a group setting) will call for the preliminary self-analysis to create the right atmosphere for group interaction. The questions presented in the self-analysis give you an insight into what people think of you as a person and direct attention to your communication strengths and weaknesses, suggesting how you may remedy deficiencies and build on your strengths.

At this point you will recognize that you probably lie between an orientation stressing concern for people and a concern for the sale. If you work toward the ideal position of being oriented toward solving the prospect's problem, you carefully organize the prospect interview and work toward the best housing decision that gives the prospect maximum satisfaction over his or her purchase.

In part, these objectives are accomplished by recognizing the formal structure of the interview with its five main parts, starting with preplanning and ending with a follow-up of the interview. By adapting your interview to its purpose (which includes interviews to secure *information,* to obtain *new information,* to make *decisions,* and to *change attitudes and behavior*), you are better able to make your interviews more professional. You follow certain broad rules that guide each part of the interview.

There are times when you are advised to use the scheduled interview that uses forms to seek information from prospects or the nonscheduled interview that calls for more skill. In each interview try to do the following:

Establish rapport.
Ask questions.
Listen effectively.
Provide prospect support.
Provide periodic summaries.
Respond to questions.

These suggestions should encourage you to develop professional interviews that concentrate heavily on direct questioning techniques that place most emphasis on the listening process. Your interview style must conform to its purpose and the relationship between the interviewer and the party interviewed. Unconsciously you adapt the interview to the formal interview structure: *preplanning,* the *opening,* the *body,* the *close,* and the *follow-up.*

REVIEW QUESTIONS

1. What is the purpose of the preliminary self-analysis?
2. Explain how you would undertake a self-analysis.
3. What is the purpose in comparing the difference between an individual's perception of his or her personality and the group's perception of the individual's personality?
4. Discuss the main advantages of the self-analysis.
5. Describe the difference between orientation toward people, the sale, and problem solving.
6. Explain the purposes and give examples of the different types of sale interviews.
7. Explain how you would structure a five-part interview.
8. Explain the differences between a scheduled interview and a nonscheduled interview. Give examples of each.
9. What recommendations do you have for establishing rapport with prospects?

3

Meeting Buyer Objections

Successfully meeting buyer objections depends largely on other sales procedures, for, ideally, every step of the sales process leads to a completed sale. In the ideal case, there would be no objections because each step in the sales process helps conclude the sale. But even assuming these ideals are reached, buyers raise objections for unpredictable and often irrational reasons.

For instance, some buyers initially object because they are reluctant to spend so much money. Some buyers raise objections as part of the negotiating process. Others require the support of the salesperson in overcoming personal doubts. And to reach a final decision, some buyers need expert help.

To work with prospects who raise these objections, first, take steps to minimize the opportunities for buyers to make objections. In the present context, these steps are referred to as methods of *conditioning* the buyer. Next, anticipate objections (this is the procedure followed by the experienced salesperson). Finally, consider the preferred ways of meeting the 12 most common objections. These objections are discussed later in this chapter.

CONDITIONING THE BUYER

There are preventive measures that minimize the possibility of buyer objections. Methods of meeting buyer objections are more effective if these preventive measures have been taken. Although their importance has been mentioned in other chapters, these preventive measures deserve repeating: know the property and know the buyer's needs.

Know the Property

You know the property if you are familiar with the property's advantages and limitations. If the backyard is too small, anticipate this possible objection by pointing out how the trees, shrubbery, and backyard fence give privacy not found in larger lots that do not have these improvements. If you know the limitations of the house (and among different buyers every house has some limitations), point out the positive features that offset limitations.

In responding to the objection that the house has inadequate window space, you could counter by noting that heating and air conditioning costs are lower, even noting that the monthly heating bill may be considerably lower than heating bills of other listed property. (In northeastern United States the utility companies recommend storm windows and a total window area equal to not more than 8 percent of the wall area.)

Some other points that offset stated limitations are listed below:

Buyer Objection	Positive Response
The bedrooms are too small.	Extra bathroom adds to convenience of the sleeping area.
There is no basement.	Utility room and storage area provide needed space at a lower cost.
The house and lot are below street grade.	The lower elevation exposes the house to cooler air.
The lot slopes too steeply.	The hillside exposure lowers heating costs by exposing the house to more sunshine.
The living room is too small.	The large family room provides more space for family activities.

The range of positive advantages that offset stated objections is virtually without limit. But you must know the details of each listed property to make effective use of this technique.

Know Buyer Needs

Carefully review the buyer qualification form; know the housing desires of both the husband and wife. This point is critical, for if you show the buyer the wrong house because you did not understand the family's true needs and financial status, the buyer may raise objections that are difficult to overcome. Their motivations as buyers should be kept in mind.

ANTICIPATE OBJECTIONS

Assuming that you know what the buyer wants to see and you know the property, your next step is to anticipate objections. If the buyer wants a large lot, know lot dimensions. If the prospect wants a study and the present owner has not furnished a room as a study, anticipate this objection by suggesting that the basement room can be easily converted to a private study. If the floor plan is too small, point out the savings in maintenance, rugs, heating, and air conditioning. Recognize the deficiencies that may be raised by the buyer so that you may give him or her compensating advantages.

THE TWELVE COMMON OBJECTIONS

Experienced brokers encourage objections. The prospect who does not raise an objection is probably not interested in buying the home you are showing. Or, worse, he or she is not interested in purchasing at any time. A person who offers objections is interested in buying but is concerned about specific features. As each objection is answered, you are that much closer to a sale because the prospect becomes more convinced that this is the best house.

If the buyer is a first owner, it is usually necessary to explain that buyers typically compromise some of their desires. Very often an added feature of the house is unexpected and offsets a feature that does not fully meet the buyer's requirements. You should know the buyer's requirements in sufficient detail so that you can identify items that have the highest priority and that, within the buyer's price range, a particular house more nearly meets the buyer's wants.

It is a well-accepted rule that objections should be met by asking why. Answers to your questions indicate the seriousness of the objection and allow you to sympathize with the prospect. Concentrate on meeting the 12 following most common objections:

1. The monthly payments are too high.
2. A new house is better than an old house.
3. The down payment is too high.
4. We will wait until mortgage interest rates decline.
5. We want to think it over.
6. The house is too far from the job.
7. The house has no basement.
8. We would rather continue renting than buy now.
9. The price is too high.
10. The house is in poor condition.
11. We don't like the neighborhood.
12. We are not ready to buy yet.

Beware of objections that are insincere. The buyer may be stalling because he or she is not interested in the house. Search for the real meaning behind the objection. The trained salesperson listens carefully, agrees with the prospect, and determines if the objection is a key objection or if the objection may be overlooked. The salesperson responds to each of these objections directly, offers explanations, and describes other features of the house.

The Monthly Payments Are Too High

Be prepared to compare the *monthly effective income* and *effective monthly housing payments*. A form for making this comparison is shown in Figure 3-1. Note that monthly effective income begins with the gross monthly pay less federal and state withholding of net income taxes. Net effective monthly income is what is left after deducting social security payments, pension payments, medical insurance, and similar payroll deductions. Although the gross monthly pay amounts to $1,875, the *net effective monthly* income amounts to $1,208.88. This is the amount the lender considers in establishing the eligibility for a mortgage (less other obligations such as car payments, alimony, and in some cases monthly utility costs).

As an alternative, review the income requirements of local lenders. Not all lenders require a statement of the net monthly income. Betty I. McDonald of Northside Realty Associates, Atlanta, Georgia, reports that Northside follows a different rule. Generally prospects qualify for conventional mortgage loans if their monthly payments (including principal, interest, taxes, and insurance) equal one-fourth of their gross monthly income. In the Atlanta area lenders qualify prospects under this general rule if the monthly debt payments do not exceed one-third of the gross monthly income. Local Veterans Administration and Federal Housing Administration qualifications deserve constant review because their regulations change and vary by region.

Next compare the effective monthly income with housing payments. With the assumed $40,000 mortgage, monthly principal and interest payments total $349.60. After adding monthly insurance and property taxes, it would appear that the monthly housing cost would equal $409.60.

Here you must determine the *after income tax* monthly payments. If the net income tax rate approximates 30 percent, the monthly mortgage payment is reduced by $107.00 to $302.60. With an effective monthly income of $1,209.04 this *after income tax* mortgage payment falls within acceptable limits. See Figure 3-1. (Remember that a married couple filing jointly reaches the 49 percent income tax bracket when their taxable income is $45,801.)

Some real estate brokers recommend that these figures be shown on a *weekly* basis in order to minimize the apparent cost of housing. Still others add additional housing costs such as natural gas, electricity, water, and an allowance for monthly maintenance. If you estimate these expenses fairly accurately, they will be helpful in showing the difference between the cost of the house being presented and the cost of other owned or rented houses. Further, if income is shown on a weekly basis, the home buyer readily sees

FIGURE 3-1. Calculating Effective Monthly Payments

Sales price $50,000
Mortgage $40,000

Down payment $10,000
Terms   9½%,   25 years,   None
     (Interest)   (Term)   (Points)

Monthly Effective Income

Gross monthly pay		$1,875.00
Less federal income tax withholding	$349.76	
Less state income taxes	86.67	
Less social security	114.94	
Other deductions		
Pension payments	93.75	
Medical insurance	21.00	
Other	—	− 666.12
Net effective monthly income		$1,208.88

Monthly Housing Payments

Monthly mortgage payments principal and interest		$349.60
Monthly property taxes		40.00
Monthly insurance cost		20.00
Total monthly cost		$409.60
Less income tax deductions		
First month's interest	$316.67	
Monthly property tax	40.00	
Total deductions	$356.67	
Income tax rate 0.30 × $356.67		−$107.00
(Decimal) (Total deductions)		
Effective monthly cost		$302.60

how much of the weekly paycheck goes toward housing.

It should be added that when you discuss monthly payments after income tax, you should remind prospects that the principal payment is recovered when the house is resold. Providing that the house sells for the original cost, or more, the principal may be regarded as "money in the bank" instead of a monthly expense.

Prospects should also be advised that under a constant level payment mortgage, monthly payments of principal and interest remain unchanged over the life of the loan. Even if variable rate mortgages are used, the index adjustment may move at a lower rate than the general price level. Consequently, it is more than likely that your prospect can anticipate higher earnings over the life of the loan because monthly mortgage payments will absorb a smaller proportion of monthly income.

A New House Is Better than an Old House

Refer the prospect to an itemized list of the actual out-of-pocket costs incurred in buying a new house. Builder-offered houses are frequently advertised in terms of a basic price available with options. The options may include housing appliances such as dishwashers, washers, dryers, refrigerators, and optional tile work, plumbing, basement finishing, and owner-constructed storm drains. Fireplaces, additional painting, insulation, and better quality hardware may raise the price several hundred dollars above the price of an older house. Compare the price per square foot of the listed house presented with the price per square foot of a new house.

Point out that the price of an older house includes landscaping. New houses typically require lawn planting, fencing, shrubs, land leveling, patio construction, and the like. Also point out that older houses typically include window treatments: curtain rods, drapery rods, and in some instances curtains, draperies, and window screens all of which may cost several hundred dollars in a new house.

Here is the place to concentrate on differences in neighborhoods. Newly developed neighborhoods run the risk of being overbuilt before the neighborhood is established and prices have stabilized. In neighborhoods that are almost fully developed the values generally are rising or are stable relative to new subdivisions that are undergoing market evaluation.

The Down-Payment Is Too High

If this is a true objection, the recommended response should indicate that final closing will take 30 days in the case of FHA financing or even longer, perhaps 60 days. This gives the prospect additional time to meet closing costs. A work sheet prepared for the prospect provides an estimate of the cash required at the time of closing. If the work-sheet procedure is used, make certain that estimates are on the liberal side. It is better to overestimate than underestimate.

Sales associates often use local rules of thumb to estimate closing costs. Closing costs and practices vary widely by region. For example, in the Atlanta, Georgia area closing costs for conventional loans approximate 3.3 percent of the loan plus $75. Closing VA and FHA loans generally cost between 2.5 percent and 3.0 percent of the loan.

More precise information is gained by completing that portion of the settlement statement that applies to the borrower. Since most buyers and sellers will be given the HUD disclosure/settlement statement, it is convenient to use this form to estimate closing costs and minimum down payments. Copies of this form may be obtained from local lenders. The form is sufficiently flexible to add customary costs experienced in your locality. Completing this form, in all its detail, allows the buyer to compare his or her available cash with the estimated amount due at closing. Regardless of the method used, it is critical that you qualify the prospect so that you show dwellings within the buyer's financial ability to purchase.

Indeed, the sale may hinge on this point. If the prospect has a qualifying monthly effective income and is sold on a particular house, consider alternative financing plans such as a second mortgage, a purchase money mortgage taken by the seller, or contracts for sale. Consider further some of the other new mortgage plans, for example, flexible payment mortgages, balloon payments, wraparound mortgages, or contracts of sale that provide for mortgage financing after equity reaches a minimum value.

We Will Wait Until
Mortgage Interest Rates Decline

Many families make payments on mortgages negotiated five, ten, or more years ago. They are accustomed to mortgage interest rates of from 5 percent to 8 percent. Understandably, current mortgage interest rates of $8\frac{1}{2}$ to 11 percent annual interest may disturb these prospects. Some buyers even multiply the number of monthly payments (300 months for a 25-year mortgage) by the total monthly payment. For example, principal and interest payments of $336 per month would be required for a 9 percent, 25-year mortgage of $40,000. The total amount paid over the life of the mortgage would be $100,800 which on its face compares unfavorably with the price of the house, $50,000.

Three points are relevant here:

1. It is unlikely that the prospect will continue to live in the house over the life of the mortgage. The average life of a mortgage is approximately seven years.
2. Because under the current law interest on home mortgages is income tax deductible, the *effective interest rate* is considerably lower. Under a mortgage

interest rate of 9 percent, a person subject to a 33 percent marginal income tax rate has an *effective* (after-tax) interest rate of 6 percent. The tax advantage increases with higher income tax brackets, which currently range upward to 70 percent.

3. If inflation continues—and there seems every likelihood that there will be a continued inflation rate of 9 percent or more per year—fixed payment mortgages are repaid with constantly cheaper dollars. This is a considerable advantage over renting because rent tends to rise with the general price level. Under a conventional fixed payment mortgage, the borrower benefits from rising prices.

To be sure, there is a possibility that mortgage interest rates may decline, favoring the person who postpones a home purchase and mortgage. However, the income tax deductibility of mortgage interest more than compensates for the possibility that future mortgage interest rates will decline.

We Want to Think It Over

After the prospect has been shown the best house available within his or her financial means, suggest that the prospect make the decision while you are there to answer questions. Point out that it is your job to help the prospect make the right decision. Refer again to the prospect's expressed needs and how this house most nearly satisfies the prospect's requirements within the preferred price range.

It may be that the prospect believes that real estate prices are "too high" and believes that prices will decrease over the next few months. Explain that construction costs have increased at an average rate of 10 percent per year (or a compound rate of approximately 7 percent per year). Current trends indicate the probability of continued increases in construction costs. Moreover, subdivision land prices have shown a dramatic increase over the last five or ten years.

Your knowledge of resales should support this point. Turn to the competitive market analysis showing resales in the neighborhood that have sold within the same price range. If this approach fails, show other comparable houses.

There is one additional point. Almost every broker has dealt with a prospect who has delayed a decision only to have another buyer purchase the house the prospect wanted. Or, conversely, if a second prospect knows that another prospect is also considering the house, the second prospect is likely to make a quick and favorable decision to buy.

The House is Too Far from the Job

Generally, prospects face increased travel time for the better housing buys. Convert the extra travel time to minutes per day. Show the advantages of sacrificing the small daily travel time in return for the advantages of this house, i.e., more square footage, a larger lot, a location closer to schools, and the like.

If it is true that the outlying houses offer more housing value for the dollar, point out that closer locations that save only a few minutes of driving time are considerably more expensive. In addition, closer in locations are usually higher density neighborhoods that have more congestion and less open space.

Finally, if you are to be convincing, you must know the best route to the job and the driving time, not the distance, from the house being presented to the prospect's employment. A highly successful saleswoman of Northside Realty Associates of Atlanta, Georgia, Colleen O'Donnell, always carries a street map whenever she shows a house. If this objection is raised, she indicates the best route to follow to get on the freeway and she quickly gives driving times to the job, local schools, and the nearest regional shopping area. This approach works; she sold 80 dwellings last year.

Consider one additional point: Outlying districts are usually closer to recreational facilities. Although the husband may have to drive a little farther to work, the rest of the family is closer to recreation and travels less. If the house is close to golf courses or other sources of leisure time frequented by the husband on weekends, the total driving time may be less in an outlying location than in a location closer to the job.

The House Has No Basement

In response to this objection, agree that a nice basement certainly contributes to housing value. But you should also add that "unless the house is especially adapted to basement construction, say for a daylight basement, basement space is usually the most expensive space in the house. Much of the space remains unused and frequently the placement of pipes and ducts will not allow for the required finished ceiling height of 7 feet, 6 inches." Frequently the basement is poorly adapted to the living area because of the limited light and ventilation.

Though the house may not have a basement, the floor plan compensates for the loss of this space with a savings in construction costs. The extra large garage and the enclosed utility room perform the same function without the expensive basement construction. Point out that the extra large closets, guest and linen closets, or added storage give equal utility without expensive basement construction—an area that remains largely unused. Also point out that unless the basement has a specific use, for a workshop, recreational room, or den, for example, in terms of its cost and frequency of use, it is the most expensive area of the house. Because of the level topography and drainage problems in some communities, basements have little utility; an example would be south Florida.

A good approach to this objection would be to start with the question: "Why do you want a basement?" Among the many suggestions that follow from answers to this question, consider these replies:

You can add an extra room on back of the house.
The backyard has space for a prefabricated storage and utility building.
You can add a childrens' playhouse in the backyard.

In short, meet the objection by discovering why the objection was raised.

We Would Rather Continue Renting Than Buy Now

There are two recommended answers to this objection: (1) There are more amenities associated with ownership than renting, and (2) given the same quality of living space, buying is less expensive than renting. In the latter case, turn to your estimate of effective net monthly cost—the monthly ownership cost less the annual income tax saving.

With this figure in mind, start your presentation with the following question: "Can you rent an apartment that has the same features for $350 a month?" Point out that renting often requires one to two months rental payment in advance, a damage deposit, and a lease that commits the tenant for one to three years. Since apartment owners face rising utility, maintenance, and operating costs, suggest that by renting the tenant risks continuing increases in rent. In contrast, the owner benefits from the equity build-up resulting from monthly payments in the mortgage principal. Be prepared to show by means of a mortgage table how much the equity increases over a five-year term. If dwelling prices increase in the neighborhood (as you are prepared to show they have in the past), the homeowner's equity usually increases with inflation.

To illustrate, consider Table 3-1 which shows the annual amount paid against principal for a mortgage of $50,000 payable monthly, 9 percent interest over 30 years. At the end of the fifth year the mortgage principal payments total $2,050. By the end of the tenth year the buyer has increased his equity in the property by $5,300, a sum that the buyer would receive if the property were resold at the original price or above.

The renter has no such economic advantage. An experienced saleswoman in Miami, Florida reminds the prospect that renters collect only rent receipts; the homeowner benefits from principal payments on the mortgage.

Close the presentation by repeating the appealing features that meet the prospect's needs. Review the appeal of the backyard garden, the play space for the children, the location five minutes from the freeway, the desirable neighbors, the extra bedroom, the added family room, and the like.

TABLE 3-1. Cumulative Equity Build-up For a $50,000 Mortgage Payable Monthly, 9% Interest Over 30 Years

End of Year	Cumulative Equity Build-Up
1	$ 350
2	700
3	1,100
4	1,550
5	2,050
6	2,600
7	3,200
8	3,800
9	4,500
10	5,300

The Price Is Too High

This is a common objection that frequently conceals the true objection. You must first ask the buyer why he or she thinks the price is too high. If you truly believe this is the real objection, turn to your competitive market analysis. Go over the prices, offerings, and listed prices of other houses having similar features in the same or similar neighborhoods. It is helpful if you have calculated the price per square foot, provided you can account for price differences between houses. Again, show that the price for this particular house is justified because of the new carpets, the extra bathroom, a more elaborate fireplace, or central air conditioning. Frequently, buyers compare prices of houses that are dissimilar in important value-determining features.

For example, assume that the husband thinks the price of the house is too much. Ask how much is too much. Assume further that the husband says "about $2,000." (This gives you the desired opening.) You then say, "About $2,000? Let's consider the real effect of that $2,000. If you buy this house, how long do you think you would live in it? At least five years? At least ten years?" The husband answers ten years. You say, "Okay, if you own the house for 10 years, that's about $200 a year or 50 weeks a year, allowing for a two-week vacation. This is equal to a weekly cost of $4 a week. You would be using the house 7 days a week for a cost of about 50 cents a day. Now, Mr. Wagner, for an additional 50 cents a day would you prefer this house to the other houses we looked at this morning?"

As a final suggestion, go with the buyer to other houses, again comparing prices and features that support the asking price. Work toward a realistic offer if, in your judgment, the listing is overpriced and the seller anticipates a lower offer.

In dealing with this issue the salesperson gives an invaluable counseling service. For here the salesperson encounters two prospects: (1) the transferee from another city and (2) the local buyer who relates current housing prices to the housing prices paid when the current house was purchased. In the former case, it is common to find that housing values vary widely among the regions of the United States. This buyer needs a salesperson to counsel him or her on local housing costs.

If the buyer is local, the agent must suggest working through a competitive market analysis to show the value of the present home and to show that the price of the new house is reasonable. Both the transferee and the local buyer are dependent on the salesperson's current knowledge of the market.

The House Is in Poor Condition

It is unlikely that every house you show will be in ideal condition. There are too many absentee owners, estate sales, foreclosed properties, and distress sales. Yet, very often these houses are "good buys," and with a little additional investment they meet the needs of your prospect. As part of your advance preparation, prepare realistic estimates on the cost of needed repairs, for example, replacing the carpets, installing a new dishwasher, or interior and exterior repainting. Point out that if the owner desires to do the work, the cost of materials will amount to "about $300" and point out that owner repairs would increase the value of the house.

Another argument in favor of buying a house in poor condition is that the buyer saves money by discounting the price according to the present condition. With the money saved, the new owners may redecorate the home according to their own personal preferences. It would be difficult to justify redecoration of a house purchased in good condition. Therefore, the house in poor condition may be redecorated to conform to the owner's taste and in harmony with the prospect's furniture, rugs, curtains, draperies, and other home furnishings.

If the price has been lowered to compensate for the present condition, this point should be verified by your competitive market analysis showing that like houses in better condition have recently sold for higher prices.

Before the listing was taken every effort should have been taken to place the house in the best possible light, but this is not always possible. In such cases, suggest to the buyer:

"Why don't you make your offer subject to these repairs?"

or, alternatively:

"Would you want to make your own repairs and have the seller reduce the asking price?"

In sum, the house in need of repairs presents added options for the buyer; the salesperson must be prepared to explain these options.

We Don't Like the Neighborhood

The best way to deal with this objection is to ask why. Is it because of the schools or the distance from employment, local shopping facilities, or access to the freeway? The reply to these questions shows the seriousness of the objection. Weigh this objection against the buyer's needs. If the objection is really not too serious, turn to the positive features of the neighborhood, for example, the twice a week garbage collection, the municipal services (sewers, municipal water), low property taxes, or other advantageous neighborhood features.

Remember that most buyers look to the neighborhood first and the dwelling second. Your presentation would be incomplete if you do not provide a review of neighborhood features.

You will probably note that values in different neighborhoods in your community are rising, stable, or declining. Before showing this house you should determine the past trends in neighborhood values. Judge each neighborhood with respect to the trend in resales, the number of new houses under construction, the percent of owner-occupancy, the number of vacancies, the quality of housing maintenance, and landscaping. The comparative market analysis should support your conclusion that values are rising or are relatively stable, thus providing good security and a favorable long-run investment for your prospect. Property owners are very interested in this latter point.

We Are Not Ready to Buy Yet

Typically, this prospect prefers to postpone a decision hoping that later on, perhaps next year, he or she could make a better buy. To overcome this objection, refer to your competitive market analysis showing housing prices of last year. Suggest that the houses currently available will soon be sold and that new listings over the next few months will probably increase in price. In addition, financing terms may be less favorable.

THE FINAL STEP

At this point you know if you have a highly motivated prospect or a prospect whose requirements are impossible to satisfy in view of the prospect's savings and annual income. Suppose you have not met the real objections of the buyer;

it would seem that you have not found the right house. If you find that you have shown the prospect every suitable house and you are not convinced that he or she should buy any of the houses shown, use the following approach:

> This neighborhood is very popular, yet we have businesses that frequently transfer employees to other locations. Because the housing market in this neighborhood is very active, we will undoubtedly have several new listings within a few days. At this time may I make an appointment for you and your wife to come back next Wednesday giving me time to select the right house for you. Would next Wednesday at 11:00 be convenient?

Make a definite appointment, but if on Monday you find a house that seems suitable, call the prospect immediately and say:

> I know we were to meet Wednesday, but this house was listed this morning and I want you to be the first to see the house, especially since it has most of the features that you need. The house is priced at the market and we expect the house to sell quickly. I told the owner to expect us tonight at 7:00. Would that be convenient for both of you?

The final rule is not to send a prospect away without setting a definite appointment to look at other houses. Never suggest that you will call the prospect at the end of the week to set up another appointment. Always make the appointment definite. If you do not, the prospect might turn to another agency.

FINAL COMMENT

Brokers are known for answering a question with another question in order to maintain control of of the interview. For instance, during the housing inspection the prospect may comment on the fact that the draperies match the living room wallpaper and then ask, "Do you think they will leave the draperies?" Definitely do not say, "No, that's personal property." Answer instead, "Would you like the draperies to stay?" If the prospect answers yes, you will probably make the sale.

Or, suppose the wife seems very much attracted to the house, but the husband hesitates. To offset his wife's enthusiasm, he may make small objections. For example, he may say that his bedroom is too small. Your reply should be, "This bedroom is too small?" Typically, the husband either validates the objection or forgets it. If the wife is attracted to the house, she herself may answer the objection.

POINTS TO REMEMBER

Almost every buyer-prospect voices objections (objections will be made even on the property eventually purchased). The skillful manner in which these objections are met may protect the sale and, at the least, will complete the sale in the shortest time. All parties in the transaction benefit from a salesperson who effectively meets buyer objections. Figure 3–2 summarizes the preliminary steps that must be taken to minimize the chance of buyer objections. These preliminary steps condition the buyer to the home you are selling. This means that, *first,* you must know the property. You must know its advantageous features and you must know its major limitations. *Second,* you must qualify the buyer and engage in sufficient conversation so that you know the buyer's true housing needs and his or her financial ability to purchase. And, *third,* you must try to anticipate objections. Prepare to agree with objections and turn to advantages that offset each objection.

In dealing with specific objections, study the recommended ways to overcome the 12 most common objections. If the prospect is a first-time buyer, explain to the buyer that most buyers have to compromise in their housing

Figure 3-2. Meeting Buyer Objections

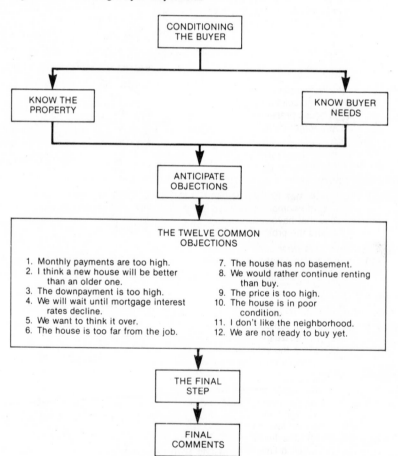

CONDITIONING THE BUYER

KNOW THE PROPERTY

KNOW BUYER NEEDS

ANTICIPATE OBJECTIONS

THE TWELVE COMMON OBJECTIONS

1. Monthly payments are too high.
2. I think a new house will be better than an older one.
3. The downpayment is too high.
4. We will wait until mortgage interest rates decline.
5. We want to think it over.
6. The house is too far from the job.
7. The house has no basement.
8. We would rather continue renting than buy.
9. The price is too high.
10. The house is in poor condition.
11. I don't like the neighborhood.
12. We are not ready to buy yet.

THE FINAL STEP

FINAL COMMENTS

purchases. (This is especially important if the buyer has in mind a "dream castle" that is impossible to realize within his or her monthly income.) In sum, this discussion has emphasized ways to meet the 12 most common objections.

1. *The monthly payments are too high.* Break down monthly payments into interest, principal, insurance, and property taxes. Show how monthly payments are reduced by income tax advantages. Compare this figure to monthly rents.

2. *A new house is better than an old house.* Inform the prospect that the items in the older house are included in the sale but if he or she purchases a new house, the cost of these items must be added to the price of the new house.

3. *The down payment is too high.* Show that the buyer has four to eight weeks to raise the down payment. Use a form showing closing cost details. Consider alternative financing plans that lower the down payment.

4. *We will wait until mortgage interest rates decline.* Explain that most buyers do not pay the full interest on the mortgage because they usually sell before the mortgage expires. Show the effective interest rate after income taxes and how fixed mortgage payments are repaid with constantly cheaper dollars.

5. *We want to think it over.* Ask why the buyer wants to think it over. Try to help the buyer reach a decision now. Show how a delay in making the decision risks losing the house to another buyer. Find out the real objection to making an immediate decision.

6. *The house is too far from the job.* Convert distance to travel time over the best route. Compare the additional driving time per day in minutes to the advantages of the house presented.

7. *The house has no basement.* Suggest that the cost of the basement is saved in this house, and point out that basement space is usually poorly utilized. Point out that the house presented has adequate storage space, extra closets, utility space, and a larger garage area.

8. *We would rather continue renting than buy now.* Review the advantages associated with ownership. Indicate that buying is less expensive than renting as shown by your calculation of the effective net monthly cost of ownership.

9. *The price is too high.* Respond by asking why the buyer thinks the price is too high. Turn to the competitive market analysis showing prices and listings of other houses that have similar features. Convert the difference between the listed price and the prospect's offer to the cost per week.

10. *The house is in poor condition.* Be prepared to discuss material and contract prices for making needed repairs. Either suggest that the prospect make an offer subject to the desired repairs or ask the prospect if he or she would want to make his or her own repairs and have the seller reduce the asking price.

11. *We don't like the neighborhood.* Determine the seriousness of the objection and weigh the final objection against the buyer's needs. If the objection is not too serious, emphasize the positive features of the neighborhood. In this case, you should know if the values in the neighborhood are increasing, stable, or declining. Judgments on these points should be based on the comparative market analysis.

12. *We are not ready to buy yet.* Suggest that houses currently listed will soon be sold and that by postponing a decision, the buyer risks not finding the house suited to his or her needs. Also suggest that housing prices are likely to increase in the next few months and that financing terms are expected to be less favorable in the future. Finally, indicate that the final closing will take several weeks, giving time to secure more cash.

The main point is this: Use a professional approach. Remember that you are the expert on each house being shown to the prospect. Your knowledge of real estate financing and the neighborhood should help the prospect find the house suited to his or her requirements. Be aware that objections may be disguised requests for additional information or they may be raised merely to support an offer below the listed price. Know how to respond to the 12 most common objections and search for the real meaning behind these objections.

REVIEW QUESTIONS

1. What preventive methods may be taken to minimize buyer objections?
2. Explain how your knowledge of the property helps to offset buyer objections.
3. Explain how you would respond to each of the 12 common objectives. Give examples in each case.
4. Discuss how you would work with a prospect who has been shown every suitable house and is reluctant to buy.

4

The Sales Process

Current trends in real estate make salespersons increasingly important. New regulations make buyers and sellers more dependent on the trained real estate salesperson. New types of mortgages complicate the purchase and sale of houses. Other market changes that emphasize the public dependence on salespersons include:

The growing importance of energy conservation in marketing houses.

Changes in communication technology: computer terminals, minicomputers, and selling applications of audio-video equipment.

The continued (and probably permanent) declining value of the dollar (inflation).

The growing importance of environmental controls.

Increasingly, buyers and sellers must turn to the well-staffed real estate firm to help them make buying and selling decisions. In turning to the services of a real estate broker, buyers must look to the salesperson as the prime force in listing and marketing houses. The firm's promotional effort, advertising, training, and reputation focus on the way in which the salesperson understands and executes the sales process. It is the salesperson who sells listed property, adjusts to the real needs of the buyer, and helps guide the prospect to the best decision.

In the last analysis, the work of the salesperson is critically important to the real estate firm and its financial success. It is the salesperson who earns income to cover the office expense, advertising charges, the use of equipment, and supporting staff. It is the successful salesperson, and his or her skill in making sound judgments, who is responsible for completed sales.

All these factors suggest that salespersons face greater challenges and better career opportunities than they did in the past. Clearly, the role of the salesperson will assume greater importance in an efficiently operating real estate market. Although the challenges to real estate salespersons will increase, the rewards will be substantial and will increase, but only if real estate selling is approached as a professional undertaking.

PROFESSIONAL SELLING

Is selling real estate a profession? Real estate authorities give various answers to this question. Probably the important characteristic that identifies the professional salesperson is a *professional point of view.* The question of professional work is not decided solely by education, experience, commissions, or communication skills. It is the attitude toward the work that controls. You are professional if your guiding principle is "What can I do for prospects?" If you ask, "What can my prospects do for me?" then you lack the attributes of a true professional.

Professional Attributes

The main point is this: The professional salesperson provides a service in meeting the needs of the buyer. In meeting these needs, not only is the salesperson proud to associate with his or her firm, but the professional continually guards and advances his or her reputation. The professional person pursues the highest personal principles and advances the reputation of the company.

Consider the main qualities associated with the professional: By using accepted communication techniques, the salesperson *gives advice* about a proposed housing purchase and *contributes to an understanding* of housing values, neighborhoods, and the advantages of a proposed purchase. In addition, the professional understands that the prospect must benefit from the sale. Only by understanding that the prospect must improve his or her circumstances by the sale will the salesperson develop long-lasting associations and repeat business from satisfied customers.

These generalizations are even more true for selling real estate than they are for selling other products. Because the real estate market is imperfect and because it is difficult for the layperson to judge the complex legal, financial, and social aspects of his or her purchase, the community is heavily dependent on the professional conduct of salespersons.

The high level of community service associated with real estate sales—at the very minimum—means that the salesperson knows the following:

1. The details on the house listed for sale: its advantages and limitations.
2. The main neighborhood and community features important to the prospect.
3. A thorough knowledge of ways to finance a housing purchase.
4. That he or she must continually learn more about real estate principles.
5. That professional selling calls for long hours, personal dedication and, above all, hard work.
6. That selling represents a personal service to the prospect.
7. That personal integrity and honesty must always be above question.
8. How to use recommended communication techniques.
9. That he or she must observe the highest ethical standards in dealing with associates and the public.
10. Recommended steps that lead to a successful record of sales.

If the real estate professional understands the importance of serving customers, he or she earns more commissions. Although salesmanship is not a profession compared to other disciplines, it is understood that buyers and prospects place considerable trust and confidence in the salesperson who is expected to act in a professional manner.

Can Selling Be Learned?

Given time, the average person can learn the technical aspects of real estate selling. Before starting a real estate sales career, the person must fulfill the license requirements. Licensing requires a minimum knowledge of real estate law, real estate instruments, real estate finance, appraising, and local, state, and federal laws governing real estate operations.

But then the question may be asked, "Are selling skills acquired by study and practice or does a good sales record follow from a 'natural' personality?" Some believe that salesmanship can neither be taught nor learned. They believe that some individuals are natural salespersons and that others just do not have the personality to sell. There is nothing the ungifted person can do to increase selling ability.

In one sense, it is probably true that some individuals are insufficiently motivated to follow a sales career. They may be successful in some other vocation, but they would probably fail as real estate salespersons. On the other hand, it is recognized that other individuals are highly qualified to succeed in real estate selling and will probably be outstanding because of their personalities, lifestyle, and their likes and dislikes.

Preferred Personality Traits. You will probably find that your associates fall into three different groups. In the *first group* are those whose inherent personal preferences and personality traits make them poorly adapted to selling. These persons are more suited to nonselling roles. Most of your associates fall into the *second group*. Their traits are average but with help and guidance they may follow successful sales careers. They are neither poorly nor exceptionally adapted to the selling task. The *third group* consists of those who have unusual backgrounds, training, and personalities. Their work habits, inherent abilities, and character combine to make them exceptional salespersons.

The last two groups will increase commissions by improving their selling skills. Even the most outstandingly qualified person must learn the requirements of the job as an architect, dentist, or lawyer would have to learn the requirements of those professions. Even the most gifted person must study real estate and the sales process if he or she is to succeed. Probably success in this area depends more on personal determination, dedication, experience, and the willingness to work hard for better than average rewards. Real estate firms and other organizations would not sponsor sales clinics and courses if the principles of good selling could not be taught and learned by the average person.

Personal Attitude Is More Important.   You can be successful without attaining perfection. Even the most talented salesperson makes mistakes. We all have certain limitations which we can never completely overcome. In some cases, you must accept a lost sale. However, a knowledge of the sales process and real estate principles will minimize sales lost because of personal deficiencies.

There is yet another aspect of the real estate profession: education never stops. In selling real estate you never reach the point where you have learned everything there is to know about selling skills. This is partly because the real estate market continually changes. Real estate laws and regulations change. New construction techniques and financing methods are only a few of the topics requiring constant review. Moreover, you never learn too much about people and how to deal with prospects. Thus, only by continually reviewing your sales effort can you hope to maintain a good record of performance. To follow this program requires development of a self-management program.

THE SELF-MANAGEMENT PROGRAM

Real estate salespersons probably have more opportunities to make profitable use of their time than do most other people in other professions. Generally speaking, they have almost unlimited flexibility in arranging their daily schedules. They also know the premium placed on actual time spent with prospects. To prove this point, take the commissions you earned last month or the average commissions earned by all salespersons in the office and calculate the commissions earned *per hour* based on the actual time spent with prospects. This figure shows the importance of maximizing selling time and minimizing selling cost.

In addition to skills in securing new listings and in selling prospects, which for the average salesperson are acquired through education and experience, the difference between the high producer and the low producer is how each one allocates time. Since each person starts the day with 24 hours, it is obvious that the one who produces the most spends his or her time efficiently and devotes the maximum time to prospects.

Budgeting Time

Self-management begins with an orderly plan for allocating time. Since salespersons typically work with a minimum of time supervision, the plan helps the salesperson work systematically. Here it is assumed that there are only two ways to increase sales commissions: sell more effectively and spend more time selling.

The salesperson who executes a plan for allocating time earns higher commissions and gains personal satisfaction in developing a good relationship with satisfied prospects. The plan minimizes nonselling time and unproductive time to the end that sales are maximized. Not all responsibilities are directly sales oriented; the time budget plan allows time for these activities. Examples would be preparing to show houses and gaining new listings. If you avoid misdirecting your efforts, you will minimize selling costs while providing service in helping families find their ideal housing. One method of initiating the time budget is to follow the five-step plan shown in Figure 4-1.

Allocating Time for Selling Functions

Offices vary on how they expect salespersons to perform office functions. With differences allowed for office needs, your daily activities should include the following:

1. Keeping records.
2. Writing ads.
3. Securing new listings.
4. Contacting prospects.
   a. Developing new prospects.
   b. Showing new houses.
5. Maintaining public relations.
   a. Developing rapport with community leaders.
   b. Doing organization work.
      (1) Churches.
      (2) Chamber of Commerce.
      (3) Real estate boards.
      (4) Other community organizations.
6. Reviewing new listings.
7. Continuing your education.

FIGURE 4-1. Initial Steps in Budgeting Time

1. *Know your prospects.*
   a. Determine their present housing.
   b. Review their financial ability and credit rating for their new house purchase.
   c. Be sure that you know their actual personal housing likes and dislikes.
   d. Determine the problems that your prospect may have in making a decision.
   e. Determine the sales aids that would help your prospect buy from you.
2. *Know your product.*
   a. Review the community and neighborhood characteristics important to your prospect.
   b. Continually review your listings so that you may emphasize the benefits of each dwelling.
   c. Review real estate financing techniques that help prospects with financial problems in buying a new house.
3. *Plan your sales presentation.*
   a. Plan your presentation from the time you first meet the prospect.
   b. Plan how you will show the house and how you will highlight amenities important to the prospect.
   c. Determine what you will say on the way to the house, how you will say it, and when you will initiate the close.
4. *Establish a daily schedule.*
   a. Decide how you will allocate time for nonselling tasks, writing ads, securing listings, and determining which prospects you will work with.
   b. Keep to the timetable for each activity you have planned.
5. *Plan daily objectives.*
   a. Stick to your objectives.
   b. Follow up your results at the end of the day.
   c. Plan work each day; work your plan.

Adapted from C. A. Kirkpatrick, *Salesmanship,* 4th ed. (Cincinnati, Ohio: South-Western Publishing Company, 1966), p. 429.

The important point is not so much how you allocate time to each of the listed activies (though you certainly emphasize time spent with prospects) but that you follow a planned schedule that will help you meet daily, weekly, monthly, and annual sales projections.

Some of the items listed above are not direct selling duties. For example, the first item, *keeping records,* provides you with a basis for making more efficient use of your time and developing new skills. The time spent in *writing ads* should be set aside during periods in which it is awkward to show houses or visit new listings. Most offices suggest that you undertake a program to acquire *new listings.* This is a good use of time that cannot be used profitably to work with prospects.

In working with *prospects,* you not only set aside time for showing selected houses to current prospects, but you also take the time to develop new prospects through your many contacts, advertising, and daily personal contacts. In part, developing new prospects is related to your personal public relations activities. In setting aside time with community leaders, you let financial institutions, local government officials, and your friends in local organizations know of your need for new listings and your reputation for service to buyer-prospects. By deliberately engaging in organizational activities of your choosing, i.e., churches, the Chamber of Commerce, the Real Estate Board, and the many community clubs, you help develop repeat business.

Finally, when you are not engaged in direct selling, you should review *new listings* and devote time to your personal *education.* The latter might include formal courses offered through the Real Estate Board or other real estate organizations, community colleges, and your own personal reading and study program. Indeed, one of the attractions of real estate is that you have ample opportunity (and possibly the responsibility) to further your own education through a self-reading program.

Planning Benefits. Most salespersons agree that they should spend as much time as possible with prospects. Yet you must spend the time in nonselling activities such as planning your presentation. Systematic planning will help you (1) identify personal objectives, (2) recognize your main selling problems, and (3) resolve these problems to meet planned objectives.

You will benefit from planning your time wisely because it will prevent you from spending time with persons who will not likely buy. Even for your active prospects, by effectively planning your presentation, you save time by showing your prospect the best selection of listings, for example, 5 houses instead of 25 houses.

There is yet another advantage: Planning prevents you from doing work in haste. Writing your advertisements should be done during quiet times so that you are under no pressure to write a carelessly worded and ineffective ad. Planning helps you to avoid rushing a prospect through a house so that you can meet another commitment. The quality and effectiveness of your showing increase by budgeting your time.

Furthermore, you minimize mistakes and oversights if you systematically plan your day. The record indicates that a given number of prospect showings result in a certain number of closed sales. If you plan your presentations, you may devote more time to direct selling which tends to increase the proportion of sales you close.

Planning Precautions. If you are to obtain the maximum benefits, you must observe certain precautions. *First,* follow company rules governing the conduct of salespersons. Usually these rules have been developed over several years of experience. Do not think that you gain by breaking company rules and policies. Your plan should be subordinate to the policies and rules of the firm.

Second, use common sense in executing the plan. There are times when you must judge for yourself whether or not you should depart from the plan to handle an unusual situation. Your plan should guide you in allocating time, but you should be ready to revise the plan to accommodate necessary and unpredictable demands.

Third, the best plan is dependent on hard work. There is no way you can plan the day to eliminate hard work. Given two hardworking salespersons, the salesperson who follows an orderly, systematic plan for using his or her time earns the higher commissions.

Evaluating the Plan Your plan should undergo periodic review. Figure 4-2 lists points to help you evaluate your plan. Depending on your particular sales organization, add other points deemed essential to your sales operation. It may be that you must devote more time to certain elements of the plan in order to maximize your sales objective, for example, education that leads to more effective selling.

Figure 4-2 covers the points considered necessary to the productive

FIGURE 4-2. Plan Evaluation

1. Have I maintained the right attitude?
2. Have I initiated a continual program of self-improvement?
3. Do I have a plan for obtaining new listings?
4. Does my plan originate new buyer-prospects?
5. Has my plan helped me to develop a good relationship with the following:
   a. My employer.
   b. My associates.
   c. My acquaintances.
   d. Community organizations.
6. Has my plan provided for a sufficient number of contacts with prospects?
7. Have I developed a plan for closing the sale with each prospect?
8. Have I planned for the best possible showing of each listed house?
9. Have I expressed appreciation to cooperating sellers and my prospects?
10. Have I made contacts with past, satisfied customers?
11. Have I developed a plan to secure new listings and new buyer-prospects from former clients?
12. Have I kept proper records so that I can evaluate my sales effort?
13. Have I shown enthusiasm in working with sellers and prospects?
14. Has my educational program kept me up to date on new developments in the community, real estate financing, construction, and regulations?

salesperson. It covers your attitude, your program for self-improvement, and your education in real estate. The points covered help you evaluate your objectives in obtaining new listings, buyer-prospects, and relationship to others, including your employer, associates, acquaintances, and organizations.

The evaluation gives you an insight into the time spent with prospects and your effectiveness in closing the sale, showing the property, and cultivating your past clients for new listings and prospects. This review enables you to analyze your selling efforts.

ANALYZE YOUR SELLING EFFORTS

Your future in real estate sales largely depends on how you develop your sales effort. Even experienced salespersons can make improvements in organizing their time and making more effective use of sales techniques. The most effective self-improvement program requires that you analyze each completed sale.

Analyze Each Sale

After closing a sale, review each step in your presentation. Ask yourself the following questions: How could I have improved my sales effort? Could I have sold the prospect with fewer showings? Did I close the sale at the appropriate time? How could I have improved negotiations with the seller?

Your answers to these questions teach you to judge your strong and weak points. Did you prepare the seller and buyer for the showing? Did you outline the neighborhood features as you approached your listed property with prospects? Did you recognize the amenities and emotional appeal of the house you sold? Did you present the house in terms of family needs? And while you were showing the house, did you interpret verbal and nonverbal communications and think of your prospect's requirements? In discussing the purchase with the prospect, did you listen effectively? Did you effectively meet the buyer's objections? If you analyze each sale carefully, you will be able to identify ways in which you may improve and avoid mistakes.

Selling Behavior Patterns

After you have analyzed several sales, you should be able to detect behavior patterns. These patterns reveal personal strengths that should be developed further and weaknesses that should be overcome or at least minimized. The salesperson who has a record of high sales volume surely follows the recommended selling procedures. Obviously, the person who has the same number of contacts but closes fewer sales does not follow the recommended selling procedures. The observed differences in selling techniques of the two salespersons make large differences in the number of sales closed.

When you are looking for sales patterns, you should consider each step of the sale separately. Start with your first contact. Determine if your telephone response encouraged the prospect to make an appointment. Consider further if you properly qualified the buyer and interpreted his or her real, not stated, wants.

Determine whether or not you have shown the house properly or have selected the right houses and presented them in a manner that would lead to completed sales. Similarly, study your closing procedures. Determine if you have learned to meet the most common buyer objections and if your negotiations in presenting offers and counter offers have created the proper selling environment for either the seller or the buyer.

By judging each step of the sale you will recognize a pattern that shows where you must concentrate on improvement. You cannot exactly imitate the successful salesperson, but you should develop your own special way of dealing with clients so that you will capitalize on your personal assets and minimize your weaknesses.

Prospect Services

The active and more successful salesperson gives priority to serving prospects. For a new home buyer, especially the out-of-town buyer, you can *perform invaluable services* not available from others. You can take your prospects to local schools, community organizations, churches, and other groups. In this regard, you anticipate the needs of your prospect and satisfy customer wants.

Your *thoughtfulness* will gain you the prospect's respect and appreciation. In showing houses, you must demonstrate a genuine willingness to serve customers. Be prepared to meet the demands of your prospect and be willing to make certain sacrifices. You will have to exercise discipline and give close attention to your prospect's requirements. In this way, you establish good client relationships that help you close the sale and you increase the chances of acquiring additional business from acquaintances of your prospect.

A related problem requires that you solve *prospect problems.* If your prospect shows a special interest in a listing that requires remodeling to meet his or her needs, help the prospect secure realistic costs. Or if the prospect has insufficient funds for closing, work with the prospect to develop a financial plan that solves a temporary problem. There are so many variations of financing plans that, given a good credit rating, you could probably develop a purchase plan that meets the needs of prospects, lenders, and sellers.

A *helpful attitude* pleases prospects. You can show how a house meets all family preferences. Your prospect will be pleased and share his or her objections with you so that you may overcome these objections by making helpful suggestions.

Give Proper Attention

Above all, be *considerate* of your prospect. Avoid criticism of any kind. Do not lose respect by criticizing other real estate brokers. By being considerate you maximize the time spent with prospects. You must establish rapport, but do not spend time in idle conversation. If your prospect talks about irrelevant topics, listen but turn soon to the subject at hand: your prospect wants your listings. Your responsibility is to keep the prospect directed toward a final sale.

Being considerate means that you *talk directly* to the prospect. You may expect the prospect's education to vary from yours. It could be more or it could be less. Never feel inferior and never convey an attitude of superiority. Look at your prospect as an individual, respect his or her attitudes, wants, and preferences, and try to understand his or her prejudices.

Show prospects proper *attention.* If your prospect talks, listen. Do not interrupt and do not show that you are bored. Establish rapport by paying attention to a prospect, but do not overdo it. Flatter the prospect's ego and reinforce confidence in you and your presentation.

THE PURCHASE DECISION

Few salespersons appreciate the complex decision-making process that faces their prospects. Place yourself in the role of a prospect and consider the many alternatives available to the family in need of new housing. First, the family must reach a decision on the need for a new house. The need may arise because the family is growing, the family wants to move to a better neighborhood, or the family has to move because of a job transfer. The simplest model of this process is shown in Figure 4-3. This model assumes that a prospect needs a new residence, which could be satisfied by rental or owner-occupancy. Therefore, the household decision maker must decide whether it is better to rent or to buy. Assuming that the decision has been made to buy, the family may more commonly select a condominium, a mobile home in an outlying area, or settle on a single-family dwelling. Among these groups are many choices. In the usual case, the family may select between new and used dwellings and among neighborhoods that vary by price, age of dwelling, location, and many other factors. Even the single-family dwelling shows differences in architectural style; for example, townhouses versus detached dwellings.

If the family has a specific preference in housing, the family must decide on housing features, namely, the functional utility of the house with respect to bedrooms, basement, carports, garages, number of stories, and the like. For example, if your prospect prefers a three-bedroom split-level house, the final decision rests on many other factors such as the down payment, available financing, the location, and the size of the lot.

The Buying Decision Model

Turn next to your role in helping the prospect reach the right decision. The process starts with the prospect's housing preferences which the prospect may or may not consciously know at the time of the first interview. Even if these housing preferences are known, they may not be verbally expressed during the initial interview.

At the same time, the prospect faces certain restraints in reaching a decision. The prospect may want a 3,000-square foot house in a subdivision of $100,000 houses, but the prospect's income and available cash may restrict

FIGURE 4-3. Prospect Decisions in Changing Residence

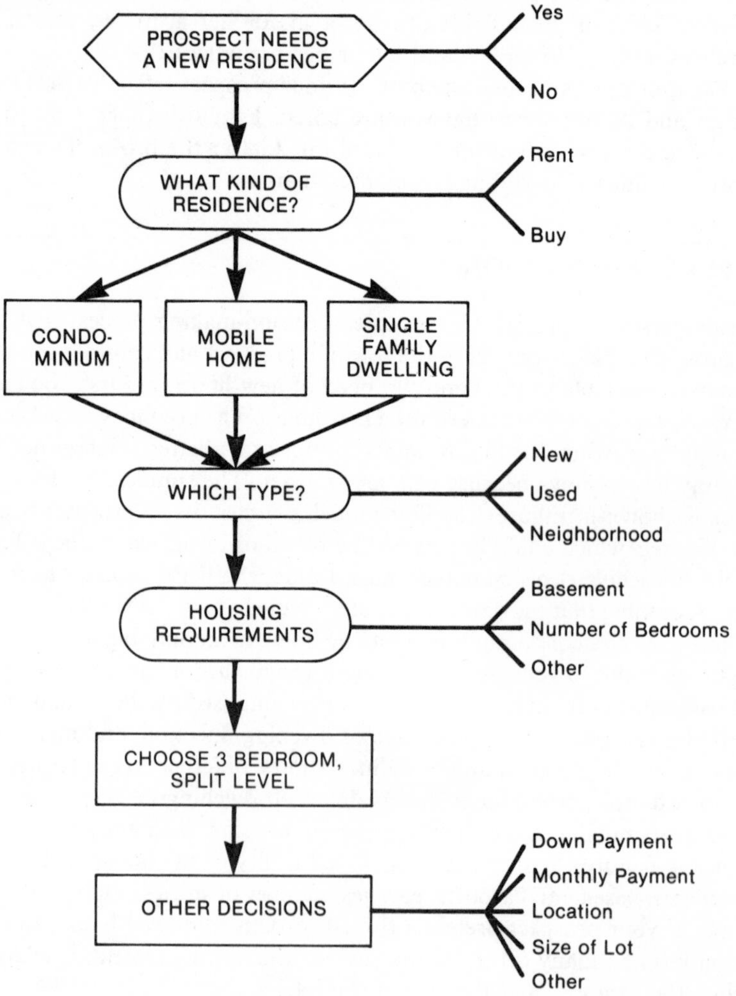

the choice to a $50,000–$75,000 subdivision. Your part in the decision-making process rests on your intimate knowledge of listings and your knowledge of local neighborhood trends, available financing, and many other details affecting housing values. These issues are illustrated in Figure 4-4.

Suppose that the prospect reaches you by telephone or makes the initial contact and a first appointment. You use the recommended communication skills to determine the prospect's realistic housing problem. You explore the prospect's interests, preferences, present housing, and family needs in order to avoid showing the "dream castle" and to direct the prospect's attention to a reasonable housing choice.

Early in the interview, you must take special care to qualify the prospect. There is no point in wasting your time and the prospect's time (and causing the seller any inconvenience) by showing houses beyond the prospect's means. Your chances of closing the sale are largely affected by your skill in carrying out these two steps.

Before the initial contact you know the details of the available listings.

FIGURE 4-4. Final Prospect Decisions in Buying a House

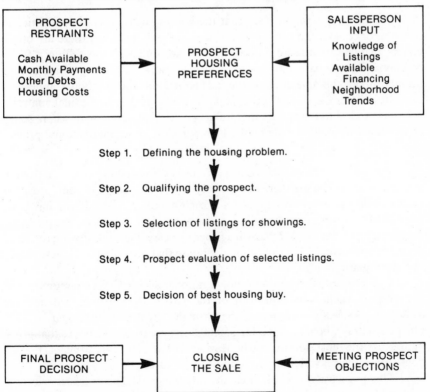

You know the physical characteristics of the property available and you recognize the special amenities of each listing that gives satisfaction. You select listings by following the proven procedures for satisfying the prospect and showing houses.

Step 4 in Figure 4-4 calls for having the prospect evaluate your selected listings. You interpret both nonverbal and verbal communication for indications of approval or disapproval. Again, you have recognized potential and stated objections, meeting each objection with points that appeal to the prospect's preferences.

This is the step that leads to eventual approval or disapproval. Your prospect responds favorably if you have learned to interpret his or her communications.

Finally, you are ready for the close. The prospect has narrowed the choice to one or two selections but hesitates to make the financial commitment. To close the sale, you must meet final prospect objections. Your skills in closing the sale help the prospect make the best housing choice.

The Decision Process

On balance, it would seem that the housing decision follows a rational selection of choices. To some extent this is probably true, but there are other factors that govern the final decision. For not only are you selling a four-bedroom, 3,000-square foot house, you are also selling the prestige of the neighborhood, the amenities of the backyard pool, the emotional appeal of good architecture, and many other subjective advantages. In the final analysis, you must appeal to the factors that influence the final purchase decision, some of which are rational and some of which appeal to other motivational principles.

The Rational Decision Process.   This is the economic view of a person as a rational decision-maker. Presumably under this concept your prospect evaluates the economic consequences of each house you offer. If you have not confused the prospect by showing too many contrasting houses, the prospect judges each prospective purchase in a progressive manner, eliminating the least desirable houses and finally selecting the house that provides the highest value, say, per square foot.

This concept of a person's being a rational decision maker assumes that the prospect reaches a final decision on the basis of the maximum satisfaction gained from selecting the house that has the greatest utility. That is, the prospect selects a house offered for $50,000 because this is the house that gives him or her the most housing at the least cost. The idea is that this particular house gives the maximum satisfaction for the price.

This purchase model assumes the following: (1) The prospect selects a house on the basis of the optimum choice that gives the greatest housing utility. (2) The prospect has reasonable knowledge of housing alternatives or virtually perfect knowledge of the market. (3) The prospect selects houses anywhere in the community—no one location has an advantage over any other location. (4) The location differs only by distance from central points.

Even the most inexperienced would recognize the fallacy of this model. We flatter ourselves if we believe that we always make the "best buy."

In fact, most of our buying decisions follow a different process. In the first place, the housing market is imperfect. The purchaser has a wide range of choices of houses: No two houses are alike; each one has certain unique features. Among the houses available for sale, probably many would adequately meet minimum family shelter needs. More importantly, salespersons realize that buyers are seldom capable of objectively judging the economic value of houses.

In short, the rational purchase decision illustrates a hypothetical situation. It is almost impossible for the prospect to obtain complete economic information about the housing market. And because each house varies so much, the buyer finds it almost impossible to make purely rational decisions. (It is recognized that the house must meet certain minimum utility needs— if the family size requires four bedrooms, a three-bedroom house would be an irrational choice.) As a consequence, salespersons concentrate on satisfying noneconomic motives.

The True Buyer Motivation. What truly motivates your prospect? In the sense used here, motivation refers to the drives, urges, wishes, or desires that initiate a sequence of events known as *buyer behavior.*[1] It is well known that every individual is strongly motivated to satisfy physiological needs: food, shelter, and clothing. But your prospect also has wants that are not motivated solely by physiological needs. Buyer behavior is explained by different motives that satisfy a *hierarchy of needs.* The hierarchy of needs was developed by A. H. Maslow in a 1943 article. See Figure 4–5.

For example, a salesperson selling coats satisfies the buyer's physiological need to be protected from cold weather. But the buyer is motivated to buy a coat for other reasons. The person would not buy a mink coat on the basis of its insulating quality but on the coat's elegant and rich appearance. The analogy also applies to listed houses. Your prospect may satisfy physiological needs for shelter from many choices, but the prospect's final decision rests on other motives.

According to Maslow, people satisfy their wants according to the hi-

---

[1]See, for example, W. J. E. Crissy, William H. Cunningham, and Isabella C. M. Cunningham, *Selling: The Personal Force of Marketing* (New York City, New York: John Wiley & Sons, Inc., 1977), p. 59.

FIGURE 4-5. Priority of Prospect Needs

PRIORITY OF NEEDS	PROSPECT NEEDS
First	Physiological
Second	Safety
Third	Love
Fourth	Esteem
Fifth	Self-Actualization

Source: These priorities were first identified by A. H. Maslow, "A Theory of Motivation," *Psychological Review,* No. 4, July 1943, pp. 370–96. For a more current explanation consult W. J. E. Crissy, William H. Cunningham, and Isabella C. M. Cunningham, *Selling: The Personal Force in Marketing* (New York: John Wiley & Sons, Inc., 1977), p. 62.

erarchy shown in Figure 4–5. *First,* individuals want goods and services to satisfy physiological needs. We must satisfy minimum requirements for food, housing, and shelter. At the *second* priority, individuals are concerned with safety (explaining why families move from declining neighborhoods that have high crime rates to new and stable neighborhoods that have lower crime rates).

At succeeding priorities, human motivation to purchase varies widely among individuals. In selling the next prospect, you must determine what is significant to your prospect, why the prospect wants to purchase, and how your listed houses appeal to his or her nonphysiological wants. For instance, Figure 4–5 suggests that individuals are guided by a *third* priority, wants related to the need for love. A house could create respect among colleagues, acquaintances, and neighbors and satisfy elements of the hierarchy, namely, appealing to a person's *esteem* and *self-actualization* needs.

To reach the highest volume of sales, you must develop skills in recognizing prospect motivation. You interpret the prospect's motivation in terms of his or her wishes, hopes, dreams, and personal aspirations. You determine the critically important factors in motivating prospects. In the qualifying interview, you identify the level of aspirations that motivate the prospect. In truth, your prospect's motivation to purchase, according to recognized authorities, is largely determined by the following four basic considerations:[2]

[2]*Ibid.,* p. 63.

1. *The Level of Aspired Achievement.* Some of your prospects constantly seek to better their status. Distinguish this prospect from the prospects who have "pie in the sky" aspirations or who are looking for a "dream castle," aspirations clearly unrealistic in terms of their financial abilities to purchase. At the other extreme are prospects who have lower levels of aspirations and are satisfied with houses that appeal to a lower level of the hierarchy of needs illustrated in Figure 4–5.

2. *Aspirations Are Self-Generated.* Satisfaction of each goal leads to other goals. The highly motivated person takes the initiative in improving and reaching aspirations. The less motivated prospect depends on others to set goals for him or her

3. *Motivated Prospects Are Flexible.* They revise their aspirations according to personal circumstances. They know when to compromise their realistic and satisfying goals.

4. *Goals Are Mutually Supportive and Free of Conflicts.* A conflict may arise in the prospect who wants a new 4,000-square foot house with financial means that restricts the choice to a new 3,000-square foot house or an older home. Goals that are mutually attractive are illustrated by the desire to live in a neighborhood that has adequate schools and shopping and well-maintained houses and lots.

A prospect whose motives are confused may want an impossible combination: a new 3,000-square foot brick veneer house five minutes from the job. Either the new house would be beyond his or her immediate financial ability to purchase or he or she would have to purchase an older home in a less desirable neighborhood in order to be within five minutes driving time from work.

These points strongly demonstrate that salespersons operate as informal, technical counselors. They help the buyer-prospect reach the best decision, building prospect confidence, and developing referrals from his or her acquaintances, colleagues, and neighbors.

The Salesperson's Goal

The interaction between the seller-prospect and the salesperson involves a complex series of steps. The final goal, however, is to close the sale so that it is mutually satisfying to both seller and prospect. The close utilizes the skills of the salesperson in guiding parties to the buy-sell decision.

The salesperson must determine the real motivations of the seller and must qualify the buyer and then anticipate and overcome the buyer's objections—and all buyers have some objections even for the house they finally purchase.

Certain obstacles that you encounter in understanding the sales process deserve repeating:

1. In your presentation of the showing, the prospect is not receiving your communications; he or she is not really listening to you or paying attention to the features of the house you show.
2. The prospect is really a casual "looker," not a serious buyer.
3. The prospect does not know you personally and does not know your company's reputation.
4. The prospect does not understand real estate procedures.
5. The prospect is not aware of your personal services that will help him or her in making a decision.
6. The prospect is unaware of your other listings that may satisfy his or her unconscious housing needs.
7. The prospect does not know how buying the house you show will give him or her the maximum benefits.
8. The prospect does not know that his or her needs will be satisfied by the house you show.
9. The prospect is unaware of real estate financing and its variations.

Finally, the housing purchase is not a simple question of accepting or declining an offer. Unlike the decision to buy a loaf of bread or a dozen eggs, the decision to buy a house is reached through a series of decisions in which the prospect must weigh substantially different features of each house and arrive at a satisfactory compromise.

Here the salesperson plays a key role, for only the salesperson is well informed about the neighborhood and the available houses that would be most suitable for the prospect. Truly, the process of buying and selling houses assumes the highest degree of complexity. Succeeding chapters explain how these problems may be minimized.

POINTS TO REMEMBER

The central role of the salesperson in the real estate office is clear. Because of the importance of this role, the question of professional status affects the conduct of salespersons, the support the salespersons are given by their employer, and more significantly, the public's attitude toward them. Real estate salespersons do not follow a profession in the sense that medical doctors, lawyers, or architects do, but their conduct must meet professional standards.

They are professional in providing service. The salesperson demonstrates loyalty—to the buyer and to the listing seller—for, on analysis, the community and, more particularly, the buyer is highly dependent on the special knowledge and services provided by professionally oriented salespersons.

Selling requires hard work and a suitable personality, but professional work requires considerable education and self-improvement. As a consequence, salespersons follow a planned self-management program that involves using a daily budget of time and a systematic plan that covers personal objectives, recognizes selling problems, and helps resolve these problems to meet personal objectives. The systematic plan includes an evaluation of past performance.

Best results are reached when the salesperson recognizes the complex decision-making process that faces prospects. In reaching a decision to purchase, it would appear that buyers make the optimum, economic, and rational choice. In reality, many houses would be suitable for the prospect in meeting shelter needs, but the prospect's final choice rests on motivations based on noneconomic factors.

True buyer motivation involves a hierarchy of needs, beginning with the satisfaction of physiological and safety needs and, more significantly, ending with benefits that meet emotional needs for love, esteem, and self-actualization. The prospect's motivation to purchase is determined by his or her aspirations. These aspirations include *aspired achievement, self-generated aspirations, flexible aspirations,* and *mutually supportive aspirations* that are *free of conflict.*

The sales process is a complex process that is aggravated by problems of communication, incomplete knowledge of the housing market, uncertainty about emotional appeals of housing ownership, and unfamiliarity with the services of the salesperson, the reputation of the firm, and the complications of making real estate transfers that involve highly technical, legal, and financial procedures.

In sum, your understanding of the sales process allows you to adapt your selling tasks to the prospect who is very dependent on your dedication to selling.

REVIEW QUESTIONS

1. Give reasons why the community depends on the professional conduct of salespersons.
2. Can selling by learned? Why or why not? Give reasons for your answer.
3. Describe the initial steps in budgeting time.
4. What are the benefits in planning your presentation?
5. What planning precautions are advised in developing a plan to budget your time?
6. Explain how you would evaluate your selling plan.

7. Give your suggestions for analyzing a real estate sale.
8. Describe the decision process followed in buying a house.
9. Contrast the rational decision process with true buyer motivation.
10. What four basic considerations determine your prospect's motivation?

Presenting Houses:
Seller Cooperation

"You must know the home you are going to show as if you had lived in it yourself," says Don D. Cooley, owner of Anthony Schools, San Jose, California.[1] Since the purchase of a home represents a major commitment, prospective buyers want details about the houses you show. Showing houses is more than a mechanical process of arranging appointments and answering the prospect's questions. Showing houses requires *housing preparation;* in other words, the house is "packaged" for sale.

Preparing the home package starts with securing *seller cooperation.* The cooperation allows you and the seller to present the house to the best advantage. When the house is "packaged" for sale, you brief the buyer before you show the house. The process of *showing the house* follows a very carefully planned presentation. Ideally, the presentation prepares the buyer for the close.

SELLER COOPERATION

Seller cooperation is necessary if you are to present the house in the best possible light. With good seller cooperation you have the maximum flexibility in arranging to show the house. Your initial step encourages the seller to create the best environment in which to show the house. Here practice varies. Some brokers furnish published lists of do's and don't's; other brokers make friendly suggestions. Both procedures work if you gain the maximum cooperation.

---

[1]Don D. Cooley, "Showing the Home and Obtaining the Offer," in *How to Negotiate in Listing and Selling Homes* (Los Angeles: California Association of Realtors.® 1977), p. 63.

FIGURE 5-1. Instructions to Sellers For Preparing a House For Showing

2768 south wadsworth boulevard · denver, colorado 80227 · 303/989-1870

PREPARATION FOR SHOWING

1. First impressions are lasting impressions. An inviting exterior insures inspection of the interior. Keep your lawn trimmed and edged - flower beds cultivated - the yard free and clear of refuse.

2. Decorate your home - a step toward a SALE. Faded walls and woodwork that looks worn reduce "desire." Do not tell the prospect how the place can be made to look - show him by decorating first. A quicker sale at a higher price will result.

3. Cleanliness is next to Godliness. Bright, cheery windows and unmarred walls will assist your sales.

4. Fix that faucet. Dripping water discolors the enamel and calls attention to faulty plumbing.

5. A day with the carpenter. Loose door knobs, sticking drawers, warped cabinet doors and the like are noticed by the prospect. Have them fixed.

6. From top to bottom. The attic and basement are important features. All unnecessary articles which have accumulated should be removed. Display the full value of your storage and utility spaces.

7. Step high - step low. Prospects will do just that unless all stairways are cleared of objects. Avoid cluttered appearances and possible injuries.

8. Closet illusions. Clothes properly hung, shoes, hats and other articles neatly placed will make closets appear adequate.

9. Dear to her heart is the kitchen. Colorful curtains in harmony with the floor and counter tops add appeal for the Lady of the House.

10. Check and double check bathrooms. Bright, clean bathrooms sell homes.

11. For the rest of your life. Bedrooms are always outstanding features. Arrange them neatly.

MEMBER OF THE NATIONAL ASSOCIATION OF REALTORS   REALTOR®

Source: F. Peter Wigginton, *The Complete Guide to Profitable Real Estate Listings: Programs of the Pros* (Homewood, Ill.: Dow Jones-Irwin, 1977), pp. 114–15.

FIGURE 5-1 (cont.)

12. Can you see the light? Illumination is a welcome sign. For after-dark inspections turn on your lights, from the porch on through. The prospect will feel a glowing warmth otherwise impossible to attain.

13. "Three's a crowd." More will lose the sale. Avoid having too many people present during inspections. The prospect will feel like an intruder and will hurry through the house. It is better to be away from the house when it is being shown.

14. Music is mellow -- but not when showing a house. Shut off the radio - it distracts. Let the salesman and the buyer talk, free of disturbances.

15. Love me, love my dog does not apply in house selling. Keep pets out of the way - preferably out of the house.

16. Silence is golden. Be courteous but do not force conversation with the prospect. He is there to inspect your house -- not to pay a social call.

17. Be it ever so humble. Never apologize for the appearance of your home. After all, it has been lived in. Let our trained salesman answer any objections that are raised. This is his job.

18. In the shadows. Please do not tag along with the prospect and the salesman. He knows the buyer's requirements and can better emphasize the features of your house when alone. You will be called if needed.

19. Putting the cart before the horse. Trying to dispose of furniture and other furnishings to the prospect before he has purchsed the house loses the sale.

20. A word to the wise. Do not discuss price, terms, possession or other features with the customers. Refer them to us. We are better equipped to bring the negotiation to a favorable conclusion with all due dispatch.

* * * * *

We ask that you show your home to prospective customers by appointment only through this office. Your cooperation will be appreciated and will lead to a more prompt consummation of the sale.

* * * * *

GEORGE REALTY CO./2768 south wadsworth boulevard · denver, colorado 80227· 303/989-1870

Advising the Seller

The George Realty Company of Denver, Colorado, offers printed instructions for the seller. The instructions begin with the following comment:

We have your home for sale because you want to sell it. With little effort on your part, this can be accomplished more quickly and at a better price. Arouse the prospect's desire for your home by making it attractive. Here are *twenty tested tips* to help us show your home to its best advantage. One of them may be applicable to you or your home. We find our efforts are most successful when the stage is well set.[2]

The 20 tips listed in Figure 5–1 suggest that the seller make minor repairs and correct for deferred maintenance. The maintenance starts with the yard and cleaning or repainting interior and exterior walls. Correcting for unsightly storage, untidy rooms, closets, and bathrooms also leads the list of prepackaging steps. The seller is encouraged to install colorful curtains and take other steps to make the house attractive. Several of the printed suggestions govern seller conduct during the showing.

Experience has shown that it is worthwhile to spend time in establishing the best possible rapport with sellers. The object is to establish a friendly relationship in order to gain their cooperation in following your suggestions.

Seller Assistance

Agreement is almost universal on the advisability of showing the house in the seller's absence. If you are showing the house by appointment, arrange in advance for the seller to leave during the showing. "Since you want to sell the house and I think we have the right prospect, please be sure you are gone by the time we arrive." If you must show the house during the seller's presence, the seller should understand that he or she should not be with you and the prospect during the showing. The seller should agree in advance to stay in the backyard or stay inconspicuously in one room, for example, the living room, while the prospect views the house.

Brokers, however, are flexible on this point. If the house has a swimming pool and the season and time of day are right, salespersons report success in having the family in the pool during the showing. The sight of a family playing together may help decide the sale.

If you want the seller to be inconspicuous during the showing and you cannot show by appointment, there is another fairly standard procedure that you can follow. After introducing the prospect to the seller, ask the seller to sit down while he and the prospect go through the house and ask the seller if he or she minds if the prospect looks at the closets. This approach calls for a very firm statement, for it is almost universally true that the seller thinks he or she knows the house better than you and would like to go through the house with the prospect. Take the initiative in showing the prospect through the

[2]F. Peter Wigginton, *The Complete Guide to Profitable Real Estate Listings: Programs of the Pros* (Homewood, Ill.: Dow Jones-Irwin, 1977), p. 114. Emphasis added.

house; under no circumstances should you allow the seller to remain with you and your prospect.

If you have not called the seller before the showing, remind the seller that when you listed the property you requested that he or she leave during the showing. Explain that it is much easier to show the house when the seller is not present: "My prospects feel more at ease and ask more questions if the owner is absent. I will lock the door when I leave."

HOUSING PREPARATION

You can be certain of one point: The seller will not get the highest price unless the house has the best possible appearance. You must caution the seller to clear the stairs of toys and other objects and that during the showing the children and pets should play outside, that the radio and TV should be turned off, and that all housekeeping should be finished.

The greatest problem is showing houses in which there are uncooperative tenants. If your appointment is inconvenient for the tenant to finish normal housekeeping, be sure to warn the prospect that the tenant has not had time to prepare the house for inspection. If the house needs cleaning, explain that a cleaning service could prepare the house for occupancy in one day. Help the prospect visualize what the house would be like if it were prepared for new occupancy.

Reconditioned Houses

Housing prospects usually prefer houses in good condition. Most sellers in turn want the highest price and an early sale. Yet because of the seller's circumstances listed houses may need cleaning, redecorating, and landscaping work. You may see the need for reconditioning, but the seller may not realize that improvements are necessary in order to maximize the price or they may be unwilling or unable to make these changes.

A house in need of minor repairs is penalized in the market. Buyers seeing the need for repainting or replacement of equipment are generally unfamiliar with the cost of building materials and labor. As a result, they discount the house by more than the cost of needed repairs.

A Reconditioning Plan.   Kenneth R. Kuhn, Vice-President of Schindler/Cummins Residential, Inc., of Houston, Texas, has developed a service to recondition unsold houses. He reports that during the 2 years his system has been in use the average selling time for a reconditioned house is between 10 and 14 days.

The system requires that an assessment of needed repairs be made at the time the listing is taken. The decision to recondition is made by the seller who follows the recommendations of the listing broker. On the seller's approval, the broker then procures bids from at least two contractors for presentation to the seller. The seller selects the contractor and pays for the repair work. Repair work is generally confined to cleaning, painting, minor carpeting, and wall papering and it generally costs approximately 3 percent of the listing price.

In one instance, a seven-room house in poor condition was purchased by an investor for $50,000. Renovation included a new sheet-rock interior, a new central air conditioning and heating system, repair of exterior brick veneer, floor refinishing, replacing screens, and exterior painting. The kitchen was remodeled. New plumbing fixtures, a dishwasher, disposal, sink, and oven were added. The total repair work cost $18,000, producing a house having a current market value of $86,500—a total gain of $18,500.[3] Note Figure 5-2 for an example of repair work that increased market value.

FIGURE 5-2.   An Example of Reconditioning a Bathroom. Note That Reconditioning Gave a Formerly Adequate Bathroom a More Modern Appearance

Source: Kenneth R. Kuhn, "The Art of Cosmetic Improvements," *Real Estate Today* (April, 1978), p. 32.

[3]Kenneth R. Kuhn, "The Art of Cosmetic Improvements," *Real Estate Today* (April, 1978), pp. 28–32.

Housing Operation.   Experienced salespersons take other measures besides asking the seller to make minor repairs. Other aspects of the house are made as attractive as possible. For example, opening draperies, turning on lights, and even placing freshly brewed coffee and freshly baked cookies or cake in the kitchen. Softly playing stereo music and a fire in the fireplace are other measures that make the presentation attractive.

These steps are considered essential, for buyers have reported that they make up their minds whether or not they like a home in the first few seconds of the inspection. If this is true, then it is essential that the house be put in the best possible light.

Preparing the Buyer

In showing a house, you must first establish friendly relations with the prospect. Know the prospect's financial ability to buy, how much cash the prospect has, and the prospect's personal preferences for a neighborhood; in addition, if you know the prospect's hobbies, likes, and desires, you are reasonably sure that a selected listing will meet the prospect's requirements.

It is further presumed that your personal appearance is good and that your automobile is suitable for the showing. Your manner is enthusiastic since you have selected the home that the prospect is going to buy.

Personal Preparation.   Your personal preparation includes a review of answers to commonly asked questions. Informative answers should be given to these questions whether you are showing your best selections to a prospect or you are preparing for an open house. Most of the questions deal with community or neighborhood facilities, for example:

1. What are the local school facilities?
   a. Primary and secondary schools?
   b. Public and private?
   c. What is the reputation of the local schools?
2. What is the driving time to the nearest shopping?
   a. To supermarkets and drug stores?
   b. To regional shopping center?
3. How far is it to the nearest limited access highway?
4. Is there an organized neighborhood or community association?
5. What are the local cultural facilities?
   a. Theatre groups?
   b. Library?
   c. Museum or other?
6. Who originally built the house? When was the house built?

7. What local recreational facilities are available and what are the driving times
to the best locations?

a. Swimming?	e. Camping?
b. Boating?	f. Tennis?
c. Skiing?	g. Golf?
d. Fishing?	

In addition to these questions, some prospects may inquire about domestic water, electricity, natural gas, and local property taxes. If you can provide this background information, you are ready to show the house.

Preliminary Points. During the initial conversation (which could be on the drive to the house), start talking about the features of the house that you know will please your prospect. It could be the swimming pool for the children, or the fenced backyard for a play area or a garden, or a basement for a workshop, or room for boat storage. If you know the neighborhood, you will comment on the houses you have recently sold and something about the neighbors living next to or near the house you are showing.

Your chances of closing begin with the features of the neighborhood that you pass while driving to the house. Your drive is not necessarily by the most direct route; if possible, you show the nearby park, new school, churches, or other neighborhood amenities. Your comments on the neighborhood schools, shopping centers, and other items of interest start your prospect thinking about how he or she would benefit from living in the neighborhood. If you know that the house has certain limitations, mention these first in order to overcome an objection which is likely to be expressed by your prospect.

For example, you might mention that if a basement den is only partially finished, it will need wallboard and painting. Or you might comment on the large family room that makes up for the living room that is smaller than your prospect desires. In short, forewarn your buyers about the less attractive features of the house so that you can give yourself a chance to mention compensating advantages.

Emotional Appeal. To help prepare the buyer, some authorities recommend a review of the emotional appeal of home ownership. Because you recognize these emotional appeals, you can better concentrate on helping your prospect reach the right decision.

1. *Security.* Real estate values tend to increase with the general price level. Your mortgage payments give you the advantage of equity build-up, providing the family with more security than it would have if it were renting.

2. *Comfort.* You can arrange your own home for personal family needs. This house has adequate closets, storage space, and large bedrooms. The location is convenient to new shopping centers, schools, and churches.

3. *Welfare of Children.* Neighborhood schools here have new playgrounds and modern, fully equipped buildings.
4. *Pride of Ownership.* Your new home will give more satisfaction. Your friends and relatives will envy your new purchase; it will give you independence not enjoyed as a tenant.
5. *Social Approval.* Your neighbors are leaders in the community. You have a doctor in the block, a lawyer across the street, and an accountant on the same street.
6. *Happiness.* "All things considered, wouldn't you be happy moving to this neighborhood? Don't you agree that this neighborhood has most of the desirable qualities you are looking for and at the same time it is minutes from your job."[4]

Showing a house starts with the first meeting with the buyer-prospect. Every aspect of your presentation is directed toward showing the house. Your success in these initial steps will make closing more likely during the presentation.

In appealing to a prospect's emotions about a home, practice presentations that stress benefits of home ownership. For example, consider the following suggestions:[5]

Avoid talking about a	Emphasize instead
Fenced backyard	Family privacy
Swimming pool	Fun and excitement
Patio	Barbeque party in summer evenings
Family room	Family leisure and games
Kitchen	Convenient meal preparation
Fireplace	Furniture placement for sitting in front of a warm winter fire
Lawn, trees, and shrubbery	Easy-chair landscaping
Living room	Entertaining friends
Sliding glass doors	Making the outdoors a part of the room

By following these suggestions you recognize that people buy benefits in a family dwelling; they do not buy a 2,500-square foot house on a 40,000-square foot lot.

SHOWING THE HOUSE

Though recommendations on showing houses vary among the leading brokers, most brokers advise against showing too many houses. If you show a prospect 15 houses in one day, the prospect becomes tired, confused, and less likely to make a decision. At the other extreme, there is a psychological purpose served in showing more than one house. By offering alternative choices, you lead the

[4]Adapted from Edward F. Rybka, *The Number One Success System to Boost Your Earnings in Real Estate* (Englewood Cliffs, N.J.: Prentice-Hall, Inc., 1971), p. 106.

[5]See Cooley, *op. cit.,* p. 63.

buyer to select the house most suited to his or her needs—you let the comparison help the buyer decide on the preferred house.

Selecting Houses for Showing

You do not show a luxury house to a family that has only the ability to finance middle-priced housing. If you show a $95,000 house to a prospect who qualifies for only a $50,000 house, he or she will look endlessly for the additional features of luxury housing not found in the more moderately priced houses. As a consequence, the prospect will tend to be dissatisfied with your other selections.

Let us say that you have selected not more than three houses to show the prospect. Preferably, one or two would be ideal since a fewer number of houses makes it easier for the prospect to make a decision. One recommended approach is to show the preferred house next to the last house presented. The first house stimulates the prospect but has certain deficiencies not present in the house that more nearly meets the prospect's needs. The third house shown should be less desirable than the second house. Your purpose in showing the third house is to encourage the prospect to return to the second house which has advantages over the first and third houses. If your seller is properly motivated, and you have qualified the buyer, you have more than a 90 percent chance of closing if you use this technique.

The Berg Agency, which has offices in five states, recommends that the first two or three houses shown should be progressively higher in price but lower than the prospect can realistically afford. The last house should be the ideal house you have selected for the prospect in the price range that the prospect can finance.

If the prospect is still undecided and unsatisfied, the Berg Agency recommends showing other houses that are higher in price until the prospect is satisfied with the features and is willing to buy. Here you must persuade the prospect to make a higher down payment and finance with a second mortgage.

Then there is the case of the experienced salesperson who concluded that for every 30 showings he averaged one sale. As a consequence, his practice was to make repeated showings from early in the morning to late at night.

The Number of Showings

In reality, the number of showings you make depends on the urgency of the prospect. A corporate executive who has two days to find a new house will appreciate your showing houses continuously until he or she makes the final decision. On the other hand, if you have a local family that wants to move to a larger house, the family will be more selective and undecided. Here you would probably be advised to confine each showing to three, or at the most four, houses at a time. Similarly, in showing luxury houses, probably one or two showings would be sufficient since these houses have so many details for the new buyer to consider.

Time of Showing

The time selected to show the house should reveal the house to the best advantage. If the house you have listed has shade trees that effectively cool the living room during the afternoon, show the house when this feature will be noted. If the morning sun shines into the kitchen, select a time of showing that reveals this condition. If you want to emphasize the backyard landscaping, play space, or garden, avoid showing the house during a heavy rain storm. Night inspections are to be avoided, if possible.

There are exceptions to this last rule, as I learned through personal experience. When I was selling my home in central Florida, a young couple came to view my house at night. They liked what they saw, but before making the final decision they came back the next morning, mainly to look at the neighborhood, exterior, and yard. It so happened that the back of the yard faced a three-acre pond in which a four-foot alligator lived. The setting was very attractive with Spanish moss trailing from large oak trees that surrounded the pond. The alligator was something of a neighborhood curiosity. At the time the family viewed the back yard, the alligator was sunning itself on the lawn. My children were old enough so that the alligator was no danger, but the prospect had a two-year old son. Needless to say, the prospect never returned after seeing the alligator. Before the house was sold the alligator was removed.

Presenting the House

As with other aspects of selling, your presentation must follow a plan. You know the prospect's needs, you have inspected the listings, and you have prepared the seller and packaged the house. Your showing starts with points you want to make on the neighborhood as you approach the listing. You know which disadvantages you will discuss with the buyer-prospect before he or she sees the house. You anticipate the strong points of the house selected for the buyer's decision and you tentatively plan the points you will make about the neighbors, the yard, the housing exterior, its architecture, and the special interior features that you want to make sure the buyer notices during the inspection.

Planning the Showing. You start by planning a tour of the house, knowing where you will begin, the procedure you will follow in going through the house, and finally how you will end the inspection in the family room where you will reemphasize the favorable points raised by the prospect and where you will counter the prospect's objections. This *advanced planning* prepares you for the showing.

When you arrive at the house, you should park across the street from the house so that the prospect can see the most attractive side of the house. If you know that the seller is at home, leave the prospect in the car while you go to the door and ask the seller to leave the house while you are showing it. If the seller cannot leave, ask the seller to be inconspicuous during the showing.

Conducting the Showing.   Go back to the car and invite your prospect into the house. Introduce the prospect and seller to each other, but use only last names. As you enter the house, take the prospect to the best room first. If you can delay the prospect in this room and discuss the main features in the house there, you build curiosity in visiting other rooms. This step is advisable because the room in which you begin the inspection is usually the room in which you end the inspection. Go to each room, open the door, and invite the prospect to enter. Open all closets. Ask your prospect to turn on the lights and open doors.

Comment only on features that your prospect may miss, for example, cedar lined closets, built-in shelves, the attic fan, silent mercury switches, or the unusual view from the master bedroom. Make sure that your prospect does not miss the advantageous features.

As you come back to the first room, it is sometimes advisable to reinspect the house to emphasize certain features that are important to your prospect. Remember, the prospect is not as accustomed to looking at houses as you are and is likely to forget some of the main features unless you talk about how the house would be ideal for the family.

In leading the prospect through the house, guard against asking questions that can be answered either "yes" or "no," for example, "Do you like the house?" Ask instead, "What is it that you like best about this house?" Some brokers advise asking, "How would you arrange your furniture in this room?" Above all, never take a defensive attitude against the buyer's objections.

Agree with the buyer's objections and counter with the positive features, explaining that few buyers find the perfect house. Every house has pluses and minuses that must be weighted according to family priorities. For example, if the bedroom is considered too small, say, "Yes, it's smaller than bedrooms of older houses, but by saving space in the bedroom, you have a larger family room."

Encourage your prospect to react to the house by opening doors and turning on appliances, lights, or other equipment. The prospect will remember a room if he or she has taken time to operate equipment, doors, and windows. Look for nonverbal communication that reveals approval or disapproval. If the prospect sees you stroke the marble-topped vanity, the prospect will likely do the same thing. As you open the closet door, have the prospect switch on the closet light so that he or she can see the built-in shelves and closet drawers. Then while going back to the most attractive room, reinforce approval by commenting on the advantages of certain features.

Presenting Open Houses

Open houses and model homes in a subdivision may promote a sale, especially in the case of subdivisions in which probably 90 percent of the sales are sold through the model home. Although open houses account only for approximately 10 percent of house sales, they have certain other advantages.

Pros and Cons. The open house appeals to buyers since they know you are actively promoting the sale. Moreover, the salesperson meets new prospects, even though a large number of them are only "lookers." By placing signs throughout the neighborhood directing prospects to the open house, you make neighboring owners aware of your firm and its selling efforts. This may help promote additional listings.

Open houses are time-consuming. A salesperson must be available on-site during open house hours. This is time that might be more profitably spent working with more active prospects. If the house is occupied, the seller may resent the parade of visitors, many of whom are not qualified or who are not really interested in buying. This is especially true of higher priced homes that are occupied by persons who prefer that the house be shown by appointment and invitation. In still other instances, the price of the house may justify the salesperson's full-time attention. Sales of luxury homes in Palm Springs, California, are often made in this way, especially for new construction.

Open House Procedures. It is best that the owner should be absent during an open house. Arrange in advance for advertising the open house in newspapers, for radio spot announcements, and for placing signs throughout the neighborhood. If the house is furnished, do not smoke while showing the house and add a discreet "No Smoking" sign at the entrance. Ask prospects not to touch the owner's personal property, but encourage their operating appliances and opening closet doors, cabinets, and other facilities. Make certain that you secure the house during the owner's absence.

More exclusive homes are shown by invitation only. This requires that you make an agreement with the owner to have the house available on a free afternoon. preferably a Saturday or Sunday between 2:00 and 5:00 P.M. Invitations are mailed to professional individuals, businessmen, and community leaders who have an interest in quality housing. Each person is sent a printed invitation on a form specially printed for this purpose. (See Figure 5-3).

You must keep the owner informed about the results of the open house. Report to the owner within at least 24 hours. If the house is very selective, advise the owner that the first showing may not result in a final sale. A letter

FIGURE 5-3. Printed Invitation for Advertising an Open House by Invitation Only

CROWL AND CYR, Realtors
are pleased to announce
their appointment as the exclusive sales agents for the
JOHN PAUL JONES RESIDENCE
1678 Manchester Park
in
Oxford Manor
You are invited to attend a preview showing of this
beautiful home and grounds on
Saturday March 12, 1971
between the hours of 2 and 5 p.m.
Messrs. Thomas P. Smith and Ronald W. Smote in attendance.

Source: John E. Cyr, *Training and Supervising Real Estate Salesmen* (Englewood Cliffs, N.J.: Prentice-Hall, Inc., © 1973), p. 143.

thanking the seller for his or her cooperation and including the names of prospects with whom you are working as a result of the open housing will help final negotiations.

Qualifying Open House Prospects. To maximize the advantages of the open house, prepare a guest register that provides space for names, addresses, and phone numbers. Prevent prospects from going through the house without signing the register. Serious prospects will offer no objection to this procedure. The guest register also helps you identify prospects when you are too busy with prospects to handle each prospect individually.

Greet the prospects at the door and say, "Please sign the register and then I will conduct you on a tour of the home." When you take a prospect through the house, ask why the prospect is looking at that particular house, where the prospect currently lives, and whether or not the prospect owns or rents. If the prospect is selling, this gives you an opportunity to offer to look at the prospect's present home to give the prospect an opinion of the home's marketability.

Or you can start qualifying prospects as they enter the open house. The direct approach is best: "Do you live in the area? Are you familiar with this neighborhood?" In fact, most salespersons do not try to sell at the open house to the first visitors. More than likely, they develop open house prospects who have needs for other listed houses. If the prospects seem generally interested, it will come out the following day when you call the persons listed in the guest register.

In order to help those new to the area, some salespersons prepare a special package that includes a map of the area or subdivision and diagrams of floor plans. Even if the house is occupied, an information packet on local schools, shopping, utilities, and community advantages is often advised.

PREPARING FOR THE CLOSE

Suppose that you have taken the recommended steps—you have prepared answers for the prospect, you have prepared the property for showing, you have made your preliminary remarks on the way to the house, and the house is properly packaged for showing.

Observing the nonverbal responses of your prospect, start moving toward the close during the showing. For example, avoid asking questions such as, "Will your furniture fit in this room?" Instead, raise the question in this way: "How would you arrange your living room furniture around the fireplace?" Or "Your king-size bed would fit nicely in the master bedroom." Or "How would you arrange your children's furniture in the second bedroom?"

Your asking questions controls the conversation. This is a way of starting your clients to think about the house and how their furniture would look in the listed house. If you end the showing in the living room and the prospect begins to discuss the placement of furniture and if you have answered all the prospect's questions, this would be an ideal time to secure signatures on a contract for sale.

At this point it would be appropriate to talk about the terms of the sale. Review the terms of the deposit receipt, add personal property that might be covered in the agreement, and if the prospect understands the purchase terms as you have listed them (the down payment, the requested financing, the closing costs, and stipulations that the buyer requests), ask the prospect to sign. Once you have the prospect's signature and check, congratulate the prospect and end the interview quickly.

It is obvious that the closing started with your initial contact with the prospect. You have learned the prospect's housing needs and you have qualified the prospect so that you can direct him or her to a suitable house. You have observed the response of the buyer, you have determined that the prospect favors the house shown, and you have met objections that are really delaying tactics of the buyer. Your positive attitude has helped motivate the buyer to sign the deposit receipt and give you a check for the deposit.

Closing the sale during the showing is more likely if you are working with a motivated buyer. You recognize the motivated buyer as one who

Wants your continuing attention.

Is confident that you will find the right house within a reasonable time.

Will be readily available to look at the houses you have selected.

Wants to hear from you regularly.

Knows that you are working to find the right house.

POINTS TO REMEMBER

Like other aspects of selling, the task of presenting houses follows a well-established procedure. In the beginning it is essential to gain *seller cooperation*—the seller's cooperation in placing the house in the best possible light, in making the house available for inspection at the prospect's convenience, and in leaving the premises as you show the house.

Housing preparation incorporates the steps you consider necessary to make the house attractive. Good housekeeping is recommended at all times. In some cases, repainting, minor repairs, and the replacement of carpets work to the advantage of the seller. In other cases, subtle means of improving the environment prove advantageous: a fire in the fireplace, children playing in the pool, and soft music.

Before you show the house, prepare the prospect by creating the impression that you have selected the best house that meets the prospect's requirements. If the house has minor deficiencies, mention these before the prospect raises an objection. On the way to the house tell the prospect about the amenities of the neighborhood and the desirable neighbors. Bear in mind the emotional appeals that go with home ownership.

Showing the house to advantage means that you select the time of showing that reveals unique features. You plan the showing from the time you park the car in a way that permits the best view of the street, neighborhood, and front of the house to the time you end in the family room where you (1) move toward closing, (2) go through the house again (depending on your interpretation of buyer approval or stated objections), or (3) show another house. How many houses you show depends on the motivation of the buyer and his or her special circumstances.

Similarly, in presenting *an open house,* you obtain the best results by asking prospects to sign the guest register which you use in following up on prospects. Salespersons report that although they may not sell the open house to visiting prospects, they obtain prospects for other listed houses. The open house requires that you ask pointed questions during the showing. You make a quick and direct effort to qualify the prospect.

The experienced salesperson moves toward closing during the showing if he or she has a motivated buyer whom he or she has carefully qualified. If you have selected a suitable house, you begin the closing by asking the prospect how his or her furniture would be arranged or how the children would use the backyard or by asking how the prospect would adapt the extra bedroom (or basement) for a favorite hobby.

In brief, presenting houses and gaining seller cooperation are not a casual undertaking; they are best arranged by carefully following frequently tested and widely accepted procedures.

REVIEW QUESTIONS

1. Why is it advisable to gain maximum seller cooperation before showing a house?
2. What advice would you give the seller for preparing his or her house for showing?
3. What suggestions would you make for reconditioning a house for sale?
4. Explain how you would "operate" a house during a showing?
5. What personal preparation should you make to prepare the buyer for a showing?
6. What emotional appeals would you stress in presenting a house?
7. How many houses would you recommend showing a prospect? Explain.
8. How would you plan a showing in advance?
9. What are the advantages and disadvantages of presenting open houses?
10. What procedures would you follow in showing open houses?
11. What suggestions do you have for preparing for a close during a showing?

Part 2

THE
SELLING
OPERATION

Securing New Listings

"Most of my listings are from builders and former prospects," says Bettye Hardeman of Northside Realty Associates of Atlanta, Georgia. Last year she sold or listed 201 houses worth $10,854,320.[1] An established salesperson, Bettye depends on *referral* listings, so-called because they are obtained from former satisfied customers and their friends.

New salespersons and expanding offices depend more heavily on *solicited* listings which concentrate on three main sources: the listing farm, for sale by owner, and "cold canvassing" by telephone or direct mail. In the solicited listings, special efforts are made to develop the *listing kit.* Further, the listing operation must now incorporate information on *energy conservation* techniques. The importance of each of these topics warrants further explanation.

REFERRAL LISTINGS

The term referral listings implies that the successful Realtor® solicits listings continually. Former customers are reminded of the need for listings by your sending anniversary cards, Christmas cards, or birthday greetings. The listings acquired from walk-in customers and incoming phone calls are few compared to the listings that result from the daily operations of the office.

The number of referral listings increases to the extent that the conduct

---

[1]This is not a misprint. Ms. Hardeman works 12 hours a day, 7 days a week—and sometimes more. She takes three short out-of-town vacations per year.

of the firm and its employees create a favorable reputation. Thus, the public relations program not only attracts new buyer-prospects but also attracts new listings.

Public Relations Techniques

When you review the reasons why owners sell houses, you will see the importance of a public relations compaign that promotes the company image. Most families sell for the following reasons:

1. The number of children and their ages make additional bedrooms a necessity.
2. Rising family incomes allow families to upgrade their housing.
3. Job transfers.
4. Death in the family.
5. Divorces.
6. Separations.
7. Grown children have moved out.
8. Retirements.
9. Decreased income.
10. Unemployment.

These are the reasons that salespersons become active in community organizations. One source suggests meeting and becoming acquainted with 25 new persons each month. Knowing the widest number of acquaintances and the frequency of moving helps you increase your chances of obtaining unsolicited listings. Since your listing success partly depends on your reputation, active participation in community organizations exposes you to an increasing number of persons who need listing services.

Next in importance are institutional advertising (in newspapers) and speeches before community organizations that acquaint the public with your services. Your community should know about the Code of Ethics that controls members of the National Association of Realtors® and their local offices. By acquainting the public with the rules governing Realtors® you help develop a reputation for honesty, competency, integrity, and fair dealing.

Former Customers

As part of the program to increase unsolicited listings, follow up on satisfied former customers. If you have sold a company employee a dwelling, the chances are that the employee will later be promoted to a new job in another location. By keeping in contact, the former customer will remember you and your firm when the family must resell the house. It pays to stop by and visit satisfied prospects, reminding them that you would appreciate their referral of friends and colleagues. Some real estate firms solicit referrals by direct mail and telephone.

Community Leaders

Certain community members have prior knowledge that a family must sell its house. Learn to know the leaders among the following:

Mortgage bankers	Savings and loan associations
Mortgage departments of commercial banks	Personnel directors
	City and county zoning departments
Building departments (or other offices that issue building permits)	Utility companies
	Post office employees
Door-to-door salesmen	Public school employees
Fuller Brush salesmen	Paper boys
Employment agencies	Chamber of commerce officials
Lawyers	Contractors and builders
Ministers	

If you have personal contacts with these people through community organizations and local clubs, you may be the first to know of an impending transfer, move, or change in family status. Thus, while you are actively participating in a planned listing program, other operations of the company and your personal conduct encourage unsolicited listings from these sources.

SOLICITED LISTINGS

Solicited listings take many forms: (1) the formally organized listing farm, which takes much time but produces good results, (2) listings gained from "for sale by owner" sources, and (3) canvassing by telephone or other means. First note that the rewards for a formally organized listing campaign are advantageous to salespersons joining an office for the first time.

Because of the high rewards gained from an organized listing campaign, some salespersons specialize in listing. These persons view the listing as they would a bank deposit. It has been proven that if the listing is properly supervised and serviced, you can expect that from 85 to 90 percent of your listings will sell. It is claimed that the return on the time spent on getting new listings is greater than the return earned on time spent with buyers. Many experienced salespeople work their listing farm for years. Other advantages cited for soliciting listings include the following:[2]

1. *Listings give more control.* Buyers are difficult to control. They vacillate among brokerage offices and are undecided in their preferences. The seller is controlled by the listing contract. As the salesperson responsible for securing the listing, you can earn approximately 25 percent or more of the gross real

[2]See Peter Wigginton, *The Complete Guide to Profitable Real Estate Listings* (Homewood, Ill.: Dow Jones-Irwin, 1977), pp. 2–4.

estate commission, a share commonly paid for the listing. If the listing is an exclusive agreement to sell, the listing person has no competition from other salespersons.

2.   *Listings make effective use of time.* If you are showing the house, you must be available when the seller has the house ready and can be absent and when time is available to the buyer. Your schedule must be continually revised to meet the needs of your sellers and prospects.

Listing enables you to control the time for your solicitation. Moreover, the listing is an effective way to use times when you cannot show a house. In addition, the listing program can be established at a set time each day with appointments scheduled in advance to make the best use of your time.

3.   *Listings represent the quickest way to develop commissions.* The listor develops business by actively soliciting business under an organized schedule. This contrasts to the salesperson who works mostly with prospects, who in turn respond unpredictably by telephone or office visits to your advertisements or for sale signs.

4.   *Listings build personal reputations.* Offices that add a salesperson's name to a for sale sign give buyer-prospects personal knowledge of your activity. If your name appears on several signs in the neighborhood, you soon gain the reputation of being the local authority on housing values. Contrast this result with salespersons who work with buyers; their names seldom appear in public as a result of their sales.

5.   *Listings provide a more stable source of commissions.* Salespersons who concentrate exclusively on buyer prospects suffer from seasonal buying variations and fluctuations in the real estate or mortgage market. A listor, who obtains 50 percent of the commission, tends to even out variations in sales. The stability is provided by more houses that are listed for sale. To obtain these advantages, the solicited listing may be gained by organizing a listing farm.

The Listing Farm

The listing farm refers to a specially selected neighborhood in which you actively solicit listings from each homeowner. Best results are obtained if the neighborhood is fairly homogeneous, that is, the houses have a fairly narrow range of prices and are of similar design and quality, and the education and the income level of the residents are approximately the same.

The neighborhood selected should have a minimum turnover factor of eight. This means that on an annual basis one out of eight houses will be sold each year. The expected rate of turnover is estimated by dividing the total number of houses, which are counted from a plat map, by the estimated annual number of sales.

Obtain information on the number of annual sales in the neighborhood from multiple listing services or public records. Some local property tax assessors record sales on a map by date of sale and price. In other communities, tax assessors have computer printouts of every sale by street address or subdivision. Alternatively, you can estimate the rate of turnover by your knowledge of past real estate transactions and the number of for sale signs and current listings of the multiple listing service. If you have 400 houses in your proposed farm, you would need anticipated future annual sales of 50 dwellings per year for a turnover factor of eight:

$$\text{Turnover factor} = \frac{\text{Total number of houses}}{\text{Number of annual sales}}$$
$$= \frac{400}{50}$$
$$= 8.0$$

The lower the turnover factor, the more successful you will be in obtaining listings. Avoid older neighborhoods in which the houses are undergoing a gradual decline in value. A neighborhood that has more than a 5 percent vacancy and a rental occupancy of over 10 percent is probably in a stage of relative decline. Instead, you should work in a neighborhood in which values are rising or that show a high degree of stability.

Maps. Before starting active soliciting, secure a good quality map of the subdivision and develop forms to keep records of your contacts. Good quality maps may be obtained from the county courthouse, the local planning and zoning office, the county assessor, the county engineer, the recording office that files subdivision plats, and commercial sources available in most communities.

Record Keeping. Ownership records are available from numerous sources. City directories, reverse telephone directories, property tax files, title insurance records, and commercial sources that supply real estate maps give this information. Property tax records are probably the best source from which to secure up-to-date ownership names.

Figure 6-1 shows the type of record system you design before you make your initial contact. Note that this form gives the address, name, phone number, year of the purchase, and whether the family owns or rents. The number of children are identified by the number of boys or girls. Two lines are provided for brief comments on prospects for listing the house. The code, which can be adapted to your special purpose, uses a circle to indicate a response from a female household member and the letter A to indicate a response from an adult male. Plus or minus signs indicate whether the response was positive or negative.

A separate sheet is prepared for each day. The date of call is in-

FIGURE 6-1. Listing Farm Record Form

SHEET NUMBER ___1___

NUMBER	NAME	PHONE	OWNT/RENT	YR PUR	KIDS	DAY/TIME	J1	F2	M3	A4	M5	J6	J7	A8	S9	O10	N11	D12	TOT
1	1868 Brewer,	696-0021	X	65	2B	Mon 3:00													
2	1870 Riley Bill, Ruth	696-0818	X	1G-1B	At														
	would like to purchase VA																		
3	1872 Thompson, Ted, Alice	696-1826	X	67	3B	At													
4																			
5																			
6																			
7																			
8																			
9																			
10																			

STREET → Pine

Source: Bruce T. Mulhearn, "The Listing Farm," in *In Search of Agreement* (Los Angeles, Calif.: California Real Estate Association, 1974), p. 14.

100

dicated by the sheet number. Each form provides for 10 entries, but you would preferably make 20 calls each day. Bruce T. Mulhearn of Bellflower, California, recommends that you make a minimum of 20 calls each day for 20 days per month. The owner's name is taken from public sources, but the additional information you list on the records is acquired by interview.

Personal Contact. It is further recommended that you make the inquiries in the late afternoon and evening. By reserving weekends to show property, you may schedule farm solicitations regularly during weekdays in the late afternoon. Avoid night calls. If your party seems irritated because you caught him or her during meal time, arrange to call back at another time. Given these points, you must adapt the presentation to your purpose. Here you would follow the preferred interviewing techniques.

Interviewing Procedures. Experienced listors say that the first call establishes trust and the second call continues to build trust while meeting objections of the potential seller. Following the preferred interviewing techniques, one authority advises (over, say, a four-month period) making four contacts to

1. Make your introduction.
2. Break down the "no" response.
3. Make your presentation.
4. Ask for business.

Others advise a more direct approach based on four probing questions. After identifying yourself and establishing rapport, ask the following questions:

1. When will you consider selling your house?
2. Which of your neighbors may want to sell their houses?
3. What do you like about this neighborhood?
4. When do you plan on selling your house?

Leave your card and then ask the prospect to call you if he or she needs real estate services. Wait a few days and then follow with a thank you note.

Meeting Listing Objections. In pursuing a listing, Roger Karvel advises salespersons working for McLennan Company of Park Ridge, Illinois, to meet the most common objections with the following responses.

1. I don't know if I want to sell now.

   What do you stand to profit by waiting? Why did you consider moving in the first place?

2. Why should I list with you?

(a) McLennan Company is 64 years old. We have more million-dollar sales-men than any other office in the area. We do substantially more advertis-ing in the media than any other firm in the area. This is the largest full-service real estate company in the area. This is the largest full-service real estate company in the northwest suburban area with a Guaranteed Sales Plan, shelter survey, sales people with long tenure, a rental department, real estate lawyers, certified property managers, and even civil engineers. We also have sold more real estate than any other office in Park Ridge.

(b) Be brief about the firm qualifications. Follow with an explanation of what the firm can do for the seller.

3. The country is going to the dogs, and I don't want to do anything right now.

Real estate values run contrary to the general economy because people have great faith in home ownership, and in times of recession inflows into savings and loans increase greatly. Real estate is traditionally the best hedge against inflation. This can be easily proven by the constantly advanc-ing prices of the homes in this area.

4. I have a friend in the business.

(a) According to John R. Clements of Clements Realty, Phoenix, Arizona, the best answer is, "Now you can have two friends" or "May I be your friend also?" This approach has the advantage of not encouraging the seller to call his friend about the doubts you raise over the friend's qualifications.

(b) Others have found it useful to respond in this way: "Is your friend full-time? How much experience does he or she have? How large is his or her office? Does he or she belong to the Multiple Listing Service? How long has the office been in business? What was his or her company's sales volume last year?"

5. I am going to put an addition on this house.

What do you really need in terms of space? Have you appraised your house? How long do you think it will take for the real estate market to recover the cost of the addition?

6. See me in a year.

"That's fine, but where are you planning to move? May we get some in-formation for you?" Alternatively, respond by saying: "I will be more than happy to contact you in a year; however, I might suggest that I contact you in about six months because we feel home values might peak at that time and you should seriously consider putting your home on the market at the best time."

7. Why should I list with a Realtor®?

a. This is our full-time business.

b. We belong to the Multiple Listing Service, the largest in the state of Illinois.

c. We are available at all hours and can show your property even when you are not in.

d. We can screen potential buyers for their financial ability better than you can.

e. Buyers will consult us about our opinion of how your house competes with the other homes for sale, but they might not be direct with you.

f. Since we offer the Guaranteed Sales Plan, we can guarantee the sale of your home and help you avoid double mortgage payments, interim financing, and storage expenses.

g. Because we act as a third party, we are able to negotiate without interference because of emotions, friendship, or personalities.

h. Buyers know that sellers are prejudiced about their houses and their values. Buyers are inclined to believe an agent more readily than a seller.

i. Remember that Realtors® have expertise in writing contracts, obtaining financing, and arranging other legal aspects of the sale.

8. I haven't found a house that I want to buy yet.

If you will provide me with the requirements for the home you desire, I will start a search program for you. In the meantime, we will appraise your home, and if appropriate, offer a guaranteed net purchase price so that you can feel free to look for another home immediately.

In developing the farm, the salesperson maintains contact with homeowners and knows the details of every home listed for sale by other firms or owners. Some salespersons practice talking to owners working in the yard. This provides an opportunity to compliment the owner and at the same time ask if he or she knows of owners who might be selling their houses. It has been proven that if a farm is developed in an orderly manner, the salesperson may expect to list *75 percent* of the properties for sale.

The Competitive Market Analysis

Special mention must be made of the competitive market analysis. The form for this analysis as developed by Clements Realty of Phoenix, Arizona, is illustrated in Figure 6-2. The purpose of this analysis is to give the seller the probable sales price. The listing price is supported by other listings and sales of similar property in the neighborhood.

Note that the form summarizes the main characteristics of the property currently for sale and includes a note on the number of days the property has been on the market. The same information is provided for recently sold property and listings that have expired over the last 12 months. This information is especially helpful in leading sellers to list the property at a competitive price. It is also invaluable in negotiating offers and counteroffers. Some offices recommend the competitive market analysis as part of the listing kit.

FIGURE 6-2. Competitive Market Analysis

COMPETITIVE MARKET ANALYSIS

CLEMENTS REALTY — Better Homes and Gardens

DATE _____

PREPARED BY _____

PROPERTY AT _____

SOLD PAST 12 MOS.	CODE	SQ. FT.	MTG.	LIST PRICE	SALE PRICE	TERMS	VOL/PG	REMARKS

FOR SALE NOW	CODE	SQ. FT.	MTG.	LIST PRICE	VOL/PG	REMARKS

EXPIRED PAST 12 MOS.	CODE	SQ. FT.	MTG.	LIST PRICE	DAYS ON MKT	REMARKS

ADDITIONAL REMARKS:

REALTOR

FIGURE 6-2 (cont.)

COMPETITIVE MARKET ANALYSIS								CLEMENTS REALTY, INC.	

PROPERTY AT _____ DATE _____

For Sale Now	BR	BA	FR	Oth	Ext. Mtg.	List Price	DAYS ON MKT.	Terms		

Sold Past 12 Mos.	BR	BA	FR	Oth	Ext. Mtg.	List Price	DAYS ON MKT.	Date Sold	Sale Price	Terms

Expired Past 12 Mos.	BR	BA	FR	Oth	Ext. Mtg.	List Price	DAYS ON MKT.	Terms		

BUYER APPEAL   MARKETING POSITION

1. Fine Location _____   1. Why are they Selling _____
2. Exciting Extras _____   2. How Soon Must They Sell _____
3. Extra Special Finan. _____   3. Will they Help Finance   Yes _____ No _____
4. Exceptional Appeal _____   4. Will they List at C.M.V.   Yes _____ No _____
5. Under Market Price _____   5. Will they Pay for Appraisal Yes _____ No _____
            Rating _____   Rating _____

Area Market Conditions _____

Recommended Terms _____

Drawbacks _____

Assets _____

Top Competitive Market Value _____ $ _____
Probable Final Sales Price _____ $ _____

Brokerage	
Loan Payoff	
Prepayment Penalty	
FHA-VA Points	
Title and Escrow	
Misc. Payoffs	
TOTAL	

$ _____

Net
Proceeds $ _____   Minus $ _____

Plus or

Form #8, 1-72

LISTINGS FROM FOR SALE BY OWNER

Acquiring a listing from "for sale by owner" is a challenge. The challenge is reduced, however, because you have listing prospects who want to sell their houses. And probably they are receptive since you can advise them on the local real estate market and other helpful ways to expedite the sale.

Answering Objections to Paying Commissions

Probably most buyers hope to save the commission. John C. Cyr of Stockton, California, has probably developed the best approach to this question. Salespersons are advised to ask leading questions when the objection over commissions arises. For example, "Mr. Owner, if you sell the property yourself, who do you think will benefit from the saving of the commission, you or the buyer?" He or she will, undoubtedly, answer that he or she, the owner, will save the commission because he or she is going to sell the house for fair market value and "not a cent less!" In this case, the salesperson counters with:

> Mr. Owner, if you expect to save the commission by selling at the fair market value, what do you think the buyer's attitude will be about this? Don't you think that he or she is also counting on saving the 6 percent by dealing directly? Surely the buyer is going to offer you 6 percent less, and perhaps even more than 6 percent less, for the property than your asking price; otherwise, why would the buyer be dealing with you? Therefore, wouldn't it be better to employ a skillful negotiator to work in your behalf, one who does this sort of thing every day and is being paid to have your interest at heart? If you will list your property for sale with us at its fair market value, we can be using our skills and techniques acquired through experience to convince any buyer that he or she should pay the full fair market value.

And further:

> Mr. Owner, if you try to sell the property yourself, you will have over 300 people in the real estate business as your competitors, but if you list your property with us, you will have these same 300 people working on your side to try to find a buyer. We are members of the Multiple Listing Service and the Stockton Board of Realtors®, and we are pledged to work in your behalf.

Also:

> Here is a list of homes that we have listed during the past 12 months and sold for the asking price! This does not mean that these owners listed their property too low but that they took our recommendation as a fair market value and accomplished their purpose in a short time and with excellent results. You, too, Mr. Owner, can have the benefit of this service if you will

give us the go-ahead to make a market analysis of your property and present you with a plan for a quick and profitable sale. Now here is how it works. . . .[3]

Another Realtor® responds to a seller who says that he or she wants to save a commission by selling himself or herself by asking the following questions?

What do you think is involved in selling your own house?

What if three couples come to your house at the same time? How would you handle this?

Do you have a work schedule that is flexible to accommodate showing your house at any hour?

Can you assist buyers in financing?

How would you screen buyers for their financial ability and true motivations?

Do you know what your competition is?

Do you think a buyer would be perfectly candid with you?

What will you do if your house doesn't sell in time to close on your other house?

What are the practical legal recourses for you if your buyer defaults?

Do you know all the pitfalls of an "Offer to Purchase" contract?

Owner Contacts

Another approach starts with a telephone call to the for sale by owner prospect. *First,* after identifying yourself and your company, ask, "Would you mind if I dropped by to look at your home?" Explain that you frequently have buyers for homes in that neighborhood and if you know the details of his or her house there is a possibility that you can be of service. The homeowner will usually let you look at the house and ask your advice. This gives you a chance to meet the homeowner face to face.

Second, during your inspection take notes and comment favorably on the housing interior and say how nice it looks. If you have the competitive market sheet, which is your listing of nearby houses for sale and neighborhood houses that have recently been sold, comment that there is no reason why the house should not sell if it is priced within the market.

Third, this is the time to ask technical questions on financing, discount points, buyer qualifications, title reports, title insurance, abstracts, and other technical points. Once you have determined his or her motivation to sell, begin closing for the listing.

At the appropriate point describe your company's services and make an

[3]John C. Cyr, *Training and Supervising Real Estate Salesmen* (Englewood Cliffs, N.J.: Prentice-Hall, Inc., 1973), p. 110.

appointment to make a market analysis of the house. Point out the importance of dealing with a reputable Realtor® and the advantages of dealing with an experienced firm in financing, selling, and qualifying the buyer.

OTHER CANVASSING METHODS

Among the other techniques to get new listings are methods of contacting certain homeowners who are likely to sell. Among the main suggestions are these points that help you build a listing bank.

General Canvassing

Call on neighboring houses when you make a listing or complete a sale; preferred practice recommends calling on five neighbors on each side of the house sold and ten houses across the street.

Continue making contacts in community organizations.

If your local board approves, interview owners of expired listings.

Continue to contact your previously sold listings.

In short, your listing program should develop every possible source. You should constantly remind your acquaintances that you need new listings, that you can give the listing personal attention, and that the services of your firm are not available from other competitors. Supplementing these procedures are telephone canvassing techniques, which are recommended by skilled Realtors®.

Telephone Canvassing

Depending on the neighborhood, you can probably expect a listing from 25 telephone contacts. Names should be taken from property records, reverse telephone directories, or city directories. Since this is a "cold" canvass, state your name and firm slowly and clearly. Call the person by name. *Always* ask if the person has time to talk to you. Repeat the name of your firm and inform your party that you (or your colleagues) have a buyer who is looking for a three-bedroom home in that neighborhood. After describing the buyer's main requirements, ask if your party knows of owners in the neighborhood who might want to sell. Do not ask the person who answers if his or her home is for sale. If the party gives you a possible lead, make the same call to the prospective client and ask for an appointment to inspect the home.

You must have a knowledge of the houses listed and recently sold in the area. You must be familiar with local property taxes, special assessments, and new construction. Dick Calafato advises this approach:

Good morning, Mrs. Archer. I was wondering if you would know of anyone thinking of selling his or her home in your neighborhood. I may have some clients who could be interested in buying a home in your area and would appreciate it if you could help me.[4]

At some point ask the further question: "By the way, when are you folks planning to move?"

Keep records of your telephone calls, name of the owner, party called, and the responses. Make the best use of your open and probing questions. For example:

Are you aware of the current property values in your neighborhood?

Have you considered investing your equity in other real estate?

Did you know that the Johnson property in your neighborhood recently sold for $55,000?

Try to make your telephone call interesting. Try to complete 25 calls an hour and develop at least one good lead per hour. Since your voice is an important nonverbal form of communication, start with a positive attitude and be prepared to give your party information of interest about property values or trends in his or her neighborhood.

On this point, the Berg Agency of Iselin and other cities in New Jersey gives detailed telephone instructions to its new salespersons and advises careful preparation:

1. Assemble and organize neighborhood information.
2. In preparing an opening statement and in making the listing presentation, salespersons are advised to
   a. Sound interested.
   b. Have the proper voice inflection.
   c. Be enthusiastic. Sound sincere and pleasant.
   d. Do not use technical terms.
   e. Use the prospect's name often.

THE LISTING KIT

The listing kit is a package you present to the seller. Included in the listing kit is a simply and effectively written listing presentation book that outlines your firm's professional services. The kit also includes aids for servicing your new listing.

[4]Dick Calafato, "How to Negotiate in Listing" in *How to Negotiate in Listing and Selling Homes* (Los Angeles: California Association of Realtors®, 1977), p. 2.

FIGURE 6-3. Itemization of The Estimated Costs for Buyer and Seller

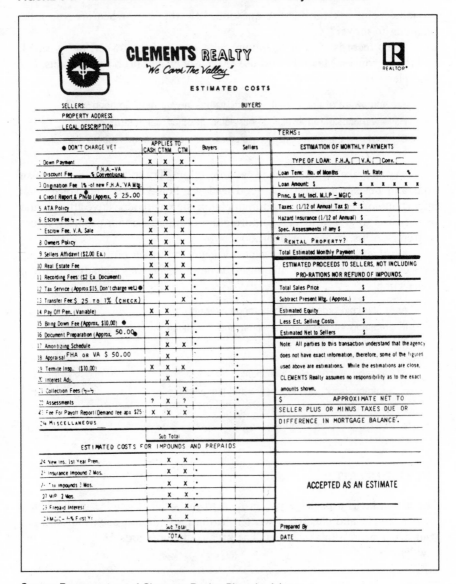

Source: Form courtesy of Clements Realty, Phoenix, Arizona.

FIGURE 6-3 (cont.)

EXPLANATION OF ESTIMATED COSTS

1. **DOWN PAYMENT:** The difference between the total sales price and the balance shown as new loan amount, or existing balance if cash to mtg.

2. **DISCOUNT:** Also known as "points". A percentage of the loan amount required by the lender. The amount of points charged fluctuate, depending on the availability of mortgage money available to the lender. On Conventional loans, this may be paid by either seller or buyer.

3. **ORIGINATION FEE:** 1% loan amount. Paid by buyer to mortgage company to originate new loan.

4. **CREDIT REPORT AND PHOTO FEE:** Charged and required by lender to obtain a financial background of buyer and to obtain pictures of home.

5. **ALTA POLICY:** Purchased by buyer to insure lender that encumbrance is a first lien on property.

6. **ESCROW FEE:** Charged by title company for their services. Fees usually split half and half.

8. **OWNERS POLICY:** Charged by title company. Owners policy insures buyer of free and clear title up to the date conveying instrument is recorded.

10. **REAL ESTATE FEE:** Amount paid by seller for real estate company to sell their home.

11. **RECORDING FEES:** Charged by the County Recorder's Office for recordation of any instrument(s).

12. **TAX SERVICE:** Required by the lender in order that the tax billings are mailed to the mortgage company.

13. **TRANSFER FEE:** Required on all cash to mortgage transactions. Mortgage company's charge to transfer loan into buyers name. Check with lender on conventional loan transfers for amount required (usually 1% loan balance). Also check for acceleration of interest rate.

14. **PAYOFF PENALTY:** Only required on conventional loan payoffs. Also known as prepayment penalty. Amounts vary, although the usual amount is 1% of the unpaid principal balance.

15. **BRINGDOWN:** Endorsement to the ALTA policy; issued by title company at the time the lender assigns their encumbrance to an ultimate investor. The endorsement insures the investor.

16. **DOCUMENT PREPARATION:** Charged by the mortgage company to prepare the disclosure statement, which is required by the government under the Truth-In-Lending Law.

18. **APPRAISAL:** Estimated market value of property as determined by a person acceptable by mortgagee.

20. **INTEREST ADJUSTMENT:** Required on all payoffs due to interest being paid one month in arrears. Always best to figure 30 days maximum.

23. **PAYOFF DEMAND:** Required by mortgage company to prepare payoff statement.

26. **MGIC REVIEW FEE:** Amount charged by Mortgage Guaranty Insurance Corporation to review buyers application and credit in order to insure loan.

The Listing Presentation Book

The Harris-Hamby Company, serving the city of Newark and New Castle and Kent counties, Delaware, has an attractive 8½" by 11" presentation book that outlines the advantages of listing with the firm. The brochure covers the following:

1. Administrative facilities.
2. Personnel background.
3. Examples of advertisements.
4. Common financing methods.
5. Services of lawyers, lending institutions, and banks.
6. Sample forms.
7. Marketing plans.
8. Trade-in plans.

The brochure, in large type for personal presentation, itemizes the company's *services,* which are explained by the salesperson. The list includes the following:

Multiple listing service	Controlled showings
Qualifying buyers	Around-the-clock phone service
Planned advertising	Client follow-up
Knowledge of financial market	Professional sales ability
Signs	Out-of-town referrals

The listing presentation book is not prepared for mailing; it is a guide for personal presentation by the salesperson. Typically, the presentation book gives major qualifications of the firm, awards and designations, professional achievements of the staff, and even letters from satisfied clients.

The Clements Realty of Phoenix, Arizona, itemizes estimated costs to sellers and buyers as part of the listing kit. This form, which is shown in Figure 6-3, is in addition to the competitive market analysis and other advertising material. Note that Figure 6-3 lists the terms encountered by Arizona buyers and sellers. Each of the numbered explanations parallels the numbered items on the buyer and seller list of estimated costs.

The marketing program is demonstrated by the reproduction of advertising and signs. In short, the listing presentation book is prepared to guide the personal presentation of the salesperson.

Other Listing Tools

Have available a 50-foot cloth tape, your listing form, and a set of mortgage tables in pocket form so that you will be ready to discuss sale terms with the prospect. The listing presentation book should include information on guaranteed sales and trade-in plans, if you make these available. Examples of company brochures, multiple listing forms, and newletters help in securing the listing.

SERVICING THE LISTING

Northside Realty Associates of Atlanta, Georgia, has developed a standard procedure for processing new listings, called the *listing caravan*. As each new listing is accepted by the office, it goes to a five-member caravan who complete the caravan slip (see Figure 6-4). The five-member caravan then reports its findings at the weekly sales meeting. During the week each salesperson is required to visit the property and become familiar with its details. At the weekly sales meeting salespersons review the activity of the listing and explain why the property has not been sold.

FIGURE 6-4   Listing Caravan Slip

```
LISTING AGENT_____BRANCH OFFICE _____
PROPERTY ADDRESS _____
IS LISTING PRICE O.K.?__YES__NO   IF NO, WHAT SHOULD IT BE?   _____
SUGGESTED REPAIRS OR IMPROVEMENTS _____
_____
_____
DON'T FORGET TO LEAVE YOUR CARD, AND BE ENTHUSIASTIC, THANK YOU.
AGENT_____BRANCH OFFICE   _____
```

Source: Form courtesy of Northside Realty Associates, Inc., Atlanta, Georgia.

You should communicate the progress of the sale to the seller on a regular basis. In a slow market the seller will be more patient if he or she knows that your efforts have been sincere. Explain to the seller your classified ad program, your telephone solicitation of prospective buyers, and direct mail.

If your initial efforts do not materialize in a sale, counsel with the seller on the asking price. In fact, if you have sent copies of your advertisements to the seller and the property does not sell, the seller will soon realize that the price is unreasonable. Keeping in continual contact with your listing seller will make it easier to negotiate the final sale, especially if your qualified buyer insists on a lower price or more favorable sale terms.

Listing Energy Efficient Houses

Approximately 70 million houses in the United States were constructed before the energy shortage started in 1974. These houses absorb almost 20 percent of the total energy consumed in the United States. Of this amount, approximately 60 percent of the energy consumed in a house is used for space heating and cooling. Consequently, national efforts seek to convert 2.5 million homes to solar heating and to retrofit approximately 90 percent of all single-family dwellings. Retrofitting refers to the addition of energy conservation devices on present dwellings.

As fuel and fuel transportation costs increase, the cost of household utilities will give the more energy-efficient houses greater value and higher marketability. New construction of energy-efficient houses, some with solar heating equipment, tends to lower the marketability of older, less energy-efficient houses.

Some lenders have observed that in some cases utility costs are greater than mortgage payments, reaching the point that loan security is in danger. Your buyer-prospect may qualify for a loan on house A, a new energy-efficient dwelling, and not qualify for financing on house B, a similar home without energy-efficient construction. It is anticipated that an increasing number of buyers will pay premiums for energy-efficient construction. Moreover, as more lenders become aware of the cost savings in energy conservation, they will grant more favorable financing to buyers of these houses. Conversely, houses not having these new features will show heavy depreciation in the market and unfavorable financing.

Listing Energy Conservation Construction

If you list an energy-efficient house, it is important that you add information not found on most listing forms. In fact, it is strongly advised that multiple listing services revise their forms so that the main energy conservation features are identified.

Consider the energy conservation construction in most houses. Although these construction features vary by location, the houses should be identified according to the following:

Windows
> Single-pane or double-pane
> Percentage of square foot area to floor area (preferably not more than 8 percent)

Exterior wall insulation
> Insulation value in R terms (R values refer to the thermal efficiency of insulation and vary by thickness and type of material)
> Moisture barrier

Ceiling insulation
> Type of insulation
> R value

Floor insulation
> R value
> Moisture barrier
> Crawl space, polyethelene covering, 6-mil thickness

Insulated exterior doors
> Metal
> Insulated with weatherstripping

Fireplace
    Exterior air vent
    Glass screen
Weatherstripping and caulking
Heating system and fuel
Solar heat
    Space heating
    Domestic hot water heating (describe main features)

In the New Orleans area the annual savings from new houses constructed according to energy-efficient principles are estimated to be from $1,429 to $1,936 for 1,300-square foot to 2,100-square foot houses having heat pumps. For houses having gas heat, the savings are slightly lower. As gas and oil prices go up, houses using fossil fuels will show greater savings. The savings summarized in Table 6-1 are compared to conventionally constructed houses having electric heat.

These savings are not realized without added costs. To list an energy-efficient house, you must be prepared to defend the extra cost of energy-efficient construction. In Table 6-2 the added cost of energy-efficient construction for a 1,816-square foot, single-story house having all electric heat is compared to a conventionally constructed house. The estimated annual savings per year are shown for each item. As fuel prices increase, these savings will be much higher in proportion to their cost. The higher fuel costs in the Northeast make these totals look even more favorable.

The figures in Table 6-2 apply to New Orleans, but similar data may be obtained from your local utility company. If you have a house that does not have these features or the owner has added these items, obtain estimates from the local utility company on how much the retrofitting saves in fuel bills.

There is one other point. Buyers may be expected to inquire about past utility costs. If you have an energy-efficient dwelling, add the following to the listing form:

1. A release from the owner (required by the utility company) to obtain the previous 12 months utility bills. Releases should be obtained for gas, electricity, and water.
2. A conversion of this cost to a cost per square foot.

These figures give the buyer a basis for comparing houses. Make further allowances for the size of the family. Domestic hot water costs more for a family that has five children than for a family that has one child. Further, if the preceding 12 months were subject to inclement weather that increased utility costs, explain that utility costs in your area were temporarily high and are not expected to be as high in succeeding years.

Solar Heating

Solar heat may be confined to heating *domestic hot water* or *space heating* and, in some instances, a combination of both. Solar heat has been used in southern Florida since the late 1920's and is proving more popular in the southwestern part of the United States. Current reports suggest that solar domestic hot water systems are feasible even for existing dwellings in the southern part of the United States.

You will probably list more solar heated dwellings as energy prices increase, as mass production lowers the cost of solar equipment, and as the government provides tax incentives to install solar equipment. Today some 20 states provide some form of property tax or income tax exemption for investment in solar heating equipment.

Typically, the solar hot water system requires solar collectors mounted on the roof and a two-tank hot water system. Storage tanks supply solar

TABLE 6-1. Typical Savings Realized From Energy-efficient Construction

New Single-Story Homes (New Orleans, Louisiana)

Floor Area (Living)	Windows	Infiltration	Walls	Ceiling	Doors	Heat Pump	Gas Heat	Total W/Heat Pump	Total W/Gas Heat
1,300–1,499	$250	$342	$166	$116	$98	$457	$379	$1,429	$1,351
1,500–1,799	277	387	174	138	86	492	409	1,554	1,471
1,800–2,100	436	424	202	160	97	617	512	1,936	1,831

Source: Unpublished paper presented by J. M. Wyatt, II, before the National Savings & Loan League Convention, Houston, Texas, October 19–22, 1977.

TABLE 6-2. Added Costs And Energy Savings of Energy Efficient Construction*

Item	Energy Conservation Construction	Additional Costs	Savings per Year
Windows (10)	Insulated	$344.00	$27.79
Walls (1,400 square feet)	Insulation board	209.00	16.82
Ceiling (1,816 square feet)	R-26 vs. R-19	164.00	13.03
Doors (3)	Insulated vs. Wood	140.00	8.72
Air conditioning and heating	2-ton heat pump, $3\frac{1}{2}$-ton base system	100.00	46.60
Infiltration	Caulking and weather stripping	100.00	39.31
TOTALS		$1,057.00	$152.27

*Single-story dwelling, 1,816 square feet.
Source: See Table 6–1.

preheated water for a second tank heated by conventional means. System controls maintain hot water at 120 degrees Fahrenheit. More complex systems integrate domestic hot water systems with an air space heating system.

Solar space heating is more complex. Collectors mounted on the roof transfer hot air to a bed of rocks or solar heated water to storage tanks. In a hot air system the dwelling areas are heated by blowing cool air from the rooms through heated rocks or through roof collectors. A system of dampers and fans maintains the selected heat level.

Solar space heating systems have low operating costs, but their initial cost is substantial. Some installations on new tract homes of 1,500 square feet during the last year cost $1,350 for materials plus installation costs of $11.70 per square foot. If you list a solar equipped dwelling, your sale will be advanced if you:

1. Secure an inspection report from a registered engineer experienced in evaluating solar systems. Lenders active in financing houses that have this equipment may require this step.
2. Obtain utility costs from the owner and convert these costs to a square-foot value on a monthly basis.
3. Make sure that solar collectors are protected by the right to direct rays of the sun. In areas where solar heating is popular, the site will be protected with solar easements.

These precautions are advised because of the mechanical problems in solar systems, especially solar collectors using solar heated water. There is sufficient evidence that the growing popularity of solar heating, especially in the southern and western states, will require supplemental material to be added to the listing form.

POINTS TO REMEMBER

Securing new listings follows from a program that maximizes listings from unsolicited sources and from a well planned campaign to solicit new listings. In the former case, salespersons gain from favorable reputations: their own personal reputation and the reputation of the firm. As a consequence, active salespersons become known in community organizations and develop acquaintances among community leaders who have special knowledge of family moves, job transfers, and other changes in family status that require the sale of a house.

Solicited listings that rely on the listing farm require the selection of a promising neighborhood in which there is a minimum rate of turnover. The listing program is undertaken on a scheduled, recurring daily basis. The objective is to become sufficiently acquainted with homeowners so that the salesperson acquires 75 to 80 percent of all houses listed.

Listings from "for sale by owners" are successful if salespersons meet owner attitudes with a planned presentation that makes effective use of probing and open questions. Other canvassing methods, such as telephone canvassing (for example, dealing with for sale by owner prospects), depend on a carefully preplanned program. Here nonverbal communication is conveyed by voice and speech patterns. A success rate of one good lead in 25 phone calls an hour is considered normal for this type of canvassing.

The listing kit is prepared to impress selling owners. It is also an aid to show the seller how the salesperson's firm and the salesperson's personal efforts are organized to secure qualified buyers in the shortest time. In servicing the listing, the salesperson keeps the owner informed about the sales program. This not only helps the salesperson acquire listings from the owner's friends, but it also develops a relationship which makes final negotiation more likely to succeed.

REVIEW QUESTIONS

1. What are referral listings?
2. Describe the public relations techniques used to acquire new listings.
3. Make a list of the community leaders who would have prior knowledge of family status and pending moves.
4. How would you benefit from soliciting listings?
5. What criteria would you apply in selecting a neighborhood listing farm?
6. Describe the minimum information recorded for a listing farm.
7. How would you repond to the eight most common objections sellers have against listing with a Realtor®? Give examples.
8. What recommendations do you have for dealing with a "for sale by owner" listing?
9. What is general canvassing? Explain fully.
10. What rules should you follow in canvassing for listings by telephone?
11. What would you include in a listing presentation book?
12. What information is recommended to emphasize energy conservation construction?
13. What are the main advantages of solar heating in your area?

7

Modern
Real Estate
Advertising

The largest single expense of a real estate office is advertising. The advertising program includes classified ads, which are the least expensive but most effective way to advertise houses, display advertising, billboards, and certain institutional advertisements that build the right image and advance the firm's reputation. Add to this group radio and television and certain other advertising specialties such as hand-outs and company prepared brochures.

In this discussion it is not implied that advertising should be considered as a panacea to boost lagging sales. Preferred practice recommends coordinating advertising with other selling activities including sales meetings, training programs, canvassing, and the like. A preliminary discussion of accepted advertising concepts supports this view.

ADVERTISING CONCEPTS

It is difficult to explain modern real estate advertising without discussing the limitations and pitfalls of advertising. That is, advertising should not be viewed as a substitute for other selling techniques. Certain practices governing the advertising program seem common to the established real estate programs. It is believed helpful to review these points before explaining specific advertising methods.

Advertising Limitations

Guard against trying to buy your way to success through heavy advertising. Experienced brokers do not view advertising as a substitute for sales training and effective leadership. Advertising is used to supplement the whole sales effort.

Overdependence on Advertising

There are real estate brokers who make less than effective use of advertising because the sales staff depends too heavily on an "effective" advertising program. The danger here is that salespersons may drop other selling techniques and wait vainly for the phone to ring and for prospects to crowd the office until every person has more clients than he or she can serve. The staff could be oversold on the effectiveness of the advertising program as a means of generating prospects, new listings, and commissions.

Some real estate brokers spend money on advertising either (1) to satisfy an unhappy seller or (2) to boost the morale of depressed salespersons. Other brokers do little to coordinate their advertising program with the listing and prospect search. By the same token, there is little merit in trying to buy out of a slow market with increased advertising.

Misuse of Advertising

Probably the more critical problem is the office that spends an above average amount for classified advertising and does not have a sales staff skillfully trained in answering the telephone. Or the staff members relate poorly to prospects who visit the office in response to telephone calls or advertisements. Or in listing, staff members do not have the required communication skills and a knowledge of neighborhoods or houses, financing, and the accepted selling techniques. In these cases, there would seem little advantage in developing an effective advertising program that generates new prospects.

In illustration, the advertising staff of the *Atlanta Journal-Constitution* made 462 calls to agency offices of Atlanta Realtors®. Calls were made from classified ads on three Sundays between 11:00 A.M. and 7:00 P.M. Agents were given Sunday and Monday to return calls. Inquiries were made so that the agent did not know that the "prospect" learned about the home from the newspaper.

The caller began with the comment, "I am calling about the home on Brookside." In this way the person answering did not know that the call was the result of the newspaper advertisement. Some 93 calls were directed to real estate offices and 369 calls were made to agents. The results are summarized in table 7–1.

Note that only 46 percent of the agents were available at the time of the call. Moreover, 27 percent of the agents did not answer; of the 28 percent of

TABLE 7-1 Results of the Telephone Response Survey

Telephone Response	Percent of Calls
No answer	27
Agent available at the time of calling	46
Answering service only available at the time of calling	28
When only answering service was available at the time of the calling:	
No message was taken	37
Message taken for the agent	63
When a message was taken for the agent:	
Agent returned the call	78
Agent did not return the call	22

the calls directed to the answering service, only 78 percent of the agents returned the call.

For the 93 calls made directly to real estate offices, the record was even less impressive: Here only 35 percent of the agents were available.

At the time of the survey, callers also rated telephone interviewing techniques. For this purpose, on the second and third Sundays the test callers were asked about the preparation and attitude of the answering agent. For the 156 calls answered in this way, the results showed:

89% of the agents *were prepared with facts* about the home advertised.
9% of the agents *were not prepared with facts* about the home advertised.
42% of the agents *asked the source of the call.*
55% of the agents *did not ask the source of the call.*
35% of the agents *were rated as excellent or cheerful.*
60% of the agents *were rated as good or friendly.*
5% of the agents *were rated as poor or unfriendly.*

The totals do not add to 100 because some of the preparation and attitude questions were not completed. Note that *9 percent* of the agents were not prepared with facts, another *55 percent* did not ask the source of the call, and *another 5 percent* were rated as poor or unfriendly. The point here is that advertising is largely ineffective unless the office and staff are prepared to make maximum use of classified advertising.

Advertising Recommendations

The importance of preparing advertising for your listed houses cannot be overemphasized. Writing advertisements may seem tedious and detailed, but it is one of the most valuable ways of spending your time. Accordingly, it is helpful to review suggestions that apply to classified advertisements, display advertisements, and other advertising devices that real estate brokers commonly use. In all forms of advertising you should:

1. Make advertisements positive; avoid negatives and stereotyped phrases.
2. Emphasize the leading amenities—every house has some unique, desirable features.
3. Be truthful in your advertisements; do not misrepresent or in any way promise features not found in the house advertised.
4. Use adequate descriptions. Long paragraphs in a classified advertisement will be read carefully by prospects. Use concrete, descriptive adjectives.
5. To make it easier for the prospect to respond, give the salesperson's name, address, and phone number. Be sure that the salesperson is available to answer the phone and is available to show the house advertised.
6. Keep records on the response to each advertisement. Eliminate ineffective ads and repeat advertisements that have a better than average response.

While these general comments apply to most written advertisements, the main problem relates to writing an appealing classified advertisement. The critical role of classified advertisements warrants a more detailed explanation.

EFFECTIVE CLASSIFIED ADS

Classified advertising should arouse the interest of the prospective buyers. The ad serves its function if prospects inquire about your advertisements. Since it is more than likely that the particular house advertised is unsuited to the prospect and since you probably have better houses for the prospect, the first inquiry must lead to an appointment. Your skill is tested when the prospect calls in response to your advertisement; you must sustain interest, stimulate further interest, and work toward making an appointment.

In creating interest, there is a tendency to overstate the listing. Best results are obtained by being truthful, sincere, and direct. In the last analysis, the most effective ad depends on your ability to (1) select the best houses to advertise, (2) select the appealing features to advertise, and (3) write the advertisement.

Selecting Houses to Advertise

Benefits realized from classified advertising depend on the houses selected for advertising. Since your object is to create interest, your chances of developing qualified prospects require that your selection appeal to the maximum number of prospects. If most buyers in your community are searching for four-bedroom, three-bath houses, there is not much point in spending advertising funds on two-bedroom, one-bath dwellings. Indeed, you are probably advised to withhold advertising if your prospects will be disappointed with the house you advertised or, worse yet, if the ad illicits few or no calls.

Probably few readers are familiar with you or the firm placing the ad. You are judged solely by the information presented in the advertisement. By advertising the best properties you have listed and not advertising houses that have known marketing deficiencies, you help build a long-run reputation. Remember that the most cleverly worded ad and the most liberal advertising budget will not overcome the marketing deficiencies in the property advertised. Consequently, your efforts must concentrate on your "choice" listings.

Selecting Features to Advertise

Assuming that you have selected the best possible listing, a listing that meets current demand, your next task is to study the property; you hope to create prospect interest by advertising features that appeal to current buyer preferences. For example, you may know that the brick veneer house with basement has a 10-inch thick concrete wall and foundation, but you will not sell the house solely on this point. The local housing market, current preferences, and the type of houses in the neighborhood dictate the items to be selected for advertising.

You must recognize that each neighborhood appeals to certain income groups, young couples, elderly couples, single buyers, or families with children. You must recognize that each house listed has at least one outstanding feature that makes the house saleable to a particular group of buyers. In other words, what particular features does your listing have as a family home?

Suppose, for instance, you have a listing for a four-bedroom house that has a fenced backyard. This house would be ideal for a young couple with several children. The occupants of the neighboring houses are couples with, typically, pre-high school children. In creating interest for this market, your advertisement should lead with a reference to children. Your heading would probably start with *attractive yard for children* or *your children will be happy here.* You create interest by appealing to emotions and not the physical characteristics of the house and lot.

To illustrate further, if the neighborhood includes a high proportion of retired couples, advertise a *retired couple's ideal house.* In the body of the ad you would add other details important to retired couples: convenience to shopping, on public bus line, quiet neighborhood, and so on.

Or suppose that your listing is an average house but that the price is below market. In your view, the house is "an outstanding buy." State this fact in the lead and give details in the ad narrative. Imply that your listed house is the best housing buy for the money. As a rule then you appeal to a prospect's preference for stable neighborhoods, a preferred lifestyle, attitudes, and emotions.

Because they are important, the physical features of the property should be reported factually and briefly but only after you have created interest. The importance of stressing physical features of the property is indicated by a survey undertaken by the *Atlanta Journal-Constitution*. The survey definitely disclosed that readers wanted facts. Tests indicated that ads that give more information get more calls. Prospects responded best to ads that included definite information on:

1. Location of the house.
2. Number of rooms.
3. Price and terms.
4. Housing design.
5. Age of house.
6. Present condition of house.
7. How house is heated.

These points deserve emphasis in the classified ad.

Writing the Advertisement

You have selected your best listings for advertising and you have identified the leading features of each house selected for advertising. Now you focus on the facts that you want emphasized. Your task is to select descriptive, creative words that elicit interest.

Creative ads avoid sterotyped phrases such as "owner must sell" or "make an offer." Equally ineffective are ads that literally copy the wording and format of competitor ads. Be original. First select a heading that creates interest and then follow with sufficient detail to arouse interest.

The Heading.   Classified ads begin with a heading associated with the amenities emphasized in the body of the ad. The more successful firms maintain a file of headings that have proven effective. Headings vary by changing market preferences and locality. There is virtually no limit to original, captivating headings that contribute to effective ads. Figure 7-1 lists headings that Rybka Realty, Inc., of Cleveland, Ohio, has found successful.

The headline has been called the single most important element in a classified ad. If the headline catches the reader's eye, he or she will look at your copy. If the headline does not attract attention, the readers will turn to other ads. For this reason, the headline serves as the key to more calls.

The Body of the Ad.   Assume that the headline offers a real benefit such as low cost or very good value. The next task is to illustrate this very good value by persuasive detailed copy. It is the preferred practice to avoid inflated or exaggerated descriptions in this copy. Describing your offer as a luxurious house, one of the best, or an executive mansion does not provide much information for decision-making purposes. More specific description is recommended.

FIGURE 7-1. Headings Found Effective for Classified Advertisements

Hearts Are Young	Spectacular View!	A Quiet Home
Designed for You	Life Begins at 40!	Garden of Ah's
Feel No Pain	Here's the Key	Storage Space?
Like Strolling?	Love Beautiful Things	Lasting Warmth
Like Golf?	Add it All Up	Get Comfortable
Enjoy Life More	Eliminate Maintenance	Star Among Stars
Country Casual	Touch of Elegance	Dining at Home
Reflects Good Taste	The Country Scene	Be A Prince
Within Your Reach	The Staying's Easy	It's Plush
Unlimited Potential	Roomy Comfort	Sunnyside
Find Relaxation	For Royal You!	For Joyful Years
Garden Lovers Only	Sheltered Location	Feel Fall Snugly
Beautiful Start	Made to Order	Seven Pines
Something for Everyone	First Class	So Rich!
Try It, Today!	Priced to Enjoy	Cream and Sugar
What Mom Wants	House Too Tight?	CHIC for Chicks
March in Before April	Hey, Look Me Over	On a Clear Day
So Nice to	If Comfort Counts	Call It Charm
Come Home to		
Join the Rent Rebellion	Helps Your Future	Dreamy Setting
Come Here Tonight	Moving With Care	Special Indeed
Get a Fresh Start	Look Once	Improve Yourself
Needs Boys & Girls	Elected for Today	Look at This!
Gentle Persuader	Wee Wonder	Scene Stealer
New Horizons	Let's Go Modern	Well, Here 'Tis
Tired of Compacts?	It's Easy to Enjoy	Professional Size
Dazzle of White	Spending Is Good	Step Saver for
		Mom
Snug Warmth	For Men Only	Luxury Without
		Tax
Gift to the Bride	For Active Living	Snug Haven
All My Lady Wants	Make a House a Home	To Love In
Cheery Childhood	Loll in A Pool	Get Compliments
Miniature Estate	Paradise Found!	Right In Step
Children Will Love It	Count the Extras	Wonderful World
Land of Lakes	Room to Grow	Glowing Address
A Sweet Deal	Why Deny Yourself?	Fire-Safe, Too
Be The Judge	Life Is Short	A Yard Wide
Budget Stretcher	For Teeny Tiny Tots	Looks Lovelier
Without A Worry	Star Bright	Entertaining
		More?
Kid-Proof	Cherished Tomorrow	Treasure Chest
She'll Thank You	Extra Privacy	Stepping Stone

Source: Edward F. Rybka, *The Number One Success System to Boost Your Earnings in Real Estate* (Englewood Cliffs, N.J.: Prentice-Hall, Inc., 1971), p. 79.

In describing the house, *dn't uz cmplx abv* (do not use complex abbreviations). Sentences or phrases are preferred to single words because they make the copy interesting and easy to read. To demonstrate the power of well written ads, the Bureau of Advertising of New York City tested these points by rewriting selected brokers' ads. The Bureau kept records of the number of calls received from the original ads and the rewritten ads. Figure 7-2 shows the results of the first test ad.

FIGURE 7-2. First Test Ad

BROKER'S AD

HASTINGS-ON-HUDSON. For grow' 'ng family. This young well planned home offers lots of living space. Lg liv rm w/cath ceiling, din rm, eat-in kit, 5 bd-rms, panel rec rm, den, 2 car gar. Ex-cellt cond. & area. $44,750. P.J. RIOLO Sole Agt. 30 Main St. 914 OW 8-1400.

6 LINES
0 CALLS

TEST AD

HASTINGS-ON-HUDSON $44,750
FOR GROWING FAMILY
This young well planned home offers lots of living space. Large living room w/cathedral ceiling, dining room, eat-in kitchen, 5 bedrooms, panel recreation room, den, 2 car gar. Excellent condition & area.
Ask for Mr. Alba
P.J. RIOLO, Sole Agt.
30 Main St. Hastings 914 GR 8-1400

15 LINES
5 CALLS

Source: *Small Talk: How to Prepare Better Real Estate Classi-fied Advertising,* (New York City: Bureau of Advertising), ANPA, no date, pp. 18–21.

The information included in each ad is the same. Note in the rewritten ad that (1) the headline stands out. (2) The headline focuses on consumer benefits. (3) The effective use of white space makes the ad stand out. (4) There are virtually no abbreviations. (5) The broker's name is easy to read.

Although the second test ad (Figure 7-3) had more lines, it received five calls compared to no calls received from the broker's ad.

Although the broker's ad of 11 lines generated 5 calls, the rewritten ad doubled the number of calls. Note again that the test ad (1) offered more information; (2) its headline had more impact; and (3) its ad copy provided

FIGURE 7-3. Second Test Ad

BROKER'S AD

WILL SACRIFICE
VA—MOVE IN—$450

7-Rm. alum. home featuring: 3
bdrms., spacious liv. rm. w-carpet and
fireplace; din. rm., fam. rm. w-fire-
place and full bath w-plumbing for
2nd bath plus covered carport and
fenced yard. All for $11,600.

AL LANNAN REALTOR
241-6326

856-6664   244-5750   856-6310

11 LINES
5 CALLS

TEST AD

$$ Dollar for Dollar $$

One of the best home values we've
had to offer you in many a day. Well-
kept all aluminum home on good size
lot surrounded by a chain link fence.
3 Nice size bedrooms, living room is
large with a fireplace and extra wide
drapes. There's a separate dining rm.;
cozy family rm. with gas log fireplace;
oil furnace; large covered patio. Ben
Davis HI. Near Fletcher Park, shops,
transportation. Bring your checkbook
—You'll want to buy it! $11,600 V.A.—
You pay closing costs—And move in!
CALL ANN for more details.

AL LANNAN REALTOR
241-6326

856-6664   244-5750   856-6310

20 LINES
10 CALLS

Source: See Figure 7-2.

relevant details and supported the headline. Note also that the adjectives described the benefits in plain language and that there were few abbreviations: nice size bedrooms, extra wide drapes, cozy family room, and well-kept all-aluminum home.

FIGURE 7-4. Third Test Ad

BROKER'S AD

LEASIDE

$5,000 down, modern square plan, 6-room solid brick family home on Donlea Drive. Bright and clean, water and oil heat. Deep lot. Wide paved drive and garage. Immediate possession. Mr. Haist, 485-6565.
L. S. SNELGROVE CO, LTD. RLTR.

13 LINES
0 CALLS

TEST AD

LEASIDE

PLENTY of room for the kids to play around this snug, solid brick home. Sparkling clean. Oil (hot water) heat. 6 rooms, 3 bedrooms, modern square plan. 220 x 135 lot, paved driveway and garage. Only $5,000 down on this $23,900 bargain on Donlea Drive. Move in now, if you like. Mr. Haist, 485-6565.
L.S. Snelgrove Co. Ltd. Realtor

13 LINES
3 CALLS

Source: See Figure 7-2.

The third test ad, which had the same number of lines as the broker's ad, gave better results (see Figure 7-4). This ad emphasized benefits: plenty of room for kids to play, snug solid brick home, sparkling clean. Note that the terms and price are given and there is more information: the actual size of the lot and the number of bedrooms.

When to Place Ads.   Sunday classified ads are the most popular source of information on new homes. Yet a survey by the Newspaper Advertising Bureau emphasized the importance of weekday ads. Of 2,007 home-buying families surveyed that moved over a 12-month period, 81 percent read classified pages on weekdays; 85 percent consulted classified advertisements on Sundays. The survey revealed that six out of ten families planning to buy or rent homes referred to newspaper advertisements on both weekdays and Sundays.

Gordon French, Real Estate Marketing Consultant of Atlanta, Georgia, reports similar results. In 378 interviews with home buyers in Atlanta (1977), it was found that buyers consulted classified advertisements according to the following schedule:

Daily	28 percent
Two to three times a week	36 percent
Sunday only	27 percent
Less than once a week	10 percent

Because of these results and because real estate offices operate weekdays (and usually evenings), it makes good sense to place classifieds throughout the week.

In administering an effective classified ad campaign, salespersons must realize the following: (1) The objective of the ad is *to encourage prospects to call;* the call should result in an appointment with the prospect. (2) Only a small proportion of prospects purchase the houses they call about—some report less than 10 percent. (3) Early in the telephone interview the salesperson should gain control of the call by asking questions instead of concentrating solely on answering the prospect's questions. (4) The classified ad, the telephone call, and the appointment introduce the salesperson to a prospect who may be directed to a house that ideally suits his or her needs and his or her ability to finance the purchase.

Evaluating Classified Ads

As part of a continuing program to make effective use of classified ads, each ad should be evaluated according to its results and the ad should be judged by means of a checklist that directs your attention to the best way of writing a classified ad. It is suggested that each ad be judged according to the following:

1. *Does the ad begin with an attention-getting heading?* The heading should be in larger type, should be sufficiently short, and should appeal to the features described in the body of the ad. An ineffective heading may cause the reader to skip to the more appealing ads of your competitor.

2. *Have you written an ad which appeals to the buyer-prospect's needs?* You may be impressed with a particular feature of the house, but your personal preferences are unimportant. You must examine the neighborhood and its occupants and determine the kind of prospect most likely to buy the house listed. Then examine the listing for features that appeal to buyer-prospects in the market for the type of house you have listed; be sure to cover these "amenities" in your ad.

3. *Have you selected the strongest appeals for the advertisement?* This requires that you emphasize the strongest amenities of each property listed.

4. *Does the ad appeal to the most qualified prospects in the market for the listing?* You must think in terms of the most likely prospects in the market for the house listed. Is the house suited to an elderly couple, a young married couple with children, single persons, a middle-income family, or a high-income family? Discourage calls from prospects who may not qualify for the house listed.

5. *Does the ad create interest and offer sufficient details to encourage prospects to call?*
6. *Have you written the ad in a direct, active style? Have you omitted ineffective, needless words?*
7. *Does the ad close with a compelling reason for prospects to call?* This part of the ad should induce prospects to call the salesperson for added information.

You should establish a routine for evaluating each ad before it is released. Keeping records of calls for each advertisement enables you to continually evaluate your judgments in writing the most effective ads. If an ad shows poor results, go back to the checklist and reevaluate judgments on these points.

DISPLAY ADVERTISING

Display advertising, though relatively expensive compared to classified advertisements, reaches potential prospects who may not consult the more detailed classified column. It combines a photograph, an effectively written ad, and a prominent exposure of the firm's name. For example, a display ad run by the McLennan Company, Park Ridge, Illinois, combined five houses in one display ad with a photograph of each house. The photograph of a contemporary brick home was accompanied by the following description:

Magnificent First Offering

This contemporary brick home is perfection-plus. Eight beautifully appointed rooms, four bedrms, two and a half baths, dramatic family room w/stone fireplace, wet bar & sliding glass doors to brick enclosed patio. *Call Gloria Petell for appointment* [telephone number follows].

In each instance, a brief description of the house ends with an invitation to call the salesperson and is printed in bold type. The point is further demonstrated by the Harris–Hanby Company of Newark, New Jersey, that advertises a split-level house with a photograph showing a large front yard.

WANT SPACE?

Then don't miss this young split-level! It offers four to seven bedrooms, 2-1/2 baths, family room with fireplace, den, two central air conditioners, appliances, flagstone foyer, and a three-car garage. Large lot features many plantings plus fruit trees and great garden. This home built by owner is an exceptional purchase.

Serviced by Dick Brunner   731-8200

$79,900   913 Nottingham Road
                                                          Newark

---

Note that the amenity of the large lot is highlighted in the heading: Want Space? Then the first lead line develops the same point: "Don't miss this young split-level" which creates further interest. "The large lot *features many plantings plus fruit trees in garden* . . . an exceptional purchase." Again the ad ends with the name of the salesperson and phone number.

These examples illustrate some common rules for writing classified ads.

1. Select only choice listings for ads.

2. Learn the main unique features that give the listed house appeal to prospects in the market for the listed house.

3. The heading selected should highlight the main amenity. It should create interest and encourage the reader to finish reading the ad. Descriptive copy is written in short sentences. Flowery, high-flown phrases are avoided.

4. Use appealing adjectives to describe the features you select, i.e., a spacious lot, exquisite colonial home with entry foyer, lovely ranch home . . . cozy split-level, nifty partial brick, ranch featuring . . . quick possession of this exceptional ranch house in Capitol Hill featuring plush carpeting.

5. Unless you are a skilled ad writer, avoid humor. Usually buyer-prospects are serious and want facts, names, places, and features.

6. Watch out for jargon. A technical term might be part of your daily vocabulary but terms like discount points, prepayment penalties, wraparound mortgages, easements, and similar terms confuse many prospects and invite suspicion. Write in plain, nontechnical terms and avoid abbreviations unfamiliar to the general public.

7. Give sufficient detail to create interest. Avoid too much detail and long descriptive copy that may cause the prospect to reject your offer before calling for additional information.

OTHER ADVERTISING METHODS

Real estate offices use numerous advertising media besides newspapers. They use institutional advertisements that build firm reputation, they use billboards, they publish brochures for direct mail, they distribute handouts to buyers and sellers, they use radio and television, and they use other advertising specialties.

Institutional Advertising

"We try to do as much as possible in all advertising fields (direct mail, outdoor advertising, newspaper advertising, novelty, area publications)," says Gordon T. Smith, owner of Volunteer Realty Company of Knoxville, Tennessee. The annual advertising budget is allocated over five major categories as shown in table 7–2. Volunteer Realty's public relations coordinator advertises more heavily from February through November, a period in which it has more

TABLE 7-2 Real Estate Advertising Budgets in Percent

Type of Advertising	Percent of Annual Budget
Outdoor	17
Classified display ads	66
Trade and area publications	7
Radio	7
Novelties	3

more heavily from February through November, a period in which it has more listings than it does the balance of the year. Generally, each house is advertised at least once every one and a half to two weeks. The firm's records illustrate the importance of multimedia advertising to produce a desired sales volume.

On examination it may be seen that much of the advertising by Volunteer Realty is not direct marketing advertising. It includes institutional advertising that places the name before the public, building a good image and explaining the services of the firm. Institutional advertising is an efficient way of adding to the company's reputation, especially important to the larger firm that has departmentalized services.

Figure 7-5 illustrates institutional advertising that is placed in local and regional publications such as real estate magazines, newspapers, brochures, and other media receiving local and broad distribution.

The advertising program of Volunteer Realty illustrates the coordination of a billboard campaign with the radio spot announcement. The advertising manager coordinates direct marketing advertising and institutional advertising among the different media.

Billboard Advertising

To make the most effective use of a coordinated advertising program, real estate firms make repeated use of unique design, color, and type face in emphasizing the firm name. Billboards that advertise the company name make maximum use of the firm's identifying mark.

Though costly and requiring professional advertising services, the billboard is frequently used to advertise a new residential subdivision. In this respect, billboards are enlarged versions of small property signs. Recommended practice limits the billboard ad to a few words that may be read in a few seconds. Figure 7-6 shows a billboard ad coordinated with a radio jingle and spot announcement. For two weeks the billboard included only the top half of the billboard: "You're next on the list!" When the bottom half of the bill-

Helping
kids
is a spotless
service.

And so is Spillbox, the household
stain removal kit. It costs just
$6 and contains 12 stain-removing
ingredients plus a government
"how to" manual.

Spillbox is available at your nearby
office of E. G. Stassens, Inc.,
Realtors, The Home Folks.

And all net proceeds from your
purchase go to support the Oregon
Museum of Science and Industry,
where kids learn what the world
is all about.

Pick up Spillbox. Clean a stain.
And help a kid. Only $6.

Realtors® National Marketing Institute 1976 Honorable Mention Institutional Advertising
E.G. Stassens, Inc., Realtors®

Source: Volunteer Realty Company, Knoxville, Tennessee.

board was added, the local radio station began playing the following spot
announcement:

Volunteer Jingle Full Vocal

See *Volunteer* to help you. We say it in our name. And even though the times
have changed, the people stay the same. We try to show you how much we
care in everything we do. At *Volunteer* we're really sincerely doing it for you.
Volunteer———*Volunteer* Realty Company———*Volunteer.* At *Volunteer*
we're doing it for you. *Volunteer*———*Volunteer* Realty.

Voice

You're next on the list—next on the list when you list your home with *Volunteer* Realty. The experienced Realtors® at *Volunteer* will be hard at work
to sell your home quickly. They're doing it for you because when the time
comes to sell your home, they know you don't want to waste time. That's
why they say you're next on the list at *Volunteer. Volunteer* Realty Company.

In this case, the jingle precedes the voice which is followed by a repetition of
the jingle. In the spot announcement the name Volunteer is repeated 12 times.

Since the spot announcement is coordinated with the billboard as well as classified and display newspaper advertising, the firm maximizes direct marketing
and institutional advertising.

Company Brochures and Newspapers

Well-organized real estate firms make frequent use of company prepared
publications. A review of current practices shows frequent use of a variety of
material. For instance, the E. G. Stassens, Inc., Realtors® of Portland, Oregon, prepare a 40-page magazine which includes display ads of the listed
houses. The following newspaper ad publicizes the magazine:

Free Magazine

We know a lot about homes, so we're sharing it with you in
our 40 page magazine. It's called Open House and it includes
142 photographs of homes for sale, plus plenty of valuable
information for home buyers and sellers. And it's free for the
asking! Call 243-6127 for your December issue, available
December 20th, or stop by any one of our 18 offices.

E.G. STASSENS, INC., REALTORS

The 8½-inch by 11-inch magazine includes considerable institutional advertising and a self-addressed, stamped postcard with an invitation to ask for additional information, for example:

We'll Answer All Your Questions About Real Estate. Just Ask!

- ☐ Marketing My Present Home
- ☐ Buying a House
- ☐ Investing in Real Estate
- ☐ Financing
- ☐ Facts about Renting vs. Home Ownership
- ☐ Real Estate Sales as a Career
- ☐ Please place my name on your mailing list for the OPEN HOUSE MAGA-
  ZINE!

Others, such as Harley E. Rouda and Company, Realtors® of Columbus,
Ohio, prepare kits for buyers and sellers. Among the material included in the
Rouda homebuyer's kit are suggestions of things for the new homeowner to
do at the new address.

At Your New Address

Obtain certified check or cashiers check necessary for closing real estate transaction.

Check on service of telephone - gas - electricity - water.

Have your stove serviced - check pilot light (if gas).

Check pilot light on hot water heater, incinerator, and furnace.

Have refrigerator - automatic washer - television set checked.

Ask mail carrier for mail; he or she may be holding for your arrival.

Have new address recorded on drivers license.

Visit city offices and register for voting.

Register car within five days after arrival in state or a penalty may have to be paid when getting new license plates.

Register family in your new place of worship.

Register children in school.

Other material in the kits supplied by Harley E. Rouda and Company help build the reputation for service to both buyer and seller.

This idea is carried further by the McLennan Company of Park Ridge, Illinois. McLennan distributes an information brochure entitled *10 Important Principles Every Homeowner Should Know.* The ten sections of this brochure cover information important to both buyer and seller:

    I. How Much Money? . . . Where to Get It . . . and How

    II. Remember the "Homeowner's Cycle"

    III. Get Professional Help!

    IV. What Kind of House and Lot?

    V. Where to Start Looking

    VI. When to Buy a House

    VII. Give Your Property Tender, Loving Care

    VIII. Should You Move or Improve?

    IX. A Good Insurance Plan

    X. Twenty-three Don'ts for Owners and Buyers

For instance, the "Don'ts" to the buyer provide helpful suggestions that include the following:

Eight Don'ts For Buyers

Don't buy a house only because it's a bargain. Buy a house you want and need—at a fair price. The fun of having bought a bargain quickly wears off, particularly if you find yourself housed in a structure that fails to fill the bill.

Don't buy on impulse. Look at the house at least twice at different times of the day. Check the neighborhood, the mortgage. Make sure the house pleases the whole family. Take your time!

Don't confuse the seller by attempting to buy personal property and real estate at the same time. Wind up your house deal first. Pick up the lawn mower and the dishwasher later.

Don't buy an obsolete house or a house that fails to meet your needs unless you know its obsolescence can be eliminated, its shortcomings removed— and the exact cost of the changes.

Don't take homeownership lightly. Your house is the biggest purchase you will ever make. Ask questions. Shop. Think. Study. Be informed. It is a big step.

Don't buy a new house in a new project if you plan to move in less than six to eight years. If you do, your buyers will gravitate to "brand new houses" being built right down the street . . . under terms you can't match.

Don't buy a house without first studying the community in which it is located. Check up on police and fire protection, zoning restrictions, garbage collection, street lighting, snow plowing, the churches, shopping centers, and the parks.

Don't overlook the schools if you have children. Your children will go to schools in the district in which you live. Pick a "poor school area" and you will have nothing to do but live with it—or sell and move into a new school district.

Advertising Specialties

The variety of other advertising specialties is virtually without limit. Sellers, buyers, prospects, and others are often given specially prepared materials, for example:

Pocket calendars	Local maps
Appointment calendars	Document folders
Six-inch plastic rulers	Home buyers guide kits
Pens and pencils	Home promotions sales kits (for seller)

Harley E. Rouda and Company includes in a kit for the home buyer "a home photo gallery," which is a color reproduction of each house Rouda lists in the Columbus area. The kit includes maps, suggestions to the buyer and seller, advantages of exclusive listing, the importance of seller cooperation, community information, and related material.

Hence, although almost all firms concentrate on classified advertisements, the advertising program is coordinated with other media for direct market or institutional advertising. In a survey of 152 real estate firms by the author, approximately 30.9 percent of the firms indicated that newspaper classified ads were most effective though other forms of advertising were utilized. Direct mail, newspaper display ads, and materials such as brochures and other company publications were next in significance. Answers to the following question are summarized in table 7–3: "Our firm finds the following advertising media effective:"

TABLE 7-3 The Allocation of Advertising Budgets

Advertising Media	Number of Firms	Percent of Total
Direct mail	27	17.7
Classified ads	47	30.9
Display ads	26	17.1
Trade publications	6	3.9
Radio	12	7.8
Television	11	7.2
Other	23	15.1
Total	152	99.7

These data suggest the relative importance of a *coordinated* advertising program. Although classified ads are the single most important expenditure, other means of advertising are necessary to support the sales program and the firm's reputation.

THE ADVERTISING BUDGET

Although practices vary widely, establishing the advertising budget is not a casual undertaking. Most firms follow established rules that seem to work in their locality.

Current Practice

Chuck Staub and Associates, Realtors® of Metairie, Louisiana, hold the advertising budget to approximately 5 percent of gross income. Depending on past success, the Berg Agency of New Jersey adjusts its budget to 6 percent of total income. A slightly different plan is followed by the Ballard Realty Company of Montgomery, Alabama. Here salespersons do their own advertising and are reimbursed up to 10 percent of net income to the company at the end of the year. Similarly, the Morton G. Thalhimer, Inc. Realtors® of Richmond, Virginia, allow salespersons to advertise up to 10 percent of the previous quarter's commissions.

In the survey of 152 brokers, the maximum allowance for advertising ranged up to 20 percent of company gross income. One firm followed a 10 percent limit on advertising, allocating 60 percent of the advertising budget for classified ads and 40 percent for institutional, image-building advertising.

A slightly different system is applied by the McLennan Company of Park Ridge, Illinois. According to Roger J. Karvel, the company forecasts the sales volume and determines the promotion effort to obtain that volume. The company adapts monthly promotion dollars to each month's projected activity and revises the forecast and promotion expense to obtain a given sales level. Some firms are less formal. Fletcher Bright of Chattanooga, Tennessee, advises that it "uses the necessary dollars to adequately expose its listings."

Budget Flexibility

Although many firms base the advertising budget on a percentage of business, there are compelling arguments against this practice. Advertising is unlike rent, electricity, heat, and other operating expenses. These are overhead costs that are relatively fixed and, in a sense, nonproductive.

On the other hand, advertising expenditures contribute to increased sales volumes: A well-designed advertising program develops new prospects and a higher sales volume. And, too, brokers should not decrease advertisement during seasonal lulls as they would for other office expenses. Reduced advertising directly decreases sales.

Size of Firm.   The proportion of gross income spent for advertising varies according to the size of the firm. The larger advertiser realizes economies of scale. Because newspaper classified advertising rates provide for a decreasing line rate based on the number of lines, the larger broker advertises at a lower cost per insertion than does the smaller firm. Moreover, if there are branch offices, the advertising cost per prospect decreases. In addition, because advertising rates vary by city and between newspapers, advertising expenses as a proportion of sales vary significantly. This is especially true since real estate commissions tend to be the same between cities.

In this respect, there is another problem. By allocating a fixed proportion of the gross income to advertising, what does the broker do when he or she has reached the advertising allocation for a specific property and it has not been sold? By withholding advertising the chances of securing a prospect are decreased. A review of the listing may indicate that you should continue to advertise.

Budgets Related to Management Problems.   Firms that have a high proportion of advertising to gross sales may also have other problems. The proportion may be high because salespersons are not skillful in handling prospects or in dealing with property owners who list the property too high. Weaknesses in telephone techniques, methods of showing the house, and skills in gaining seller cooperation may be other deficiencies that make the advertising budget appear high in relation to sales volume.

Budget flexibility allows for changes in the number of listings, sales volume, and new salespersons. In short, a planned advertising budget is required not to save advertising expenses but to make the maximum use of advertising funds. You should make a sales forecast; then plan and adapt the advertising and other selling techniques to reach the sales projection, which, in turn, is based on reasonable objectives. Hence, the advertising budget should not be viewed as an inflexible proportion of gross sales.

Advertising Policy

The *Chicago Tribune,* which has the largest circulation for classified advertisement in the Chicago metropolitan area, is utilized heavily by the William L. Kunkel & Company Realtors® of Chicago, Illinois. The company has an established policy of using classified advertisements 365 days a year on the theory that the company does not know when buyers of real estate are in the market. Experience indicates that a consistent advertising program succeeds. Whatever the rule, advertising must follow company policy. Clearly, it is inadvisable to make damaging budget cuts because of temporary decreases in sales.

Advance Planning.   Most firms prepare an advertising expense budget based on the previous year's profits. This has the advantage that adequate funds are provided for advertising from the previous year's earnings. In contrast, if the preceding year was a year of an unusually low sales volume, it may be advised to increase the advertising budget on grounds of a more favorable forecast and not on below average earnings of the past year.

Realistically, the budget is based on an estimate of forecasted sales. The advertising budget, depending on the firm's past experience, should be the amount necessary to realize the anticipated volume. The budget should be earmarked monthly and allocated to institutional, display, classified, and other advertising.

Review the Forecast.   The annual forecast should be reviewed monthly and adjusted accordingly. Some firms adjust advertising expenses after a quarterly projection; other companies concentrate on the best season or decrease ads during bad weather. Still other companies set aside funds in years of high sales volume to supplement the advertising budget in the less active years. By establishing a reserve, the advertising budget follows a planned sales program.

Another approach is to base advertising on the number of salespersons, the office location, and current market conditions. Once a plan is established it is inadvisable to deviate from the plan. That is, a real estate broker should not buy his or her way out of a slow period with heavy advertising—there are too many other variables in the sales effort. And, finally, it is not advised to spend advertising money without studying the results.

Advertising Records   This last suggestion requires that records be kept on the success rate of each advertisement. Records on classified ads should be maintained and should indicate the number of calls received from each ad. The time of the call, the date, and the name of the salesperson taking the call should be entered.

Some offices prepare a classified ad scrapbook in loose-leaf format. Each page has a copy of the advertisement with a record of its cost, the replies received from the advertisement, and a rating of the quality of replies, for example, the numbers 1, 2, 3 representing good, fair, and poor. The local weather noted for the day the ad appears helps to interpret the effectiveness of the ad. A study of these results over time gives an insight into the effectiveness of a classified ad program. Other offices add to this scrapbook a camera record of billboards, special signs, and window displays with their costs, results, and a statement of how each expenditure increased buyer-prospect inquiries.

POINTS TO REMEMBER

Although it is the largest single expense for a real estate office, advertising is no substitute for professional selling techniques; advertising merely supplements the whole sales effort. Advertisements should be positive, emphasize leading amenities, and be truthful in every respect. They should be continually tested, reviewed, and improved by evaluating the results of advertising.

Effective classified ads turn on the proper selection of houses to advertise. The emphasis is on features that appeal to your most likely prospect. In writing the ad, particular attention is paid to the heading which must create interest and capture the reader's attention. The body of the ad gives sufficient detail to encourage the prospect to call. A review of common practice shows the dependence on adjectives that appeal to the emotions. That is, do not write "a seven-room house." Write "a *sprawling* seven-room house." Then test the ad by using a checklist that covers the recommended content of advertisements.

As display advertising reaches prospects who may not consult the more detailed, classified columns: (1) Select only choice listings for presentation. (2) Emphasize the unique features that appeal to the most likely prospect. (3) Select a heading that highlights the main amenities. (4) Lastly, in the body of the ad use appealing adjectives that invite further inquiry. Avoid humor and jargon and give sufficient detail to create interest without causing prospects to reject the house you offer.

Preferably, institutional advertising will be coordinated with other advertising methods. Billboard advertising, for example, may be coordinated with newspaper displays and radio spot announcements. The more successful firms rely on company brochures and specially printed newspapers and pamphlets that advertise the firm's name and listed houses. Advertising specialties cater to the buyer and seller's needs; home promotion sales kits and home buyer kits are among the more popular specialties.

The advertising budget, which may be based on a percent of gross sales, follows a planned program. Advertising as a percent of gross sales varies according to the size of the firm and the skill and training of the sales staff.

The less efficient salespersons may show an unreasonably high advertising allowance not because of excess advertising but because of poor sales techniques.

The best procedure allows for budget flexibility based on advanced planning; that is, the budget should be earmarked monthly and allocated to institutional display, classified, and other advertising to reach a projected sales volume. The sales forecast is reviewed periodically to adjust the advertising budget to meet changes in market conditions or the firm's objectives.

The advertising program is reviewed on the basis of accurate records maintained on classified and other published advertising. Keeping a file of advertisements (the number of calls and related details) helps to identify the ads that give the best results and the ads that are weak performers.

REVIEW QUESTIONS

1. What factors can you cite as limitations of advertising programs?
2. In what way are management policies related to advertising effectiveness?
3. What general advertising recommendations apply to classified, display, and other advertising methods?
4. What physical features should be stressed in advertising houses?
5. What is the significance of a heading in classified advertising? Give an example to illustrate your answer.
6. List the recommendations that you would make in writing a classified advertisement.
7. What arguments may be offered in favor of placing classified ads during the week?
8. What points would you make in evaluating a classified ad?
9. What type of advertising would you recommend to promote the firm's reputation?
10. Explain how you would establish the firm's advertising budget.
11. What type of advertising policy would you recommend for real estate brokers?

8

Qualifying the Prospect

The house you listed last week may be ideal for your prospect, but the final sale depends on your skill in qualifying the buyer. Unless you know your prospects, their needs, and their financial status, you will not reach your maximum sales volume. Consider the salesperson who listens carefully to the husband and wife, learns their housing preferences, and shows them houses priced from $65,000 to $70,000. Only after three weeks does the salesperson learn that they cannot arrange more than a $10,000 down payment and a $30,000 mortgage. To avoid such an impasse, arrange your initial interview to (1) know the buyer and (2) obtain prospect financial data.

KNOW THE BUYER

Jack King of E. G. Stassens, Inc., Realtors® of Portland, Oregon, advises sales associates to qualify a buyer at the buyer's residence. Mr. King reasons that buyers are more relaxed at their homes, thus making it easier to establish rapport and engage in more meaningful communication. More importantly, the sales associate learns the lifestyles of the prospects, their furniture arrangements, and other likes and dislikes important to their new homes.

In your first contact with the buyer, in the home or office, start the interview by asking, "How did you learn about our company?" This starts the interview on a friendly basis and allows you to progress smoothly into the qualifying interview. Rich Port, a Realtor® in La Grange, Illinois, advises his sales staff to (1) be pleasant, (2) sell yourself, and (3) get the prospect to relax.

With this beginning, the salesperson moves to buyer qualification by asking direct questions.

Remember that some buyers, especially first home buyers, may express a desire for an ideal home that is beyond their financial capability to buy. Here you must listen attentively, ask leading questions, and establish a friendly relationship before seeking financial information. Find a common ground by asking such questions as: "Where do you work?" "Where are you from?" Then ask questions about the prospect's housing needs. At an early point you should have answers to these questions:

> Do you have a specific neighborhood in mind?
>
> What type of house do you prefer?
>
> Do you own your own home now?
>
> How many children do you have?
>
> Before you buy a new home, do you have to sell your present home?
>
> Have you seen other houses that you like?

To better serve the buyer, you should slowly progress to the *prospect interview sheet* that establishes the financial status of the buyer-prospect. You will soon learn that the first-time buyer usually misunderstands the type of house that he or she can afford. Even the experienced buyer may not understand that his or her current income warrants higher monthly payments. Finally, the prospect interview sheet helps you identify the buyer's motive.

Before you present the prospect interview sheet, you must establish rapport with the prospect. At the appropriate time, start the qualifying interview by asking, "Would you mind if I ask you a few questions so that I can exactly understand your preferences?" Then you should fill out a prospect card by asking questions in this approximate order:

1. What is the correct spelling of your name, your address, and your phone number?
2. How many are in your family (learn the first names of the wife and children)?
3. How much of your savings do you plan to use as down payment?
4. What type of financing do you prefer? Are you eligible for Veterans Administration financing?
5. Do you presently own or rent (if the prospect owns, find out the address of the house; if your prospect is renting, find out the monthly rent)?
6. Where are you employed?
7. What type of work do you do?

Note the form shown in Figure 8-1. In soliciting this information try to determine what needs seem more pressing. If the husband needs basement space for his woodworking equipment, there would be little point in showing houses that have no basements. The purpose of the checklist in Figure 8-1 is really to find out which of the expressed housing requirements may be compromised.

FIGURE 8-1. Confidential Home Requirements

```
                    CONFIDENTIAL HOME REQUIREMENTS

Date _____

Deed to be made to:     Mr. _____
                        Mrs. _____

Present Home Address    _____
                        _____ Present Phone No. _____
Presently Employed by Whom _____
                Position _____
With whom will you be associated in Winston-Salem? _____
Position with Firm _____ Phone No. _____
Name and age of children _____
                         _____
Others living in the home: _____
How long have you been looking for your new home? _____
How soon will you need your new home? _____ Why _____
Rent or own present home? ____ Is it on the market now? ___ Price _____
Will you need the Equity from present home to invest as a down
payment? _____
What type of loan do you wish to secure? _____
How much of your money will you have available to invest in your
down payment and closing costs? _____ Is this flexible? _____
What price range home do you have in mind? _____
Would you go higher if we found the "right" home? _____
Maximum monthly payments (one-fourth of monthly net income): _____
Approximate annual income _____
Long term debts: (over 12 months)    _____
                                     _____
                                     _____
                        (Net) _____

Type House      _____  Special Requirements:
No. of rooms _____   _____
Bedrooms        _____  _____
Baths           _____  _____
Age             _____  _____
Negative Requirements: _____

If a home were found today which fits your needs, are you in a
position to make a decision? _____
Is there anyone else who must approve your purchase? _____

                    Sales Representative: _____
```

PROSPECT FINANCIAL DATA

After a friendly relationship has been established, take special care in securing financial and employment data. If the maximum down payment is conditional on the sale of the present home, make certain that the proceeds of the sale will be sufficient to cover the down payment and closing costs of the listed houses. The monthly payment, it will be noted, includes property taxes and insurance. The employment data should provide sufficient information to indicate the probable credit status of the husband and wife. If income is derived from other sources, try to identify the certainty of this income for mortgage qualification purposes.

Detailed Qualification Forms

Some brokers recommend detailed qualification forms. In this case, the income is more detailed; money from overtime, other income, and the list of assets suggest the amount of money that will be available to cover the closing costs and the down payment. Listing the liabilities showing installment payments and other liabilities, such as child support and alimony, gives greater insight into the prospect's credit status. Other brokers estimate the net monthly income, multiplied by $2\frac{1}{2}$, to suggest the maximum housing price. This is a useful rule of thumb for eliminating houses that the prospect may not be able to finance.

Financial Questions. Obtaining credit information is a highly skilled operation. In some cases, the same question must be approached in numerous ways, for many buyers withhold information because they fear that they will be sold something they cannot afford. Information on the prospect card may very often be obtained by indirect questions such as:

How much money do you want to pay down on a house?

If we could find a house today that meets your standards, could you make a down payment of $5,000 to $10,000?

Suppose we could find a house available for the amount you want to pay down ($10,000). Could you spend an additional $3,000 on interior decorating?

Do you have any other real estate or other investments such as saving certificates, bonds, stocks, or life insurance cash value that could be used to purchase your new home?

Do you have relatives to assist you temporarily in financing the best house for you?

If we found the right house today, could you save another $4,000 if the seller would postpone final closing for three months?

The best interviews take place where personal questions may be asked in privacy and free from interruption. In asking questions, encourage prospects to talk about their families, hobbies, social interests, business expectations, and their community and civic activities.

Prospect Requirements. During the interview try to learn how urgently the buyer needs a house. It makes a difference if the family is temporarily living in a motel and needs a house within the next few days or if the family is currently living in a dwelling that must be sold before the family can buy another house.

FIGURE 8-2

Salesman _____

Date: _____

Confidential
Home Requirements and Survey

(1)	Name _____ Address _____	
(2)	Bus. _____ Address _____	
(3)	Home Phone _____ Bus. Phone _____	
(4)	No. in Family _____ Children's Ages _____	
(5)	Other Family Members _____	

	Possession	Renting or	How Long
(6)	Needed When_____	Sell First_____	Looking_____

			Down	Monthly
(7)	Price $ _____ To $ _____ Max. $ _____		Pmt. $_____	Pmts. $ _____

	Necessary Anyone	Subject to
(8)	Else See Home _____	Transfer _____
(9)	Other _____	

(10)	CHOICE FACTORS	REQUIREMENTS	HOME "A"	HOME "B"	HOME "C"
(11)	Type - 1st. - 2nd.				
(12)	Construction - 1st. - 2nd.				
(13)	Age Home - 1st. - 2nd.				
(14)	Area Pref. - 1st. - 2nd.				
(15)	Bedrooms - No. & Sizes				
(16)	Den				
(17)	Baths				
(18)	Living Rm. - Style & Size Prefs.				
(19)	Dining Room Size				
(20)	Kitchen - (T.S.)				
(21)	Recreation Rm.				
(22)	Basement - ½ - Full				
(23)	Workshop - Oth. Spa.				
(24)	Fireplace				
(25)	Storage - Extra				
(26)	Heat & Fuel				
(27)	Air Conditioning				
(28)	Garage, Carport or off St. Park.				
(29)	Lot Size & Type Trees, Gard., Etc.				
(30)	Price				
(31)	Down Payment				
(32)	Possession				
(33)	SUMMARY				
(34)	School Req.				
(35)	Shopping				
(36)	Transportation				
(37)	Any other Special Req.				

A more detailed itemization of prospect requirements has been developed by Harris-Hanby/Realtors® which they call the "Confidential Home Requirements and Survey." See Figure 8-2. This one-page form itemizes some 23 housing features that represent preferences of the prospect. Space is provided for rating three listings shown to the prospect.

Although this form does not concentrate on the prospect's financial resources and credit, space is provided for the minimum–maximum price, down payment, and monthly payments which indirectly solve the same problem. An example of a more detailed buyer qualification form that includes leading questions to guide the interview has been developed by Chuck Staub and Associates, Inc., of New Orleans, Louisiana. See Figure 8-3(a).

Note that question 3, "What special features do you desire?" and question 4, "How soon do you require occupancy?" Help to estimate the motivation of the buyer. The reason for buying and the urgency with which the prospect must acquire new housing are indicated in question 4. Question 7 leads to the first appointment.

Also note that the detail on the husband's and wife's income, including income from various sources and their outstanding debt, gives greater insight into the couple's ability to finance their purchase.

The reverse page of the form, shown in figure 8-3(b), covers the main features of the house. The salesperson's interpretation of the buyer's impression of the house is noted under remarks.

You will soon develop skills in understanding the real needs of buyers who may have difficulty in focusing on housing that they can afford. In particular, review features of the prospect's present home that are especially attractive to the family. Learn why the family wants to sell the home and those features that the present home lacks. In some instances, it is difficult to learn the express needs of the prospect. To obtain the prospect's reaction, the experienced salesperson may deliberately show houses other than the one he or she expects to sell. By studying the prospect's reaction to a specific house, the salesperson gradually learns the prospect's true attitudes toward housing preferences.

Emotional Factors

It is probably true that most salespersons in dealing with prospects concentrate on practical housing needs. To be sure, the financing, the number of rooms, the location, the lot area, and the neighborhood are significant. Yet, because a number of houses may satisfy these physical requirements, it is probably safe to say that the sale rests largely on emotional attitudes toward home ownership.

The importance of this point has led E. G. Stassens, Inc. of Portland, Oregon, to recommend that in qualifying buyers emotional factors be consid-

FIGURE 8-3(a)

```
                    CHUCK STAUB & ASSOCIATES, INC.

                    SALES APPROACH ACTION SHEET

NAME_____PHONE_____

ADDRESS_____DATE_____

1.  "In what area do you prefer to live?"_____

2.  "How many in your family?"_____Adults:_____Children:_____Ages:_____

    Bedrooms:_____Baths:_____Sq.ft:_____Schools:_____

3.  "What special features do you desire?"_____

4.  "How soon do you require occupancy?"_____

    Reason for buying:_____

    Sell First?_____Rent?_____Urgency_____

5.  "How much of your savings do you feel you want to invest in a home as a down payment?"

    _____Maximum monthly payment desired:_____

    Price of home:_____Type of Financing:_____

6.  "Have you seen any homes that appeal to you?" Yes_____No_____

    How many have you seen?_____

7.  Wouldn't it make sense?_____1st Appointment (Alternate Choice)_____

    _____Location:_____ _____
```

NEED DETERMINATION
CONFIDENTIAL HOME SURVEY

```
Husband Employed by:_____Wife Employed by:_____

How long:_____How long:_____

Husband Income:                         Wife Income:
  Salary_____           Salary_____
  Commission_____           Commission_____
  Bonus_____           Bonus_____
  Overtime_____           Overtime_____
  TOTAL_____           TOTAL_____
```

OUTSTANDING INSTALLMENT OBLIGATIONS:

DEBTOR	AMOUNT/MO.	REMAINING BALANCE	TIME REMAINING

FIGURE 8-3(b)

CHOICE FACTORS		REALTRON CODE	PREFERENCES	WHY DO THEY WANT THIS?(SPECIFIC NEEDS)
TYPE	One Story	1		
	Two Story	2		
CONSTRUCTION	Brick	1		
	Frame	2		
BEDROOMS	One Bedroom	1		
	Two Bedroom	2		
	Three Bedroom	3		
	Four Bedroom	4		
	Five Bedroom	5		
OCCUPANCY 30 Days or Less		11		
GARAGE/CARPORT		12 / 23		
LIVING ROOM Comb. or Sep.		X		
BATHS # desired		13		
DEN or FAMILY ROOM Size		14		
NEW CONSTRUCTION/AGE		16		
DINING ROOM		17		
BUILT-IN KITCHEN		18		
FIREPLACE		19		
SWIMMING POOL		20		
CENTRAL AIR CONDITIONING		24		
SCHOOL REQUIREMENTS		X		
SHOPPING/CHURCHES		X		
TRANSPORTATION/RECREATION		X		
FINANCING DETAILS		X		
NECESSARY ANYONE ELSE SEE HOME		X		

PRESENTATION

DATE		REMARKS:
		COMMENTS:

ered before determining physical housing needs. Lloyd D. Werner, director of training for E. G. Stassens, Inc., reports

> . . . we teach that the most motiviating considerations are a buyer's emotional needs which include such things as the comforts that a buyer derives from home ownership, the social considerations associated with a new home, and the pleasures, hobbies, and plans for children centering around a new home.

So while satisfying shelter needs serves as the prime motivation, leading opinion recommends emphasis on how family members view the home as meeting their emotional feelings about family living, recreation, and their general lifestyle.

THE TELEPHONE INQUIRY

Telephone inquiries cost money. The advertising cost, management expense, and personnel time may raise the cost of a single telephone inquiry to as much as $50. All these time-consuming, costly efforts must bring prospects to the office. For this reason, it is essential to follow accepted telephone practices. Remember that the telephone interview usually represents the initial contact which sets the tone for the office call and final sale.

Specific Suggestions

You must know the list of houses advertised for the coming week. To respond properly, review information—and in detail—on the houses advertised. Have prospect cards, pen, and pencil always at hand. The Berg Agency with several offices in New Jersey advises its staff to:

1. Prepare an opening statement.
2. In answering calls, identify yourself and the company on all calls.
3. Avoid slang or meaningless expressions.
4. Be enthusiastic, sound interested, sound sincere and pleasant.
5. Do not use technical terms.
6. Use the prospect's name often.
7. Thank the person for calling, and after telling the person your name ask for his or her name and phone number.

A friendly beginning leads your prospect to the right response. Try this beginning: "Good morning. Thank you for calling the ABC agency. This is Bill Smith speaking."

The Sincere Caller. Suppose the caller read a recent advertisement and calls. Assume the caller starts with the following statement: "Could you tell me about the three-bedroom split-level house you advertised for $50,000? I would like to know the address of the house."

You would answer (expressing your answer in very positive terms), "Yes, I know that house very well. It is a three-year-old house in one of our better neighborhoods, and I would certainly appreciate showing you and your wife this home."

If the caller continues to insist on the property address, say, "I am very sorry but because the owners have listed their house only with us, they have insisted, and we have agreed, not to give out the address over the telephone."

At this point emphasize the special attention you could give the caller if he or she would arrange for an appointment. "I will be happy to meet with you to see the house inside and out. Would 4:00 P.M. today be good for you or would you prefer to come in later?"

If the caller wants more information about the advertised house, explain further that there are other houses he or she would probably want to see.

As the telephone conversation progresses, start asking questions: "Do you have children?" "Are you looking for houses in our neighborhood?" "Are you looking for a house that has a basement?" As you ask these questions, create interest in your advertised house. For instance, "Yes, adjoining the kitchen is a large family room with a fireplace." Or, "The house has a double attached garage. Do you have one or two cars?"

If your caller asks for more information, offer to pick your caller up and show him or her the house. At the same time mention that you have other houses in the same area that you can show for comparison. Then, if your caller is agreeable to meeting you at their home, ask for the name and then try this approach.

The Cautious Caller.   In the course of handling telephone inquiries you will encounter the caller who is afraid of the salesperson. The person is calling to get the address so that he or she may look at the property alone—and even try to deal directly with the seller. Withhold the address and ask questions in order to learn more about the caller. "What area are you interested in?" "What type of home are you looking for?" "What price bracket are you interested in?" Eventually you partly qualify the buyer: "The house you are inquiring about is available by assuming the loan. How much of your savings are you and your husband willing to invest in a new home?"

Although the interested buyer will answer your questions, remember that the telephone interview is for a single purpose: to obtain an appointment. This is no place to sell the property. You must work toward a qualifying office interview. If the caller is serious, he or she will answer your questions, allowing you to separate the interested buyer from the curiosity seeker. Work toward obtaining the caller's name and address at some point in the interview; you can follow up on the call later.

If you use a prospect card to guide the interview, gradually work toward completing the form to the point that you secure an appointment. Get to know the prospect. Continually remind the caller that you have other houses in the neighborhood that have similar features that he or she may want to review also. The key questions guiding your interview would turn on questions taken from the prospect qualifying sheet.

Now suppose the caller starts out by saying:

I am calling about that three-bedroom house with a fireplace and full basement that you advertised in today's paper.

The salesperson would preferably respond by saying:

Yes, that is one of our new listings of a three-bedroom house in a very popular neighborhood. I believe that house is also available by assuming an existing mortgage with a 9 percent interest rate. That house also has an unusually large dining room and basement. Are you especially interested in a house that has a large basement?

To the caller who insists on the address, say, "You should really see the inside of the house. It has an unusually nice kitchen and family room." Some experienced telephone interviewers remind the caller: "In addition to the house at 1235 Holly Lane we have two other houses in that neighborhood that you should see. May I show you these houses this afternoon at 3:00 o'clock?"

During the course of the interview listen attentively and ask questions that help you qualify the buyer.

1. How many children do you have?
2. Are you interested in a particular neighborhood?
3. How much of your savings do you want to invest in a house?
4. How far is your husband willing to drive from his job? (This gives you a clue to where the husband works.)
5. About how much do you want to pay for a house?
6. Are you looking at new houses or older houses in good condition?
7. Are you eligible for Veteran's Administration financing? Would you consider a FHA mortgage?
8. Do you own your own home? When are you planning to move?
9. Do you have your present home listed with a real estate broker?
10. Are you planning to sell your house before you buy a new one?
11. How old are your children?
12. Would it be convenient for me to show you this house and other houses in the neighborhood today at 3:00 o,clock?

These are typical questions that help you work toward making an appointment and arranging for the 30-minute to one-hour qualifying interview. These questions help you to study the needs of the prospect and select houses that would probably meet the prospect's requirements.

The importance of asking the right questions has led Northside Realty Associates of Atlanta, Georgia, to prepare an *incoming call register* placed next to office telephones (see Figure 8-4). Note that the reminder restates the goals: Create a favorable image and make an appointment as soon as possible. Note further that the last reminder question presents the question: "What is a convenient time for an appointment?" Without these aids, money spent on advertising and listing programs is largely wasted.

FIGURE 8-4. An Example of an Incoming Call Register

```
                           NORTHSIDE REALTY ASSOCIATES, INC.
          FILE REF.____     700 DALRYMPLE ROAD
                           ATLANTA, GA. 30328
                           Incoming Call Register

                      GOALS  1. Create Favorable Image
                             2. Make appointment soon as possible
                           REMINDER QUESTIONS
     Name?    Address?    Phone No.?    What area preferred?    What type home?
     What price range?  How many in family?    Ages?    What area work in?    Will you
     sell present home?   Any special requirements?    Would you like list of available homes
     in preferred area?   What is convenient time for appointment?

     Ad Reference_____ Date_____      Family Information_____
     Address of Home in Ad_____       Now Owns or Rents_____
     Name of Caller_____    ▶  Date and Time of Appointment_____
     Address_____Phone_____         Comments_____
     Area Desired_____       _____
     Special Requirements_____       Follow Up_____
     Type of Home_____Price Range_____       _____
     Type or Place of Employment_____       _____
```

Telephone Courtesy

There are certain rules of courtesy that must be followed in answering a business phone. In real estate this point is especially important since the caller is probably responding to one of two information sources: either your caller has cruised a neighborhood and jotted down several phone numbers from for sale signs or the caller has taken a list of phone numbers from newspaper for sale advertisements. As a consequence, the caller wants questions answered in the shortest time. Remember that the caller is not committed to your listing and, therefore, any unfavorable reply would encourage the caller to go on to the next telephone number. To minimize this possibility, carefully observe the following rules governing telephone courtesy.

Answer the Telephone Promptly. Assume that the caller has other persons to call about houses for sale. A delay in answering suggests that the office is poorly staffed or that the office is indifferent to inquiries, and, worse yet, that the work is poorly organized. Your professionalism begins with a prompt answer to phone inquiries and the observance of other telephone courtesies.

Ask Frequent Questions. When the caller requests information on your listing, answer his questions then ask the caller qualifying questions. This gives you control of the interview and provides you with information on the buyer's needs. Salespersons report that callers usually buy houses other than the ones they initially ask about. Your skilled questioning guides your buyer to the right selection.

Do Not Make the Caller Wait. Suppose the caller wants to know the age of the dwelling or the size of the lot or whether the floors, ceilings, and walls are insulated. Or suppose the salesperson accepting the call is not thoroughly familiar with the property advertised. In these circumstances, do not make the caller wait while you study the record or seek the answer from others. Instead, offer to call back in 15 minutes. Or if the inquiry requires additional information from the local planning or zoning office or tax assessor, tell the caller that you will call back as soon as you have the correct information. It is extremely discourteous to ask the caller to hold the line while you desperately search for additional information.

Listen to Your Caller. It is assumed that you have information that the caller is likely to want. After giving this information, listen to the caller without interruption. Answer questions directly with information and respond with appropriate questions. At the end of the interview let the caller hang up first.

Give Your Caller Your Undivided Attention. In a busy office, especially during the peak hours, you may face interruptions from other incoming calls, the office staff, and other salespersons. Resist these interruptions. Do not talk to other people in the office when you are on the telephone. Make your colleagues understand that under no circumstances will you be interrupted while answering a telephone inquiry. Do not ask your caller to stand by while you service another incoming call. Your caller should be made to feel that at that moment he or she is your single most important interest.

THE WALK-IN PROSPECT

Typically, the walk-in prospect comes to the office after seeing a for sale sign or reading your advertisements. If the prospect asks about a house that has a for sale sign, generally he or she wants to know the price and certain other minimum details, for example, the number of bedrooms, and baths. The buyer may be reviewing several houses in the neighborhood and may wish to leave as soon as he or she has gained the wanted information.

Interest the Prospect

Your first task is to interest the buyer so that you can discover his or her motivation in buying and start the qualification process. After you greet the walk-in prospect, suppose the prospect says that he or she wants information on "that white house you have for sale on Broad Street." Immediately ask the prospect to sit down while you get the details on the house.

Show enthusiasm: "That's one of our best listings." You should have a certain measure of privacy to gain personal information about the buyer. Avoid the temptation to show the house before you qualify the prospect.

This is the time to start the qualification sheet. You should explain that to serve the prospect's needs and get the best financing, you must have certain personal information.

Prospects Responding to a Classified Ad

The prospect who responds to an ad will probably want to know the location and address of the house so that he or she may drive by in order to make his or her own first inspection of the house and probably several others. Ask the prospect to sit down (in privacy) while you give information on that particular house. Avoid showing the house without knowing the prospect's motivation and other needs.

For example, it may turn out that the wife insists on a fireplace in the new dwelling. You would be wasting your and the prospect's time by showing a house that does not have a fireplace even though the house is suitable in other respects. Without the buyer qualification, you would not know the importance of a fireplace, and your prospect would have no way of knowing the details of the house before inspection.

Moreover, you may discover that the house has an added feature that would be very attractive to the buyer that may overcome the lack of a fireplace, for example, a basement recreation room large enough for a pool table. After conducting the qualifying interview—say 30 to 60 minutes—you have an opportunity to select other houses for the prospect to inspect.

Once you have qualified the buyer and have selected three or four houses for inspection, slip out and call the owners, letting them know that you have a prospect to see their houses. Most brokers recommend that you show the prospect a specific house that you think most nearly meets his or her requirements. The prospect should be aware that you have selected the ideal house; show the other houses only after the prospect has expressed objections that you cannot overcome. Some brokers even show houses that they do not expect to sell in order to make a favorable comparison to the selected house.

The Follow-Up Letter

A letter is recommended if the buyer has raised valid objections to the homes you have shown. The letter serves as the basis for follow-up calls, and it reminds your prospect of the firm's name and your personal knowledge of the market. Adapt the letter to your situation by (1) *thanking* the prospect for calling on your firm; (2) *giving* additional features of the home which you believe are of special interest to the prospect; (3) *reminding* the prospect that you have new listings available each week; and (4) *asking* the prospect to visit or call you again, giving your office hours and your office and home telephone numbers.

This letter gives you an opportunity to call the prospect again a few days after he or she has received your letter. Such a letter is shown in Figure 8-5. Note that the letter thanks the prospect, provides additional information, reminds the prospect of new listings, and asks the prospect to call again.

Prospect Records

Qualifying the buyer is a progressive procedure. Carefully maintained records on homes shown each prospect help guide the final closing. There is an added benefit in using the letter shown in Figure 8-5: The letter helps establish a claim for a commission in disputed cases. Chuck Staub and Associates, Realtors®, of Louisiana, go further and require a prospect client sheet for sales, planning, and evaluation purposes. Each prospect has a sheet indicating the objective, sales approach, buyer need determination, a plan of presentation, and a closing plan. Each of these steps has space for an evaluation (see Figure 8-6).

There is an added point made by Thomas W. Lambe, Jr., of Lambe–Young Gallery of Homes, Winston-Salem, North Carolina. According to Tom Lambe, sales associates are trained to ask questions from the prospect qualification form, for, in their experience, people give more correct anwers and more information than if they were only asked these questions in casual conversation. In Lambe's view, the prospect form creates a more professional, businesslike impression.

POINTS TO REMEMBER

Qualifying the buyer saves time for both you and your prospects. By economizing on your time, you more efficiently serve your principal, the seller. After a friendly relationship, has been established, you should ask direct questions about the prospect's housing preferences. The Prospect Interview Sheet summarizes points important to your sales effort. Many brokers prefer the detailed

FIGURE 8-5. Prospect Follow-up Letter

ABC REALTY
Box 1000
Hometown, U.S.A.

August 30, 19___

Mr. and Mrs. James Woodruff
430 Westview Drive
Hometown, U.S.A.

Dear Mr. and Mrs. Woodruff:

Thank you for inquiring about our recently advertised home on 1120 Broad Street, N.E.

Since showing you this house, the owners have added a new range top and reminded me that the house was originally constructed five years ago by Hopely Construction Company, one of our community's best builders of fine homes.

Later in the week, I will call you about our new listings which seem especially suited to your requirements. If you have additional questions about the house we advertised, please note that our office is open from 9:00 a.m. to 6:00 p.m. daily and Sunday from 2:00 to 6:00 p.m. Our office telephone number is 548-5882 or please feel free to call me at home, 542-2126.

Thank you again for letting us help you find a new home.

Sincerely,

Sam P. Johnson

qualification form which summarizes the income, assets, and liabilities of both husband and wife.

A combination approach is shown in the form in Figure 8-4. This form summarizes housing preferences and financial data and provides a record of prospect presentations.

FIGURE 8-6(a)

Corporate Headquarters:
3220 NORTH TURNBULL DRIVE • METAIRIE, LOUISIANA 70002 • 504/888-9261

REALTOR®

SALES PLANNING/SALES EVALUATION

Salesman _____ Date _____

Prospect/Client _____

PLAN	EVALUATION
Objective	Results
Approach -- Plan	Approach -- Evaluation
Need Determination -- Plan	Need Determination -- Evaluation

We Enjoy Our Work Because   *We Solve Your Problems*

FIGURE 8-6(b)

PLAN	EVALUATION
Presentation -- Plan	Presentation -- Evaluation
Action Closing -- Plan	Action Closing -- Evaluation
Objection -- Plan	Objection -- Evaluation

Learning Experience -- What did you learn in the contact that you can use in future sales interviews?

Telephone inquiries should lead to an office call. Special attention is given to the caller who wants the address of an advertised house. The skilled interviewer responds to information requests by asking questions that help qualify the prospect and that encourage the prospect to visit the office for an inspection of the house interior and other listings in the same neighborhood.

Common telephone courtesies must be observed: Answer promptly, ask frequent questions, do not allow the caller to wait, listen, and give the caller your undivided attention without interruption.

Walk-in prospects are equally important. Try to interest the buyer and discover motives for his or her interests. The next task after showing houses is to continue with a followup letter thanking the prospect, citing additional features of the home that you have shown, reminding the prospect that you have new listings, and asking the prospect to visit or call again. Finally, the best procedure requires that you keep prospect records that plan your sale from the initial interview to the final closing plan.

REVIEW QUESTIONS

1. What are the arguments in favor of qualifying the buyer in the buyer's home? Explain how you would arrange qualification in the buyer's home.

2. What are the main elements of a prospect interview sheet?

3. Give examples of financial questions that would help you to qualify your prospect.

4. What questions would help you determine the emotional factors expressed in a prospect's preference for a new home?

5. What specific suggestions would you make for answering a telephone inquiry?

6. What questions would help you gain an appointment from a telephone inquiry?

7. Discuss five rules of telephone courtesy.

8. Describe how you would qualify a walk-in prospect.

9. What is the purpose of prospect records? What information do they include?

9

Knowing the Product

It is fairly clear that the salesperson provides certain services to the buyer and seller: The buyer-prospect is dependent on real estate brokers to provide a central clearing place for offers to sell. Similarly, the seller lists property with a real estate broker in order to reach the largest number of buyers and to gain the best price.

Ordinarily both buyer and seller are misinformed about real estate topics; typically, they are not very knowledgeable about housing values, current financing terms, and neighborhood trends. They make general conclusions from a single sale and they make erroneous judgments on the basis of hearsay. Indeed, buyers and sellers look to real estate brokers as a central market much as those who deal in stocks and bonds operate through their brokers and the stock exchanges.

To perform this marketing service, *the salesperson must know the product.* The prospect turns to the salesperson to find the house that has the highest utility for residential purposes at the lowest possible price. Moreover, prospects will increasingly consider the energy efficiency of both new and used housing. As a result, the salesperson must learn to evaluate energy conservation construction, including solar energy. Further, prospects look to the salesperson for judgments on the neighborhood—its locational advantages, its physical, economic, and social characteristics, and its trend in value.

According to Edward M. Klein of Morton G. Thalhimer, Realtors® of Richmond, Virginia, knowing the product helped sell a large subdivision of ranch homes. The City of Richmond converted to natural gas which was new to the community and which was used to heat homes of the new subdivision.

Because prospects were uncertain about heating costs, Thalhimer obtained from the utility company a letter in which were reported estimates for heating each home. Copies of the letter were given to salespersons and were used to overcome prospect reluctance to buy gas heated homes—a case in which knowing the product promoted subdivision sales.

This chapter focuses on these main elements: *housing design, energy conservation construction,* and *neighborhood characteristics*—all a part of knowing the product.

Do not misunderstand the purpose of this chapter. The agent's role is not to criticize listed houses but to provide the buyer and seller with information to help them make decisions. By knowing the product, the salesperson is able to emphasize certain advantages that compensate for housing deficiencies. Because he or she knows the product, the salesperson is able to help the seller list the house at a realistic price. The listed price should measure the main appeal of the house in view of its main advantages and known limitations.

HOUSING DESIGN

When a buyer is judging houses, he or she considers the floor plan, the architecture, and the site. Be prepared to discuss the architectural style if this seems important to the prospect. The site is important not only because of family tastes and outside activities. How the dwelling and site are oriented are also important. Certain site arrangements reduce heating and air conditioning costs.

The Floor Plan

In stressing the advantages of a house, it is helpful to recognize desirable floor plans. The floor plan adapts the house to three main functions: It provides a *sleeping area* (the bedrooms, bathrooms, and dressing rooms), the *living area* (the living room, dining room, family room, den, recreation room, and enclosed porches), and the *service area* (the kitchen, utility room or laundry, and other specialized work areas). Connecting these three areas is the circulation system of the hallways, stairs, and front and rear entrances.[1]

Before we discuss these points further, we shall review some common floor plan deficiencies. Floor plan standards vary according to the value of the house; a 720-square-foot house priced at $38,000 will have certain compromises not found in a $80,000 dwelling. If you encounter floor plan deficiencies, look for offsetting features. The more common floor plan limitations fall into six categories:

[1]For additional information, consult George F. Bloom and Henry S. Harrison, *Appraising the Single-Family Dwelling* (Chicago: American Institute of Real Estate Appraisers, 1978), Chapter 10; F. Peter Wigginton, *Residential Real Estate Practice* (Indianapolis: Bobbs-Merrill Educational Publishing, 1978), Appendix E; and Henry S. Harrison, *Houses* (Chicago: National Institute of Real Estate Brokers of the National Association of Realtors®, 1973), Chapter 3.

1. No guest closet and no entrance way from the front door to the living room. No comfortable eating space in the kitchen area.
2. No separate dining area or a dining room that does not leave convenient access to the kitchen.
3. Bedrooms and bathrooms visible from the living room or entrance foyer.
4. No outside entrance to the basement.
5. A poorly located family room.
6. Numerous doors and windows that limit the placement of furniture.
7. No garage or only a one-car garage.

The Sleeping Area.   Bedrooms should be separated from the living and service areas and preferably reached directly from a hallway. Ideally, the bedrooms are in the quietest part of the house. The Federal Housing Administration and lenders generally consider the minimum bedroom area as 80 square feet (8 feet by 10 feet). In part, the minimum area depends on the bed arrangements.

Bed Style	Minimum Area
Single bed	8'10" × 10'0"
Double bed	10'0" × 11'6"
Twin beds	11'6" × 12'0"

A room of 120 square feet (12 feet by 10 feet) would be preferred for a single bed; a room 14 feet by 12 feet would be more suitable for a twin-bed arrangement.

The closets should have a minimum depth of at least 2 feet and a width of 3 feet or more. A typical arrangement is shown in Figure 9-1.

In middle-priced housing the three-bedroom house having two bathrooms seems fairly standard. One bathroom serves the master bedroom and there is another full bath accessible from a hallway and the bedroom area. Higher-priced housing may require one bathroom for each bedroom. Bathrooms should be accessible from bedrooms without exposure to other areas of the house, especially the living areas. The placement of bathrooms and closets should provide soundproofing between bedrooms.

The Living Area.   The living area should be proportional to the total square foot floor space. The living area should not serve as a hallway and should supplement the dining room and outdoor recreational space, for example, screened porch, patio, or deck.

As a general guide, a living room for a three-bedroom house should measure 12 feet by 18 feet. Preferably, the room should be rectangularly shaped because a square room makes furniture arrangement awkward. Typically, one wall should be devoted to a fireplace, built-in shelves, or cabinets and there should be one long wall for a couch or sofa. The exit should be at

FIGURE 9-1. Minimum Bedroom Floor Plan Requirements

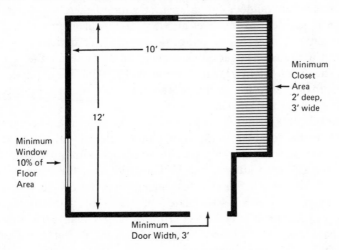

FIGURE 9-2. Living Room Floor Plan

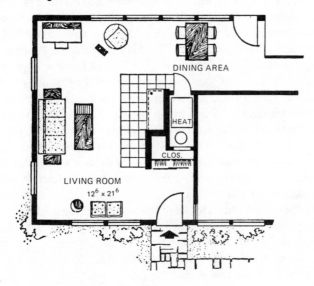

one end of the room; ideally, the living room should be placed in a dead-end area where there would be no through traffic. A dead-end location and blank living room walls allow for grouping furniture around a 10-foot conversation area. A larger room should have space for additional conversation centers. A typical floor plan is shown in Figure 9-2.

Service Areas. Good design requires direct access from the kitchen to the dining area, outdoor eating area, or patio; if there is a family room, the kitchen should provide a clear view of the play area. Usually, the kitchen would be close to the garage or carport. The utility of the kitchen is reduced if the kitchen serves as a main traffic route for the rest of the house. The floor layout should be compatible with the total floor area since approximately 10 percent of the total cost of the three-bedroom house is spent on the kitchen.

Considerable weight is placed on the working triangle—a triangle determined by the location of the refrigerator, kitchen sink, and the range top and oven area. A working triangle is found in the five basic kitchen layouts: the L-shaped kitchen, the U-shaped kitchen, the corridor- or gallery-shaped kitchen, the straight-line layout, and the combination kitchen and family room. For a 1,400-square-foot house, the kitchen area should measure at least 10 feet by 12 feet. Houses of less than 1,000 square feet should have less kitchen space, typically 8 feet by 10 feet. See Figure 9-3 for typical kitchen floor plans.

The counter height should be 36 inches over drawer and cabinet space. Although cabinets may be placed at different heights to suit the original occupants, departures from the 36-inch standard may restrict resale. The standard counter width is 25 inches with a minimum base cabinet frontage area of 6 feet (10 feet is recommended). There should be from 1 foot to 2 feet of counter top on each side of the built-in range and ovens; there should be approximately 18 inches of counter top on the handle side of the refrigerator and from 2 feet to 3 feet of counter space on each side of the sink.

Laundry facilities are found in the kitchen, the attached garage, carport, or basement area. The compactness of the automatic washer/dryer combination usually recommends a kitchen location. This location minimizes plumbing and drainage costs. The more expensive house will have a separate utility room next to the kitchen. This room will have its own bath, counters, storage space, and room for ironing and sewing.

Learn the good features found in the best floor plans. Although you will not lecture prospects on floor plans, knowing the preferred floor plan will enable you to prepare for buyer objections. Your knowledge here may be the deciding factor in helping the buyer make the final decision. Points that add to the desirability of a house include the following:

1. Private access to bedrooms and bathrooms.
2. Convenient access from kitchen and living room to the dining area.
3. Rooms that are in the right proportion to the total floor area.
4. Adequate storage space for the size of the house.
5. Proper placement of doors and windows.
6. A play area within view of the kitchen.

FIGURE 9-3. Kitchen Floor Plans

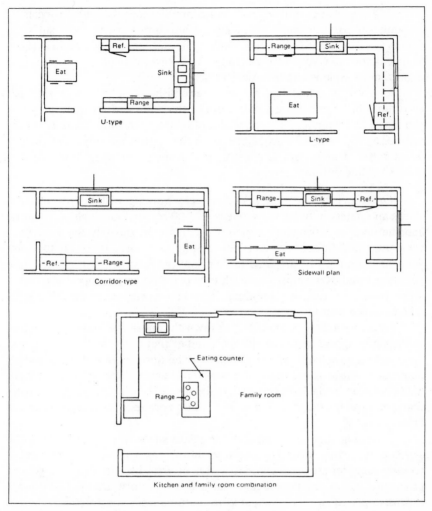

Source: William M. Shenkel, *Modern Real Estate Appraisal* (New York: McGraw-Hill Book Company, 1978), p. 405.

In this analysis, it is presumed that interior finishing is attractive and suitable for the house. Although you would not find marble floors in a modest three-bedroom house of 1,500 square feet, there is a preferred floor plan given the architectural style and total floor area. Learn to recognize the most desirable features of floor plans for the types of houses that you most commonly list and sell.

Judging Architecture

The importance of dwelling architecture depends on your prospects. If a significant part of your listings has architectural appeal, learn sufficient details to be informative. If you are selling houses that are of historical significance, know how your listing demonstrates historical authenticity, a factor important in establishing historical value.

You will also find that houses in established neighborhoods are built according to the prevailing architecture of the times and are easier to sell if you have at least a minimum knowledge of their architectural features. At the very least, you should be acquainted with the relative advantages of the different types of architectural construction, namely, the main advantages of houses of different floor levels.

One-Story Houses. Suppose you are working with a prospect who shows an interest in two houses: one is a 2,000-square-foot single-story house and the other is a two-story structure having approximately the same floor area. One of the favored houses is not one of your listings. If you are to insure your sale, you must be prepared to point out the relative merits of the house you have listed. Remember that each type of house has an appeal over other types. By asking searching questions, learn how to emphasize the advantages that your prospect favors.

Certainly a large group of buyers favor the one-story house, a house that is especially appealing to the elderly, families that have small children, and families that have handicapped members. In addition, note that the one-story house saves the stairway space of a two-story house. Moreover, the one-story house is easier for the homeowner to maintain and repair. One-story construction is more adaptable to adding rooms, patios, porches, fireplaces, and garages or carports.

Offsetting these advantages is the relative lack of privacy between the sleeping and living area. The one-story house has a low-density use and it requires more lot area per square foot of floor area. Because there is a greater proportion of roof and floor area to wall space, one-story construction is more expensive per square foot compared to multiple-story construction.

One and One-Half-Story Houses. In some neighborhoods the one-story house has lost favor to houses of one and one-half stories. If it is assumed that the lot area is the same as that of the one-story house discussed above, added space is gained at a relatively low additional cost by raising the pitch of the roof and by adapting construction to the second story. Generally, the floor area is approximately one-half of the first-story floor area. It depends on the pitch of the roof and the addition of window dormers. Heating costs compared to one-story construction are less because of the smaller perimeter of the enclosed living area. Construction costs per square foot tend to be less than for the one-story house of similar area and quality.

Shoulder height in second-story rooms may be limited, which, of course, affects furniture placement. The window area tends to be limited, and if there is inadequate insulation, the second floor will have greater temperature extremes in summer and winter. Added space must be provided for stairways. If the second floor is limited by electrical and plumbing facilities, it may not compare favorably with a one-story house.

The Two-Story House. These houses have three unique advantages: (1) The two-story house gives *greater privacy;* the sleeping area is generally on the second floor, thus giving maximum privacy from the living area. (2) The two-story house (per square foot) is *less costly* than the same floor area on one story. The lower per unit cost follows from the relatively low roof and floor space in proportion to the wall area. (3) The two-story house is *more adaptable to the small lot,* that is, more floor area can be provided per square foot of land area.

To be sure, these advantages are not without certain compromises. To some prospects, climbing stairs would be inconvenient. The sleeping area has relatively poor access to outside space. The house is difficult to remodel or to expand because the design requires additional space for access to the second floor.

Split-Level Houses. In the beginning split-level houses were placed on sloping lots. The sloping lot allowed a ground-level entrance to the first floor; excavation costs are lower. It should be added that split-levels provide for a more functional separation of living areas. Sleeping areas are usually confined to the upper or lower levels and the living and service areas are placed on ground-level. And like the two-story house, the cost per square foot of living space and associated heating costs tend to be lower per unit than for one-story construction. Stairway access to the different levels may be viewed by some as a distinct handicap for much space is lost in stairways. Some people object to the appearance of a split-level house on a level lot.

Architectural Style

If architectural style has a bearing on the saleability of the house, be prepared to help the buyer recognize the main architectural features. You will find a knowledge of architecture helpful in selling luxury houses, houses in newly developed neighborhoods that have the latest architectural features, and houses in older neighborhoods that show past architectural preferences. Here the range in style is almost without limit. Architectural style varies by geographical area, by neighborhood, and by age of the house.

Early architecture followed practices taken from European cities. Examples are the Early American two-story houses which are shaped like boxes and have flat roofs and the New England farmhouses with their steep-pitched roofs. If your listing includes architectural styles taken from Early Colonial styles, learn the appeal of the Dutch Colonial house, the Southern Colonial with its two-story columns, and some of the English and French influences. The early French styles of New Orleans and the Spanish architecture of southwestern United States deserve added study if you have these houses in your inventory. If you are working a new subdivision which has a dominate architectural style, for example, the contemporary house or houses that rely partly on solar energy, make certain that you can explain their main design features.

The Residential Site

At this point you are aware of family housing needs. With respect to the site, you know the attitude of the family toward a fenced-in backyard, an attractive lawn area, landscaping, the privacy afforded by the site, the availability of garden space, and room for recreational vehicles. Also remember that a prospect looks to you for product information. Your selling task will be easier if you respond to buyer motivation by explaining certain other features of the site that add to its value, namely, the *physical nature* of the site, the *local climate, housing orientation,* and even the unique *landscaping* which may lower monthly heating and air conditioning costs.

To explain these points, focus on the *microclimatic* effect of the site, the housing orientation, and landscaping. Your ability to point out these factors builds prospect confidence and gives you the edge in competition with other salespersons. Every site within a community has a different relation to the weather that affects heating and air conditioning expenses.

Topography. The importance of topography varies between geographic locations. Even the altitude makes a difference. If temperatures in the higher elevations drop one degree Fahrenheit for each 300 feet, a lower elevation can make large differences in housing comfort. Because cold air flows like water, a site in the lower elevations tends to be cooler, especially at night, compared to higher elevations. In the colder areas a lot on the slope that receives large amounts of radiation from the sun is preferred to the lot on a level site.

Site Orientation. Further, the direction of orientation has an effect on living comfort. Generally speaking:

1. For warmth in winter and coolness in summer, houses should face south.
2. Houses facing southeast and southwest are colder in winter and warmer in summer.

3. East and west exposures are warmer in summer and colder in winter than houses facing south, southeast, and southwest.

In large measure, a house should be oriented on the site so that it takes advantage of seasonal variations in air temperature and sunlight. For example, in the cooler zones houses whose longitudinal accesses are oriented east of south give the best heat distribution, especially if they are halfway up the slope. In more temperate locations a house oriented farther east than south gives the best degree of comfort. The upper locations are preferred if the site is protected from winter winds.

In hot areas of the south, lower hillside locations that have afternoon shade that benefit from cool air flow are preferable. In more humid areas, sites are preferred that are exposed near the crest of a hill to gain from cooling breezes. Southern and northern slopes are more desirable than the eastern and western slopes because they receive more radiation from the sun. For example, in Phoenix the best orientation (to minimize exposure to sun radiation) is 32 degrees east of south. In the New York–New Jersey area the best orientation is $17\frac{1}{2}$ degrees east of south.

Landscaping. Direct the prospect's attention to the beneficial effect trees have on heating and air conditioning. In the winter evergreen trees provide windbreaks that reduce heat loss and restrict drifting snow. In the summer grass and leaves absorb radiation and cool the air through evaporation. Deciduous trees placed close to houses provide generous shade at the right season, i.e., during the hot summer months. Even vines cool by evaporation and provide shade, which is important to sunny walls in hot weather. Note that the trees give their best performance on the east-southeast and on the west sides of the house. A house that has an overhang reduces radiation at midday. In the early afternoon trees in the southwest corner protect the west side. The best housing shape and vegetation for different climates are shown in Figure 9-4.

As an illustration, consider the optimum site conditions for Miami, a city that receives an average of 60 inches of rainfall, primarily in the summer months. Here high elevations on the windward side are desirable and houses should be sited on the southern and northern slopes. High rectangular buildings are preferred. There should be shade protection on all sides exposed to the sun, especially on the roof and on the east and west sides.

Water drainage must be away from the house and the site must be graded to encourage the run off from heavy rains. Trees should be high branching so that they do not interfere with breezes. Low vegetation, preferably, should be kept away from the house in order to allow a free flow of air movement. The building should be elongated and oriented 5 degrees east of south. Houses should be painted in a color that reflects light and reduces absorption of sunlight.

FIGURE 9-4. Preferred Housing Shape and Placement of Trees by Climate

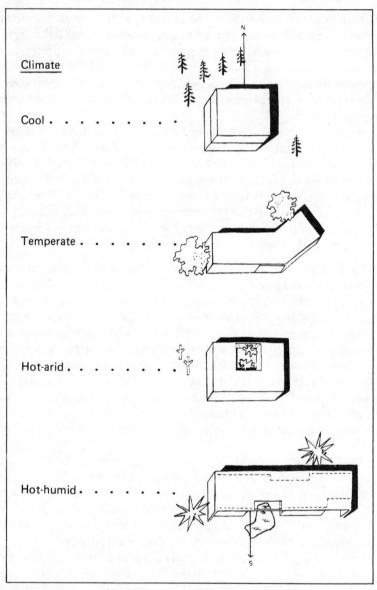

Source: Victor Olgyay, *Design with Climate: Bioclimatic Approach to Architectural Regionalism* (copyright © 1963 by Princeton University Press): Fig. 174, p. 89. Reprinted with permission of Princeton University Press.

ENERGY CONSERVATION

Energy consumed in residential buildings accounts for 13 percent of the total energy consumed in the United States. Resident use of natural gas absorbs *25 percent* of the total national consumption. Space heating accounts for 60 percent of all energy use in commercial, residential, and industrial activities. Residential space heating absorbs 10.8 percent of the total United States energy consumption.

The impact of rising energy prices and building values will be appreciated when it is realized that the over 70 million dwellings listed in the 1970 census were constructed during a period of relatively low energy prices. Because of these relationships, the 1978 Congress authorized a 15 percent income tax deduction up to $300 for the first $2,000 spent on home insulation, storm windows, and other energy conservation methods. Moreover, 1978 legislation authorized a maximum federal income tax credit of $2,200 for investment in solar energy systems. At this time 16 states have granted some form of property tax exemption for solar residential energy systems. Six other states have granted state income tax incentives to encourage investment in solar energy.

These developments are forcing more buyers and sellers to consider the energy efficiency of houses. Because of rising costs of fuel, the informed salesperson will counsel buyers and sellers on the impact of energy conservation on housing prices. Generally, this will require the revision of listing forms and other real estate documents to show the degree of energy efficiency for each house. Accordingly, this discussion centers on methods of determining energy efficiency and ways to judge the effectiveness of solar energy systems.

Energy Conservation Construction

You will encounter buyers who will ask about insulation: insulation beneath floors, between the walls, and above the ceiling. Not only must you know about the kind of insulation but you must also know about the quality of the insulation. Quality is measured by the *R value* of insulation. The R number refers to the resistance to winter heat loss or summer heat gain. The R value of insulation is plainly marked on insulation packages and vapor barriers. The R value varies according to the thickness of the insulation and the material. The R values for selected insulation materials are shown in Table 9-1.

The types of insulation material include:

1. Mineral wool.
2. Cellulose fiber.
3. Vermiculite and perlite.

4. Foams (polyurethane, polystyrene, or urea formaldehyde).
5. Reflective foil.

TABLE 9-1.   R Values for Selected Insulation Materials

	Batts and Blankets			Loose Fill	
R Value	Glass Fiber (in.)	Rock Wool (in.)	Glass Fiber (in.)	Rock Wool (in.)	Cellulose Fiber (in.)
11	$3\frac{1}{2}$–4	3	5	4	3
19	6–$6\frac{1}{2}$	$5\frac{1}{4}$	8–9	6–7	5
22	$9\frac{1}{2}$	6	10	7–8	6
30	$9\frac{1}{2}$–$10\frac{1}{2}$	9	13–14	10–11	8
38	12–13	$10\frac{1}{2}$	17–18	13–14	10–14

¹Single story dwelling, 1,816 square feet.

Mineral wool, fiberglass, or rock wool are the most widely used types of insulation. They are available in blankets, or they may be cut to 4-foot or 8-foot lengths for insulation between wall studs, above the ceiling, and between floor joists. Loose fiber is poured or blown under attic floors. Pneumatic equipment is used to blow insulation above ceilings or between walls.

Older Homes.   If you have an older home listed, you should obtain information on how it is insulated. Advise your prospects of the savings that are gained by adding the conservation measures recommended for existing houses:

1. Attic insulation to the recommended R value.
2. Exterior wall insulation with blown or foam insulation.
3. Floor insulation beneath crawl spaces.
4. Polyethylene ground moisture barrier in crawl spaces (6-mil thickness).
5. Insulation of heating and cooling ducts if they pass through unheated space.
6. Insulation of water heater in unheated space; thermostat turned to 120 degrees Fahrenheit.
7. Caulking around windows and doors, foundation sills, and at points where pipes, wires, and electrical outlets break the wall surface.
8. Window and door weatherstripping.
9. Storm windows; tight-fitting fireplace damper and glass fireplace screening.
10. Shower head flow restrictors and insulation of hot water pipes in unheated areas.

Although these points cover the existing home, new housing construction developed to maximize energy conservation techniques will show even greater savings in heating and air conditioning. Depending on the degree to which energy prices increase and on the local temperature, newly constructed houses that conform to energy efficiency requirements will show a higher value. Conversely, older construction not having energy saving features will be less in demand and lower priced.

New Houses. New houses will show a wide range of energy conservation innovations. If the house has crawl space, there will be 6 inches of fiberglass matting under the floor and the ground area will be covered with a polyethylene vapor barrier. Exterior walls will have built-in insulation of R-18 and $3\frac{5}{8}$-inch fiberglass mats and a 6-mil polyethylene vapor barrier over the mats against interior Sheetrock. A 1-inch Styrofoam sheathing having an R-5 value will be applied to the exterior framing before a brick veneer exterior is added.

Experience has shown the superior insulation ability of exterior metal doors that have foam cores and factory-installed magnetic weatherstripping similar to refrigerator door gaskets.

New construction will show double glass windows that have factory-applied weatherstripping throughout the house. Storm windows will be standard construction features in newer buildings. Fluorescent lights will replace the less efficient light bulbs. Attic insulation for an air conditioned house will have at least an R-38 value. Window areas will probably be limited to 8 percent of the floor area in the living area. Foam sealing will be applied to all openings around windows, doors, plumbing, and electrical holes. Plumbing will be found on the inside wall to avoid breaks on the outside wall. Overhead lighting will be minimized in order to reduce ceiling heating losses. Wiring will be placed at the bottom of wall studs; wall outlets and light switches will be placed away from outside walls.

The Value of Energy Conservation Construction

The thermal efficiency of a house, to be sure, is very important. It will grow even more important as energy prices increase and as federal and state governments provide incentives for energy conservation construction. It has been predicted that many prospects will inquire about past utility bills. Lenders are already judging mortgage credit partly on the amount of the monthly utility costs.

Consequently, Realtors® must increasingly supply this information on listed houses. To expedite the sale of an insulated and thermally efficient house, present the local utility company with a waiver from the owner in order to determine the total energy used over the past 12 months. Convert total kilowatt-hours, for example, to British thermal units (BTUs) (with the help of the local utility); then show the number of BTUs per square foot of dwelling area. This figure will give you a standard to measure against other houses.

SOLAR ENERGY

Solar energy systems provide space heating or domestic hot water; some systems provide both. Their feasibility varies geographically and according to projections on future energy costs. Generally, as fuel prices increase, solar systems will prove increasingly economical.

The feasibility of solar energy varies widely over the United States. Today domestic hot water systems are practical in southern states and in parts of the northeastern United States that pay relatively high fuel and fuel transportation costs. The temperature, cloud cover, humidity, and wind are among the factors that create solar climatic zones. Most authorities, for example, believe that solar energy will remain uneconomic in the Pacific Northwest mainly because of the extensive cloud cover and availability of low-cost hydroelectric power.

Solar heating and hot water systems consist of two basic elements: (1) a means of capturing radiant energy and then converting it to heat energy and storing the heat in some insulated device, and (2) delivering the stored energy to a hot water or space-heating system. The two elements are referred to as the *collector system* and the *delivery system.*

FIGURE 9-5. Component Parts of a Solar Energy System

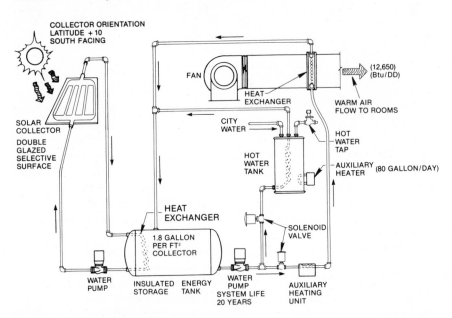

Source: *Solar Energy for Space Heating and Hot Water* (Washington, D.C.: Energy Research and Development Administration, 1976), p. 2.

A typical arrangement of the component parts of a solar energy system is shown in Figure 9-5. Note that the solar roof panel functions much as a greenhouse; heat is removed from the collector by water that circulates under the panel. The heated water then passes to an insulated storage tank from which it moves to the heat exchangers or a space-heating unit when sunlight is unavailable.

Recent reports indicate, depending on the location, that between 55 percent and 80 percent of the space heating may be supplied by solar heating. Most auxiliary systems account for between 50 percent and 80 percent of the heating and hot water energy requirements. It is believed that a correctly designed system for a 1,500-square-foot house would save approximately $366 at today's natural gas prices in Maine and approximately $195 a year in Nevada. Much higher savings would be experienced in comparison with the cost of heating a building with electricity.

Depending on the sophistication, the cost of the energy system for space heating and hot water ranges from $8,000 to $24,000 in Maine for a 1,500-square-foot home to $2,000 to $6,000 in Nevada. Evidence shows that there is considerable market acceptance of solar energy systems. In a recent survey of residents of Miami, Florida, who owned houses that have solar hot water heating systems, it was found that current users found solar hot water heaters very appealing. Another 43 percent of the homeowners surveyed, who had no firsthand experience with solar hot water heaters, said that they would choose a home equipped with a solar hot water heater system. In a survey of 60 current users of solar hot water heating systems, 77 percent approved of their systems.

The Department of Housing and Urban Development has sponsored 40 solar energy projects throughout the United States. In one project 22 families purchased homes equipped with solar heat. The prices of the houses ranged from $50,000 to $80,000. The solar home buyers tended to be well educated and to have few if any children. In the Montbello section of Denver, 19 out of 25 solar heated homes were sold the first weekend they were offered for sale. The total price of a house not having the solar heating system was $48,000; solar equipped houses were sold for an additional $8,000 to $9,000.

Mortgage lenders, such as the Midland Federal Savings Association of Denver, Colorado, grant mortgages on solar heated houses provided:

1. The solar heating system is designed by a registered mechanical engineer.
2. An auxiliary heating system supplements the solar heating system.
3. The appraisal of solar heated houses is adjusted for the extra cost of the solar system.

The popularity of these systems will increase to the extent that (1) state and federal laws provide tax incentives for installations, (2) mass production lowers the initial cost, and (3) energy prices increase.

KNOW NEIGHBORHOOD FEATURES

Neighborhoods are homogeneous groupings of similar houses. Often neighborhoods may be associated with a central facility such as a school or community shopping center. Your prospects will judge the neighborhood according to its physical, economic, and social features.

Physical Features

Physical features include the street layout, paving, sidewalks, street lighting, and the like. If the neighborhood has municipal sewers, storm drains, curbs, and streets sufficiently wide for on-street parking, be sure your prospect knows about these features, especially if your prospect has considered other neighborhoods.

Topping the list of physical advantages is *access.* Access should be judged according to the driving time to shopping, employment, and the freeway. If you consider public transportation an important feature, explain how the neighborhood is served by mass transit.

Be prepared to explain how the neighborhood benefits by public or private schools; know the grades taught in the local schools. At some point show how the surrounding land use contributes to stable neighborhood values.

Economic Features

Economic features that you may stress turn on local employment trends, the low-vacancy rate, and the high ratio of owner occupancy. If families are employed by many different industries, neighborhood values tend to be more stable than if they work in a single industry or government installation. Be prepared to respond to questions about property taxes. Determine the date of the last valuation, the current assessment rate, and if a future revaluation has been scheduled.

Be sure to discuss the availability of domestic water and its source and cost; the availability of cable TV service and garbage pickup, and charges for the sewage system. Find out if special assessment districts have been formed to finance playgrounds, parks, or street improvements.

Social Features

Learn the typical income, education, and age of the household head and the family size of the neighborhood for your listed property. Buyers in new suburban neighborhoods prefer a fairly high degree of social uniformity. It is helpful if you can explain why present occupants were originally attracted to the neighborhood. Identify the age of the neighborhood and the main advantages that encourage people to continue to live there. Local community organizations, such as garden clubs, or associations that operate the nonprofit swimming pools or playground facilities tend to preserve neighborhood desirability.

Characteristics of Stable Neighborhoods

Help the prospect identify factors that contribute to stable and rising property values. Look for these *physical* features that insure neighborhood stability:

> Good property upkeep.
> Sound structural building condition.
> Homogeneous housing types.
> Well-maintained landscaping.
> A location convenient to shopping, employment, and freeways.

Indicate how a neighborhood illustrates these favorable physical factors.

Turning to the *economic* features associated with stable or rising neighborhood values, consider the following:

> High rate of owner occupancy.
> Rising resale values.
> Financing available on favorable terms.
> A high local confidence in the neighborhood's future.

Your local study should verify that these economic conditions support property values. Explain how the main sources of employment and the typical occupations support values, for instance, managerial or executive, skilled workers, professional people, and other groups who have a vested interest in maintaining the quality of the neighborhood.

Social features associated with stable and rising neighborhood values commonly include the following:

> Moderate to upper incomes.
> High school education and above.
> Family-oriented or childless adults.
> White-collar or skilled blue collar workers.
> A socially cohesive neighborhood.
> Good neighborhood reputation in the community.
> Neighborhood considered as safe.

In the final analysis, your prospect must be assured that the house you are showing is in a neighborhood that serves his or her needs and that he or she will be compatible with other neighborhood occupants. In some respects, the neighborhood's quality and future override the characteristics of the dwelling and its site. In short, build prospect confidence by knowing product housing design, the degree of energy conservation construction, and the quality of the neighborhood and its relative stability of property values.

POINTS TO REMEMBER

Successful selling rests largely on knowing the product: the *housing design,* and under current energy conditions, *energy conservation construction* and *neighborhood characteristics* that insure stable and rising values. The degree of residential utility depends on the floor plan and housing architecture. Concentrate on the three functions served by a dwelling: the sleeping area, the living area, and the service areas. If the house in question has an unusually well-designed floor plan (among other things, rooms that are in the right porportion to the total floor area, adequate storage space, and the proper placement of doors and windows), be ready to point out these special features.

Be acquainted with the advantages of the one-story, one and one-half-story, two-story, and split-level house. Since you know the needs of your prospect, show how architecture serves his or her special needs. If the architectural style contributes to the house's appeal, know something of the architectural background of the neighborhood and the particular house you have listed.

Learn how the particular site adds to energy efficiency—an important point in addition to the topography, drainage, landscaping, play area, garden space, and outside living advantages.

Energy conservation construction affects both new and existing homes. It would be helpful to ask your local utility company the minimum recommended R values for ceiling, floor, and wall insulation. As utility prices increase, brokers will find an added sales appeal in explaining past utility prices per square foot on the energy efficient houses they have listed. Indeed, some buyers may ask you to calculate the energy savings on added energy conservation construction.

If the house and site are suitable for solar domestic hot water or space heating, learn how the house may be remodeled for solar energy. If the house has solar equipment, go to the lender, the local utility company, and experienced contractors for details on the system. Market acceptance of solar energy partly depends on the salesperson's skill in presenting the solar equipped house and the degree to which local energy prices increase.

It is more than likely that your prospect is unacquainted with details of the neighborhood. Your knowledge need not be encyclopedic, but you should have a good knowledge of the physical, economic, and social characteristics of the neighborhood. Know its age, main physical features, accessibility, and the characteristics of the neighborhood residents: their main sources of employment, incomes, education, family sizes, and typical ages. Indeed, this part of the sales presentation may be more convincing than explaining features of the listed house.

REVIEW QUESTIONS

1. Describe the three main functions of a house.
2. What are the main limitations commonly observed in floor plans?
3. What are the minimum requirements for bedrooms?
4. What are the minimum requirements for the living area?
5. What are the main components of kitchen floor plans?
6. Explain the relative advantages of one-story, one and one-half-story, two-story, and split-level houses.
7. What factors would you consider in judging a residential site?
8. What effect does the direction of orientation have on living comfort? Give examples to illustrate your answer.
9. Explain the main elements of energy conservation construction.
10. How would you describe solar energy facilities to a prospect?
11. What are the main precautions that lenders take in granting mortgages on solar heated houses?
12. What main energy conservation features would you include in a listing?
13. Describe the physical, economic, and social features associated with stable or rising neighborhoods.

10
Negotiating Skills

To a large degree, the successful salesperson is a successful negotiator. The emphasis on negotiation follows from the nature of the product. To sell houses, the salesperson copes with complex emotions associated with home ownership, the neighborhood, and family welfare.

Complicating the issue is the fact that buyers and sellers of houses face a highly imperfect market. Each house is so different that it is difficult to make rational price comparisons. It is difficult to get information on prices and available prices require skillful interpretation. The lack of market knowledge on the part of buyers and sellers places heavy demands on a salesperson's negotiating ability.

Surely, the work of a salesperson closely conforms to the definition of negotiation: *A process of finding a compromise that is mutually acceptable.* The definition implies that the buyer and seller who close a sale each gain less than a total victory. Each gains less than the best possible outcome based on the first offer or counteroffer. Because the buyer and seller have direct conflicts of interest, each one depends on the salesperson to negotiate a close.

This chapter first covers the role of the salesperson as a negotiator and then deals with the basic rules of negotiating before describing the technical process of negotiating. The final part includes suggestions on negotiating the offer and counteroffer.

THE NEGOTIATING ROLE OF SALESPERSONS

To a large extent, the salesperson acts as a biased mediator. As an agent of the seller-principal, legally the salesperson serves the seller. The seller expects to sell at the highest price and employs the broker to represent his or her interests. It is presumed that the agent will sell or negotiate for the highest price.

In another sense, the salesperson may be biased in favor of the buyer-prospect since the sale will not be completed until the interest of the buyer is served. In mediating a final close, the salesperson may negotiate with a bias in favor of the buyer.

FIGURE 10-1. A Model of the Negotiating Process

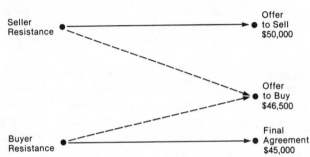

The position of the real estate salesperson is illustrated in Figure 10-1. The seller, in listing a house, offers to sell under a stated price and terms of sale. The buyer, in considering the offer to sell, makes an offer to buy at the lowest price. The salesperson, in attempting to mediate these differences, must judge the resistance or "toughness" of both the buyer and seller.

For example, a seller considering a larger house in a more expensive neighborhood may be under no immediate compulsion to sell and would be a relatively tough negotiator. A buyer transferred to a new city has a limited number of days in which to make a housing decision for an impending family move. In Figure 10-1, for instance, the buyer rejects the offer to sell for $50,000 and offers to buy for $45,000.

Agreement is reached only if the final compromise is mutually beneficial. For instance, the buyer might agree to $46,500 provided the seller finances the additional $1,500 with a three-year note repayable $500 a year with 10 percent interest. The sale is closed after the salesperson, sensing the resistance of both parties and their willingness to compromise, centers on points believed subject to negotiation, in this case, the price and method of payment.

Negotiating Authority

In the process of listing, selling, and closing the sale, the salesperson assumes many negotiating roles. Negotiation starts with listing the property. You negotiate with "for sale by owner" and you negotiate the listing in competition with other real estate firms. Even the type of listing is negotiated: a negotiation in which the seller has options ranging between the open and the exclusive right to sell listing. In these cases, the salesperson assumes the true role of negotiator.

In closing the sale, however, the salesperson, acting as an agent, has no direct authority to negotiate for either party. Rather, the salesperson mediates the closing with final negotiations subject to approval in writing by the buyer or seller. This lack of authority means that negotiations proceed only after advance preparation which gives the salesperson an insight into the points that are most likely to be subject to compromise. Indeed, the imagination, skill, and experience of the salesperson determine whether or not the parties reach an agreement.

Basic negotiating rules are followed in showing a house since most home buyers must reach a final compromise. Early in the selling process the salesperson must learn points on which the buyer is most likely to compromise. The salesperson must also determine how urgently the buyer wants a particular listing. In short, the salesperson must interpret the *toughness* of the buyer if the original offer to sell is unacceptable.

Points of Negotiation

Your ability to close by skillful negotiation ranges over a wide number of topics. Selling houses is more than reaching agreement on the price; in fact, the number of issues subject to negotiation gives the salesperson many possible items on which compromises may be reached. The final sale comes after a series of negotiations has resulted in a mutual agreement in the best interest of both buyer and seller. This point is reached depending on

1. The equitable fairness of the buyer and seller.
2. The degree to which the buyer and seller openly state their positions and skillfully evaluate the position of the opposite party.
3. The salesperson's skill in negotiating with the buyer and seller.
4. The willingness of the buyer and seller to avoid an impasse by making compromises.
5. The relative bargaining power of the buyer and seller.

This discussion of negotiation covers closing the sale for the buyer and seller, but the basic principles of negotiation apply to other personal relationships encountered in listing and selling. Actually, the final price may be accompanied by compromises in sale terms and many other factors which in turn are subject to negotiation. Consider a partial list of factors subject to negotiation with sellers and prospects:

Negotiating with Sellers
The type of listing.
The listing period.
The real estate commission.
The trade-in value.
The terms of sale.

Negotiating with Prospects
Method of payment, the down payment, closing costs.
Personal property.
Method of paying for personal property.
Time of possession.
Homeowner warranty plans.
Repairs and maintenance.
Unlisted property included in the sale (extra land or personalty).
Rental terms for immediate occupancy.

Numerous variations of these points are possible, for example, in financing. The central task is to determine from both parties which items are subject to compromise. Professional negotiation of each of these points is a method in which the salesperson deals with buyers and sellers and, by the specialized process of communication bargaining, both parties reach agreement on the sale.

Negotiation is essential in selling houses because typically the seller is not the sole source of available housing. Usually, sellers are unable to take an inflexible position because buyers usually have other opportunities. Similarly, in an active housing market, buyers are in a weak position because the seller may negotiate with other buyers. Hence, persuasion and logical argument are used to convince buyers and sellers to reach a final agreement.

It is much like playing poker. Although there is a large element of chance, the salesperson who prevails is the one who knows the rules and understands each party's bargaining position. The negotiator, observing the code of real estate ethics, conducts the negotiation according to accepted negotiating rules.

Real estate brokers often feel that they are placed in an adversary position like the prosecutor, who prosecutes, and the defense attorney, who defends. For the seller's and buyer's mutual benefit, the salesperson must help both make sacrifices and resolve their differences.

BASIC RULES OF NEGOTIATING

Real estate salespersons conduct two forms of negotiation: *sequential* and *overall.* Their personalities and attitudes must adapt to the requirements of either form. These points deserve brief comment before proceeding with a more detailed discussion of the generally accepted negotiation rules.

Forms of Negotiation

Sequential negotiation refers to the separate negotiations of each issue. As the negotiation progresses, firm agreement must be reached on each point before moving to the next issue. Salespersons practice this form of negotiating when they present an offer that requires the seller to approve purchase terms different from those originally agreed upon in the listing.

Suppose, for example, that the seller agrees to accept the buyer's price. But if the sale is to be closed, the seller must be convinced that it is to his or her best interest to accept a second mortgage on the property in lieu of additional cash. Once the seller has agreed to a second mortgage, the closing proceeds to terms of repayment. The final negotiations then progress to the sale of personal property and the price, i.e., curtains, draperies, furniture, rugs, and the like.

The danger in proceeding from point to point is that the negotiation will end if the parties fail to agree on a single detail. For example, if in the preceding case the seller does not agree to a second mortgage, the discussion would probably end then and there. Reaching an impasse on a single point bars the negotiator from trading off one concession against another.

The *overall negotiation* avoids this situation. A final agreement between the buyer and seller does not represent an agreement on several single issues one at a time; it represents a final resolution of all points of disagreement.

On the one hand, the seller may be firm in asking for $75,000 cash. With a $60,000 first mortgage available, let us say that the buyer agrees to pay $10,000 down and execute a purchase money second mortgage in favor of the seller for the balance. Here the negotiation should not be limited solely to the purchase terms; the salesperson, knowing both parties, may resolve all issues fairly and reasonably by seeking compromises on other issues such as personal property or date of occupancy or other issues on which either party is likely to concede. In sum, closing the sale may require that both parties make concessions on a number of individual points. By negotiating all issues together, concessions made by one party represent payments for concessions granted by the other party.

The skilled salesperson negotiating on an overall basis attaches considerable importance to both verbal and nonverbal communication. The willingness of the buyer or seller to make concessions can be shown by facial expressions, tone of voice, or body movements. Buyers and sellers very often unconsciously show the importance of specific issues and the relative order of their priorities.

Requirements of a Negotiator

To negotiate on an overall basis, the negotiator must demonstrate a suitable negotiating personality and, above all, must negotiate in the right frame of mind. The right frame of mind depends on understanding the philosophy of negotiations, a knowledge of interpersonal relations, communication techniques, argument, and persuasion. Chances of a successful outcome increase as the negotiator wins the goodwill and respect of both the buyer and seller. He or she must have a good knowledge of the neighborhood, the house, and the needs and desires of both the buyer and seller. A good negotiator concentrates on developing other helpful attributes:

1. The ability to think clearly and rapidly.
2. The ability to speak well.
3. The ability to analyze what the buyer and seller are communicating.
4. The ability to remain objective and impersonal.
5. The ability to interpret another's frame of reference.

The salesperson must approach the seller with an offer or counteroffer refreshed and ready to negotiate. He or she must be free of personal problems and must not be burdened by end of the day fatigue. The salesperson must be able to listen and express himself or herself clearly but not glibly. Negotiating requires patience and letting the other person explain his or her position. The skillful negotiator must continually reevaluate positions on negotiable points.

More importantly, the negotiator must be good humored, realizing that not all negotiations are successful. In a sense, salespersons acting as negotiators are coordinators who convey information to buyers and sellers, giving both parties the advantage of their specialized skills and real estate knowledge.

Basic Rules

The purpose of the negotiation is to arrive at an agreement that is both fair and reasonable to both buyer and seller. In approaching the seller with an offer, or the buyer with a counteroffer, the salespersons gains skill in learning which points each party may concede. A successful outcome turns on determining which party can be expected to change his or her position.

In working to bring the buyer and seller together on the price, terms of sale, or other issues, the final outcome will depend on (1) the relative bargaining power of the buyer and seller, (2) the advance preparation of the salesperson, (3) the degree to which the interest of the buyer and seller is compatible or conflicting, (4) how much importance the buyer and seller attach to the elements of the sale—the price, terms of sale, personal property, or closing costs, and (5) the motives of the buyer and seller.

Predicting the Final Outcome.   The seller who is under little compulsion to sell, for example, the seller who occasionally searches for a larger home in a better neighborhood, is under the least pressure to make a buying decision. This seller would also probably price his or her own house above the market in order to raise equity. Negotiating a fair listing price, gaining an exclusive right to sell agreement, or reaching a final decision when offers are presented may be fairly remote.

When a buyer makes a lesser offer, he or she establishes a range between that offer and the listing price within which the parties will eventually reach an agreement. At this point the salesperson should ignore the other terms of sale and direct attention to sales and listings of similar houses in order to gain the seller's acceptance of the offer.

Agreements between the buyer and seller are more likely if the differences between the buyer and seller are small. Here the salesperson helps compromise differences between the buyer's offer and the seller's asking price by negotiating other concessions. Much depends on how skillful the salesperson is in interpreting the strength of the buyer's willingness to buy and the bargaining power of the seller in holding out for a higher price.

If the buyer's offer is considerably less than the seller's asking price, there may be little hope of compromise. The salesperson must then help the buyer reevaluate his or her housing needs, preferences, and financing ability to purchase a home and then review with the seller the asking price in the light of recent transactions, listings, and current offers. A counsel with both parties, though not resulting in an immediate compromise, may encourage both the buyer and seller to change their positions.

Preparation for Negotiation.   Although preparation varies according to the role assumed by the salesperson, each negotiation calls for advance work. When soliciting a seller for a listing or when presenting a seller with an offer below the listed price, *in advance* you must (1) be sure of your facts, (2) begin your negotiations only after you have identified your objective, and (3) plan your negotiating strategy.

You could plead that you lack the time, but you must overcome this obstacle. Your recognized skill, experience, and training will be of little avail if you do not have the facts about your company, the benefits that the owner would gain by listing through you, and the points to offer in support of the exclusive right to sell agreement.

There is the related question of assembling the necessary *technical knowledge.* When you deal with buyers and sellers, you rely on variable rate mortgages, homeowner warranties, guaranteed sale plans, and other technical arrangements. Make sure that you have the main points of these agreements well in mind if they are negotiable terms. When you are estimating the final cash payment to the seller, you must have sufficient facts to make reasonable estimates of the after income tax cost of housing. If your prospective buyer is currently a renter, you must assemble the information on the after tax cost of home ownership for your presentation.

Your position as negotiator requires still other preparations. You must estimate the time available for *discussion*. If you present the buyer's offer and you believe that it will take 30 minutes to go through an analysis of similar house sales, you might risk the sale if the seller has only 10 minutes before leaving for a bowling game.

At the other extreme, limit your interviews to not more than an hour (and in most instances this is probably too long). An hour of discussing real estate matters seriously tries the seller's concentration.

There are other instances in which you might determine that negotiations need a second person, for example, the sales manager. If the negotiation is a difficult one, a *second person of authority*, one who is familiar in every detail with the local real estate market, might support the buyer's offer of $5,000 below the listing price.

Real estate brokers take special care to create a *stable atmosphere* for negotiations: in the seller's home, in the privacy of the real estate office, or in the buyer's home. The atmosphere must be free of disturbances, of distracting telephone calls, and of interruptions by friends or other employees.

Digressions. You are sitting in the living room of the listed house summarizing the points that the buyer has mentioned as being specially appealing to him. The prospect turns on the television set and watches the baseball game. He starts talking about the club standing in the league and why this game is so important. The possibility of moving to a trial close looks dismal and you wonder how you can salvage the presentation.

The prospect who digresses from your presentation has three possible problems: (1) The prospect is not aware of your objective. (2) The prospect has not prepared an objection to your presentation and is evading a decision. (3) The prospect has reached a limit to further concentration. In these circumstances, digression makes it difficult to revert to the subject at hand. If while discussing a complex mortgage purchase agreement you detect a slackening of the prospect's concentration, drop this line of presentation and come back later when the prospect shows less fatigue.

Interpret a digression as the prospect's inability to cope with the subject. In these circumstances, stop the discussion and attempt to maintain conversation at a more trivial level but leave the presentation open for the next discussion. At this point, it is necessary to establish a point of further reference for a repeat presentation.

THE PROCESS OF NEGOTIATION

The salesperson serving as a mediator between the buyer and seller assumes that both parties will agree on the outcome with the highest possible advantage. It is also a fact that most buyers and sellers will agree to a fair solution and that they will eliminate proposals disliked by both parties.

Some authorities feel that successful negotiation depends on judging the buyer's and seller's degree of *toughness* (toughness here refers to the general level of their demands). As a general rule, the degree of toughness is closely correlated with deadlines which either party must reach. The further the deadline, the greater the toughness. Thus, a seller who leaves town because of a job transfer would be reluctant to leave a vacant unsold house. Similarly, a buyer whose family must have new housing within 30 days will probably have a low degree of toughness.

In this instance, negotiation is really a game in which buyers and sellers are relatively free to make choices as they desire. The central issue for the salesperson is to determine the best choices for the buyer and seller so that when the game is over each party wins.

In this regard, the salesperson succeeds in helping both parties reach an agreement only if the salesperson anticipates what the buyer or seller will do about considering offers and counteroffers. Ideally, the salesperson would anticipate a buyer's reaction to a seller's counteroffer; the salesperson should be able to anticipate how much pleasure would be gained by the buyer and seller in reaching an agreement on points subject to negotiation. If the salesperson negotiates so that both parties gain pleasure from the transaction, and if the pleasure in both cases is greater than the pleasure that would follow from a disagreement, then the sale will be closed.

Judging Negotiating Strength

Buyers and sellers show different degrees of willingness to negotiate, depending mostly on their relative degree of competitiveness or tendency toward cooperation. If we rank, for example, a buyer showing a marked degree of competitiveness with a seller who tends to be very cooperative, they maximize their position somewhere between two extreme negotiating positions.

Suppose, for example, you have a highly competitive, resistant buyer and a highly cooperative seller who wishes to sell before an impending move at the end of the month. They are likely to reach an agreement at the 5–5 point on the negotiating grid shown in Figure 10-2. Buyers and sellers, variously ranked on this grid, show different relative negotiating positions for each sale. That is, there is a point that balances the buyer's competitive attitude with the seller's relative degree of cooperation. There are other cases in which the role of the seller and buyer would be the reverse of the position shown in Figure 10-2.

FIGURE 10-2.   The Buyer and Seller Negotiation Grid

THE COMPETITIVE BUYER		Slightly Cooperative	Somewhat Cooperative	Moderately Cooperative	Quite Cooperative	Highly Cooperative
	Slightly Competitive	1-1	1-2	1-3	1-4	1-5
	Somewhat Competitive	2-1	2-2	2-3	2-4	2-5
	Moderately Competitive	3-1	3-2	3-3	3-4	3-5
	Quite Competitive	4-1	4-2	4-3	4-4	4-5
	Highly Competitive	5-1	5-2	5-3	5-4	5-5

THE COOPERATIVE SELLER

When you present an offer to a seller, remember that the seller's bargaining position is largely determined by how much he or she knows about the buyer's attitude toward the house and terms of sale. The salesperson who works with both buyer and seller gains an insight into what is important in helping the buyer and seller reach a mutual compromise. The final willingness to reach an agreement depends on the answers to the following leading questions:

1. What specific objections does the buyer have to buying this particular house?
2. What features does the buyer dislike about other houses you have shown?
3. What special features of this house are most important to the buyer?
4. Does the buyer believe the statements you have made about the house and neighborhood?
5. What indications has the buyer given you that he or she wants to buy this house?

In guiding the parties to an agreement, your judgments about the toughness of both parties, their willingness to compromise, and the points on which they may reach an agreement depend partly on the questioning techniques you used during negotiations. The common questioning rules should guide your negotiations with buyers and sellers.

Negotiating Questions

Early in your interviews you establish rapport. In the initial meeting it is helpful to establish rapport by avoiding "taboo" subjects and concentrate on topics that appeal to prospective clients. You must not introduce controversial political, religious, or ideological subjects. You must not discuss your illnesses. Discuss these topics only if the client introduces them. Listen sympathetically but make no personal commitment.

In your search for topics of mutual interest, you have learned that people usually select their automobiles with considerable care. This is a good and safe topic for establishing good relations. If you have learned what your prospect's hobbies are, you have another suitable topic for establishing the right relationship. Clothing is another topic for discussion—at least it is better than making trite comments about the weather.

Questions to Avoid. Good questioning techniques avoid questions that *reveal lack of knowledge* on the part of the salesperson. Your objective is to become confident enough so you automatically avoid questions that suggest that you do not know the details of real estate finance, construction, or other matters important to your presentation.

Similarly, a question is a poor substitute for your *lack of attention.* If your mind wanders while your client is talking, your later questions will reveal that you did not listen carefully.

The questions you ask *must not embarrass* your prospect. And you must ask questions at the appropriate time and be able to ask questions in proper form.

There is also the problem of following up on questions that are poorly answered. Salespersons may be inclined to give up too easily on questions that are avoided or poorly answered. Try to think your question through in advance and follow the acceptable negotiating questioning techniques.

Questions for Negotiation. The negotiator develops skill in using five kinds of questions, each question serving a different purpose: (1) questions that attract attention; (2) questions that ask for information; (3) questions that give information; (4) questions that start the prospect thinking; and (5) questions that encourage the prospect to make a decision.

1. *Questions That Attract Attention.* These questions are also known as the *ritual questions.* They are questions such as, "Could you help me determine your housing needs?" "Could you tell me if you have the next hour free?" "Would you be available to look at houses this afternoon?" Like the question, "A beautiful day, isn't it?" these questions break ground for further discussion. They create little anxiety.

2. *Questions That Ask for Information.* These questions usually start with the words who, what, when, where, should, shall, could, will, for instance,

or for example. They may create anxiety in the prospect if the prospect has reason to withhold information. These questions apply especially to qualifying the buyer and to learning prospect objections. Presenting the information-type question gives the salesperson an insight into the real motives for purchasing.

3. *Questions That Give Information.* Questions that start, "Have you considered a second mortgage?" lead to an explanation of alternative financing means. These questions begin with the words because, if you, did you, or would you. This form of questioning gives the salesperson an excellent opportunity to supply the prospect with new information.

4. *Questions That Start the Prospect Thinking.* "To what extent are the front and back yard important to you?" "Would you prefer a split-level house or a two-story house with basement?" The key words starting these questions include how, why, did, would, and describe. If your prospect feels threatened, your asking this kind of question will develop anxiety in him or her.

5. *Questions That Encourage the Prospect to Make a Decision.* The better salesperson is skilled in avoiding yes/no questions and in leading the prospect to a decision by asking, "Which do you prefer, a three-bedroom house with basement or a three-bedroom house with a family room?" "Would your sofa look better in this corner or against the wall?" "Would you prefer to send your children to the public school or to the private school?"

Tie-Down Questions. The general format of these questions is adapted to one other questioning device: the *tie-down question.* The tie-down begins with the words doesn't it, didn't it, wasn't it, couldn't it, wouldn't it, don't you agree, as you say, aren't they, wouldn't they, and hasn't she. All of these questions ask for yes responses.

For instance, as you drive through the neighborhood, you confirm its attractiveness by asking, "Houses in this neighborhood have well-maintained landscaping, don't they?" Or as you show the house, you ask, "This is an extra large master bedroom, isn't it?" The central idea here is to build toward a series of "yes" answers on the details that help confirm and carry forward the final decision.

The more experienced salesperson never uses the tie-down without being absolutely sure that a positive response will result. The danger is that additional obstacles will be created if the response is negative. If you do not know the real needs of your prospect, you might ask, "The back yard has an unusual number of shade trees that make it especially attractive, don't you agree?" If your prospect answers that he or she needs a sunny back yard for a greenhouse, you have presented a tie-down question that illicits a negative response.

In preparing questions in advance, make sure that you avoid a canned presentation. Your questions should have sufficient variety and should be sufficiently learned so that you can easily move through the conversation without overusing a single questioning technique.

The Last Question.   It has been said that the person who asks the last question controls the conversation. In reinspecting a house with a prospect who shows considerable interest, suppose the prospect says, "The lined draperies match the carpet. Are the draperies included?" The inept salesperson would reply, "No, that is the personal property of the seller." Or "No, that's not included." Here it is best to answer the question with a question: "They do match the carpets, don't they? Would you want the draperies included in the sale?" Or in looking at the attractive patio, the prospect notes a natural gas barbeque and asks, "Do you think the seller would include the barbecue?" Instead of answering, "No, that's not in the listing," ask another question: "Do you think your family would like that?" If the answer is "yes," your prospect is probably ready for the close.

When you are negotiating for the down payment, work for the largest possible deposit, for, in most cases, the prospect wants to make the smallest down payment. Instead of asking directly how much of a deposit the prospect wants to make, open the negotiation with, "We generally ask prospects to make a 5 percent or 10 percent earnest money deposit. Which one would you prefer?"

NEGOTIATING THE FINAL OFFER

Among salespersons experienced in closing, some encourage buyers and sellers to submit offers and counteroffers, reaching final agreement by negotiating acceptable compromises; some wrongly interpret buyers and sellers who have not agreed on the final price; and some wrongly give up on the sale when the seller rejects the buyer's first offer. A seller asking $60,000 for his or her five-year-old house might negotiate on other details with a buyer who offers $55,000. Under these conditions, reaching an agreement requires that the selling broker develop a *closing strategy,* learn to handle the *"last and final offer,"* and deal competently with the *final contact.*

The Closing Strategy

Closing strategy refers to the *skillful management in reaching your goal,* the completed sale. It refers to your method of conducting the closing negotiations. Strategy is based on preplanning which reduces the possibility of buyer or seller resistance.

In interpreting buyer and seller negotiations, you will observe three negotiating positions: the offensive, the defensive, and the defensive-offensive positions.

Seller Strategy. Consider first the position of the seller. The seller offers the house for sale based on an interpretation of current demand, the competition for buyers, and closing costs. If the property is listed at a competitive price, the seller in this instance is justified in being on the offensive.

1. *Offensive Strategy.* If the seller assumes the offensive position (and the salesperson is a party to this tactic), the buyer learns early in the negotiation that the seller knows the local housing market and the relative bargaining position of buyers. In short, by requiring that the buyer prove that the seller's offer is unfair, the buyer must adopt a counterstrategy and show that the seller's price or terms of sale are unacceptable.

The point here is that both parties must move toward the best and most reasonable price based on the salesperson's knowledge of the market. The seller assumes the offensive by staying with the offer unless the buyer (or salesperson) presents information that justifies lowering the sales price. If this information is forthcoming, the offensive-type seller would normally reconsider.

2. *Defensive Strategy.* If the seller adopts a defensive position, the buyer has an advantage: The buyer may offer less than the asking price and face no valid objections from the seller.

3. *Defensive-Offensive Strategy.* The seller adopts a defensive-offensive strategy if he or she offers the house for sale based on the best analysis of the current housing market but reserves acceptance of an offer until the buyer (with the help of the salesperson) demonstrates that the original listed price is *not* reasonable. In the latter instance, the seller's defensive-offensive position transfers the burden of negotiation to the buyer, who is then forced to be offensive and to convince the seller that the listed price, which on its face seems fair, is not acceptable.

Probably most of your listings cover the defensive-offensive strategy. When you present the offer to the seller, he or she defends the original price against the lower offer of the buyer and looks for an opportunity to be offensive, thus weakening the buyer's offer.

Here the salesperson's role is very plain. If the buyer makes an offer of $55,000, reasoning that the seller's asking price of $60,000 is too high, the seller would be advised not to take a defensive position by explaining why the price is *not too high* but move to the offensive and question reasons for the lower offer. The salesperson may help both parties reach an agreement by reviewing similar houses recently sold and listed.

If the buyer and seller seem locked in one of these negotiating positions, the salesperson then reviews the important elements that determined the price of the house listed for sale. The salesperson negotiates with both parties by reviewing the factors that are important to the current price. If the buyer has no support for his or her "lower than the listed offer," then the salesperson would be advised to change the topic and negotiating tactics. The obvious inference is that the buyer had no justification for the offer and was offering the lower price simply to see if by chance it would be accepted. If it is assumed that your buyer is qualified, this procedure is especially effective for the buyer who makes an extremely low initial offer.

Buyer Strategy. Generally speaking, buyers usually use offensive strategies, but the tactics used to approach the closing vary. Probably most buyers try to negotiate on *the most important issues first*—such as the asking price—on the grounds that if the most significant issues are resolved first, it is easier to resolve the minor details.

Other buyers may insist that the seller take a second mortgage as part of the purchase price, believing that the first issues to negotiate should be those from which the buyer *expects the most opposition.* It is the understanding of such buyers that if the more irritating terms of the offer are resolved, the more important issues, such as the price, may be more readily negotiated.

You will encounter other buyers who work toward a close by deciding first on the *least important issues,* establishing a pattern of agreement that deals progressively with the more significant issues. Early agreement on the purchase of personal property as part of the sales price is a case in point.

In contrast to the seller, the buyer has three basic choices in acting offensively: (1) He or she may reveal *no position,* (2) reveal a *minimum position,* or (3) reveal the *minimum in a final offer.* Suppose that the buyer is undecided about accepting the seller's offer to sell at $75,000.

1. The first choice is illustrated by the buyer who at no time reveals his or her true attitude toward the price. The salesperson works toward the close, let us say, by asking if the prospect would make an offer if the washer and dryer were included in the sale. The salesperson then proceeds point by point to other issues, such as, "Would you be willing to pay a second mortgage?" Next, the salesperson works toward an offer—point by point—until the buyer moves toward making an offer at or near the seller's offering price.

2. The second negotiating offensive strategy requires that the buyer reveal his or her maximum offer which must be realistic. If the buyer makes an unreasonably low offer, the sale may be lost or the seller may adopt a counteroffensive position by asking the buyer to justify the offer. If the buyer has no realistic basis for the offer, the buyer is not bargaining in good faith and probably is not in the market for the house.

In the last analysis, the salesperson encourages both parties not to make offers and counteroffers simply to compromise but to make concessions only if the other side has earned it and to offer convincing, logical evidence that either one's position (if not right) is at least stronger and more logical than that of the other party.

3.   The third and last offensive tactic of the buyer can be illustrated by an offer to buy at $64,000 under a 90 percent mortgage providing that the seller includes the draperies and carpets as part of the sale. By revealing his or her maximum price and acceptable terms, the buyer has little bargaining room. The sale will be based on the salesperson's ability to convince the seller that the offer is reasonable.

The Real Estate Market.   In part, the role assumed by the buyer or seller depends on the current market. When operating in a buyer's market, the buyer is advised to negotiate with the seller to meet the buyer's price and terms of sale. If their position is more equal, the buyer is advised to state the minimum price only as an initial offer, encouraging the seller to take a more realistic position. Here both parties are ready to make mutually agreeable concessions. The last alternative assumes that the buyer has made a final offer that has caused negotiations to break down; the seller is unconvinced that the buyer's first offer is true.

The Last and Final Offer

In interpreting the last and final offer, do not always take the offer at its face value. Remember that if the party making the final offer is not believed, then his or her bargaining power is weakened. It is imperative that you reduce to writing the exact words of the party making the final offer. In approaching the final offer with a counteroffer, introduce new alternatives and solutions. The last and final offer requires that the negotiator do the following:

1. Test the party making the final offer by suggesting an alternative offer that still meets buyer and seller objectives.
2. Counter the final offer with a plan adaptable to changing negotiating circumstances.
3. Do not encourage the buyer or seller to make a counteroffer along the same line or in the same form as the one he or she rejected.

On the third point: If the seller offers to sell under stated terms and price but rejects the buyer's offer to make a second mortgage in favor of the seller, counter this proposition by some other form of financing which does not require the seller to assume the second mortgage.

Elaine Schiff, a Realtor® in Louisville, Kentucky, makes a special effort to keep negotiations alive for buyers and sellers who make "the final offer." For instance, if the seller lists for $60,000 and another agent submits an offer of $55,000, both making the final offer, she keeps the negotiations active by stating, "Mr. Seller, rather than kill the offer and perhaps lose it forever, will you come back with a counteroffer to the asking price of $60,000?" She uses this approach if the purchaser interprets the seller as being stubborn and unwilling to compromise.

The Final Contact

Your final presentation to the buyer and seller (for an offer or counteroffer) should be planned to resolve points of disagreement, making it easy for the prospect to make a transition to another line of thought. In failing to close, make certain that the prospect terminates the interview with a pleasant memory, regardless of the outcome.

In part, this is a matter of creating the right conversational atmosphere. The final contact must end on a positive note just as the initial contact provides for continued negotiations. If earlier discussions have shown favorable results, they provide points of reference for the final interview. If the seller has rejected the buyer's offer and your buyer is unreasonable, show respect for the buyer's position: "I understand your position on this property. Suppose we meet in my office at 4:00 o'clock next Wednesday. We have some new listings in process; one of them may be just what you are looking for."

In other words, if the situation is a difficult one, the final contact should leave open the possibility of showing other houses on a specific date and time. Make your prospect understand that refusal to meet the seller's price in no way prejudices future showings. Close on a positive note. "Of course, I will continue to look for a home that meets your needs. Let's meet next Wednesday at 4:00. If we list a suitable house before this time, I will certainly call you."

POINTS TO REMEMBER

Salespersons negotiate directly with sellers over the listing and with buyers over terms of the proposed sale. In other respects, the salesperson acts as a mediator in negotiating the final sale. Defined as the *process of finding a compromise that is mutually acceptable,* the negotiating authority of the salesperson is limited to helping the buyer and seller reach an agreement. It is limited because the salesperson is not a party to the contract and, unless given specific authority in writing, cannot bind the principal.

Negotiating may take the form of *sequential negotiation.* Sequential negotiation requires firm agreement on each point before moving to the next point. The danger here is that failure to reach an agreement on a single issue may jeopardize further negotiation. It is difficult to trade off one concession against another concession in sequential negotiation.

Overall negotiation refers to a final resolution on all points of disagreement. By negotiating all issues together, concessions of one party represent payment for concessions by the other party.

The successful negotiator gains skill in determining which points the buyer and seller may concede. The final outcome depends on the *relative bargaining power* of the buyer and seller, the *advanced preparation* of the salesperson, the degree to which the buyer's and seller's *interests are compatible or conflicting,* the *information* that the buyer and seller have on the importance that each attaches to elements of the sale and their *motives.* In the last analysis, the salesperson working toward the close must be sure of the facts, identify negotiating objectives, and plan the negotiating strategy.

Special care is given to asking questions that are suitable for negotiation: namely, questions that *attract attention,* questions *that ask for information,* questions that *give information,* questions that *start prospects thinking,* and questions that *encourage the prospect to make decisions.* The *tie-down* questions end with the words doesn't it, didn't it, wasn't it, couldn't it, and so on. They build yes responses which lead to a final close. The tie-down is used only when you are sure that you will get a positive answer.

Closing strategy—the skillful management in reaching your goal—requires a planned method of conducting closing negotiations. Sellers and buyers may very easily assume the *offensive,* the *defensive,* and the *defensive-offensive* positions.

A seller who lists the house at the competitive market price assumes an offensive position. But, if the property is overpriced, the seller may adopt a defensive position which gives the buyer an advantage. An offer below the listed price will elicit no valid objections from the seller.

A seller adopts a defensive-offensive position if the house is listed for sale on the best analysis of the current market but reserves acceptance of an offer until the buyer (or the salesperson) demonstrates that the original listed price is *not* reasonable.

Generally speaking, buyers usually use offensive strategies. Some buyers negotiate on the most important issues first. Other buyers decide first on the least important issues, thus establishing a positive pattern of agreement. In making an offer, the buyer assumes an offensive position by revealing no position on price, revealing a minimum position, or making a minimum and final offer. In part, the suitability of these buyer-seller strategies depends on the local real estate market.

The last and final offer is not always accepted at its face value. Salespersons are advised to test the party making the final offer by suggesting alternatives to meet the objectives. If an offer has been rejected, avoid making a counteroffer along the same line or in the same form as the final offer; originate some other plan of action. The final contact must end on a positive note and leave open the possibility of showing the buyer other houses.

REVIEW QUESTIONS

1. Define the term negotiation.
2. Describe the salesperson's negotiating role.
3. Explain five factors that determine final mutual agreement.
4. Differentiate between sequential and overall negotiations. Give examples of each.
5. Explain the main requirements of a successful negotiator.
6. What steps are advised in preparing for negotiation?
7. Explain three possible problems that cause prospects to digress.
8. What determines the final willingness of buyers and sellers to reach an agreement?
9. What kinds of questions would you purposely avoid asking during negotiations?
10. Give examples of five kinds of questions that serve different negotiating purposes.
11. What is a tie-down question and what is the last question?
12. Give examples of the offensive, defensive, and defensive-offensive strategies used by the seller.
13. Give examples of the three strategies used by buyers negotiating a final sale.
14. What are the three offensive positions usually taken by the buyer?
15. Explain how you would interpret the last and final offer.
16. What suggestions would you follow in making the final contact with either buyer or seller?

11

Closing the Sale

Real estate selling places you in an either/or situation. Either you close the sale or you fail to close, thus losing the sale. Then you must repeat the close after selling other prospects. As a consequence, failure to close wastes your good efforts in prospecting for listings, working with the seller, and showing houses.

Since closing is such a critical part of selling, you must be familiar with the recommended techniques used to close the sale. The techniques are many and varied. You will find that the circumstances that you and your prospect face conform to a series of common situations, each of which has a recommended closing procedure. You can learn these procedures as you learn other steps in selling. Before turning to closing recommendations, consider the main reasons why salespersons fail to close.

REASONS FOR FAILING TO CLOSE

There are three basic reasons why a salesperson may fail to close: (1) The salesperson lacks personal confidence—in himself or herself, the company, or the saleability of the listed house. (2) The salesperson feels insecure and guilty about persuading prospects to buy. (3) The salesperson has done a poor job of selling. This is probably the most important reason for the salesperson's failing to close. This point covers a broad category of faults, any one of which may cause the prospect to reject the offer.

Personal Lack of Confidence

Some salespersons have little confidence in selling prospects. They are not convinced that the listed home is a "good buy." Or they do not have confidence in their employer. If the salesperson believes that the house selected is a second-rate house available only at an inflated price, he or she will find it difficult to close under any circumstances. The way to a quick and successful close depends on the salesperson's attitude. The salesperson must show enthusiasm and convey this enthusiasm to the prospect by working for a close.

The salesperson who lacks confidence, for whatever reason, should counsel with his or her supervisor. If it can be shown that the lack of confidence is unjustified, then the salesperson will not hesitate in moving toward the close. A salesperson who has any doubts is in a poor position to close the sale.

Personal Guilt Feelings

Guilt feelings arise from misconceptions about selling real estate. The salesperson who assumes that selling is a matter of begging the prospect to buy tends to act as an intruder who imposes his or her will on the prospect. Such a salesperson is poorly suited to selling.

The salesperson should act in a *service* capacity, helping the prospect find needed housing. The service role benefits sellers who wish to sell in the shortest time at the highest price. Negotiating so that both parties are satisfied should remove any guilt feelings. Overcoming (conscious or unconscious) feelings of guilt requires a change in attitude that emphasizes services for which rewards are gained in the form of real estate commissions and, to be sure, personal satisfaction.

Poor Selling Tactics

It has been repeatedly shown that this factor is the leading cause of failure to close. Poor selling may encompass the failure to read nonverbal communication which means that the salesperson never really knows when it is the right time to initiate the close. A common fault is the salesperson's tendency to overemphasize personal needs and underemphasize prospect needs.

Salespersons may not succeed because of circumstances out of their control. Some prospects, who work slowly toward a decision, need additional time. Instead of forcing a premature closing and thus losing the sale, the salesperson should finish the closing at another time. Closing often requires that the salesperson be flexible and adjust his or her selling techniques to meet changing prospect attitudes.

General Rules for Closing

Before considering the practical closing techniques, it seems advisable to consider the general rules for controlling the closing process. Some rules are extensions of the procedures followed in other aspects of the sale. Other rules apply specifically to closing.

At the closing you are likely to encounter slight disagreements between husband and wife or about the terms of sale offered by the seller and counter-offers of the prospect. It is important to maintain rapport, to maintain a friendly attitude, and to demonstrate your willingness to help the prospect and seller. Here it is essential that you prevent arguments.

When the time of closing seems at hand, make certain that you have the required material for closing: various papers, forms, and the like. Carry an extra pen; you do not want to be caught at closing without getting a signature.

Equally important are other aspects of the closing: you must not beg for the sale. You are moved to close by your dedication to solving a purchase decision, you are providing a service important to the buyer and seller, and because prospects may feel uneasy, you proceed to the closing smoothly and painlessly. This means that you give the closing your undivided attention. You provide an atmosphere that is free from telephone calls and personal interruptions.

You encourage the prospect to think of himself or herself as the owner of the listed property: You interpret prospect reactions, you study attitudes, and you move quickly toward the close as you reiterate the benefits of the sale.

Figure 11-1 summarizes the general "Do's" and "Don'ts" for closing sales. Preferably, closing is an informal process conducted in a friendly, pleasant atmosphere. Avoid giving the prospect any opportunity to withdraw. Ask your questions by using open questions. Do not ask closed questions, for they

FIGURE 11-1. Do's and Don'ts in Closing Sales

DO'S
1. Maintain a friendly attitude at the close; avoid arguments by being friendly even though there will be minor disagreements.
2. Before closing, be sure that you have the necessary deposit receipts, pens, and forms.
3. Realize that begging for a sale looks bad and turns the prospect away.
4. Ask the prospect to approve the offer instead of asking the prospect to sign.
5. Make it possible for the prospect to reach an easy decision.
6. Close in a protected setting. Avoid interrupting phone calls or other distractions.
7. Treat each prospect as you would your listings. Direct the closing to the prospect's preferences.
8. Lead the prospect to think as an owner of the new home you show.

will end the discussion. Avoid making unauthorized promises or promises that cannot be fulfilled. Finally, give prospects every opportunity to make a decision.

TIME TO CLOSE

Ideally, you close when (1) you know that the prospect has firmly decided to buy the listed house; (2) you have prepared the prospect so that every possible contingency has been anticipated; (4) your prospect expresses a willingness to sign the deposit receipt; or (5) your prospect accepts the terms offered by the seller. While this is the ideal result, you must take certain preliminary steps before you decide on the closing effort.

You close when you have finished selling the prospect. Your closing techniques include certain subtle tests that help strengthen your prospect's desire to buy. You stress the *advantages* considered attractive to the prospect and *not the disadvantages* of other houses. Once you have counseled the buyer on financing terms, you have a clear idea of the terms that the buyer expects. If you have finished your sale, you search for clues that indicate the right time for closing.

Interpreting Prospect Clues

A salesperson is never 100 percent sure that the prospect is ready to buy, but he or she should be able to judge time to close by studying certain clues. The alert salesperson recognizes the buyer who comes close to buying, then withdraws, then again moves toward a decision to buy. The salesperson notes these reactions and acts at the appropriate time. Clues are both physical and spoken.

Physical Closing Clues. Observe actions and movements, especially interactions between husband and wife, their glances, the nodding of the head, the facial expressions showing approval and disapproval. A movement of the body, a shrug of the shoulders, the manipulation of cigarettes, pipes, glasses, or briefcases are among the many forms of nonverbal communication that recommend closing or additional reinforcement.

Spoken Clues. Try to interpret comments that indicate favorable reactions, for example:

"Our present house does not have a modern oven and range."
"Our bedroom furniture would fit in the master bedroom."
"Would the seller accept a lower down payment?"
"Would the house qualify for a $60,000 mortgage?"
"When could the seller give possession?"
"Are the draperies and TV antenna included in the sale?"
"We would have to move in by May 15th."

Though you have not completed your presentation, stop if you sense an opportunity to close the sale. The prospect's questions may be such that you can quickly progress to the close rather than continue the presentation. Figure 11-2 lists other physical clues, comments, and questions that suggest the time of closing.

Certainly, purchasing a home is more than a casual undertaking. Some buyers must have time to make up their minds about the numerous details. In contrast, corporate executives, more accustomed to buying homes, typically

FIGURE 11-2. Prospect Closing Clues

Physical Clues

1. The prospect returns to the kitchen, opening and closing doors and turning switches off and on.
2. The prospect lingers in the backyard, showing personal approval of landscaping or play area.
3. The prospect reads the Homeowners Warranty Plan.
4. The prospect nods in agreement with the salesperson's statements.
5. The prospect studies the contract for sale or deposit receipt.

Prospect Comments Showing Willingness to Buy

1. "We always wanted a microwave oven."
2. "The house seems well insulated."
3. "The bathroom carpets and vanity are attractive."
4. "The kitchen is well laid out."

Questions That Indicate a Close

1. "What are the monthly utility costs?"
2. "How much would be required at closing?"
3. "When can the seller give possession?"
4. "Are the draperies included?"

---

make quick decisions. Recognizing that details are less important, (for example, the color of interior walls, the drapery material, the type of kitchen range and oven), this prospect knows the type of house wanted (probably because the risk is reduced by company employee transfer policies) and early in the presentation is likely to give clues to the time of closing.

Prospect Differences. Guard against the prospect who appears interested but is really not ready to buy. You detect an interest in the middle of your showing and though you attempt a close and fail initially, you continue the presentation by trying several closes as you proceed. If you do not follow this procedure, you may miss the ideal time to close. It is similar to taking a photograph. You have to take many pictures before you get the best one.

Assume that you have made your major presentation, shown the house, and believe that prospect objections, for the most part, have been satisfied. You have answered all questions and resolved the main problems facing the prospect. In these circumstances, do not postpone closing in the belief that you will find a better opportunity during the next appointment. There is a real danger that later the prospect will cool off, thus making it even more difficult to close than if you had moved to the close at the proper time.

You are not limited to just one closing attempt. It is a universal complaint of real estate brokers that salespersons do not try closing enough. And, further, the initial failure to close discourages subsequent efforts to closing.

The record reveals that the best salespersons attempt numerous closings. It is probably true that most real estate sales are made only after making several attempts to close. If a buyer cannot make up his or her mind easily, there is a decided advantage in making repeated attempts to close, for even this buyer is eventually likely to change his or her mind. In deciding when to close, salespersons rely heavily on the trial close.

The Trial Close

You rarely find "the magical moment" when the close should be made. There is the wrong notion that since closing is a separate step, you should only start the close at the end of your presentation. Because the closing is the end result of the entire presentation, you arrange each part of the showing and the interview to reach a buying decision. But closing is not just a matter of reaching the final closing point. You have been using the trial close continuously throughout the presentation.

Consider the trial close not so much as a separate step in the selling process but as a natural sequel to the presentation. In other words, if you detect an implied consent when you show the house or during the interview, make the trial close. Hopefully, the "trial" close will become a "final" close, even though the "magical moment" occurs early in the selling process.

Trial Close Defined.   The trial close refers to any attempt to determine if the prospect is ready for a final decision. In this context, the trial close defines any unsuccessful close. Recognize and accept the fact that not every attempt to close results in a sale; the trial close that results in failure or postponement creates an opportunity to reinforce the real advantages of the purchase or, alternatively, to overcome objections more effectively. Hence, even though the attempt to close results in several "trials," each one is a sincere effort to arrive at a final buying decision. Continue the selling effort until you reach another point appropriate for the close.

Trial Close Objectives.   On analysis, trial closes are arranged so that a negative reaction will not risk the chances of reaching a buying decision. Trial closes should give the salesperson information with which to proceed toward a positive reaction.

In this respect, the trial close meets three objectives: (1) It is a relatively safe way to ask the prospect for a decision; if it succeeds, you have a completed sale. (2) In a sense, it is a way to test prospect attitudes; the trial close shows the degree to which the prospect is acting favorably toward the home and also shows whether or not the prospect is fully convinced and ready to buy. (3) The trial close guides the salesperson and prevents prospects who are not ready for the final close from making negative and final decisions.

CLOSING TECHNIQUES

You should learn each of the suggested closing techniques so that if the occasion recommends a closing, you are ready with one of the tested methods. This recommendation serves your interest because you are not restricted to a single closing technique. Depending on the selling technique that you use, there is a closing method that is appropriate at the time. Recognizing that there is no one best method, you use several methods until the prospect signs. You will probably begin with the most effective closing method and if that does not work, you try other techniques.

The Assumptive Close

It is assumed that you have vigorously applied your selling skills before the showing. You have adequately qualified the prospect; and you know what the prospect wants; you have prepared the prospect for the showing; and you know the house and neighborhood.

In taking these initial steps, you have demonstrated enthusiasm and you assume that the prospect will buy. You have narrowed the choice and you have satisfactorily met all the prospect's objections. Your remaining task is to resolve the minor details and fill out the contract for sale. "Shall we ask for possession on the 15th of next month?" "Suppose we require the seller to include the draperies?" "Shall we ask the owner to replace the bathroom carpet?" "If the seller agrees to accept a second mortgage for $3,000, would you be willing to pay $5,000 down?"

These questions assume that the prospect will buy. If you get favorable responses to these questions, you are one step away from the completed sale. While you are talking, you start filling out the deposit receipt, the address, the date, and other minor details. If your prospect is ready, he or she will not feel forced. You are only taking the natural step which gives the prospect the pleasant sensation of finally reaching a decision. For this reason, do not hesitate on the assumptive close even though it is a bold step. This method of closing has proven to have been successful too often not to be tried.

Summarizing Advantages

Recall that your prospect looks to the benefits realized from owning a home and not the house itself. As a reminder, home ownership confers, among other benefits:

Security.
An investment against inflation.
Advantages of the neighborhood (especially for children).
Personal satisfaction in owning a superior house.
Facilities for entertaining friends: a swimming pool, a backyard barbecue, or other amenities.

A summary of these advantages appeals to the insecure prospect who has seen several houses and seems overly concerned with minor details. The salesperson has the advantage of knowing, through asking probing questions and interpreting nonverbal responses, the more important ownership advantages that appeal to the prospect.

For prospects who are distracted by details, the summary has the advantage of directing attention to the more significant features and offsetting the tendency to forget the less important points. By directing the prospect away from small details, the summary has the further advantage of reinforcing the more significant benefits.

Summarize in Logical Sequence.   It is helpful to give the summary in a logical sequence. The sequence may follow the *order of presentation* in which benefits have been explained, for instance, the neighborhood, the convenience of the location, the outside attractiveness of the house, the new kitchen appliances, the roominess of the family room, or the financing. A presentation in this order reminds the prospect of the points that you made at the beginning of your presentation.

An equally effective way is to summarize *in reverse order,* that is, beginning with the last point you made and working in logical steps backward to the first point you made when you drove the prospect through the neighborhood. Summarizing in reverse order lets the prospect think of the benefits still on their minds.

Summarize the Points of Common Agreement. In other instances, it will prove more beneficial to start the summary on points least likely to encourage prospect objections. If you are showing the house to the husband and wife, begin with points that they commonly agree on. Follow with the next point most likely to be accepted, and proceed to other accepted points that lead the prospect to eventual approval. Each time your prospect agrees with a point, he or she is less likely to disagree with the next benefit you stress. By developing a series of positive agreements you move toward a positive time to ask for the signature.

As you finish the summary, ask for a deposit. If your summary has touched on the significant points, which repeatedly have shown how the prospect benefits from buying this home, the prospect should be sufficiently interested to sign the deposit receipt. The summary helps the prospect reach the final decision.

The Direct Close

There are two situations in which the direct close is recommended. If your prospect is an experienced homebuyer, if the prospect has approached you with a fairly fixed set of requirements, and if the prospect is pressed for time, he or she usually appreciates a straightforward presentation and your direct, however blunt, request to sign the contract for sale. Your judgment here is critical. The direct approach may create irreparable, psychological barriers for the insecure, undecided buyer.

The second kind of prospect is the person who has consulted other brokers. Every device to sell the prospect has failed and you stand a large chance of losing the sale. If you have selected the house that you feel is ideally suited to the prospect and without question is your best listing for the prospect, state flatly, "This is the house for you. Give me your deposit and sign this receipt."

Chances are that if you are refused, you would have lost the sale anyway. But the prospect may react favorably to your instructions. The direct approach resolves the prospect's problem and avoids the added inconvenience of searching for other houses that will probably not be as suitable as your listed house.

The Balance Sheet Approach

You have worked with your prospect for two weeks. Today you have shown your prospect three houses, one of which you consider as the ideal purchase. You have established rapport and you know in some detail the prospect's major requirements. You know that the prospect must compromise some of his or her demands, but in view of the prospect's particular wants, the house you have selected has the more important features he or she wants.

You realize that the prospect is hesitating and is carefully weighing the respective benefits of this house. In this situation, your best response is as follows:

> On the left side of this paper let's make a list of the specific things you like about this house. First, you like the large master bedroom, right? And you know that your utility bills will be lower because of the special energy conservation construction. Not many houses have 12 inches of ceiling insulation. In this house you also have a daylight basement and a large attractive recreation room.
>
> Now, on the right side of this paper let's make a list of your main objections. This house costs $10,000 more than you originally planned to spend. Let's see how much more that would be with a $9\frac{1}{2}$ percent, 25-year mortgage. My calculations show that this would increase your monthly payments by $87.40, which is less than $3.00 a day. In addition, you don't like to drive 20 miles to work, but since you are only one-half mile from the freeway entrance, that gives you a driving time of 25 minutes. Let me list your other objections."
>
> Note that your list on the left gives advantages that offset your objections. Since you will be living in the house at least until your children finish high school, on balance this looks like a good buy, don't you agree?

Real estate brokers refer to this as the *Benjamin Franklin* close. The story is that Benjamin Franklin would draw a vertical line in the middle of a paper and then label one side "yes" and the other side "no." After writing all the affirmative arguments on one side and the negative arguments on the.other side, he would reach a final decision. In the same way, the salesperson helps the prospect identify the reasons for making the purchase. Generally, the advantages outweigh the objections.

Closing on a Single Objection

Let us say that your prospect states a specific preference for a house that has a basement, or a brick exterior, or one story, or a maximum down payment or price. With the exception of this one item, the house you show meets the the prospect's needs. Or suppose the house meets the wife's approval, but the husband balks because of this single objection. In this case, ask pointedly "If this objection were removed, would you buy?"

By gaining this admission, the trained salesperson works to overcome the objection. Your familiarity with the house and the prospect's wants gives you the opportunity: "The lack of a basement is offset by the large garage and more than adequate storage and closet space." "The cedar shakes will outlast your ownership of the house." "The insulated, cedar siding has advantages over an uninsulated, brick veneer exterior."

If the objection turns on price and financing, work toward different financing plans that overcome objections about the down payment, monthly payments, and the price. Convert these costs to prices per day. Show that the benefits the prospect will receive by this purchase are more than offset by the added cost.

This approach concentrates on the single objective and helps the prospect reach a compromise on the final objection, which is usually a minor point. You would be doing your prospect a disservice if you do not help direct attention to the many benefits that offset the single and last objection.

Closing on Minor Details

It is easier for a prospect to make decisions on minor details than on larger details. The prospect is almost ready to say "yes" but shows some hesitation. You close by casually suggesting an incidental point.

You believe, for instance, that the prospect likes the neighborhood and wants this house with its three large bedrooms and a den for a study; the prospect would also consider assuming the present mortgage. Your prospect has noted that the custom-made, lined draperies in each room match the new-looking carpets. You initiate the close by asking: "Why don't we make the seller an offer for $70,000 and ask that the draperies be included in the price?"

In truth, a home purchase calls for decisions on countless details. You have determined that the prospect has reached a favorable decision on each detail. You work toward the sale by focusing attention on the last detail. As a closing device, you help the prospect make a normal transition to the buying decision. If your prospect fails to close on the detail, start moving smoothly to the next closing opportunity.

The Scare Technique

Probably overused and certainly abused by the less experienced, this technique is a negative form of close. You try to panic the buyer into making a decision by saying, "This is a popular neighborhood and you realize the house has been listed for only one week. One of our other salespersons has a prospect who is also seriously considering this house. I doubt that the house will be on the market next Monday."

This is also known as the "standing-room-only" approach. It is only useful if you can honestly tell the prospect that the house is a "good buy" and if you personally believe that it will not be on the market for more than a few days.

Your reputation will suffer if you use this approach as a lazy way to force the close. If your prospect believes that you are not sincere and that you are trying to scare him or her into making a decision, then you have lost the sale. The method should only be used for special situations. You must be truthful and you must be able to verify your case. There have been situations in which a delay of a few hours has disappointed a prospect who really wanted the house but delayed making a decision until it was too late.

The Alternative Choice

Suppose you have selected a particular house that meets your prospect's needs but in order to offer a contrast, you show a slightly inferior house in the same neighborhood. You make it difficult for the prospect to remain undecided if you ask, "Do you want the brick veneer house on the corner or the frame house with the basement?"

Both houses have features that are important to the prospect. But suppose the main objection to the brick veneer house, which is the prospect's preferred choice, is the price. By reviewing the features of each house, and especially the features of the brick house, with the features that please the prospect, you make it difficult for the prospect to reject the offer.

This approach rests on the principle that as the number of alternatives increases, the process of decision making is more difficult and more likely to be postponed. The skillful selection of the alternatives, which are kept to a minimum, decreases the likelihood of the prospect's making objections and it makes it easier for you to guide the prospect to a final close.

FAILURE TO CLOSE

The closing steps outlined here assume that you eventually lead your prospect to the closing by using one or a combination of the suggested closing techniques. You are studying your prospect's behavior and you frequently ask probing questions.

As a matter of fact, the skillful use of questions, in itself, represents one method of closing. Use the questions to cover the details of the sale; for example, ask questions like the following:

"What do you like about the kitchen appliances?"
"What kind of vegetables would you grow in the garden?"
"Would you want an attic fan installed to supplement the air conditioning?

Figure 11-3 illustrates how these probing questions help move your prospect toward a close.

Reasons for Closing Failures

Not all your showings will result in sales and not all prospects will buy from you. After each interview remember to thank your prospect for considering your houses and make sure that your prospect leaves in a good frame of mind. Always remind the prospect of your name, address, and phone number.

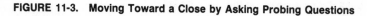
FIGURE 11-3. Moving Toward a Close by Asking Probing Questions

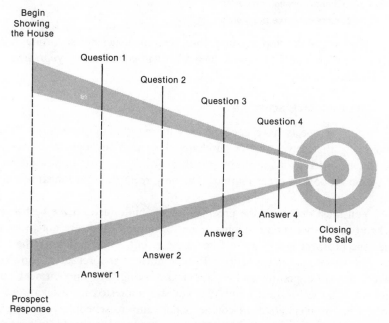

Adapted from H. B. Rames, *The Dynamics of Motivating Prospects to Buy* (West Nyack, N.Y.: Parker Publishing Company, Inc., 1973), p. 147.

It is helpful to give out brochures or other printed handouts as a reminder. Maintaining good relationships creates the right atmosphere for a repeat interview.

Immediately after terminating an interview, make notes of everything you have learned about the prospect. Write your impressions of how the prospect responded to each house. Outline the mistakes that you think you might have made in dealing with the prospect and outline how you propose to avoid repeating these mistakes. If your prospect offered objections, consider how you could have handled these objections more effectively.

List all the reasons for your failure to close. The list would probably include at least some of the following points:

I could not answer the prospect's questions.
The house was not properly prepared for showing.
I did not brief the prospect properly before the showing.
I did not identify the main sales appeal of the house.
I did not ask the prospect the right questions.
I did not show the prospect the right houses.
I qualified the needs of the prospect poorly.
I irritated the prospect.

I did not ask for a closing at the right moment.
I did not show enough enthusiasm.
I failed to counter the prospect's objections.

The list you develop will help you overcome deficiencies. Although you will not develop a perfect record, such a list will contribute to your program of self-improvement.

The Call-Back Schedule

Some prospects have good reasons for postponing a decision. Before committing themselves to the purchase, they must arrange their personal finances in order to make the required down payment or they want more details on schools or other matters. The only recourse is to schedule a call-back.

You must deal with the prospect who is undecided on the best neighborhood or the best house for his or her purposes. Take care not to antagonize the prospect by trying to force a close, but try to minimize the time spent in irrelevant conversation. If you must make repeated showings, make a definite appointment for your next meeting. The appointment for a call-back lets the prospect know that you are interested in resolving his or her housing problem. It gives you an opportunity to schedule your time effectively and it prevents the prospect from becoming irritated by repeated calls for a later appointment.

You will make a good impression by taking out your appointment book and writing the date and hour of the call for your next interview. Through this the prospect learns that you are serious and he or she will be more likely to keep the appointment.

You prepare for the follow-up interview and the call-back the same way you would for an initial showing. If you are calling unannounced, give a good reason for making your repeat call. For example, you have new information on the house: The seller has lowered his offer or a new school has been proposed in the neighborhood. You try a new approach in succeeding interviews. You make the presentation personal and you show interest in the problem. Remember that you should always leave the door open for another contact.

The Closing Attitude

To succeed in closing, you must be convinced that the house offered is the best value for the prospect's needs. You must convey the impression that if the prospect does not buy this house, the prospect is really not in the market for a house *at this time*. In your personal view, the prospect will not find a better house than the house you are showing.

Encourage the prospect to consider all the alternatives open to him or her. For example, the prospect could

1. Maintain his or her present residence.
2. Find a way to make a larger down payment so that better housing can be purchased.
3. Take a part time job, work overtime, have the spouse get a job; or take other (legal) steps to increase monthly income and qualify for a higher mortgage.
4. Go to a neighborhood of lower-priced houses (which might increase driving time and add travel expense).
5. Purchase this house because it provides the greatest possible benefits for the prospect's present needs and within his or her price range.

In truth, selling houses is a complicated process. In this work you grow like a tree—the real estate sales tree of accomplishment shown in Figure 11-4. You start with a minimum knowledge of real estate details: house construction, financing, appraising, and regulations among other topics. You concentrate on securing listings, gaining seller cooperation, and preparing the house for showing. Turning next to prospects, you plan the sale as a general would plan a campaign. If you follow the leading selling suggestions, you reach the top of the tree: you close the sale.

POINTS TO REMEMBER

Salespersons experiencing an unusually low number of closings fail to close because of (1) a personal lack of confidence, (2) personal guilt feelings, and (3) poor selling tactics. Besides overcoming these deficiencies, the salesperson should follow these general rules: maintain a friendly attitude, make it easy for the prospect to reach a decision, close in a protected setting and early in the interview, let the prospect think of himself or herself as the occupant and owner of the house you show. Above all, don't appear anxious, don't apologize about the showing, don't make promises that cannot be fulfilled, and don't ask closed questions.

The best time for closing is indicated by your interpretation of physical clues, the prospect's comments, or the prospect's questions. Given favorable clues, rather than wait for the "magical moment" you make repeated trial closings. The trial close is a relatively safe way to ask for an early decision; it tests prospect attitudes and it guides the salesperson in avoiding a final, negative decision by a prospect who is not ready to buy.

In applying closing techniques, you use the *assumptive close*—you assume at the outset that the prospect will buy. In other instances, it is to your advantage to *summarize advantages* and end with the request for a deposit. The *direct close* is recommended for the experienced homebuyers who have

FIGURE 11-4. The Real Estate Sales Tree of Accomplishment

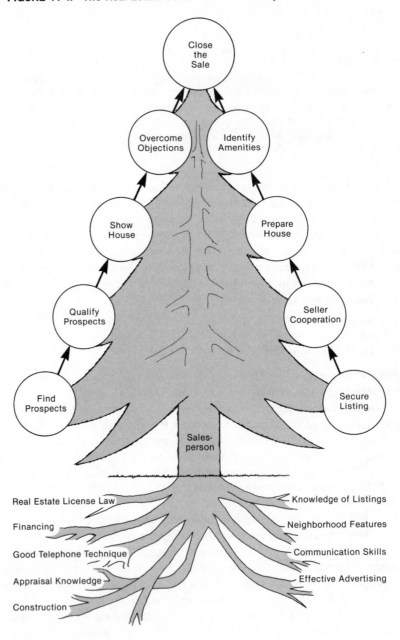

preconceived ideas of their needs. The direct close may work if you have the ideal house for a prospect who is also considering other alternatives. In other situations, the *balance sheet approach* (the prospect weighs the advantages against the objections) may lead to the final decision. *Closing on a single objection* or *closing on minor details* are other methods that lead to an early close. The *scare technique* and *closing by the alternative choice* are still other methods that may be used in combination with other types of close.

Analyze your failures. After having worked with numerous prospects, you will recognize deficiencies that you may be able to minimize in your next presentation. Concentrate on developing good call-back procedures, thus leaving the door open for another contact. Develop a positive closing attitude and, if the prospect is undecided, ask the prospect to consider other alternatives. These alternatives usually narrow down to four or five choices that indicate whether or not the prospect really wants a new house at this time.

REVIEW QUESTIONS

1. What are the main reasons for failing to close?
2. Discuss the recommended do's and don'ts for closing sales.
3. When is the best time to close?
4. Explain what the physical and spoken clues to closing are. Give an example of each.
5. What is a trial close? Explain how you would initiate a trial close.
6. Explain and give an example of an assumptive close.
7. Explain three variations of closing by summarizing advantages.
8. Describe the direct close. When is it recommended?
9. Give an example of a balance sheet approach to closing.
10. What are the advantages of closing on a single objection? Explain fully.
11. When would you recommend closing on minor details? Explain thoroughly.
12. Do you consider the scare technique a valid closing method? Why or why not? Give reasons for your answer.
13. When is the alternative choice method of closing recommended? Give an example.
14. What are the five alternatives generally available to the prospect who fails to close?

Part 3

IMPROVING THE SALES ORGANIZATION

12
Selecting
Qualified Salespersons

Recruiting is probably the most critical part of improving the sales organization. A sales incentive program, sales training, and the best advertising program will not overcome the limitations of unqualified or unmotivated salespersons. One authority who specializes in qualifying salespersons reports that 30 percent of the salespersons account for 70 percent of the sales volume. In a review of several thousand salespersons, it was concluded that one-half of the real estate salespersons should not be on the sales staff; these are the persons who do not cover their assigned overhead.

Further, there is a common misconception held by new salespersons that passing the state real estate license examination qualifies them as successful salespersons. The more experienced, however, know that the real estate license laws only protect the public from technically unqualified persons. Although license laws legally qualify a person as a real estate salesperson, they do not evaluate the qualities that are associated with successful selling.

Therefore, this chapter identifies personal traits found helpful in selecting qualified salespersons. The chapter begins by reviewing the qualities of the successful salesperson. A discussion on preferred recruiting practices follows this section. The last two sections discuss recommendations on helping newly selected salespersons and methods of screening employees. Most successful real estate brokers have instituted a formal procedure to screen prospective real estate agents as explained in this chapter.

QUALITIES OF SUCCESSFUL SALESPERSONS

A five-year study of more than 3,000 salespersons and applicants identified three main factors that explained failure among real estate salespeople. The factors cited include: (1) the selection of salespersons from other real estate firms solely because of past experience, (2) recruiting programs confined to applicants who met relatively high minimum educational qualifications, and (3) appointment of salespersons on the basis of overall personal characteristics without regard to their job assignment.[1]

To guard against hiring unproductive salespersons, real estate brokers vary widely in their recruiting practices. Some firms through experience have adopted relatively inflexible guidelines for qualifying prospective salespersons. Others rely more on the interest, motivation, and personal qualities of the individual.

Guidelines to Salesperson Selection

Some notably successful firms prefer women for selling houses; other firms favor men to sell commercial, industrial, and income properties; and at least one company requires applicants to meet five minimum requirements:

1. A college degree or adult education beyond high school.
2. A family person who has no serious personal problems; the ability to live six months without income.
3. A past record of success and not necessarily in the real estate industry.
4. Selection only on the basis of at least four counseling sessions one week apart.
5. Successful qualification through a sales aptitude test.

It would probably be difficult to consistently apply these and other rigid minimum standards for employment. Too many exceptions have been noted among successful sales organizations that have not applied these inflexible rules. In selecting potential salespersons, practice ranges from brokers who rely on a formal qualification process and the employment of outside counselors to brokers who depend on a more subjective process based on the past experience of the firm.

Formal Qualification Procedures. Herbert D. Weitzman, writing in *Real Estate Today,* reports that the Henry S. Miller Company of Dallas, Texas found that interviews to qualify potential salespersons were unreliable because "some applicants were faking the interviews, telling sales managers what they wanted to hear."[2] Because the firm employed too many people who were

[1]David G. Mayer and Herbert M. Greenberg, "How to Choose a Good Salesman," *Real Estate Today* (January, 1970), p. 64.

[2]Henry D. Weitzman and Robert W. Eichinger, "The Statistics Behind Success," *Real Estate Today* (April, 1978), p. 11.

unsuccessful, a more formal process of qualifying salespersons was initiated in 1969.

The system combines (1) a professional consulting opinion on the applicant's assets and liabilities and (2) information gathered through interviews, reference checks, and credit checks. The procedure requires that the applicant complete a battery of questions that measure intelligence, interests, motivation, emotional composure, interpersonal style, management strength, achievement orientation, and work style. The results indicate that the responses to the questionnaire are not as significant as the psychologist's *interpretation* of the responses to the questions.

1. *Applicant Test Questionnaire.* Applicants are first screened during a preliminary interview by a personnel officer and head of the sales division. If the interview is successful and if the references are satisfactory, the applicant answers eight sections of questions which take approximately two and a half hours. The answers to each section are sent to professional psychologists for evaluation. Applicants are measured according to 45 character traits divided into eight major categories. Each trait is measured on a scale from one to nine.

Results of the battery are compared to judgments formed from interviews and background information. If the judgments formed from the interviews and the interpretation of the answers to the questionnaire vary, management seeks an explanation why an individual performs differently in the two qualification methods.

According to Weitzman, the firm searches for qualities that indicate *strength and stability.* Persons showing extreme values are common to the instant, high achiever. These persons are avoided because the firm does not want to devote personnel time and resources to the "superstars" who are likely to leave the firm after a short-term employment. As do most real estate offices, the Henry S. Miller Company prefers a steady, sound achiever over a short-term, high achiever.

Moreover, sales managers in the Miller Company may employ persons who have a record of success who do not rate high on the questionnaire. A person who seems strongly motivated, who sincerely desires to work with the firm, and who has a record of past success qualifies for employment.

According to the Miller Company, eight years of experience with this system reveals that its salespeople have characteristics that differ markedly from the characteristics of the general population. The differences were noted in five main areas. These differences between the personalities of salespersons and the personalities of the general public are listed in Figure 12-1.

2. *Salesperson Personality Profile.* Although this survey is limited to salespersons who deal with commercial properties and is based on a limited sample, generalizations on this comparison seem reasonable. For example, salespersons appear more *objective, intelligent, results oriented,* and *practical*

FIGURE 12-1. Real Estate Salesperson's Personality Profile Compared to the General Public's Personality Profile

Compared to the General Public the Average Salesperson Is **More**	Compared to the General Public the Average Salesperson Is **Less**
1. Intellectual abilities and style	
Objective Intelligent Results oriented Practical	Organized Academically oriented Detail oriented
2. Work task interests	
Entrepreneurally oriented	Needful of work variety People oriented Of a personal risk taker Needful of thinking Mechanically inclined
3. Achievement drive	
Able to work alone Needful of recognition Needful of rewards	Organizationally rebellious
4. Emotional development	
Emotionally stable Restrained and controlled Stress tolerant Emotionally secure	
5. Interpersonal style and skills	
Assertive and aggressive Self-confident Driving and energetic Comfortable with people Persuasive	

Adapted from Herbert D. Weitzman and Robert W. Eichinger, "The Statistics Behind Success," *Real Estate Today* (April, 1978), pp. 14–16.

than does the general public. They also appear less organized and less inclined to engage in academic studies or intellectual reading. They seem to be more concerned with broader topics and less detail oriented.

In being judged on work task interests it was found that salespersons are more interested in selling, owning, or renting things and in being in reasonable control of their worlds; that is, they are *entrepreneurally oriented*. The results indicated less need for work variety and fewer personal risk takers. In addition, salespersons are less mechanically inclined than the general public.

In being judged on relative drive it was found that salespersons display more *ability to work alone* than is typical of the general public. They also have more *need for recognition and rewards.* They are less hostile toward organized authority and tend not to rebel against organized activity.

Successful salespersons are *emotionally more stable, tolerant of more stress,* and more *emotionally secure* than is the general public. Their interpersonal style gives them more self-confidence, aggressiveness, drive, and energy. Similarly, they are *more persuasive* and generally more *comfortable with people.*

In addition, according to this source, it is important that the sales applicant belong to community organizations such as school organizations or church groups because this indicates that the person relies on other people for guidance and assistance. A person likely to remain with the organization and become a steady producer must show past evidence of a positive willingness to be dependent on others and the support services that the company provides salespersons.

Less Formal Selection. Some companies have learned by experience to qualify salespersons on the basis of personal ability and character. Although specific requirements to qualify salespersons vary among brokers, most authorities agree on certain general qualifications desired in real estate salespersons. Typical qualifications would cover five characteristics important to successful real estate sales:

1. *Drive and motivation.* This characteristic refers to the willingness to work hard. Long hours and interrupted personal schedules—even during the weekend and holidays—are required of salespersons. The applicant must have sufficient drive to ensure that he or she will call back on prospects and personally persuade prospects to look at other houses. Making personal calls, responding to advertisements, and canvassing door to door require a high degree of motivation and considerable self-discipline.

In the final analysis, it is not the lack of technical knowledge that divides high-producing salespersons from the unsuccessful; it is the strong, driving motivation that leads to more effort. Without this quality, other personal attributes are of little advantage.

2. *Aggressiveness.* To be sure, salespersons should not be offensively aggressive. Yet, the record shows that the self-assertive, enterprising person is not discouraged easily and is one who has the ability and confidence to pursue prospects.

3. *Ability to handle people.* This trait breeds confidence among prospects and creates the right rapport so that prospects and clients find it easy to deal and talk to the salesperson. This salesperson is enthusiastic and cheerful. The best traits are found in people who have sufficient self-control to continue a persistent, tactful approach in understanding the other person's point of view.

4. *Knowledge.* Not only must the salesperson have a good memory, but he or she must also have sufficient knowledge of financing, construction, and real estate law and instruments so that he or she may help the buyer and seller comprehend the complicated real estate transaction.

5. *Self-respect.* Self-respect leads the salesperson to take the initiative in completing the sale. He or she is sufficiently motivated to develop a spirit of competition. A salesperson who has this personality trait appreciates an attractive office that has adequate equipment and furnishings so that the individual feels proud of his or her office and desk.[3]

Personal Attributes

Research has shown that successful salespersons have a high degree of ego drive and empathy. The *ego driven* salesperson enjoys persuading other individuals as a means of personal gratification. His or her self-esteem is enhanced by successful persuasion and is diminished by a failure to persuade. A completed sale gives the ego driven individual a feeling of satisfaction which adds to personal pleasure.

Empathy refers to the ability to sense accurately the reactions of another person. Persons who have this characteristic recognize the clues provided by others and react effectively to these clues. Empathy allows the salesperson to perceive another person's feelings without necessarily agreeing with those feelings.[4]

Another source divides the qualities required of salespersons into *essential traits* and *desirable traits.* This source regards judging salesperson applicants to be the most important part of selecting, training, and supervising real estate salespersons. The *essential traits,* according to this source, include four items:

1. *Intelligence.* Not the Ph.D. variety, but sufficient intelligence to think and act for themselves. It also makes them easily trainable.
2. *Good attitude.* This goes hand in hand with intelligence and is the ingredient that makes them easy to work with.
3. *Well motivated.* Whether money-motivated or recognition-oriented, a strong motivational factor is necessary in the successful person.
4. *Empathy.* "The imaginative identification of one-self with another person." In other words, the ability to place yourself in someone else's shoes and look at any situation from his or her point of view.[5]

[3]For example, see *Increase Real Estate Office Profits* (Los Angeles: California Real Estate Association, 1965), pp. 109–110.

[4]See Herbert M. Greenberg and Jeanne Greenberg, "Selecting Top Producers," *Real Estate Today* (September, 1974), p. 4.

[5]John E. Cyr, *Training and Supervising Real Estate Salesmen* (Englewood Cliffs, N.J.: Prentice-Hall, Inc., 1973), p. 66.

The *desirable traits* include four additional items:

1. *Education-minded.* A good education not only denotes intelligence, but it also indicates a strong desire to succeed and a willingness to sacrifice for that success.
2. *Aggressiveness.* It takes more than the average amount of aggressiveness to be successful. However, too much aggressiveness may be offensive to prospects.
3. *Well-organized.* A top salesperson organizes his or her time and efforts to get the maximum mileage out of both. However, we have all seen salespersons who are so busy keeping organized that they never get any selling done.
4. *Industriousness.* The hard worker by virtue of his dogged "stick-to-it-iveness" can oftentimes make up for other deficiencies.[6]

Supplementing these points are other qualities that salesperson applicants should have: (1) *normal mental and emotional stability,* (2) *intellectual capacity* to take real estate courses and instruction, (3) *no prejudices and biases* that might adversely affect performance, and (4) *good oral ability.* If these minimum requirements are met, it is held that other attributes may be acquired by the properly motivated salesperson. The next issue is to maximize the chance of securing the best qualified applicant through an organized recruiting program.

THE RECRUITING PROGRAM

The best sources of new salespersons are recruiting programs (neighborhood coffees, license preparations courses, career nights, and so on) and experienced salespersons who have worked for other firms.

Some real estate brokers consider recruiting a continuous process that builds a good local image. The firm's reputation gives the established company a ready supply of qualified people who seek employment. Others plan to reach this point by a carefully designed recruiting plan. Clearly, the best advice is to take as much time as necessary to secure the most ambitious people who have the aptitude and temperament for real estate sales.

Better quality recruiting means less time in training and less time wasted in motivating people who are not capable of being motivated; better quality recruiting develops a staff in which each person bears at least his or her proportion of overhead.

Recruiting New Salespersons

The Hardin & Stockton Company of Kansas City, Missouri, recommends for every house sold that the new buyer arrange for a neighborhood coffee paid for by the office. The coffee meeting introduces the new buyer to

[6]*Ibid.*

the neighbors and at the same time shows that the company is interested in its clients. More importantly, the meeting gives the salesperson an opportunity to discuss a real estate sales career with neighbors. The company reports that many qualified applicants have been obtained this way.

As a further inducement to qualifying applicants, some firms sponsor license preparation courses. These courses are offered to applicants who have been screened through aptitude tests and interviews. The company provides training aids, lectures, and sample license examinations. After passing the state real estate license examination, the applicant is further instructed in the firm's policies and selling techniques.

Recruiting Sources.   Still others, like L. James Koutnik, owner of Western Realty Company, Inc., Twin Falls, Idaho, sponsors a career night which is an employment seminar for the public. For this meeting, which is widely advertised, material is prepared showing what a prospective salesperson must do to pass the state real estate examination, the firm's training program, the salesperson's duties, and the potential income of a salesperson. An organization of 18 salespersons, the company reports an annual rate of turnover among salespersons of less than 25 percent.

Other common sources for recruiting salespersons include the following:

Statewide newspaper advertisements.
Referrals from sales staff.
Classified display ads.
Salespersons from other brokers who call the firm.
Personal knowledge of the individual.
Walk-ins.
Old town families.
Customers.
Real estate schools and license preparation cram courses.
Contacts from property management.
Business college graduates.

Some firms that have strong reputations have no organized program for recruiting. Other firms rely on their personal knowledge of acquaintances and contacts from property management operations. Still other firms regularly recruit among educational institutions such as private real estate schools, license preparation cram courses, and business college graduates.

Continuous Recruiting.   As does the selling process, recruiting constitutes a continuous program. The more prominent firms advertise that the firm wants qualified applicants. Some firms attract likely candidates by making their needs known during meetings of professional and trade associations and club and community organizations. The main object is to maintain a continuing list of qualified candidates to fill vacancies promptly and to meet the staff needs of the expanding office.

Other prospects are secured from employment agencies and from newspaper want ads. The E. G. Stassens Company of Portland, Oregon, has recruited successfully by running a two-week advertisement in the employment classified ad section.

> If you are seriously thinking of a full-time career in Real Estate Sales, join Oregon's fastest growing team of professional "HOMEFOLKS."
>
> Stassens is currently serving the Portland area with 18 offices and our new Lake Oswego office will be opening after the first of the year to help meet our ever-increasing demand.
>
> We offer the best in all areas—from a proven training program to award-winning advertising campaigns—we are behind you 100%!
>
> Call Bob St. Aubin, Director of personnel, 243-6115, and become acquainted. He'll sit down and help you discover your place with Stassens Realtors®.

By running these ads, a sufficient number of qualified persons may be obtained for instruction in passing the state license examination and for instruction in real estate sales.

Recruiting from Other Real Estate Firms

Critically important are the reasons why a salesperson changes firms. In a given locality incentives, commission rates, and support facilities usually are relatively similar. It may be that the so-called experienced salesperson who wants to change employers does not have a successful sales record. He or she may think that his or her selling success will improve by changing firms. In reality, this person will have the same work habits, motivation, and probably the same sales record he or she had in the other company.

Be more receptive to the salesperson who reports that his or her current employing broker is not supporting the sales staff. If your office has the reputation for being a professional operation, dissatisfied employees from other firms will approach your office. Most brokers are advised to ask permission of the applicant to call the present broker for a reference. If permission is not granted, there is probably a valid reason for not hiring the salesperson. Typically, the salesperson seeking a change in companies believes that the change will improve him or her. Ask the salesperson why he or she thinks that he or she will do better with your firm than with the present employing office.

The Qualifying Interview

The first interview screens new applicants for further interviews and testing. This interview identifies the overly sensitive, critical person who has a negative attitude and who relates poorly to others. Before the initial inter-

FIGURE 12-2. Suggested Questions for the Salesperson's Initial Interview

1. **Sales experience**
   Describe your sales experience.
   Why do you like selling?
   What was your method of compensation?
   What was your annual income?

2. **Other employment**
   Summarize your work experience over the last five years.
   Who was (were) your employer(s)?
   What was (were) your job title(s)?
   What was (were) your salary(ies)?

3. **Family status**
   What is your marriage status?
   How many children do you have and what are their ages?
   Is your wife employed? If so, where is she employed?

4. **Real estate interest**
   Why do you want to sell real estate?
   What special preparation or courses have you taken?
   Are you licensed?
   Do you have friends in the real estate business?

5. **Financial requirement**
   What minimum income do you require?
   How much do you expect to earn in real estate sales?

6. **Personal work habits**
   How many hours a week are you willing to devote to real estate sales?
   Can you work nights? Weekends? Holidays?

view, new applicants are asked to complete an interview questionnaire. Suggested questions are given in Figure 12-2.

In reviewing the written application with a prospective salesperson, ask these questions:

What do you consider to be your strongest qualities?
What do you consider to be your greatest weaknesses?

During the qualifying interview it must be determined why the person is giving up his or her last position and possible seniority benefits. What does the person lose by changing jobs and what does the individual expect to gain by changing?

After the initial interview a more comprehensive application is recommended. For the most part, the application expands on the most essential points of the initial interview. There is the further requirement that the applicant sign a statement at the end of the form attesting to the truthfulness of the answers and giving the employer authorization to check references.

Among the more significant points covered by an application form are the following:

1. Reasons for applying to the company.
2. Past criminal record.
3. Organization affiliations.
4. Special qualifications for real estate work.
5. Financial ability to meet living costs while training.
6. Physical conditions that might impair ability to work.
7. Past employment record (with references).
8. Marital status.
9. Desired income.
10. Educational background.
11. Personal references.

It is fairly clear that the answers to these questions will give the employer sufficient information to decide on the advisability of a follow-up interview. This form may be used in planning or predicting the success the applicant may have in company training programs. Personal references allow the company to eliminate applicants who may have questionable backgrounds. More significantly, motivations for applying encourage the employer to ask the applicant to make a fuller statement about his or her motivation.

Judging Motivation

According to experienced real estate brokers, the importance of a strong motivation often more than compensates for other suspected personal weaknesses. In this respect, the motivating force may take different forms. In the words of Mary Dot Klock, a sales associate with Klock Company Realtors® in Miami, Florida, her motivation is the desire to win:

> I love to win. I love the feeling of achievement that real estate sales give me. I also like the idea of having a new career. So many women raise their families and after their children leave play tennis or bridge every day. They feel useless. When women are raising children they are stimulated. But cleaning house or playing tennis or bridge is certainly not challenging. They need something else to do.

The initial interview may identify other equally valid reasons for wanting to work as a sales associate. James Mueller, executive vice-president of Miller, Cowherd & Kerver, Inc., Realtors® in Fort Lauderdale, Florida, states that his initial motivation was financial:

> The reason I went into real estate was that I could not see much of a future in the job I had. I had gone to work for a food service corporation immediately after college. I knew that I would be able to earn a salary within a certain

range for a certain number of years. Maybe, some day, I would get a big office and be a vice-president. By that time I would be 45 years old. What was the point of living like that? . . . Money was positively my first motivation.[7]

While money was the initial motivation for James Mueller, others report a personal satisfaction in helping prospects find the required housing. For instance, in handling corporate transfers in which the prospects have three or four days to select a new residence, experienced salespersons take pride in finding the right house for the prospect in two or three days, leaving one day for relaxation and vacation. In other words, the motivation for employment must rest on grounds other than dissatisfaction with the present job (for example, because of the inability to get along with others).

WORKING WITH NEW SALESPERSONS

A critical step is taken the first day the new salesperson reports for assignment. Because the employing broker usually has had several years of experience, there is an inclination for him or her to assume that the new salesperson is ready to deal with prospects after successfully passing the state license examination. When I first started out in real estate, my broker directed me to the state license manual listing rules and regulations and to the listing file. Beyond that I was given no explanation of the company's policies, procedures, or selling techniques. My product knowledge was very minimal. As a result, my association with this firm was short-lived.

In this regard, it has been observed that too many brokers allow their salespersons to drift and after providing a desk, telephone, and a briefing of office procedures, the new salesperson is left alone. For the office that does not have a full-time sales manager who concentrates on training, there is no substitute for personal interest in new salespersons by the employing broker. On this point Percy E. Wagner, of Chicago, Illinois, one of the nations's leading real estate professionals, advises:

> . . . there is nothing like the feeling that the "boss" really wants to help you. If the broker has time to give attention to the newcomer, I believe it would save a lot of dropouts.

Expressing personal interest in the new salesperson begins with the initial indoctrination.

Initial Indoctrination

The initial indoctrination is considered more important than a knowledge of the listing inventory. Time must be spent in ensuring that new employees have at least a minimum understanding of the following:

[7]"Self-motivation: The Power Behind the Sale," *Real Estate Today* (May/June, 1978), pp.4–6.

Company policies and procedures, including services offered by the company.

The current market for houses, including houses listed for sale and active buyers in the market.

Communication techniques covering questioning techniques, listening habits, and proper interviewing methods.

Company recommendations in qualifying buyers.

Preferred methods of presenting an offer.

How to show a house.

Techniques of closing the sale.

The importance of the first point has led the larger firms to write policies and procedures manuals. Some companies have construction, development, management, appraisal, and even financing services. Each of these functions overlap; for example, managing rental houses provides an important source of listings. Similarly, knowledge of the local market enables the new employee to concentrate on buyer-prospects who are most likely to buy.

The introduction to communication skills cannot be overemphasized. Few people newly employed as salespersons have the requisite communication skills to maximize their selling efforts. Preferably, communication skills should be demonstrated by the experiences of other salespersons in dealing with buyers and sellers. Time spent on this topic proves profitable to both the individual and the firm.

Developing Product Knowledge

It is assumed that this instruction is in addition to an organized weekly sales meeting in which listings and prospects are covered. For even with the requisite selling skills, the salesperson must have a superior knowledge of the neighborhood and the houses offered for sale.

One prominent broker advises newly appointed salespersons to inspect five listings each day. At the end of five days the salesperson has a close familiarity with 25 houses. At the end of the first month, the salesperson should have personally inspected and reviewed 100 of the houses in the listing inventory. In fact, it is not uncommon for salespersons specializing in dwelling sales to have personal, detailed knowledge of from 100 to 150 houses.

EMPLOYEE EVALUATION

In part, the evaluation process identifies unproductive employees and helps ensure that salespersons make the best use of their time. Time should be allocated to (1) acquiring new listings, (2) interviewing prospects, (3) showing property, and (4) negotiating offers or counteroffers. The person responsible for the sales staff helps salespersons avoid wasting time on unmarketable houses or unqualified prospects.

Daily Activity Reports

It is assumed that the supervisor knows the daily work schedule of each salesperson. Percy Wagner, in the real estate business since 1928, recommends that every agent submit daily reports. The daily report can be a brief memorandum, but it should show the following:

1. The hours spent on the job.
2. The names and addresses of persons telephoned, interviewed, or written.
3. The purpose of each contact or interview.
4. Results of personal contacts.
5. Special problems encountered.
6. Suggestions, recommendations, and requests for help.
7. Reports, comments, and other relevant matters.
8. Requests for a personal conference with the sales manager or broker.[8]

These reports should be turned in at the end of each day so that the sales manager may review them early the next morning. This review acquaints the management with marketing problems and it serves as a basis for determining the need for personal counsel with individual staff members.

More specifically, daily reports enable the supervisor to observe—on a continuing basis—progress, personal attitudes, and work habits. A review of dress and speech patterns reveals the degree of motivation and the ability to accept disappointment. Personal conferences are recommended on a regular basis to monitor personal performance.

Time Allocation

Most authorities recommend sales quotas. If quotas are established, the salesperson should understand the minimum volume required as qualification to remain employed. Quotas should be increased (if they are reasonable) as a means to stimulate the maximum sales effort.

Another technique is to encourage salespersons to establish weekly, monthly, and annual goals. A record is kept of new listings, listings sold, total transactions, sales volume, and total commissions earned for each month. Realistic goals are put in writing to remind the salesperson of the required progress. In this way, the sales manager counsels the salesperson on methods of best meeting personal goals.

The salesperson is encouraged to allocate time as needed to reach goals. One source recommends that a salesperson's time be allocated as follows:

[8]Harry Grant Atkinson and Percy E. Wagner, *Modern Real Estate Practice* (Homewood, Ill.: Dow Jones-Irwin, Inc., 1974), p. 123.

Class A. Time spent face to face with a party who signs a listing or purchasing agreement.

Class B. Time spent preparing for "A" time—for example, time spent in arranging for listings, making appointments, preparing presentations, and planning negotiations.

Class C. Time spent on other real estate activities such as record keeping, sign posting, writing correspondence, and attending meetings: sales, association, and other real estate conferences.

Class D. Nonreal estate activities such as coffee breaks, personal business, recreation, social and family life.

Time classification reveals time devoted to "nonproductive" activities. If these records are kept, e.g., the daily report, time records, sales records, and progress made in meeting goals and quotas, supervisors will have most of the information they need to make personal evaluations.[9]

Personal Evaluation

In addition to the suggested system of records and reports, each salesperson should have a periodic personal evaluation made by the sales manager or broker. Even though the evaluation is informal, it allows each salesperson to learn his or her strengths and to minimize or overcome weaknesses. The evaluation also indicates to what degree performance is explained by circumstances beyond an individual's control. More than likely, the evaluation will show low performance because of poor use of time, undeveloped skills, poor attitudes, or weak motivation. Finally, the evaluation identifies consistently unacceptable performance which will encourage transfer or separation from the company.

Evaluations are recommended monthly in the case of new employees and at least every six months for more experienced staff. Best results are obtained if the evaluation rests on objective criteria. This requires planning on the part of the supervisor and a rating of the desired qualities of real estate salespersons. A form for evaluation may follow the format listed in Figure 12-3.

If an evaluation form is used, it requires a summation of the daily reports or other records of each salesperson. Note that the evaluator must establish units of measurements to rate each performance. The unit could be a percentage of the activity believed reasonable. For example, a unit of measurement for meeting customer-prospect contacts would be the number of contacts per day, week, or month. The numerical rating would show the degree to which the individual met established quotas. In the end, the overall rating rests on the final judgment of the supervisor.

[9]*Real Estate Sales Handbook,* 7th rev. ed. (Chicago: Realtor® National Marketing Institute of the National Association of Realtors® 1975), p. 46.

FIGURE 12-3.   Salesperson's Evaluation Rating

Job Evaluation	Numerical Rating (0–10)
1. Meeting quotas	
2. Customer satisfaction	
3. Satisfactory reports	
4. Compliance with policy and procedures	
5. Personal attitude	
6. Product/knowledge	
7. Prospecting for listings	
8. Planning	
9. Time utilization	
10. Qualifying prospects	
11. Appearance and manner	
12. Communications effectiveness	
13. Rapport	
14. Showing houses	
15. Closing	
16. Handling objections	

Source: Adapted from William Wachs, *How Sales Managers Get Things Done* (West Nyack, N. Y.: Parker Publishing Company, 1971), p. 93.

During the evaluation interview an individual should be praised for his or her strong points. Then there should be a discussion of the problems that the salesperson has encountered that may affect performance. It should be explained to the salesperson that the evaluation is a regular procedure and is designed to help each salesperson develop the largest possible sales volume— and highest attainable personal income.

POINTS TO REMEMBER

It is fairly clear that the selection of successful salespersons has more importance than listing and selling houses. A person who does not have the proper motivation and requisite abilities wastes his or her own personal time and efforts; in addition, the salesperson absorbs costly resources of the sponsoring broker. For this reason, real estate firms have developed guidelines for more efficient salesperson selection.

The guidelines take the form of formal qualification procedures starting with a qualifying interview and a professional interpretation of qualification questionnaires. The less formal means of selection concentrate on recognizing personal ability and character. Minimum qualification requirements vary among brokers, but most brokers agree that salespersons must have (1) *drive and motivation,* (2) *aggressiveness,* (3) the *ability to handle people,* (4) a *knowledge* of real estate matters, and (5) *self-respect,* which leads the salesperson to take the initiative in completing a sale.

Desirable personal attributes include a high degree of ego drive and empathy. There are also the *essential traits,* which include intelligence, a good attitude, motivation, and empathy, and the *desirable traits,* which include education-mindedness, aggressiveness, being well organized, and industrious.

Recruiting for new employees starts with building a good reputation which encourages applicants to apply on their own initiative. Some organizations regularly solicit applicants from friends, acquaintances, customers, and like contacts. If salespersons from other organizations apply, the firm makes careful inquiry into the reasons for the desired change of employment.

The qualifying interview provides additional information to indicate the degree of motivation and the desirability of undertaking further interviews, testing, and reference verification. After a new salesperson has been hired, training begins with the initial indoctrination of company policy, communication techniques, trends in the local real estate market, and product knowledge.

Special attention is given to employee evaluation, preferably through daily activity reports and studies of the salesperson's time allocation. A personal evaluation tests the degree to which the person has met established goals and quotas. Here, the sales manager helps the individual to minimize or overcome personal weaknesses and to build strong points.

REVIEW QUESTIONS

1. In your view, what guidelines to salesperson selection would you recommend?
2. Describe formal qualification procedures.
3. Compare the real estate salesperson's personality profile to the profile of the general public.
4. What five characteristics typically qualify salespersons?
5. What personal attributes are associated with successful salespersons?
6. What are your recommendations for recruiting new salespersons?
7. What facts are identified in the first qualifying interview?
8. What is the purpose of an employee evaluation?
9. What procedures are recommended for making personal evaluations?

13

Incentive Plans to Increase Sales

Salespersons and their employing broker have mutual interests. No incentive plan will overcome poor relations between salespersons and their employer. Not only must the salesperson observe real estate license laws, acting as agent of the listing seller and serving the buyer-prospect, but the salesperson must also meet the approval of his or her employer and serve the company objectives.

COMPANY OBJECTIVES

The role of salesperson calls for extra effort to provide maximum service to the company and to demonstrate a competitive spirit. But at the same time, the salesperson works toward the company's success. For, in the final analysis, salespersons depend on the services of the broker—supervision, advertising, and public relations. Accordingly, salespersons should be asked to give time to the nondirect selling activities that are necessary to company operations.

Long-Range Goals

In the course of their work, salespersons are inclined to develop negative thoughts which are partly minimized by incentive compensation plans. For instance, salespersons may believe that they are overworked when they consider only the short-term rewards. This view emphasizes company operations from a personal, short-sighted outlook. He or she may not recognize that the real estate business shows variations from year to year or even from one month to the next. Try taking a longer look (a career-oriented attitude); recognize the fact that salespersons depend on a steady, annual growth and a constantly improving firm reputation.

In other words, the salesperson assumes the role of an employee who must contribute to company operations that are mutually beneficial, even though not all selling duties involve direct selling. Salespersons who contribute their fair share of time to company operations meet management approval, thus gaining appreciation and resulting in improved firm operations.

Relationship with Supervisors

The sales supervisor knows more of the salespersons' abilities (and weaknesses) than any one else in the office. The supervisor, who has had considerably more experience, can help direct efforts to maximize sales. For this reason, the relationships between salespersons and the supervisor are critical to good sales performance.

Cooperating with your supervisor means that you prepare the required company reports in detail and turn them in promptly. Developing good relations with your supervisor calls for a willingness to spend extra time in order to increase sales. Cooperation calls for carefully planning your work and it calls for keeping current on important real estate developments. If the relationship between you and your supervisor is a good one, you will more likely seek help on problems beyond your immediate control.

Supervisors use various incentive plans as a means of advancing salespersons relationships with customers, the community, and the firm. Incentive plans involve morale building techniques, special compensation plans, which, in themselves, provide added incentives, and motivation techniques that rely on contests to increase listings and sales. Even though a competitive spirit overrides most aspects of a sales career, real estate offices must develop group loyalty and a spirit of teamwork. Incentive plans and sales contests tend to be more effective if employee morale is good.

INCENTIVE PLANS

Incentive plans such as bonuses and sales contests should not be viewed in total isolation. They are a part of the general problem of managing the sales force. Sales contests in their many forms are more effective if other important aspects of sales management contribute to professional operations. For example, it is presumed that the firm employs only qualified salespersons, that company policies, which have been adequately explained, contribute to stable growth; and that a continuing educational program is part of the office operation. In this environment the various incentive plans help increase sales.

The Sales Management Program

Sales contests and other incentive compensation have certain prerequisites. They are not substitutes for frequent personal contact between the supervisor and salespersons. Each salesperson should be personally known to the sales manager and treated as an individual and as a productive, dedicated sales professional. The sales manager should regularly observe the daily operations of the salespersons, identifying their strengths and helping them to overcome personal weaknesses. The manager should periodically rate the salespersons and communicate with each salesperson daily to review his or her problems and achievements.

Management Sales Support

Management supports sales with more than good supervision, advertising, and sponsorship of incentive compensation plans. Management uses the best techniques in arranging regular *sales meetings,* in providing a workable system of *sales records,* in encouraging attendance at *real estate conventions,* and in helping with company *contests* and *bonus plans.*

Sales meetings coordinate methods to stimulate sales, thus giving salespersons the maximum help available. By exchanging experiences, problems, and courses of action, salespersons are better able to reach solutions and refine their selling techniques. Sales meetings concentrate on "how to do it" issues.

Sales records, including telephone and advertising results, should be tabulated (daily, weekly, and monthly), put in written form, and distributed among all salespersons. Sales managers analyze the information in these reports for the benefit of each salesperson who may then measure his or her personal record against the average sales activity of all salespersons. A system of reports encourages salespersons to plan work, analyze their personal productivity, and measure their personal effectiveness. In this respect, contests encourage performance above normal expectations.

Regular attendance at *real estate conventions* is essential to efficient sales performance. Real estate conventions, as well as the regular meetings of the local real estate board, or state and national meetings, expose staff members to the current and significant issues and to ways of solving common problems.

Contests supplement these management tools by capitalizing on the competitive spirit, a prerequisite to the selling task. Most salespersons tend to be highly competitive, but contests stimulate and motivate them to make even more effort. A special contest, organized on either a group or individual basis, is directed to a singular purpose: to increase sales. Some critics question contests, but if their deficiencies are recognized, they can be used as an added means of managing the sales force.

MORALE BUILDING TECHNIQUES

Morale building originates with management. Although employee participation is essential, certain group activities help develop a spirit of cooperation, for it is vitally important to maintain good personal relations among salespersons, especially since the salesperson selling the house may depend on information provided by the person who secured the listing. The more common activities that build group loyalty include:

1. Office membership in a bowling league.
2. Annual outings planned and conducted by the staff.
3. Christmas parties.
4. Annual bonuses.
5. Flowers and messages to sick employees and their families.
6. Birthday cards.
7. Appropriate recognition of births, marriages, deaths, and other events of employee families.
8. Office bulletins and company publications for employees.
9. Special breakfasts, luncheons, and dinners to celebrate employment anniversaries with appropriate gifts at the end of five, ten, or more years of employment services.[1]

These and similar programs help maintain good relations between the employing broker and the sales staff in addition to building a spirit of cooperation and teamwork. Compensation plans and other motivating techniques tend to be more effective if there is a high level of employee morale.

Compensation Plans

Employee compensation may be adapted to incentive plans based on a system of bonuses. Instead of supporting contests, McKay & Poague, Inc., of Chicago, provides regular incentives in order to increase sales by using a system of additional commission compensation. Salespersons earn additional compensation under the following circumstances:

1. When a sales associate earns $10,000 for the company during a fiscal year, his or her commission is increased an additional 5 percent for every additional sale closed for the balance of the year.
2. When a sales associate produces $15,000 profit for the company, in addition to the additional 5 percent commission, a $1,000 additional commission is paid to the sales associate.
3. The sales associate receives an additional 5 percent for a 10 percent increase in commissions earned over $20,000.

---

[1]Harry Grant Atkinson and Percy E. Wagner, *Modern Real Estate Practice* (Homewood, Ill.: Dow Jones-Irwin, Inc., 1974), p. 100.

Such a plan provides an automatic incentive on a longrange basis. The company pays the usual commission of 50 percent to the salesperson when the salesperson sells his or her own listings. Therefore, a salesperson earning commissions over $20,000 receives 60 percent of the total sales commission for additional commissions earned in the same fiscal year. To be eligible for the added commission, the salesperson must close the sales before the end of the fiscal year.

In addition to this incentive commission schedule, the company gives a dinner at the private country club for the sales associate and his or her spouse who leads in monthly sales. The same courtesy is extended to the salesperson who has secured the most listings in a given month.

To encourage more exclusive listings, in addition to the regular commission, the company gives a five-dollar bill at the weekly sales meeting to the salesperson who has brought in a new exclusive listing during the week. The five-dollar amount may not be too impressive, but it does remind the staff of the need for more exclusive listings and it gives recognition to the salesperson who performs.

A similar philosophy is followed by the Laura McCarthy, Inc., Realtors® of St. Louis, Missouri. Over a five-year period the company developed from a one-office organization of 22 agents to a three-office organization of 60 agents and it increased it sales sixfold. During the annual sales meeting the company revises its bonus structure according to a progressive percentage rate. In a recent year, bonuses for commissions over $9,000 were listed as follows:

Commissions Earned	Percent of Bonus
$ 9,000–$11,999	4
$12,000–$14,999	6
$15,000–$17,999	8
$18,000–$20,999	10
$21,000–$26,999	12
$27,000–$32,999	14
$33,000–$40,000	16

The company chose the bonus plan after the company discovered that its operating costs were increasing at a greater rate than its sales volume. The bonus plan increases the percentage commission awarded as sales increase and in this way the company attempts to overcome the rise in operating costs.

Other firms, as a regular practice, award a plaque to the salesperson who has had the highest monthly sales and to the salesperson who has secured the most listings during the month. Some companies treat the whole staff to lunch or dinner if monthly sales exceed some minimum stated amount.

The William L. Kunkel & Company, Realtors® of Des Plaines, Illinois, gives bonuses to increase the supply of listings. For example, for the month of May salespersons were given gift certificates for new listings according to the following schedule:

Starting May 1st and continuing to the end of May, you will receive bonuses for listings as follows:

Number of Listings	Gift Certificate
First	$10.00
Second	$20.00
Third	$30.00
*Fourth	$40.00
Fifth	$50.00
Sixth and over	$50.00

*An additional cash bonus of $100.00 is paid to all salespeople who produce four (4) or more listings during the month of May.

Call your old customers, call your friends, call your neighbors, call your relatives, canvass your territories, and tell everyone we need good saleable homes in all price ranges.
BUSINESS IS GREAT—GO GET THE LISTINGS!!

The same company gives a $500 check and a turkey to anyone who makes ten sales or listings during October and November. It should be noted that these bonus plans are in addition to the regular sales commission. The bonus plan, which supplements the regular commission schedule, follows certain specific rules:

1. The sales commissions are based on the calendar year.
2. The bonus payments are paid on the commissions paid to the salesperson during the calendar year. Bonus payments based on previous year's earnings are not counted as current earnings.
3. To participate in the plan, salespersons must be working with the company at the end of the year and they must have earned a minimum of $_____ for the year. A new salesperson qualifies if he or she has earned an average of $____ per month from the time of employment.

From the minimum commission schedule, salespersons earn a bonus on the amount earned graduated from 3 percent to 10 percent. The bonus percent increases with an increase in sales; that is, the percentage goes up as the salesperson's volume is reached. These bonuses are paid at a yearly banquet for salespersons and their spouses. At the annual dinner it is recommended that management give special recognition to the three top salespersons and that the outstanding new salespersons (salespersons employed less than one year) be given a special award.

Other Commission Bonuses

Particular attention should be given the commission split, for this method of compensation may, in itself, provide incentives for extra performance. Though practices vary according to local custom, most companies pay 50 percent of the commission for the sale, providing the salesperson listed the property sold. The division of commissions between the "lister" and the salesperson who sold the house depends on the local real estate market, the company's reputation, and advertising policy, among other factors. Some offices reportedly pay as little as 7 percent of the commission for listing new houses. The salesperson who sells under these circumstances receives 43 percent of the commission plus an incentive bonus if the minimum sales quota is met.

It is more common to allocate 20 percent or 25 percent of the total commission for the listing. Depending on the local market, the person who secures a new listing can be rewarded with a higher percentage if the company needs listings. In a buyer's market, in which the company must concentrate on sales and not on listings, a broker tends to pay a greater share to the salesperson who sells and a lesser share to the salesperson who gets the listings.

Some companies prefer to pay the listing fee from the total commission and then divide the remaining commission between the selling person and the company. For example, a $6,000 commission might be divided by granting 15 percent ($900) to the person who secures an exclusive listing; the remaining $5,100 would be split equally between the salesperson and the company.

An alternative plan is to divide the total commission equally between the company and the salesperson. The latter would receive 20 percent for the listing and 30 percent for the sale.

The compensation system must be arranged according to the services provided the staff. More fringe benefits that help salespersons add sales and provide for a higher volume might be more attractive than a larger commission share with fewer helpful services. In short, the compensation system represents an integral part of an incentive plan to increase sales.

SALES CONTESTS

Sales contests have mixed acceptance. Their benefits depend on the purpose of the contest. The three categories of contests are as follows:

1. Contests in which salespersons complete with other salespersons.
2. Contests that organize the staff into competing teams.
3. Contests in which salespersons are individually rewarded and compete only with themselves.

Some firms reject contests and rely on a graduated commission schedule which automatically and regularly rewards extra effort. Other firms use contests to solve a temporary problem, for example, the lack of listings or a temporary sales slump. Still other firms schedule regular contests as part of their long-range plans for a progressive growth in sales. There are probably few firms that do not rely on some form of organized incentive program. A review of contest limitations and benefits will explain the differences in the popularity of contests.

Contest Limitations

A poorly organized contest may create problems which will be difficult to resolve. *First,* salespersons, in shifting their time to the contest, may postpone or neglect other responsibilities such as writing good ads, keeping records, making follow-up calls, and performing other nondirect selling activities.

For instance, contests to increase sales may cause staff members to neglect prospecting for new listings. Conversely, rewards offered for new listings may cause staff members to neglect the selling responsibility. In the case of contests for new listings, salespersons may bring in unsaleable listings, i.e., listings of marginal properties, in poor condition, and in declining neighborhoods which are overpriced.

Second, contests in which rules are loosely drawn may increase hostility among salespersons or between salespersons and the contest supervisor. If the interpretation of contest rules is subject to personal value judgments, feelings of resentment against the favored salesperson or against the authority of the supervisor result in sales *disincentives* and not in incentives that encourage more effort.

Third, contest objectives may be abused. Salespersons may withhold sales or new listings so that they can submit them during the contest period. Sales credited to the contest may fail to be closed after the contest ends. Furthermore, overaggressive acts may create ill will among prospects and clients. Inadvertent mispresentations may be made by overenthusiastic salespersons who pursue short-run contest rewards at the sacrifice of long-term business.

Fourth, repeated reliance on sales contests usually rewards the same few salespersons, thus demoralizing those who lose repeatedly. To prevent this possibility, two remedies are available: (1) Design the contest so that each salesperson wins something. After reaching a certain sales plateau, the individual selects from a list of prizes. When the salesperson reaches the next plateau, he or she qualifies for an additional prize. (2) Form sales teams that generate group spirit among the staff. Try to divide teams evenly according to sales ability.

For example, in the Berg Agency of New Jersey, Jerry Salomone divided branch offices into team A and team B. Beginning on November 1 and ending on December 19, each office gained one point for each sale and two points for selling a Berg listing. A trophy was awarded to the winning team at an annual company-sponsored dinner. When Jerry Salomone announced the contest, he said, "The only difference between a winning team and a losing team is the attitude, enthusiasm, and effort put forth." In order to win over the previous year's contest, 294 points were needed. Jerry Salomone included in the announcement, "Things are looking up this year and we should surpass that mark easily." Either approach removes the adverse effect of coping with those who lose repeatedly.

Another team effort has been developed by E. G. Stassens, Inc., Realtors® of Portland, Oregon. Branch offices are divided into political parties as shown in Table 13-1.

Cash awards are given to winning salespersons at the weekly branch meetings and biweekly group meetings. The winning political party is the party that receives the greatest number of "votes" during the contest period. A bonus of $1,000 is divided among the qualifying participants. To qualify, the salesperson must list a minimum of three properties during the contest.

In addition to the $1,000 awarded to the winning party, qualified salespersons who list a minimum of three properties are allowed to throw darts at balloons which are equal in number to $1\frac{1}{2}$ times the number of listings. Balloons are marked for payments of $5 and $20. One dart is given for each new listing. The person who secures the highest number of listings may throw darts at

TABLE 13-1   Branch Office Teams Organized for Listing Contests by E. G. Stassens, Inc., Realtors®

Party	Branch	Number of Sales-persons	Yearly Total Listings	Monthly Average Listings
I (Whigs)	Oregon City Gateway Hillsboro	43	395	49
II (Tories)	Gresham Sunset Vancouver West Portland	44	377	54
III (Federalists)	Hollywood North Aloha	48	393	49
IV (Independents)	Milwaukie Beaverton Luxury Homes	49	416	52
V (Revolutionists)	Southeast Barbur Midway	50	402	50

balloons priced from $50 to $300 and is paid $15 additional for each listing sold through the end of the year.

Contest Benefits

Some contests provide benefits that are difficult to realize in other ways. Their primary purpose is directed toward increasing earnings—an increase in business shared by the salespersons and the company—but the benefits center around selected objectives.

Salesperson Recognition.   A brief review of the more popular contests shows a fairly significant number of contests that give salespersons special recognition for accomplishing above normal goals. This is a form of ego satisfaction necessary to individual salespersons that goes beyond monetary rewards.

Contests arranged so that salespersons earn recognition for extra effort automatically produce financial rewards and high earnings. These contests provide awards in the form of certificates, plaques, trophies, and newspaper announcements. Within the company, a posted reward roster is another tangible way of recognizing individual contributions. The special recognition provided for salespersons who demonstrate exceptional performance is considered one of the leading benefits of sales contests.

Improved Work Habits.   Since contests reward persons who perform above the norm, contests encourage salespersons to develop more efficient work habits. Contests that award added points for attending sales meetings (and on time), attending educational conferences, and completing real estate courses and the like are cases in point.

Since the bonus or contest award follows only after added effort, the individual gains lasting benefits realized from superior, continuously applied effort. Thus a 60- or 90-day contest may produce permanent benefits because it creates financial rewards for consistently more efficient use of time.

Improved Staff Interpersonal Relations.   Contests organized around teams and contests that allow each salesperson to win—assuming extra effort results—provide financial benefits realized by working together. If the contest brings husbands and wives together socially (at an award banquet, luncheon, or other activity), salespersons tend to be supportive of the efforts of others. They tend to work for the benefit of the group, thus increasing the sales potential of each person.

Adds to Job Satisfaction.   Contests provide an extra reward by breaking the daily routine. Not only does the contest improve morale, but it also makes work more enjoyable, thus offsetting the daily frustrations inevitably encountered by salespersons. Properly organized, the contest adds personal job satisfaction and, at the same time, allows individuals to benefit from their improved performance.

Organization of Contests

Contests often concentrate on the off season: October, November, and December. Since in some regions these are slow selling months, it is advantageous to organize a listing contest at this time in order to generate listings for the following spring. The larger agencies sponsor contests for new salespersons who are given an incentive to compete with salespersons who have more seniority. Preferably, for new employees, the reward system should allow each person to win.

A contest for new salespersons, called the *quick-start contest,* was established by the Berg Agency under the supervision of Joe Cervasio. The announcement of this contest is shown in Figure 13-1.

This contest rewards sales associates for completing a company-sponsored training school and securing a minimum number of new listings. In illustration, to enter the contest a salesperson must have four *90-day listings accepted* by the office manager. Under the 90-day contest, new salespersons are rewarded according to commissions earned, $4,000, $3,000, and $2,000. The merit in this contest is that each salesperson is rewarded according to his or her productive efforts without creating conflict between the new sales associate and the experienced staff.

A variation of the listing contest has been organized by E. G. Stassens, Inc., Realtors®, which awards salespersons for new listings. Rules for the listing contest are shown in Figure 13-2.

The contest awards salespersons 500 points per acceptable listing. Each point is redeemable at one cent. The salesperson who does not have a new listing for the preceding week contributes 50 cents toward the cost of the luncheon given at the end of the contest. The grand prize is paid not to the individual but in the form of a prize that benefits the office. Note that branch managers are encouraged to form teams within the office in order to promote "more team cooperation" and "competitive spirit."

The McClennan Company has sponsored a contest for residential salespersons. Credit is given for new listings or sales. Sales or listings gained in a three-month period entitle the salesperson to a wardrobe selected from a wholesale catalog according to the following schedule.

1. One transaction that closes during the contest period will win a $50 wardrobe.
2. Two transactions closed during the contest period will win a $200 wardrobe.
3. Three or more transactions during the contest period will win a $500 wardrobe.

In planning a contest, John E. Cyr advises that sales contests should have simple and easily understood rules and that they should be limited to

FIGURE 13-1. Quick-Start Contest for New Sales Associates

This is to formally introduce you to the "Quick-Start" contest for New Sales Associates. We at Berg are particularly excited about what this can do in the way of assuring your future success in the Real Estate Industry. An exciting array of prizes will be awarded to those who qualify in the three categories identified below. All of the Managers, Regional Managers, Jerry Salomone, our President, and Kenneth Berg, our Chairman, will be watching your progress closely. So, let's take a look at the rules of the contest:

1. In order to qualify, the new Sales Associate must have completed *all* of the classes in the New Sales Associates Training School.

   A. If the associate has not finished with his assigned class, he makes up the days in the next class (and the next class *only*), and will enter *that* class's contest.

   B. Any business achieved during the class *you complete* is counted in the contest.

2. Weekly Activity Reports, initialed by your Manager, and signed by you, MUST BE SUBMITTED EACH WEEK OF THE CONTEST (to be mailed on Monday following the Sunday that ends the week) to: Mr. Joseph Cervasio, The Berg Agency, 75 Lincoln Highway (Route 27), Iselin, N.J. 08830. If you are out sick, please note this information on your Activity Report and send it to our attention.

3. In order to qualify, you must have *written* four 90-day listings, each accepted by your Manager.

4. The contest lasts for 90 days after your last class. (However, as noted above, business achieved during the class from which you *graduate* is counted.)

5. To win a first-place prize, you must have $4,000 in production commissions written in process; a second-place prize, $3,000 in process, and a third-place prize, $2,000 in process.

The prizes are:

First Place	*VALUE*
1. The "Lead the Field" Motivational Cassette Tape Program by Earl Nightingale	$150
2. A Cassette Tape Recorder	$45
3. A Calculator	$60
4. A Polaroid Camera	$66
5. An attractive Plaque for your Office	—
Total Value	$321

Second Place

Choice of any two of the above or the "Lead the Field" Motivational Cassette Tape Program by Earl Nightingale.

Third Place

A Calculator

A Class Progress report will be sent to all Managers, Regional Managers, and Contestants each month of the contest. Let's begin to test ourselves now. "Lead the Field" from the start!

Source: The Berg Agency, Iselin, New Jersey.

FIGURE 13-2. A Listing Contest Organized By E. G. Stassens, Inc., Realtors®

1. Contest to run 60 days consecutively.

2. Listings are to be 90 day exclusive or longer.

3. All listings will count except lots or land.

*4. If lots or land are sold during contest they will receive full listing credit.

5. All contestants must obtain a minimum of three listings during the contest period to qualify as a contestant.

6. After qualifying, all listings will count for full point credit.

7. Salesmen to receive 500 points per acceptable listing.

8. The company will issue prize checks weekly to be distributed at weekly sales meetings by Branch Managers.

9. Prize checks to be redeemable at the rate of one cent per point in the Dahnken's Catalog.

10. Winners may spend the checks at will or accrue to end of contest.

*11. In addition, each Branch will form two teams, with the losing team buying lunch for the winning team at the end of the contest. Each Tuesday when prize checks are awarded, the salespeople who do not have a listing for the last week will contribute fifty cents to a kitty, with the amount collected to apply to the cost of the luncheon at the end of the contest.

12. A secret Grand Prize will be the object of a treasure hunt to be conducted by the branches during the contest.

13. The top branch each week will be given a clue to the treasure.

14. Grand Prize to be something useful to the branch, i.e., AM/FM Stereo.

15. Grand Prize winner to be announced at end of contest.

16. Weekly top office to be determined by ratio of number of salesmen to listings obtained.

17. Grand Prize winner and winning team to be announced at General Meeting following contest.

*18. Item eleven not mandatory but strongly recommended to all branch managers to help create more team cooperation and competitive spirit.

19. Establish reporting system to keep all offices informed daily of individual progress.

20. Pre-manufacture and distribute score boards which are to be kept up daily.

21. Score sheets to be turned in at end of contest.

*Indicates changes.

a short period, say 90 days. Contests for short periods are more easily sustained and are more effective because the rewards are earned relatively quickly.[2]

Note also that contests can be adapted to the current problems of the office. The main purposes of contests promote:

[2]John E. Cyr, *Training and Supervising Real Estate Salesmen* (Englewood Cliffs, N.J.: Prentice-Hall, Inc., 1973), p. 90.

1. New listings during off selling months.
2. Higher sales volume.
3. Combination of increased sales and listings.
4. Sales and listings among new employees.
5. Sales in particular neighborhoods (or branch offices).

Contest rules can be structured so that salespersons are rewarded for attending sales meetings or performing other office duties. Points may be given for these activities considered essential to the sales effort. An office that wants more exclusive listings to advertise or that needs to close sales within a shorter time period or that needs to improve advertising writing may design contests covering these activities. Team contests are useful in improving sales or listings in a particular neighborhood branch office. If sales are consistently declining, a sales contest may reverse the downward sales trend.

Minimum Contest Requirements

Note that contests reward performance for only "above normal" achievements. Therefore, contest minimums are set above what salespersons are normally expected to achieve. Note that in some of the examples cited, salespersons do not qualify as participants unless they have met a certain minimum quota, i.e., three minimum listings or three closings during the contest period.

In addition, best results are achieved if rewards can be earned by using extra effort but not superhuman effort. The contest should reward activity that leads to personal profit for the salesperson and adds to the company's earnings. Rewards may be either in the form of money or personal luxuries such as cameras, radios, clothing, or the like. Plaques, trophies, and certificates are popular awards because they give added personal recognition in addition to monetary rewards.

The best contests produce the maximum number of winners. Particularly in the team-oriented contest, members of the group gain mutual rewards by the extra group effort. Ideally, everyone who works a little harder gains personal rewards or recognition.

The Long-Range Plan

Contests should have long-range objectives. Contests should not be considered a one-time operation to overcome a temporary problem such as securing new listings. Contests should be adapted to different times of the year and according to variations in the local real estate market. They should be adapted to the training program and to new employees. They should be skillfully planned so that they improve employee morale, continually calling for extra effort in times of declining business. They should also develop group spirit.

Forecast Objectives.   Such a long-term program forces the company to develop long-term objectives in which contests add to other programs of the company such as advertising, hiring new employees, or expanding branch offices. Therefore, the first task is to forecast reasonable objectives, say over the next five years. Real estate services and office operations should be planned over the next five years and goals and quotas should be set for each year. The plan for the current year should show forecasts by quarters and months.

Budget Contests.   Budgets for office operations should include planned contests. Out-of-pocket costs, such as promotional materials, supplies, prizes, awards, entertainment, and administrative costs above the normal costs of sales management, should be included. Contest costs should be compared with forecasts of contest results. Here contests must be identified according to their purpose, method of compensation or rewards, and expected staff participation.

If contests are planned in detail, repetitious contests are avoided and the contests are directed to critical company issues. Planned contests might be directed to new listings, improved work habits, rewards for educational achievements, and increased sales volumes. Keeping records of contest results and comparing these records with planned objectives make it easier to change contest rules, compensation, and administration of the contest.

The staff must be aware of the objectives of the contest. Management should announce the contest, giving details and proposed objectives, and probable earnings which are realistic expectations resulting from contest participation.

POINTS TO REMEMBER

Incentive plans promote company objectives. They further long-range goals and they improve relationships with supervisors. Commissions, bonuses, and sales contests, however, are not substitutes for personal contact between supervisors and salespersons. Instead, they coordinate management sales support in the form of sales meetings, sales records (and their interpretation), and training and educational programs, including real estate conventions. A review of selected bonus plans indicates that incentives and rewards apply only to above average performance. These bonus plans stimulate sales activity during temporary sales slumps and they help resolve company problems, for example, an inadequate number of saleable listings.

Sales contests have certain limitations; they may misdirect time from noncontest responsibilities such as writing classified ads, keeping records, making follow-up calls, and promoting a favorable company reputation. Further, misinterpretation of contest rules increases hostility and acts as a disincentive to more work. In other cases, contest objectives have been abused, i.e., sales are deferred until the contest period and overenthusiastic contestants misrepresent their listings. Poorly administered contests have the effect of rewarding the same persons and demoralizing those who lose repeatedly.

If these objections are minimized, contests create certain benefits: They give salespersons recognition for extra work, they tend to improve work habits, they promote improved staff interpersonal relations and, in other respects, increase job satisfaction.

In organizing a contest, most offices sponsor contests during the off-season or, alternatively, they design a contest for new employees. Preferably, contests reward performance for only above normal achievements.

Best results are obtained if rewards are given for extra but not superhuman effort. The better contests allow each person to earn rewards through extra work: Contestants compete only with themselves and not with each other. And the final point: Contests follow long-range objectives and are a means of supplementing the company's other selling programs. Ideally, contests are budgeted on a regular, recurring basis.

REVIEW QUESTIONS

1. What is the main purpose of an incentive plan?
2. In what way can management support the sales effort?
3. What would you advise doing to build staff morale?
4. Explain how compensation plans provide for automatic incentives.
5. Show how real estate commissions and their calculations provide incentives for extra performance.
6. Explain the three main kinds of sales contest.
7. What are the recognized contest limitations? Do you agree? Why or why not?
8. Explain four contest benefits.
9. How would you adapt sales contests to long-range objectives?

14

Sales Motivation: The Sales Meeting

The skillfully conducted sales meeting serves many company functions. An essential part of sales supervision, the sales meeting is especially helpful in motivating salespersons. In this respect, many brokers consider the sales meeting one of the more effective sales management tools. This chapter discusses selling motivation, sales management tools, sales meetings, and role playing.

SELLING MOTIVATION

The sales meeting supports personal motives for selling. It stimulates individuals and it helps to overcome poor selling techniques.

Salesperson Wants

Usually, the salesperson works to maximize personal income. He or she has a need for a minimum income to meet the costs of living or a need for a secure and stable income to maintain his or her lifestyle. Accordingly, real estate salespersons depend on incentives—incentives that provide direct rewards for good selling performance.

Since most salespersons work on a straight commission, they benefit from a compensation plan that pays for work largely under their own control. And for the most part, straight commissions tend to be proportionate to individual performance and sales volume. To be sure, real estate sales vary according to the local economy, mortgage credit availability, national economic conditions, and the like. Yet, with a system of incentive bonuses, commissions, and contests, individuals tend to be rewarded according to their hard work, training, and skill.

Advantages of Straight Commissions.   In contrast to a straight salary, a straight commission is paid for job performance only. Under a straight salary, the employer buys the individual's time. Working for straight commissions may, in itself, provide the highest motivation since *personal accomplishments are paid according to productivity*—the number of listings or sales completed. Unusually hard work or superior performance may be rewarded by commission rates that are progressive, that is, once sales reach a minimum volume, the percentage share earned by the salesperson increases. However, even the constant rate commission tends to increase pay proportionately with increased performance.

Clearly, straight commissions provide strong selling incentives. The higher the sales volume, the greater the commissions. Under commissions, therefore, salespersons are given *considerable freedom on the job,* a feature that often attracts the better salesperson.

Straight commissions may be varied to meet management purposes. Bonuses, contests, and compensation plans may be varied to increase the number of listings or to stimulate more selling effort during a sales slump or off-season sales. Commission payments adapt easily to different groups; for example, they give added incentives to the new salesperson. Since management controls the selling costs, such as advertising and office expense, selling costs may be more easily budgeted under commission plans. For instance, if the income of the company and salespersons increases or decreases with total sales, budgets may be revised to meet the changing market.

Disadvantages of Straight Commissions.   Straight commissions *provide minimum management control over staff.* The real estate broker, unlike the sales manager of a retail store, has much more difficulty controlling salespersons because they work much like independent business persons. This reason alone warrants frequent meetings to explain company interests, train, advise, and review sales reports.

Straight commissions are subject to considerable fluctuation. In large measure, this disadvantage is offset by training and superior management. There is also the related danger that salespersons working solely for commissions would neglect nondirect selling jobs. Moreover, disputes may arise over who is entitled to commissions. Disputes over commissions are usually settled through local real estate boards, however.

Reasons for Selling Failure

For the moment, let us assume that the salesperson has met the minimum job qualifications, is reasonably motivated, and is not limited by personal circumstances. The final determination of job success then hinges on management efficiency. Management efficiency, in turn, is judged on the way management reduces friction between salespersons and management.

Selling success (it is assumed that the person selected has been properly screened) clearly depends on management functions. Though not the sole means of motivating, guiding, and training staff, sales meetings remove some of the main frictions between the sales staff and the sales manager or real estate broker. In a study of 405 sales managers, 41 percent listed poor communications as causes of friction between salespersons and the company. Although the survey covered nonreal estate salespersons, the findings seem equally valid for real estate sales. These items are summarized in Table 14-1.

TABLE 14-1. Leading Causes of Friction Between Salespersons and the Company

Cause	Percent
Poor communication	41
Unfair compensation	21
Weak leadership	19
Disagreement with company policies	18
Reports	17
Inadequate recognition of performance	17
Personality clashes	16
Management's ignorance of sales persons problems	15
Poor cooperation	13
Salespersons not company oriented	11
Lack of proper training	11
Lack of initiative	11

Source: Charles Atkinson Kirkpatrick, *Salesmanship*, 6th ed. (Cincinnati: Southwestern Publishing Company, 1976), p. 555.

It is seen in Table 14-1 that poor communication heads the list by a wide margin, a point that may be overcome by holding weekly sales meetings. Unfair compensation is not too relevant in a straight commission payment plan. Sales meetings help minimize the complaints about weak leadership, personality clashes, management's ignorance of salespersons' problems, poor cooperation, lack of initiative, and salespersons who are not company oriented. Hence, the sales meeting should be integrated as part of the tools available to sales supervisors.

SALES MANAGEMENT TOOLS

Since most real estate salespersons work on straight commission, the central problem is to encourage salespersons to make effective use of their time. And since they work relatively independently, the main emphasis is on persuasion: persuasion to plan work, observe the code of ethics, and follow company policy. To carry out these objectives and give each salesperson a strong motive to sell, management relies on a fairly limited number of management tools. Among these tools, sales meetings play a central role in guiding sales activity.

Directing Salespersons

Personal communication heads the list of ways to guide salespersons. Personal contacts keep the sales manager informed on the activities of the sales staff, especially the new employees. Knowing individual strengths and weaknesses helps management form in-house training programs and select the main topics for sales meetings. Sales meetings assist the staff in advertising effectively. The salesperson benefits from the supervisor's personal observation of his or her daily sales performance. Preferably, these daily evaluations are made in frequent personal interviews with the sales staff. Although they are time-consuming, there is no substitute for these personal contacts between the supervisor and salespersons. In this way, the sales supervisor learns of individual problems, either personal or job-oriented.

Sales contests, which are treated in a separate chapter, are more specific. They are adapted to the overall sales objective and provide additional motivation. Contests that are directed to a single purpose, run for a limited length of time, and have easily understood rules promote mutual objectives.

The most important tool of all is the sales meeting: the regular meeting of the local real estate board, the real estate convention, and the monthly meeting of other real estate organizations. Although they are mostly educational and very beneficial, professional meetings do not substitute for sales meetings, which are more frequent and far more adapted to selling.

The importance of personal recognition should not be overlooked. Salespersons functioning in a highly competitive field require support in the form of peer recognition and approval by superiors. Sales commissions override other considerations, but bonuses, certificates, and other organizational awards are also important. The recognition of accomplishments and superior performance all represent available management tools.

Evaluating Performance

Real estate brokers would be remiss in their responsibilities if a program of evaluating performance was not an integral part of motivating salespersons. The evaluation rests on personal contacts which give a subjective insight into individual performance. And while commissions measure the sales record, the reports required by management explain why selected salespersons experience problems in closing sales.

Some offices require a daily time sheet showing management how each salesperson spends his or her time. In addition, a daily log of telephone calls, another useful report, helps management determine if salespersons could improve telephone techniques. For instance, suppose the telephone log indicates a low appointment rate. This means that the individual should practice the recommended ways of handling telephone calls.

The evaluation must not concentrate on sales volume alone. The quality of performance must also be studied. Here the sales manager is more concerned with the personal activities of salespersons in promoting company good will, developing repeat prospects, maintaining a professional appearance, and keeping the automobiles clean and in good repair. Personal habits should be judged impartially with respect to how salespersons conform to behavior that maximizes long-range company goals.

The need for sales meetings that guide real estate salespersons is indicated by Table 14-2. The table summarizes the various roles of a salesperson and itemizes the salesperson's behavior patterns in each category. Note that the behavior pattern may vary from the ideal. For instance, bypassing your supervisor when you want something in a hurry or breaking rules if you think it is in the best interest of the company are behavior patterns that can be remedied by sales meeting programs.

SALES MEETINGS

Primarily, sales meetings show salespersons how to maximize the value of their time. The range of topics could cover each chapter in this book and more.

Weekly Sales Meetings

As a general rule, though using various formats, weekly meetings concentrate on three general topics:

1. Reviewing listings.
2. Reviewing current market trends.
3. Increasing sales motivation.

The listings review circulates new information on the properties listed. The reasons why specific listings have not sold are discussed and additional information on new listings received during the week is introduced. Current

TABLE 14-2. The Role of a Real Estate Salesperson

The Role of a Salesperson	Salesperson Behavior Patterns
Observe company rules	1. Use personal discretion in interpreting company rules that apply to a particular sale rather than checking with your sales manager.
	2. Bypass your supervisor when you want something in a hurry.
	3. Accept judgment of your sales manager as final.
	4. Break rules if you think it is in the best interest of the company.
Cooperate with others	1. Join with another salesperson to call on a difficult prospect.
	2. Work as a team with other salespersons in the same office.
	3. Work on company advertising with another salesperson.
Exercise independence	1. Set your own work hours independently as long as you are meeting the sales quota.
	2. Be left alone by your sales manager unless you need help.
	3. Determine the way you do your selling.
Support company goals	1. Have the final say about a work assignment.
	2. Ask your sales manager for help in closing a difficult sale.
	3. Ask your sales manager to overcome difficult sellers and buyer-prospects.
	4. Be consulted on office decisions that affect you.
	5. Determine your sales quota.

market trends, on occasion, might be covered by guest speakers such as local officials, mortgage bankers, savings and loan officers, attorneys, contractors and builders, or others willing to talk on informative subjects.

Some companies devote one meeting a month to sales education. Sales education might cover company policy, sales forecasts, and a review of preferred practices in gaining listings, new prospects, and other aspects of the selling process.

More specifically, outside speakers and supervisory staff arrange sales meetings to review:

The latest information on listings.
Trends in the local real estate market.
Company sales policies.

Selling skills.

Methods of improving effective work patterns.

Salespersons should have up-to-date knowledge on listings and how they conform to current markets. New tax appraisals, new sources of mortgage credit, changes in the interest rate, new companies moving in, and major construction likely to affect the housing market, for example, a new shopping center, are typical topics discussed at sales meetings.

Salespersons must be reminded of the company policies on sharing commissions with outside firms, trade-in housing plans, homeowner warranties, and advertising budgets. Sales meetings should periodically reintroduce topics, such as effective listening techniques, interviewing, meeting prospect objectives, proven ways to close a sale, negotiating counteroffers, and a host of other related topics.

Weekly sales meetings provide the best way to improve—on a continuing basis—sales performance. It would be difficult to overemphasize a review of methods to use time efficiently—a topic deemed especially important to a staff compensated by straight commissions. Since salespersons must work independently on prospects with minimum supervision, they require frequent support in devoting the necessary time to direct selling.

Above all, sales meetings should be conducted on a positive note. At all costs, controversial discussions that lead to hostility, arguments, and further misunderstanding must be avoided. If the meeting develops in this way, the meeting should be terminated and the problem should be handled on an individual basis. Other purposes of the sales meetings are as follows:

1. They allow management to motivate salespersons at least once a week by providing progress reports, new ideas, or listing prospects.
2. They keep salespersons informed on new listings, financing, and changes in listing prices.
3. They bring the sales force together, making it unnecessary to contact each individual to discuss new programs, common problems, and new ideas for advertising, office procedures, and sales campaigns.

The Sales Meeting Agenda

It is strongly advised that a well-planned agenda be followed. A planned agenda does not bore the staff but stimulates and adds to the prospects for increasing sales next week. The planned agenda provides for stable meetings that follow a predictable pattern, but not every meeting has to follow the same format. Special programs that break the usual format should be planned in order to create maximum interest. Special care should be taken to time the meeting so that the objectives of the meeting can be accomplished in the time allowed. The agenda could be formed around the more common topics recommended for the weekly sales meeting.

Review Past Sales.   If the salesperson has closed a sale during the past week, ask for comments on how he or she made the final closing, the skills used to negotiate the final offer, or the financing procedures that were adapted to buyer and seller circumstances.

Discuss a New Listing.   The person responsible for the listing should highlight the points that would be significant to the buyer. If a committee has reviewed the listing and its price, a report by the committee may lead to a quick sale if the listing is properly presented in the weekly meeting.

Cover Current Mortgage Trends.   Guest speakers from finance or government agencies would be helpful here. Time should be devoted to a specific selling tool. If someone has knowledge of new publications or periodicals he or she feels would be important to office policy, these should be recommended for discussion at later meetings.

The Sales Meeting Format

Sales meetings should cover the necessary topics, but there is no reason to use the same format at every meeting because the meetings will become monotonous and dull if that is the case. There are many different ways to present information to the group and there are many instructional aids that promote the purpose of the sales meeting.

The meeting must start on time. If there are habitual late comers, steps should be taken to avoid interruptions. The audience should be made comfortable. The audience must be able to hear the speaker. There should be proper lighting, training material should be tested for burned-out bulbs, and other equipment should be tested to make sure that it is operating correctly.

Regardless of the format adopted, there are certain preliminaries that should be followed. After the meeting has been opened, the person leading the meeting

Welcomes those in attendance.
Introduces guests and newcomers.
Makes announcements about the next meeting and other announcements.
States the objective of the meeting.
Follows the agenda.
Observes time limits closely.
Thanks participating guests.
Closes the meeting on a positive note.

The body of the meeting is devoted to the main objective and the presentation is adapted to the size of the group. Generally speaking, the body of the meeting will have one of five presentations: (1) a lecture, (2) a discussion, (3) a demonstration of new products or procedures, (4) audio-visual material, and

(5) role playing. Preferably, each week is varied with one of these presentations in order to give weekly meetings increased interest.

The Lecture Technique.   In some circles the lecture is considered the least effective way of teaching. It is especially ineffective if the lecturer is inexperienced. If the lecture is to be informative, it should concentrate on a few main points. It should be brief and it should be supplemented with points written on a flip-over chart or chalkboard or with handouts. Nothing dulls the enthusiasm so much as a rambling, descriptive, poorly organized lecture. Look for a lecturer who has an attention-getting introduction, an organized talk that has a theme, well-developed main points, and a brief summary.

The Discussion Meeting.   The discussion session may be adapted to many objectives. The group may be asked to present views on a sales problem: "How should we increase our listings?" "What are your suggestions for improving the effectiveness of our ads?" "Are we using the best telephone interviewing techniques?"

Alternatively, the discussion could start with a presentation of a case study that demonstrates a recommended selling technique. Then the salespersons could be asked to comment on which points were effectively made and what procedures they would recommend as alternatives.

In a discussion meeting it is important to close with a general statement of the principles that were emphasized in the discussion. The principles will be learned more easily if the discussion involves all participants. The group leader should direct questions to those who have not volunteered discussion. A few persons should not be allowed to dominate the discussion. Long-winded discussions can be cut off by asking, "Let's hear from someone else on this point," or "How do the rest of you feel about this point?" If someone brings up points that are not suggested by the agenda, the leader of the meeting should ask that person to talk to him or her about these points after the meeting.

Audio-Visual Equipment.   Public libraries in most metropolitan areas lend films, slides, tapes, and other materials significant to the business community. The National Association of Realtors® and its affiliates have prepared numerous visual aids that are available to member organizations to help improve sales ability. If a firm has a policy to demonstrate or some techniques to emphasize, it is relatively easy for the firm to obtain an overhead projector for group presentation of a main point or procedure.

If audio-visual equipment is used, the meeting should close with a brief discussion of the points raised and how these relate to the salespersons' individual work. The audience should be reminded of the main points made in the presentation and there should be a discussion on how these points apply to their office.

ROLE PLAYING TO IMPROVE SELLING

The availability of television equipment and video tape that allows immediate playback on a television screen provides an extremely effective method of improving interpersonal relations. The larger firms might even justify purchasing this equipment. Since video equipment includes portable TV cameras that operate from battery packs or a car cigarette lighter, the equipment has considerable flexibility, thus justifying an investment for training purposes. Some companies use color equipment for preliminary screening of houses for prospects. Most major cities have firms that rent equipment on a daily or hourly basis.

Role playing may assist in developing favorable interpersonal relations among real estate salespersons. Figure 14-1 shows six interpersonal relations encountered by salespersons, ranging from the employer-broker to the seller-principal and buyer-prospects. The salesperson has direct relations with each of the six categories shown in Figure 14-1, but each of these parties has interpersonal relations with each other that include the real estate salesperson. Role playing using audio-video equipment helps salespersons develop effective interpersonal relations with each of these groups.

FIGURE 14-1. Interpersonal Relations Shared By Real Estate Salespersons

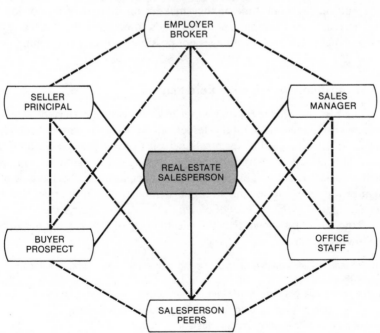

The Purpose of Role Playing

Audio-video equipment permits participants to play assigned roles, which are recorded on television video tape and which can be played back immediately. This lets salespersons see themselves as others see them—a very powerful learning technique.

Undesirable nonverbal communication techniques, such as nervous body twitching, poor eye contact, poor listening, or personal nervousness, are readily detected. Roles are selected that demonstrate how salespersons handle a specific issue. In this way, salespersons see their own limitations for themselves. Therefore, it is usually unnecessary to call weaknesses to their attention.

Role playing is also supportive. Good techniques are demonstrated and become obvious to the group and tend to be copied. In sum, role playing:

1. Simulates actual experience encountered in selling houses.
2. Demonstrates preferred ways to sell houses.
3. Allows participants to experiment in handling actual problems without being penalized for mistakes.
4. Gives participants practice in refining sales techniques.
5. Identifies personal problems that would be undetected under normal selling situations.

In other words, role playing gives salespersons practice in selling techniques and, at the same time, if they make a mistake, they do not lose the sale. Therefore, the learning experience tends to be accelerated. Clearly, role playing provides training advantages not possible under other teaching procedures.

Suggestions for Effective Role Playing

The best use of role playing is not to demonstrate preferred techniques by the more experienced, skillful salesperson. Role playing can be much more effective: It must be used by each salesperson to learn preferred selling techniques. This can be accomplished only by letting each person see himself or herself in selected roles. Through group participation salespersons learn to recognize their weaknesses and strengths demonstrated in the roles that have been selected. *It is the individual playing the role who learns the most.*

Experience has shown that the effectiveness of role playing is increased by following certain rules:

1. Preselect cases adapted to actual selling scenarios encountered by salespersons.
2. Keep the role playing demonstration short—from five to ten minutes.
3. Design role playing for learning a single, preselected technique.
4. Require all salespersons to participate in a "role."

5. Keep the role playing group small—10 to 25 persons is ideal. Organize several smaller groups if the sales staff is larger.
6. Do not be overly critical of role playing participants. They will quickly observe their mistakes during the playback.
7. Make positive comments on preferred techniques used by the role players; offer alternative suggestions on ways of relating to the prospect or seller.

In the ideal role playing plan, a case is presented that emphasizes a specific problem, for example, meeting a given prospect objection. One person is selected to play the role of the prospect and another person is selected to play the role of the salesperson. After the role is filmed, the group is shown the playback for comment. The group is asked to comment on the salesperson's questioning techniques and the other ways that the salesperson handled the prospect. Everyone in the group must play a role. In this way, the group tends to be supportive and undue personal criticism is avoided.

Introducing Role Playing

The first time role playing is introduced, participants will be reluctant to act before a camera for a group showing. Yet it is necessary that each person act naturally. The supervisor of the role playing session should do everything possible to relax the participants. The first presentation should be a demonstration showing how the supervisor proposes to develop selling skills.

The supervisor should take the role of a salesperson and have one of the sales associates act as a property owner. The supervisor, in the role of the salesperson, does exactly what the recommended procedures say not to do. For example, the supervisor and the sales associate act out the following scene: A prospect enters the office. The salesperson is sitting with his feet on the desk. While the salesperson and the prospect are talking, the salesperson frequently blows smoke in the prospect's face, rudely interrupts the prospect, and deliberately makes the prospect wait while he answers the telephone and fills out forms. The salesperson makes misrepresentations and overstatements and generally demonstrates incompetent performance.

When this scene is played back, the group relaxes because each person understands that the tape is not a threatening device but a valuable instruction tool. The first case selected should be played by the more experienced, outgoing persons because they will be less sensitive to group criticism.

As the role playing progresses, added interest could be developed by rating each person on a scale from 1 to 10 and asking the group to vote on the presentation. These points should be accumulated and then divided by the number voting in order to produce an average rating. The person who earns the highest point value in the same role playing scene could be presented a reward at the end of the series.

Role Playing Organization

Role playing using video tape recording equipment is ideally adapted to helping salespersons refine their selling techniques. The sales supervisor may use this procedure to develop skills in areas that need attention. Some of the more popular role-playing topics would include the following:

Qualifying prospects.
Negotiating an offer below the listing price.
Telephone interviewing techniques.
Listing a "for sale by owner."
Negotiating an exclusive listing.
Meeting prospect objections.

Cases may be specially structured to give practice in listening, in interpreting nonverbal behavior, or in the effective use of probing questions. Before the role-playing sessions begin, the participants should review communication skills, interviewing techniques, and recommended company suggestions for responding to prospects and sellers. The purpose of role playing is to learn recommended techniques in simulated, real-life situations.

Preselected Cases. Suppose that listing a "for sale by owner" house is the case selected for practice. Role participants should be given a typed case that describes the roles they will play. For example, the salesperson playing the part of the seller would be identified as one who recently placed a want ad to sell a $75,000, four-bedroom, three-bathroom home. Role playing begins by filming the salesperson's visit to the home of the seller. The seller states (on camera), "I want to save the real estate commission." From this point each participant acts out his or her role as he or she would in actual situations. The salesperson tests his or her technique before the sound and video equipment and the other party makes the objections commonly encountered in the field.

After the role is played for five or ten minutes, the scene is played back. If a good point has been made or if someone says that the salesperson could have responded in a slightly different manner, the recording should be stopped and there should be a discussion.

One special advantage of the recording lies in this ability to stop the presentation, ask for discussion, or repeat the scene for discussion purposes. With repeated role playing by different persons in the audience, the group soon learns how to handle a real-life situation which is designed to be as realistic as possible.

Unknown Cases. An alternative method, one that is recommended once the participants have gained more experience in role playing, is to develop a sales problem that is unknown to one of the role-playing parties.

In illustration, suppose that your group wants to develop skills in negotiating for an exclusive listing with a seller who prefers an open listing. To establish this case, send the person playing the salesperson's role out of the room and then instruct the other participant to act out the part of a seller who is willing to give only an open listing. Provide the acting seller with the facts that he or she will argue: "By giving an open listing I have several brokers selling my property." "An open listing will give me the highest price." "I will sell the property faster with an open listing." Add other arguments that agree with your actual experience.

The person playing the seller's role will be given these questions in advance. Once the party assuming the role of the seller has been properly briefed, call the salesperson and briefly explain that he or she is talking to a seller who wants to give an open listing instead of an exclusive listing. The role playing (and camera) start with the introduction of the salesperson at the home of the seller.

Again, after ten minutes of role playing, replay the tape, stopping the tape at each point that the salesperson meets the objections of the owner in granting an exclusive listing. Ask for group comment on the good points demonstrated by the salesperson. Discuss alternative ways in which the salesperson might have handled the interview. At every opportunity comment on recommended communication techniques, including gestures, facial expressions, and body movements.

The value of this presentation lies in the extemporaneous reaction of the salesperson. There is no chance to prepare in advance. If the proper response has not been learned, it will be revealed during the presentation and the salesperson will concentrate much harder on learning to apply his or her arguments.

Role Playing to Improve Communication Skills

If the number of appointments from your telephone calls is dropping or if the number of sales closed from office visits seems low and declining, the problem might lie in interviewing techniques. Role playing is the ideal way to learn the use of probing questions and listening habits.

Suppose that your group wants to study interviewing techniques in qualifying prospects who responded to your advertisement. Structure the role so that the person playing the role of the prospect forces the salesperson to utilize the recommended communication skills. Let the prospect ramble on and evade the salespersons questions and see how the salesperson leads the prospect back to the central problem. Or suppose that the prospect is evasive about his or her financial status. See how the salesperson gets the required information. Or suppose that the prospect is buying his or her first house and describes a dream castle. The prospect wants a $75,000 house but has the financial means to buy a $40,000 house in an older neighborhood.

If every salesperson practices selected sales situations, he or she will rapidly learn these skills in a pleasant, nonrisk environment.

POINTS TO REMEMBER

Salespersons work to maximize personal income. Under the straight commissions system, salespersons are paid according to their productivity. This form of compensation gives considerable freedom on the job, but it gives management minimum control over staff time. Because of this, there is often poor communication between management and salespersons which causes friction between the employer and staff. Sales meetings provide a means of overcoming these deficiencies.

Weekly sales meetings generally concentrate on a review of listings, current market trends, and various means of motivation. In addition, the sales meeting keeps salespersons informed on new listings and brings the sales force together to discuss new programs and common problems. Ideally, the sales meeting has an agenda and follows a standard meeting format.

Sales meetings normally follow one of five methods of procedure: the lecture, discussion, demonstrations, audio-visual presentations, or role playing.

Role playing allows participants to play assigned roles, which are recorded on television video tape for immediate playback. Salespersons in reenacting a sales situation see themselves as others see them. Sales techniques are rapidly learned because the method gives practical experience in recommended selling techniques. Role playing allows for trials without penalties for mistakes, such as a lost sale.

The most effective use of role playing requires that the cases actually be adapted to selling scenarios. The cases are selected for demonstrating or practicing a single selling method. Each staff member should participate in playing the various roles.

The playback gives the group an opportunity to view the way in which the salesperson handles the sales situation. Group comment on good and questionable techniques helps refine the sales method.

An alternative role-playing procedure is to have one member of the group develop a critical selling problem which is unknown to the salesperson selected for the demonstration. This practice permits the salesperson to view his or her response to real-life selling situations under controlled conditions. Thus, role playing with video tape has considerable flexibility in covering the numerous steps in the sales process.

REVIEW QUESTIONS

1. Explain the advantages of working for straight commission.
2. Explain the disadvantages of working for straight commissions.
3. What are the main three general topics covered by weekly sales meetings?
4. What are the principal purposes of sales meetings?
5. Explain the preferred sales meeting format.
6. Review the main features of five meeting presentation methods.
7. What advantages may be cited in support of role playing?
8. Explain how to increase the effectiveness of role playing.
9. Indicate how you would use preselected cases for role playing.
10. How would you present unknown cases for role playing?
11. Indicate how you would introduce role playing to a new group.

REVIEW QUESTIONS

Part **4**

THE
TECHNICAL ASPECTS
OF
SELLING

15

Federal Regulations Affecting Real Estate Brokers

There are federal laws that directly affect the operations of real estate salespersons and their employers. Some of the legislation has stimulated the real estate market, for example, the Equal Credit Opportunity Act which extended more mortgage credit to families with working wives. Other laws require salespersons to observe the new regulations on real estate brokerage operations.

Salespersons must understand the new laws so that they will be able to answer any inquiry from a prospect; they must recognize the rights of parties under these new laws; and they must advise prospects when legal counsel is advised. The laws that directly control real estate operations include the following:

Interstate Land Sales Full Disclosure Act (Public Law 90-448, August 1, 1968, as amended).

Real Estate Settlement Procedures Act of 1974 (Public Law 93-533, as amended in 1975, Public Law 94-205).

Truth in Lending Act (Public Law 90-321, 1968, as amended).

Equal Credit Opportunity Act of 1974 (Public Law 90–321).

Civil Rights Act of 1968 (Public Law 90-284) as amended by the *Housing and Community Development Act of 1974* (42 U.S.C. Sec. 5301).

Certain other acts, while not directly controlling salespersons, affect the real estate market. This legislation includes national environmental controls that bear on local real estate markets. As late as the 1960's, real estate investors, developers, and brokers, for the most part, dealt only with local and state laws controlling real estate; namely, real estate license laws, subdivision regulations, zoning regulations, and various other codes on buildings and housing. Today real estate operations must conform to the new federal laws affecting land use. Many states have new environmental laws that parallel federal laws. Environmental laws are explained in the last part of the chapter.

INTERSTATE LAND SALES FULL DISCLOSURE ACT

It is unlawful to sell subdivision lots over interstate boundaries unless the subdivision is registered with the Secretary of Housing and Urban Development. Registration is accomplished by providing the Secretary with a Statement of Record that includes the following:

1. The name and address of each person having an interest in the lots of the subdivision.
2. A legal description of the total area included in the subdivision and a statement of the topography, including a map showing block dimensions and streets.
3. A statement of the condition of title to the land.
4. A statement of the present access to the subdivision, availability of sewage disposal facilities, the location of the subdivision with respect to nearby municipalities, the nature of improvements to be installed, and the schedule for completion.
5. If there is a blanket encumbrance, a statement of the consequences if an individual purchaser fails to fulfill the obligations of the encumbrance.
6. Copies of articles of incorporation, instruments by which the trust is declared or created, copies of articles of partnership, and related papers showing ownership.
7. Copies of the deed establishing title to the subdivision.
8. Copies of all forms of conveyances to be used in selling lots.
9. Copies of instruments creating easements or other restrictions.
10. Certified financial statements as required by the Secretary.
11. A statement of terms, conditions, prices, and rents.

On receipt of the Statement of Record from the subdivider, the Secretary issues a *Property Report* which includes certain statements believed important *to a prudent* purchaser. The report, according to the law, may not be used for promotional purposes and the seller may neither advertise nor represent that the Secretary approves or recommends the subdivision.

Purpose

The purpose of the Interstate Land Sales Full Disclosure Act is to discourage fraud, misrepresentation, and deceit in the sale of subdivision lots over interstate boundaries. The law considers that no fraud is committed if the purchaser has adequate information. The Act covers subdivisions of 50 or more lots offered for sale or lease as part of a common promotional plan. Unless the subdivider complies with the Act, it is unlawful for any developer or any agent to use any means of transportation or communication in interstate commerce to sell subdivision lots.

Exceptions

The exceptions to the Act include:

1. Sales to contractors required to construct buildings within two years.
2. Real estate sold under court order.
3. The sale of mortgages or deeds of trust.
4. Securities issued by a real estate investment trust.
5. The sale of real estate owned by government or its administrative agencies.
6. Cemetery lots.
7. Sales for the purpose of constructing buildings.
8. Sales of real estate which are free of all encumbrances if the purchaser has inspected the lots which he or she proposes to purchase.
9. Lots of five acres or more.

The Act requires that the purchaser be given a copy of the Property Report in advance of the contract or agreement for sale. Failure to issue the proper report to the purchaser is grounds for considering the contract of sale voidable at the option of the purchaser.

Administration

If the developer violates this law, the purchaser can bring suit to recover his or her purchase price, the cost of improvements, and reasonable court costs. In addition, the Secretary has the right to issue an injunction or restraining order to enjoin illegal acts or practices. The Act provides power to subpoena witnesses, books, and papers and to levy a fine of not more than $5,000 or imprisonment of up to five years or both.

Furthermore, the developer must list unusual conditions relating to the location of the subdivision. Adverse influences such as air pollution, possible floods, or limitations on the availability of water, electricity, telephone service, and sewage disposal must be noted and explained.

The Statement of Record requires a detailed list of municipal services to the subdivision, including local services such as fire and police protection, garbage collection, schools, shopping facilities, public transportation, and related services. Special risk factors must also be listed. Some statements include comments that the future value of land is very uncertain: For example, "Do not count on appreciation. Future land values are uncertain." In the

Report prospects are further advised that unless they acknowledge a waiving of revocation rights, the purchaser has 48 hours after signing to revoke the contract.

Thus, when a purchaser buys land subject to the Act,

1. The purchaser must be given a Property Report for land sold subject to this law.
2. The purchaser who is not given a Property Report at least 48 hours before signing has the right to cancel and the developer must return earnest money, unless the purchaser waived the right to cancel in writing.
3. If property is misrepresented to the purchaser, the purchaser may sue the developer under this law.

Figure 15-1 illustrates the purchaser's acknowledgment which is included as part of the Home Site Purchase Agreement prepared by the ITT Community Development Corporation for the Palm Coast Subdivision in Flager County, Florida. The acknowledgment states that the purchaser received and examined a copy of the Property Report as required by federal and state laws. Note that the agreement includes the statement of the option to void the contract if the buyer did not receive a copy of the Property Report in advance or at the time the agreement was signed.

FIGURE 15-1. Purchaser's Acknowledgment of Receipt of Property Report

PURCHASER'S ACKNOWLEDGMENT

Purchaser hereby acknowledges that before he signed this Purchase Agreement he received and examined a copy of the appropriate property report, public offering statement, prospectus or public report required by Federal law and by the laws of Florida, as well as any property report or other appropriate documents, if any, required by the laws of the state of _____.

This contract is subject to the Conditions of Sale printed on the reverse side and the guarantees below, which the Purchaser has read.

YOU HAVE THE OPTION TO VOID THIS CONTRACT OR AGREEMENT IF YOU DID NOT RECEIVE A PROPERTY REPORT PREPARED PURSUANT TO THE RULES AND REGULATIONS OF THE U.S. DEPARTMENT OF HOUSING AND URBAN DEVELOPMENT IN ADVANCE OF, OR AT THE TIME OF YOUR SIGNING THE CONTRACT OR AGREEMENT; AND YOU HAVE THE RIGHT TO REVOKE THE CONTRACT OR AGREEMENT WITHIN 48 HOURS AFTER SIGNING THE CONTRACT OR AGREEMENT IF YOU DID NOT RECEIVE THE PROPERTY REPORT AT LEAST 48 HOURS BEFORE SIGNING THE CONTRACT OR AGREEMENT.

Signed by the Purchaser(s)_____, 197____.

_____(SEAL)   _____(SEAL)
            Purchaser   Purchaser

WITNESS: APPROVED AND ACCEPTED BY
                                                ITT COMMUNITY DEVELOPMENT CORPORATION

_____   By_____
                                                          Authorized Signature

_____   Date_____

STATE OF FLORIDA ⎱ ss
COUNTY OF DADE ⎰

I HEREBY CERTIFY that on this day, before me, a Notary Public authorized to take acknowledgements, personally appeared the person who signed this Agreement on behalf of the corporation and whom I know to be the agent of ITT Community Development Corporation and he acknowledged that he executed this Purchase Agreement in the name of and on behalf of the Corporation, that he was duly authorized by the Corporation to do so; and that this Agreement is an act of the Corporation.

Witness my hand and seal at Miami, Dade County, Florida,_____, 197____.

This instrument was prepared by

                                                _____
                                                Notary Public, State of Florida at Large

    5225 Northwest 87th Avenue, Miami, Florida 33166

REAL ESTATE SETTLEMENT PROCEDURES ACT (RESPA)

The purpose of the 1974 Act, as amended in 1975, was to "ensure that consumers throughout the nation are provided with greater and more timely information on the nature and cost of the settlement process and are protected from unnecessarily high settlement charges caused by certain abusive practices that have developed in some areas of the country."

Accordingly, agencies financing one- to four-family dwellings subject to this law must observe settlement rules. Federal regulation has been interpreted to include mortgages advanced by agencies and institutions supervised by the Federal Reserve Board, the Federal Home Loan Bank Board, the Federal Deposit Insurance Corporation, the Veterans Administration, and federal agencies that buy and sell mortgages in the secondary market. Because mortgage lenders are subject to at least one of the regulatory agencies, most one- to four-family dwellings are covered.

Exemptions

Mortgages on property of more than 25 acres and home improvement loans are exempt. Loans to finance the purchase of a vacant lot or constructing a house are not covered. Similarly, loan assumptions (providing the assumption fee is less than $50) and short-term construction mortgages, land sales, and contracts and loans to finance the purchase of property for resale are also exempt. Crop loans and loans for purposes not involving the transfer of title are not covered.

Lending Duties

While the burden of compliance is placed on lenders, lenders are partly dependent on real estate brokers to supply certain information to borrowers. Lenders have the duty to supply borrowers with three types of information:

1. *Settlement Cost Booklet.* This booklet, which is prepared by the Department of Housing and Urban Development, must be given or mailed to the borrower within *three business days* of the time of the written loan application. The Settlement Cost Booklet provides an explanation of (1) each settlement cost, (2) the standard real estate settlement form, (3) escrow accounts, (4) the choices available to buyers in selecting persons to perform services incident to settlement, and (5) the unfair practices and unreasonable, unnecessary charges to be avoided by the prospective buyer. The table of contents for this booklet indicates the detailed information available to buyers (see Figure 15-2).

FIGURE 15-2

**Table of Contents of the Required Settlement
Cost Booklet***

Settlement Costs: A HUD Guide. Rev. ed. (Washington, D.C.: U.S.
Government Printing Office, June 1976), p. 40.

---

2. *Advance Disclosure of Settlement Costs.* Lenders are required to give
a "good faith" estimate of the settlement charges. Printed forms included in
the Settlement Cost Booklet may be used for this purpose. This estimate must
be supplied at the time of loan application.

3. *The Uniform Settlement Statement.* The buyer and seller must be
given a prescribed form which the borrower has the right to inspect during the
business day before final closing. This statement, conforming to debit and
credit closing statements, lists settlement charges such as, real estate commis-

sions, lenders fees, escrow reserve amounts and title charges. The statement requires prorates normal to closing a real estate transaction. The form lists charges paid by the buyer and seller.

Other Requirements

One of the purposes of the Act was to further the national housing goal of encouraging homeownership by regulating certain lending practices and closing and settlement procedures in federally related mortgage transactions to the end that unnecessary costs and difficulties of purchasing housing are minimized, ...

Accordingly, Section VIII of the Act prohibits payments of fees, kickbacks, or anything of value merely incident to the real estate settlement. Payments of split fees or percentages of any charge made or received other than for *services actually performed* are prohibited. The Act prohibits referral fees and unearned commissions paid as a portion of attorney fees by the lender or real estate agent for the referral of prospective clients.

Further, the Act prohibits selection of a title insurance company by the seller; the law prohibits forcing the buyer or borrower to purchase title insurance from a particular company. Violation subjects the seller or lender to penalties, which are paid to the buyer, equal to three times all charges made for the title insurance.

The amount of the escrow collected for property taxes and insurance is generally limited to the actual amount required to pay annual property taxes and insurance premiums.

Because of the far-reaching implications of this Act, salespersons are advised to read the Settlement Cost Booklet because it summarizes the rights of the prospect in closing the sale and loan.

EQUAL CREDIT OPPORTUNITY ACT

In the past, mortgage lenders discounted all or part of that portion of family income earned by the wife. It was reasoned, especially for a young couple, that the wife's income was temporary and that the income from this source would terminate with pregnancy.

Federal Reserve Regulations

Legislation and regulations of the Federal Reserve Board have changed these practices. Under new regulations, it is also much easier for a single person to obtain mortgage credit. The right to discount the income of a married woman in judging the maximum allowable mortgage is seriously limited. The Equal Credit Opportunity Act which amended the Consumer Protection Act provided:

It shall be unlawful for any creditor to discriminate against any applicant on the basis of sex or marital status with respect to any aspect of a credit transaction.

The Act reads further:

The Congress finds that there is a need to ensure that the various financial institutions and other firms engaged in extension of credit exercise the responsibility to make credit available with fairness, impartiality, and without discrimination on the basis of sex or marital status. . . .

1976 Amendments

As required by the Equal Credit Opportunity Act amendments of 1976, it is now unlawful to discriminate on the basis *of race, color, religion, national origin, and age* in addition to *sex*. In compliance with this new legislation, the Federal Reserve Board under *Regulation B* has issued rules that affect mortgage processing:

1. *Credit scoring on the basis of marital status.* The Regulation forbids the use of sex or marital status in credit scoring systems.
2. *Reasons for denying credit.* Upon the request of an applicant, creditors are required to provide the reasons for terminating or denying credit.
3. *Childbearing.* Creditors may not inquire into birth control practices or into childbearing capabilities or intentions, or assume, from her age, that an applicant or an applicant's spouse may drop out of the labor force due to childbearing and thus have an interruption of income.
4. *Income.* A creditor may not discount part-time income but may examine the probable continuity of the applicant's job. A creditor may ask and consider whether and to what extent an applicant's income is affected by obligations to make alimony, child support, or maintenance payments to repay the debt being incurred. *But the applicant must first be informed that no such disclosure is necessary if the applicant does not rely on such income to obtain the credit.* Where an applicant chooses to rely on alimony, a creditor shall consider such payments as income to the extent the payments are likely to be made consistently [emphasis supplied].
5. *Recordkeeping.* Creditors must keep applications and related materials, including any written charges submitted by the applicant alleging discrimination, for 15 months following the date the creditor gives the applicant notice of action. For all accounts established on or after November 1, 1976, the creditor must identify for consumers reporting agencies or others to whom the creditor furnishes information those accounts that both spouses may use or for which they are both liable, so that the credit history can be utilized in the name of each spouse. The creditor is required to inform holders of accounts of the borrower's right to have credit history reported in both names.

If the Act is violated, applicants are allowed to seek actual and punitive damages up to $10,000.

The Act has been interpreted to allow lenders to request and consider any information that might be considered about the spouse. If the applicant applies on the credit worthiness of the spouse, lenders may require signatures of both husband and wife or where state law requires both signatures to pass clear title, to create liens, to waive potential property rights, or to assign earnings.

TRUTH IN LENDING ACT

The Truth in Lending Act, originally passed in 1969, requires lenders and real estate brokers to make certain disclosures in advertising real estate credit terms. *Regulation Z,* issued by the Board of Governors of the Federal Reserve System, details the administrative requirements of the Act. Regulation Z applies to any organization that extends or arranges credit for which a finance charge is or may be payable or which is repayable in more than four installments. The Federal Trade Commission enforces advertising rules which must be observed by real estate brokers and salespersons.

Of interest to real estate salespersons are the rights under certain circumstances to rescind credit contracts and to make full disclosure in advertising credit terms.

Right of Rescission

Generally speaking, borrowers have the right to cancel a credit transaction three days after loan approval. However, the Act exempts first mortgages to finance a customer's residence. First mortgages of dwellings *not purchased as a residence* and *second mortgages* may be canceled within the three-day limit. Other lenders must show the total dollar amount of finance charges, but lenders extending real estate credit are exempt from this provision.

Hence, in real estate it is not necessary to show total mortgage payments in the case of first mortgages on dwellings. Moreover, it is unnecessary to show total cash price, total financing, and other charges in the sale of a dwelling.

Advertising

Real estate brokers may not advertise that a buyer "may assume an 8 percent mortgage." Advertisements must read "assume an 8 percent *annual percentage rate* mortgage." The provision of the Act governing the real estate advertisements states:

No advertisement to aid, promote, or assist directly or indirectly any credit sale including the sale of residential real estate, loan, or other extension of credit, other than open end credit, subject to the provisions of this Part, shall state (1) the rate of finance charge unless it states the rate of that charge expressed as an "annual percentage rate," using that term.

Abbreviations are not allowed. When specific credit terms are mentioned, advertisements must give full disclosure of all credit terms. The advertisement may not read "no down payment" without disclosing (1) the selling price, (2) the dollar amount of the down payment, (3) the number of monthly payments, (4) the dollar amount and payment periods, and (5) the mortgage interest rate shown as an annual percentage rate. It is important to express the annual percentage rate after the discount points, which may be taken from published annual percentage rates assuming various discount and mortgage terms.

FAIR HOUSING LAWS

Fair housing is enforced under two laws. The first is an 1866 law that states that

> . . . citizens, of every race and color . . . shall have the same right, in every State and Territory in the United States, . . . to inherit, purchase, lease, sell, hold, and convey real and personal property [42 *U.S.C.* Section 1982 (1970)].

A Supreme Court decision ruling on this law held that the 1866 law "bars all racial discrimination, private as well as public, in the sale or rental of property, and that the statute, thus construed, is a valid exercise of the power of Congress to enforce the 13th Amendment." (*Jones* v. *Mayer*, 392 U.S. 409 1958). As a result of this decision, it is unlawful to discriminate in housing on account of race.

The second law is much broader. Title VIII of the Civil Rights Act of 1968, as amended, requires real estate brokers to observe fair housing requirements and requires that builders and sponsors of FHA financed housing prepare affirmative fair housing marketing plans. Current legislation bars discrimination based on race, color, religion, sex, or national origin in the sale or rental of most housing and in the sale of vacant land offered for residential construction or use. Specifically, the 1968 Act states, "It is the policy of the United States to provide within constitutional limitations for fair housing throughout the United States."

Prohibited Acts

Acts prohibited by the fair housing laws cover several forms of discrimination:

1. Refusing to sell or rent to, deal, or negotiate with any person.
2. Discriminating in terms or conditions for buying or renting housing.
3. Discriminating by advertising that housing is available only to persons of a certain race, color, religion, sex, or national origin.
4. Denying that housing is available for inspection, sale, or rent when it really is available.
5. "Blockbusting" for profit, persuading owners to sell or rent housing by telling them that minority groups are moving into the neighborhood.

6. Denying or making different terms or conditions for home loans by commercial lenders, such as banks, savings and loan associations, and insurance companies.
7. Denying anyone the use of or participation in any real estate services, such as broker's organizations, multiple listing services, or the facilities related to the selling or renting of housing.

Applying to approximately 80 percent of residential properties, the Civil Rights Act of 1968 covers houses owned by private individuals listed with a real estate broker for sale or rent. Included are houses owned by persons who have more than three houses or who in a two-year period sell more than one house in which the individual was not the most recent resident. Moreover, there must be no discrimination in the sale or rental of apartments of five or more units—they are automatically included; however apartments with fewer than five units are covered if the owner does not reside in one of the units.

Exemptions

If a broker is not used in the sale or rental, houses owned by an individual who has three or fewer houses are exempt, provided discriminatory advertising is not used and provided no more than one house in which the owner was not the most recent resident was sold during any two-year period.

Provided that discriminatory advertising is not used, the Act further exempts rentals of rooms or units in owner-occupied dwellings of from two to four families. Dwellings owned by churches that are operated for other than a commercial purpose are exempt if the religion does not restrict membership on the basis of race, color, or national origin. Private clubs that own and operate residential property for noncommercial purposes have the right to rent or sell residential property to its own members.

Enforcement

Real estate brokers are required to display fair housing posters. According to the Civil Rights Act of 1968, real estate brokers or others shall post and maintain a fair housing poster at their place of business or where a dwelling is offered for sale or rent. Figure 15-3 illustrates a fair housing poster available from the Department of Housing and Urban Development. These posters are required to be prominently displayed and readily apparent to all persons seeking housing accommodations and brokerage services. Regulations define failure to display the fair housing poster as evidence of discriminatory housing practices.

The Secretary of Housing and Urban Development may be informed by complaints filed either with the Secretary or directly to federal, state, or local courts. Courts may grant injunctions or temporary restraining orders or offer other appropriate relief. Actual damages and punitive damages of up to $1,000 may be awarded.

FIGURE 15-3. Fair Housing Poster Required By Fair Housing Laws

**EQUAL HOUSING
OPPORTUNITY**

We Do Business in Accordance With the Federal Fair Housing Law

(Title VIII of the Civil Rights Act of 1968, as Amended by
the Housing and Community Development Act of 1974)

IT IS ILLEGAL TO DISCRIMINATE AGAINST ANY PERSON BECAUSE OF RACE, COLOR, RELIGION, SEX, OR NATIONAL ORIGIN

- In the sale or rental of housing or residential lots
- In advertising the sale or rental of housing
- In the financing of housing
- In the provision of real estate brokerage services

Blockbusting is also illegal

An aggrieved person may file a complaint of a housing discrimination act with the:

U.S. DEPARTMENT OF HOUSING AND URBAN DEVELOPMENT
Assistant Secretary for Fair Housing and Equal Opportunity
Washington, D.C. 20410

Affirmative Marketing Plan

The Department of Housing and Urban Development requires an affirmative fair housing marketing plan for developers of federally assisted or insured housing. The purpose is to attract "those persons who traditionally would not have been expected to apply for housing, primarily blacks, Spanish-Americans, Orientals, and American Indians." Today these marketing plans are required of all subsidized and unsubsidized housing developments. If a salesperson is selling houses subject to these regulations, the developer must

Maintain an equal opportunity hiring policy for persons selling or renting housing.

Display the HUD fair housing slogan in any printed material for promotion of sales or rentals.

Post a sign on project sites that advertise HUD equal opportunity statements.

Even before the project is approved, the developer must submit an acceptable market plan as a condition for federal assistance. The plan must be complete in every detail: It must describe the marketing methods and the target minority group and it must detail any planned advertising, including the advertising media, frequency of use, copies of brochures, and written copies of radio announcements. The sales and marketing staff must be reviewed by HUD for experience in marketing to racial and ethnic groups.

FEDERAL ENVIRONMENTAL CONTROLS

Historically, private property rights were largely restricted by local land use controls. Local zoning ordinances, building codes, and housing codes are typical regulations that govern land use and its improvement. Today, real estate owners face numerous federal laws that not only affect property rights but also largely control the use of land, which markedly changes real estate values. A brief review of the main legislation shows the degree to which property owners—and especially members of the real estate industry—must observe environmental controls.

The National Environmental Policy Act (NEPA)

Under this Act, passed in 1969 (Public Law 91-190, as amended), it became national policy to encourage "harmony between human beings and the environment and to promote efforts to prevent environmental damage and stimulate health and welfare." Federal legislation requires an environmental impact statement on major federal actions that significantly affect the quality of the environment. (It should be noted that several states have enacted similiar legislation that controls land use within state boundaries.) The environmental impact statement must review:

1. The *environmental impact* of the proposed action.
2. Any *adverse environmental effects* that cannot be avoided should the proposal be implemented.
3. *Alternatives* to the proposed actions.
4. The relationship between *local short-term uses of the environment* and the maintenance and enhancement of *long-term productivity.*
5. Any *irreversible* and *irretrievable* commitments of resources that would be involved in the proposed action should it be implemented.[1]

---

[1]*Public Law* 91-190, January 1, 1970. Emphasis supplied.

Since 1969, environmental impact statements have been required for the construction of power plants, high-voltage transmission lines, the routing of highways, public parks, federally assisted housing projects, and ski resorts, among other projects. Under current regulations, housing developments insured by the Department of Housing and Urban Development must have an environmental impact statement for projects of more than 500 units. Some state laws require similiar statements for smaller projects.

The National Flood Insurance Program

The *Flood Disaster Protection Act of 1973* (Public Law 93-234, as amended) provided for flood insurance and is required for FHA and VA mortgages in designated flood hazard areas. The Federal Insurance Administration (FIA) of the Department of Housing and Urban Development has identified some 21,000 flood-prone communities that have a risk of at least one flood every 100 years.

After a community is notified by the FIA that it is in a flood-prone area, the community has one year to adopt flooding prevention measures. These measures include zoning that prohibits new construction in flood hazard areas and regulations that require buildings in flood hazard areas to be placed on stilts, piling, or additional land fill.

Premiums.   If special flood hazard measures are adopted in the community, residents may purchase flood insurance at subsidized rates under an emergency program. For example, single-family dwellings were originally insured for flood insurance for a maximum of $35,000 at an annual premium of 25¢ per $100. Other structures may be insured up to $100,000 under the emergency program. The law provides for insuring the contents of single-family dwellings to a maximum of $10,000 at a slightly higher annual cost— a 35¢ premium per $100 of contents.

The 1977 amendments raised maximum insurance limits for single-family dwellings to $185,000. The premiums under the *regular,* nonsubsidized rates are based on actuarial studies undertaken by the FIA and vary from community to community.

Insurance Coverage.   Flood insurance covers damages from water overflow, the runoff of surface waters, mud slides, and the subsidence of land along shorelands caused by oceans or waves. Bills, money, manuscripts, stamps, or coin collections are exempt. Certain site improvements are excluded (fences, swimming pools, wharves, piers, docks, driveways, and landscaping). Personal property such as motor vehicles, trailers, aircraft, and boats are not covered.

Although insurance is not required other than for FHA, VA, or other federally assisted loans, lenders in nonparticipating communities are not eligible for flood insurance programs. If there is a flood, nonparticipating communities are not eligible for federal financial assistance in the case of widespread flood damage.

In each state the FIA has designated a representative to provide forms and other information to local insurance agencies. Flood insurance maps may be secured from designated state agencies. Flood insurance may be purchased from any licensed insurance agent who works through the state designated representative. Regional offices of the FIA under administration of the Department of Housing and Urban Development provide local information on the flood insurance program.

Air Pollution

Under authority of the Clean Air Amendments of 1970 (Public Law 91-604, as amended), the Environmental Protection Agency imposes certain restrictions on transportation in some 30 cities. These cities are encouraged to reduce air pollution by promoting mass transportation, car pools, and staggered working hours, by reducing the number of parking spaces in the central city, and by using other related measures. The Agency establishes air quality maintenance areas that have the potential for exceeding national air quality standards over the next 20 years.

Real estate developments are affected in that the Agency may control developments that have parking spaces which attract automobiles that pollute air above acceptable standards. To the extent that the Agency regulates transportation that might pollute the air, local land use and its value may be affected.

Water Pollution

Water pollution controls may be restrictive to new subdivisions that have problems in controlling sewage. The Federal Water Pollution Control Act Amendments of 1972 (Public Law 92–500) provide for the elimination of pollutants into navigable waters by 1985 and water quality that protects fish and wildlife by July 1, 1983.

Area-wide waste treatment management plans have been developed to control water pollution from *point* and *nonpoint* sources. Point sources refer to direct discharges of effluent into navigable waters. Nonpoint sources refer to water runoff from agriculture, mining, construction activities, or even parking lots. Area-wide waste treatment plans may restrict building permits issued for construction of roads, parking lots, and buildings. For example, a municipal permit must be obtained from the Environmental Protection Agency for the operation of any public sewage waste treatment facility.

Rapid growth communities having a population of under 10,000 may be required to (1) increase the capacity of their waste treatment or (2) slow their population growth. Some 38 standard metropolitan statistical areas, identified as high-growth areas, are now subject to sewage hookup restrictions. If your area is identified as a limited growth area subject to these restrictions, you have probably encountered certain limited growth policies, primarily, higher restrictions on land use density, withholding of building permits, various zoning restrictions, and similar measures.

Noise Pollution

The location of airports and industrial facilities and the operation of transportation equipment may come under the office of Noise Abatement and Control of the Environmental Protection Agency. This agency, which was created by the Noise Pollution and Abatement Act of 1970 (Public Law 91–604, as amended), was directed to identify sources of noise and to determine:

1. The effects of noise at various levels.
2. Growth of noise levels in urban areas to the year 2000.
3. The psychological and physiological effects of noise on humans.
4. The effects of sporadic extreme noise (such as aircraft near airports) as compared with constant noise.
5. The effects of noise on wildlife and property (including values).
6. The effects of sonic booms on property (including values).

Because of the undesirable impact of noise on residential property, the Department of Housing and Urban Development prohibits federal assistance to dwellings subject to high noise levels as defined in the Act.

Coastal Zone Management Act

Enacted in 1972 (Public Law 92–583, as amended), this act affects land use and water development in 30 states. The law seeks to:

1. Preserve, protect, develop, and, where possible, restore coastal resources.
2. Assist states in the wise management of their coastal resources by the formulation of effective management programs.
3. Encourage federal agencies engaged in activities in coastal areas to work closely with designated state agencies responsible for coastal zone management.

Mainly, the law depends on state administration. Federal grants help states identify coastal zone boundaries and develop local authorities to control land and water uses that have a significant impact on coastal waters. The management plans developed under this law coordinate local, area-wide, and interstate agencies. Coastal zones extend inland from the shoreline, including land uses that have a direct and significant impact on coastal waters.

If you work in an area that operates under a coastal zone management plan, population and economic development of coastal areas must be arranged to protect and preserve living marine resources and wildlife. The Act controls the overall ecological, cultural, historic, and aesthetic values in coastal zones deemed "essential to the well-being of all citizens." Even natural and scenic characteristics fall under the Act.

POINTS TO REMEMBER

To a large degree, federal regulations that must be observed by salespersons and brokers either (1) protect the public from fraud and misrepresentation, such as the Interstate Land Sales Full Disclosure Act, or (2) protect various rights of parties to a real estate transaction. In addition, there are federal environmental controls that supplement the "preregulations" of zoning and building codes with a case-by-case processing of real estate projects subject to federal and, in some instances, state environmental laws.

The Interstate Land Sales Full Disclosure Act provides information believed important to a prudent purchaser who decides to buy subdivision lots out of state. Failure to observe requirements of this Act allows the buyer to rescind the purchase and may subject guilty parties to fine and imprisonment.

The Real Estate Settlement Procedures Act is directed largely to lenders advancing mortgage credit. Salespersons have a vested interest in administration of this law since the sale and financing are so highly inter-related. As presently written, the law requires the lender to give the bor-rower the Settlement Cost Booklet, an advance disclosure of settlement costs at the time of loan application, and the uniform settlement statement. The borrower has the right to inspect the statement during the business day before final closing. Moreover, kickbacks, fees, and other payments for favors other than for services actually performed are prohibited. The pros-pect has the right to select a title insurance company; the lender is re-stricted in the amount of escrow collected for payment of property taxes and insurance premiums.

The Equal Credit Opportunity Act makes it easier for a single person to finance a real estate purchase. Moreover, families with working wives may qualify for higher-valued mortgages since lenders may not discount the income of the wife in calculating the maximum allowable mortgage credit.

The Truth in Lending Act requires that brokers advertise annual per-centage interest rates and other credit terms if advertisements mention credit. A borrower does not have the right to cancel a credit transaction three days after loan approval for a first mortgage on a dwelling purchased as a residence.

Brokers are required to display the *fair housing* poster and are subject to actual damages and $1,000 punitive damages for violating the fair housing law. With minor exceptions, it is unlawful for a real estate broker or salesperson to discriminate in the sale or rental of housing because of race, color, sex, religion, or national origin.

Environmental controls limit real estate developments that must have environmental impact statements, which are required by some states. Federal agencies proposing projects that significantly affect the quality of the environment must prepare environmental impact statements. The National Flood Insurance Program makes flood insurance mandatory in designated flood hazard areas for FHA and VA mortgages. Communities not participating in flood plain prevention measures are ineligible for federal disaster relief from floods. Federal controls on air pollution illustrate the trend toward regional control of real estate developments. Although a project may comply with local zoning, planning, and building regulations, the project may not be approved if the project attracts traffic and increases air pollution beyond acceptable limits.

Similarly, controls that affect *water pollution* directly limit population growth and development in problem areas. Some 38 standard metropolitan statistical areas are now subject to sewage hookup restrictions. Even *noise pollution* caused by industrial operations or air traffic may be such that vacant land may be considered unsuitable for subdivision or urban development.

The Coastal Zone Management Act restricts development in some 30 states. The law encourages states to develop a coastal zone management plan to safeguard coastal resources, including marine and wildlife. The Act may extend to ecological, cultural, historic, and aesthetic values "considered essential to the well-being of all citizens."

REVIEW QUESTIONS

1. What is the Statement of Record required to sell subdivision lots over interstate boundaries?
2. What is the purpose of the Interstate Land Sales Full Disclosure Act?
3. Explain the information included in a property report.
4. What specific duties does the lender have under the Real Estate Settlement Procedures Act?
5. How does the Equal Credit Opportunity Act and Regulation B of the Federal Reserve Board affect the market for real estate?
6. What advertising rules must real estate brokers observe in order to comply with the Truth in Lending Act and Regulation Z of the Federal Reserve Board?
7. What specific acts are prohibited by fair housing legislation?
8. What are the provisions for the enforcement of fair housing legislation?
9. Explain the purpose and content of an affirmative marketing plan.
10. What information is included in an environmental impact statement?

11. Explain how the Flood Disaster Protection Act of 1973 affects the market for FHA and VA insured mortgage loans.

12. In what way are real estate developments affected by the Clean Air Amendments of 1970?

13. How do water pollution controls affect the market for new subdivision houses?

14. What is the purpose of the Coastal Zone Management Act?

16

Understanding Home Ownership Advantages

How do you deal with prospects who are not aware of all the advantages of owning a home? The prospect turns to you for help in solving housing needs. Your help is especially needed for the prospect who hesitates and prefers to rent or keep his or her present home because the monthly payments are lower. This prospect benefits from your understanding of home ownership advantages, namely, the *amenities, economic advantages,* and *tax advantages.*

In directing attention to selected amenities you emphasize the housing features that appeal to most buyers. The economic advantages are not as easily understood. These include the *imputed income* of homeowners, certain advantages arising because of *inflation,* and the benefits of *equity build-up* which the owner receives from constant-level mortgage payments. The income tax advantages include mortgage interest and property tax *deductions from ordinary income* and, under certain circumstances, *exemption from capital gain taxes* —advantages gained by homeowners which are not enjoyed by renters.

HOME OWNERSHIP AMENITIES

The amenities of home ownership are the pleasant satisfactions that are not received in the form of money. They cover tangible and intangible benefits of ownership.[1] Another author defines amenities as "some feature, refinement, or latent value that a prospective buyer discovers in a property that gives him so

---

[1]Byrl N. Boyce, ed., *Real Estate Appraisal Terminology* (Cambridge, Mass.: Ballinger Publishing Company, 1975), p. 9.

much pleasure that he cannot resist the urge to make it his home."[2] In this sense, amenities refer to "pleasure" motives that stimulate the decision to buy. In this book it is convenient to consider the amenities of the community, neighborhood, and house.

Community Amenities

At the outset, it is presumed that you know the important facts about your dwelling. At this point you are encouraged to learn the features of the community that make the community more pleasant—features that supplement common locational advantages, for example, the proximity to schools, shopping centers, employment, and freeways or mass transportation.

To emphasize the community, keep the definition flexible. If you are working in a large metropolitan area, the community would probably refer to a district in the city such as Ballard or Queen Anne Hill in Seattle, Washington. In smaller cities such as Athens, Georgia, or Beaumont or Port Arthur, Texas, the community might refer to a school district, a city, a county, or group of counties. In some northeastern states, such as Connecticut or Pennsylvania, townships are more important.

Your buyer-prospect should know how the community's land use restrictions support housing values. To explain this point, you need information on the minimum allowable lot size, minimum floor areas, or restrictions on the type of construction, for example, all houses (in a subdivision) must be brick veneer.

This information is obtained from the local planning or zoning office, recorded subdivision plat books, deed restrictions, or other community land use controls. Some homeowner associations enforce land use controls that tend to enhance value. For instance, the model home association code published by the Urban Land Institute includes the provision that

> No building, fence, wall, or other structure shall be commenced, erected, or maintained upon The Properties, nor shall any exterior addition to or change or alteration therein be made until the plans and specifications showing the nature, kind, shape, height, materials, and location of the same shall have been submitted to and approved in writing as to harmony of external design and location in relation to surrounding structures and topography by the Board of Directors of the Association, or by an architectural committee composed of three (3) or more representatives appointed by the Board.[3]

This control ensures property owners that adjoining property will be unlikely to decrease the value of their ownership.

In the more restrictive subdivisions, similar amenities are added by

---

[2]Arthur Brown Sherman, *How to Exploit Amenities and Hidden Values in Selling Real Estate* (Englewood Cliffs, N.J.: Prentice-Hall, Inc., 1959), p. 3.

[3]*The Home Association Handbook* (Washington, D.C.: Urban Land Institute, 1964), p. 392.

landscaping requirements and land use controls that prohibit the location of air conditioning units on the front or side of the house or that prohibit unsightly television antennas. If your community enforces land use controls that add amenities, you should explain them to interested prospects.

In sum, what creates pleasantness in the community? Is the community noted for its theater group? Is the local high school band noted for winning state awards? Does the city support an organized recreational program in the public parks? Does the community sponsor a swimming team? In short, tell your prospect about the unique features of the community that make it pleasant.

Neighborhood Amenities

Similarly, neighborhoods have amenities. Some amenities are readily apparent. Others are hidden. Amenities that you can see are dominated by the attractiveness of the houses in the neighborhood, the condition of their landscaping, and how well the houses are maintained. Street maintenance, sidewalks, and storm sewers create different degrees of pleasantness and to be sure, neighborhood services like street lighting, shopping districts, public transportation, and the closeness to traffic routes, schools, churches, and other facilities add to neighborhood amenities.

But if your prospect is new to the neighborhood, discuss the *hidden* amenities. It would be more than helpful if you identify neighbors: Where do they work? How long have they lived there and what are their hobbies? You establish the character of the neighborhood for the prospect by describing the people who live there, especially the neighbors surrounding the listed property.

Families who have children have special needs. If the house you are showing is next to a neighbor whose children are playing in the front yard every afternoon, be sure to show the house to a family that has children of the same age group. By knowing about families that have children in the immediate area, and their approximate ages (know also about the reputation of the local school), you turn children into an asset which, for some families, would be a considerable neighborhood amenity.

Amenities of the House

It is assumed that you know your product, the square foot area, the lot size, and other physical characteristics, but do you know which amenities should be emphasized? You will be dealing with older houses that have special features not found in new construction and you will be dealing with new houses that have certain design and construction features that give these houses special appeal.

Amenities of the Older House.   The older house is likely to have an architectural design not found in new construction. If the architectural design has some historical appeal, learn more about who designed the house, who constructed the house, and what special features identify the architectural design.

The older house tends to show more owner individuality. Bedrooms may be converted into special-purpose rooms such as sewing rooms, dens or studies. Over the years property owners convert space to new uses and add rooms, restore interiors, and make additions to the landscape that may appeal to your prospect. The present owner and neighbors may give you hints on points that may be useful in your presentation.

Amenities of New Construction.   Increasingly, new houses show certain energy cost-reducing construction. Know how new construction reduces annual utility costs. Generally, you will find that the new house conforms to new floor plan preferences and that the house is ideally adapted to the site.

The new house has probably been constructed with more care taken in arranging color schemes and in using interior finishing materials; appliances will be new and the latest models. If you include appliances in the mortgage, this, in itself, represents an amenity, for your prospect not only buys the house but also a house equipped with the latest kitchen equipment. It will pay to learn about the appliances if this is the type of house you have listed.

In short, your prospect wants to know the main details of the house, details which usually include the locational advantages, the physical characteristics of the house and lot, and the minimum financing requirements. But in addition to these features, which are usually shown on the listing form, you have an added responsibility: You must know how the community, the neighborhood, and the house add to amenities that will give your prospect the maximum satisfaction and the most pleasant house for his or her needs.

ECONOMIC ADVANTAGES

In the present context, economic advantages refer to the benefits owners gain independently of certain income tax advantages: (1) There is imputed income. (2) Homeownership represents a hedge against inflation. (3) Because of amortized mortgages, owners gain from equity build-up (that amount of the mortgage payment that repays the principal).

Imputed Income

In one sense, a house is a consumer good that provides shelter services. In another sense, a house is an investment that earns income. The buyer-investor makes a down payment and pays operating expenses in the form of interest charges on the mortgage, monthly utility expenses, and charges for needed repairs and maintenance. In return, the owner gains from housing services, representing a return on his or her investment over monthly operating costs. The services rendered by a house, namely, housing "shelter," can be considered a form of imputed income earned on invested capital—the down payment.

You can stress this point by comparing housing services to the market rent for the property listed. Your prospect has the option of making the down payment and occupying the house—and gaining from housing services—or renting; owner-occupants gain from income earned "in kind" on invested capital—the down payment.

Strictly speaking, housing services are a form of imputed income received by owners that is not subject to income taxes. Suppose, for instance, you deposit $10,000 in a local savings and loan association. Your $5\frac{1}{2}$ percent interest earns an annual income of $550 which is taxed as ordinary income for federal and possibly state personal income taxes. If you invest $10,000 in a house and occupy it as your residence, you receive income not in the form of interest payments on a deposit but in the form of housing services, which is not taxable.

Therefore, homeowners gain from the imputed income from a house which is income tax exempt. In comparison, the renter, at least for most investments, must pay income taxes from earnings on his or her invested capital.

Hedge Against Inflation

Today most buyers anticipate future price increases. Many authorities regard inflation as a permanent feature of the economy. This does not mean, however, that all houses will increase in value or that the house you sell today will automatically sell later for more money. Housing prices are affected by many local and national events, for example, declining employment, shifts in population, changes in transportation, catastrophic events, and many other factors.

Construction Cost Increases. Average construction costs have increased every year since 1947. Three construction cost indexes are reported in Table 16-1. Note that construction costs from 1967 through 1978, as reported by the American Appraisal Company, increased by 140.9 percent. Similarly, the Boeckh index for the same period indicates that residential costs have increased by 135.9 percent. Similarly, the series reported by Engineering News-Record shows a construction cost increase of 147.8 percent from 1967 through 1978. All three series are diagrammed in Figure 16-1.

The Rising Consumer Price Index. Other evidence of continually rising prices lies in the consumer price index. Table 16-2 indicates the changes in the consumer price index from 1967, the base year. Note that from the base

TABLE 16-1. Three Construction Cost Indexes Showing the Annual Percent of Increase

Year	American Appraisal Company Average Costs, 30 Cities (1972 = 100)	Annual Percent of Increase	Boeckh Indexes: Average, 20 Cities Residential Costs (1972 = 100)	Annual Percent of Increase	Engineering News-Record Building Costs (1972 = 100)	Annual Percent of Increase
1967	66	—	68.6	7.3	64.4	—
1968	71	7.6	73.6	8.2	69.2	7.5
1969	77	8.5	79.7	8.3	75.8	9.5
1970	83	7.8	89.0	5.4	80.2	5.8
1971	92	10.8	91.1	8.5	90.5	12.8
1972	100	8.7	100.0	9.8	100.0	10.5
1973	111	11.0	109.2	9.2	108.5	8.5
1974	117	5.4	118.0	8.1	114.9	5.9
1975	125	6.8	125.9	6.7	124.5	8.4
1976	137	9.6	136.2	8.2	135.9	9.2
1977	146	6.6	148.5	9.0	147.3	8.4
1978	159	8.9	161.8	9.0	159.6	8.4
Percent of Change 1967 to 1978		140.9		135.9		147.8

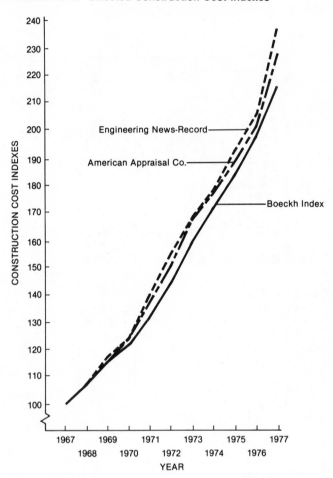

FIGURE 16-1. Selected Construction Cost Indexes

CONSTRUCTION COST INDEXES

Engineering News-Record

American Appraisal Co.

Boeckh Index

YEAR

Source: Table 16-1.

year through 1978 consumer prices increased to 195.4, which over 11 years is an average annual increase of 8.7 percent. The data also indicate that the consumer price index has increased some 32.5 percent from 1974 to the end of 1978—an average annual increase of over 8.1 percent. A 7.25 percent compound rate of change is equivalent to a doubling of prices every ten years. Figure 16-2 shows these data.

Housing Price Increases. Another indication of the trend in housing values is given by the price index covering sale prices of a series of new one-family houses. This index is published by the U.S. Bureau of the Census.

TABLE 16-2. Annual Change in the Consumer Price Index

Year	Consumer Price Index	Annual Percent of Increase
1967	100.0	–
1968	104.2	4.2
1969	109.8	5.4
1970	116.3	5.9
1971	121.3	4.3
1972	125.3	3.3
1973	133.1	6.2
1974	147.7	11.0
1975	161.2	9.1
1976	170.5	5.8
1977	181.5	6.5
1978	195.4	6.7

FIGURE 16-2. Consumer Price Index 1967-1978

Source: Table 16-2.

Although this series refers to national trends, local housing prices may be expected to move in the same direction but at varying amounts. These data are summarized in Table 16-3.

Based on 1972 prices, this index shows a price increase for each year since 1965 when the index was started. The annual average price increase ranges from 3 percent (1967 and 1970) to 00.0 percent recorded for 1978. It will be observed that since 1973 the index increased by more than 8.4 percent each year. These trends are illustrated in Figure 16-3.

If these trends prevail, the national average price of new houses will double in less than ten years. These various price series suggest that housing prices tend to move upward with the general price level, thus giving homeowners a convenient hedge against inflation. No such protection is presently afforded other intangible assets, savings deposits, for example.

Although there is no assurance that a particular house will experience a price increase, there is a tendency for real estate prices to move in sympathy with the general price level. In some communities the housing prices have moved up much more rapidly than the consumer price index or other price series have. In still other instances, examples may be found in which real estate prices have moved downward. However, if housing prices have declined, there is usually a valid and predictable explanation, for example, a one-industry town lost its main source of employment, a military base was abandoned, a government defense facility closed down, or the population changed, thus creating a local housing surplus.

But for the neighborhoods that attract buyer-prospects, you can probably advise your prospect that home ownership—at least in the past—has served as a hedge against inflation.

Ownership Leverage

The advantage enjoyed by the owner varies according to the original equity. Suppose, for example, that the house is purchased for $50,000. If the owner finances with a $45,000 first mortgage, the required original equity would be 10 percent of the price, or $5,000. Without considering the mortgage equity build-up, a 10 percent price increase over his or her ownership would double the ownership equity interest. These relationships are shown in Table 16-4.

Table 16-4 shows the appreciation in the original equity for selected equity percentages ranging from 5 percent to 40 percent. Assume a price increase of 10, 20, 30, and 40 percent; note how the owner gains from leverage. For example, for a 10 percent price increase and a 10 percent equity, the owner increases his or her equity interest by 100 percent ($5,000 to $10,000). With a 20 percent price increase, a sale price of $60,000 increases the equity interest to $15,000, a 200 percent increase. Under these assumptions, the proportionate

TABLE 16-3. Price Index of New Residential Sales,
1965–1978
(1972 = 100)

Year	Price Index	Percent of Annual Change	Year	Price Index	Percent of Annual Change
1965	71.2	—	1972	100.0	6.5
1966	74.2	4.2	1973	108.9	8.9
1967	76.4	3.0	1974	119.1	9.4
1968	80.3	5.1	1975	131.0	10.0
1969	86.5	7.7	1976	142.0	8.4
1970	89.1	3.0	1977	159.3	13.0
1971	93.9	5.4	1978	182.1	14.3

Source: U.S. Bureau of the Census, *Statistical Abstract of the United States:* 1977 (99th ed.) Washington, D.C., 1978, p. 786.

FIGURE 16-3. Price Index of New Residential Sales 1967-1978

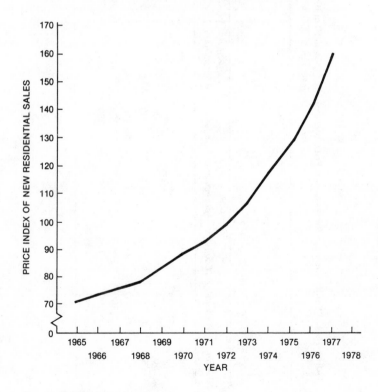

Source: Table 16-3.

TABLE 16-4. Equity Increase for Assumed Price Increases for Original Equities Ranging from 5 Percent to 40 Percent
Original Purchase Price: $50,000

Original Equity		10 Percent Price Increase (Sale Price = $55,000)		20 Percent Price Increase (Sale Price = $60,000)		30 Percent Price Increase (Sale Price = $65,000)		40 Percent Price Increase (Sale Price = $70,000)	
Percent	Amount	Equity	Percent of Appreciation	Equity	Percent of Appreciation	Equity	Percent of Appreciation	Equity	Percent of Appreciation
40	$20,000	$25,000	25	$30,000	50	$35,000	75	$40,000	100
35	17,500	22,500	29	27,500	57	32,500	86	37,500	114
30	15,000	20,000	33	25,000	67	30,000	100	35,000	133
25	12,500	17,500	40	22,500	80	27,500	120	32,500	160
20	10,000	15,000	50	20,000	100	25,000	150	30,000	200
15	7,500	12,500	67	17,500	133	22,500	200	27,500	267
10	5,000	10,000	100	15,000	200	20,000	300	25,000	400
5	2,500	7,500	200	12,500	400	17,500	600	22,500	800

increase in equity increases as the amount of the equity is lowered and as the future sales price increases.

Equity Build-Up

Even if there is no price change, owners benefit from savings realized from mortgage principal payments. If the constant-level mortgage repayment plan is used, the proportion of the monthly mortgage payment going to principal gradually increases each month. For example, a 9 percent, 20-year mortgage of $40,000, 25-year term, would require a monthly payment of $373.20, or $4,478.40 annually. After the first year, approximately $720.00 is paid toward principal. During the fifth year approximately 23 percent of mortgage payments go to mortgage principal. During the fifth year the mortgage principal payments—for that year only—equal approximately $1,034.

Thus, even with no change in price and assuming that the prospect resells the house at the same price, mortgage principal payments are a form of forced savings that give the owner increasing equity each year, in itself a substantial economic advantage over rental status.

The proportion of mortgage payment going to principal depends on the interest rate, the length of the mortgage, and the length of time the owner holds the property. Table 16-5 illustrates how equity increases over the first 15 years

TABLE 16-5. Accumulative Equity Build-up over 15 Years for a $40,000 Mortgage, 9¼ Percent, 20, 25 and 30 Year Term

	Term of Mortgage		
End of Year	20	25	30
1	$ 720	$ 400	$ 240
2	1,480	880	520
3	2,320	1,360	800
4	3,280	1,920	1,160
5	4,280	2,520	1,520
6	5,440	3,160	1,880
7	6,680	3,880	2,320
8	8,040	4,680	2,800
9	9,520	5,560	3,320
10	11,200	6,520	3,920
11	13,000	7,600	4,560
12	15,000	8,760	5,240
13	17,200	10,040	6,000
14	19,600	11,440	6,880
15	22,240	13,000	7,800

for mortgages of 20, 25, and 30 years. For this illustration, a $9\frac{1}{2}$ percent interest, $40,000 mortgage is assumed.

Table 16-5 shows that the 20-year mortgage provides considerably more equity build-up. At the end of the first year the hypothetical prospect has increased his or her equity by $720. At the end of the fifth year $4,280 has been added to the owner's equity. If there is no change in price, this amount accrues to the owner from the proceeds of the sale. Figure 16-4 shows how equity build-up accelerates further during the final years of the mortgage.

At the end of the fifth year, 25- and 30-year mortgages show an added equity accumulation of $2,520 and $1,520. It should be noted that although the 30-year mortgage provides less equity build-up, it is partly offset by the

FIGURE 16-4.   Accumulative Equity Buildup over 15 Years, 20, 25, and 30 Year Term, $40,000 Mortgage, $9\frac{1}{4}$ interest

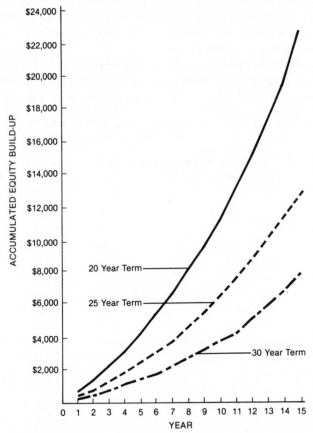

Source: Table 16-5.

increased income tax deduction of interest. For example, during the fifth year, 90 percent of the mortgage payments for a 9 percent, 30-year mortgage goes to interest—compared to a 25-year mortgage—giving more of an income tax deduction but less mortgage equity build-up.

INCOME TAX ADVANTAGES

Income tax advantages arise from the deductibility of mortgage interest and property taxes from federal personal income taxes. Most states that levy a state personal income tax permit the same deductions. In addition, on resale, provided the homeowner purchases another house as a residence, the homeowner may postpone capital gain taxes.

Income Tax Deductions

As an illustration of personal net income tax advantages, assume a purchase price of $62,500 and an 80 percent mortgage of $50,000, 25-year term, $9\frac{1}{2}$ percent interest. Monthly mortgage payments, principal and interest, would be $437.00. Interest payments in the first year would total $4,744. If the annual property taxes were to approximate two percent of the value of the house, the estimated annual property tax would be $1,250, giving a total personal income tax deduction of $5,994. These figures are summarized below for the first year of the mortgage:

Mortgage		$50,000.00
25 years, $9\frac{1}{2}$%		
Monthly payment		$ 437.00
Interest, first year	$4,744	
Annual property tax	1,250	
Total deduction		$5,994

At this writing, married couples filing joint returns are liable for a 49 percent marginal income tax rate for that portion of their taxable income over $45,800 and under $60,000; single persons pay the 49 percent rate for income over $34,100 and less than $41,500. As taxable income increases, the rate increases to a marginal rate of 70 percent for that portion of a single persons taxable income over $108,300. Since the rate varies for each bracket (See Table 16-6), the average rate is always less than the marginal rate. For instance, a married couple having a taxable income of $43,900 and filing jointly would pay a tax of $11,903, as shown by the bracket rates of Table 16-6. (A tax of $8,162 on income of $35,200 and $3,741 [43%] on the balance of $8,700). This would be equivalent to an *average* tax rate of 27.1 percent, although the *marginal rate* on income over $35,200 and not over $45,800 is 43 percent.

The effective monthly payments tend to be reduced according to the

TABLE 16-6. Marginal Income Tax Rates for Married Individuals Filing Joint Returns

Taxable Income		Tax Rate in Percent
Over	Not Over	
$ —	$ 3,400	—
3,400	5,500	14
5,500	7,600	16
7,600	11,900	18
11,900	16,000	21
16,000	20,200	24
20,200	24,600	28
24,600	29,900	32
29,900	35,200	37
35,200	45,800	43
45,800	60,000	49
60,000	85,600	54
85,600	109,400	59
109,400	162,400	64
162,400	215,400	68
215,400	—	70

average tax rate. If the prospect is subject to an *average* tax rate of 50 percent, his or her total tax deduction for the year would be $2,997 ($5,994 × 0.50), or $249.75 monthly. An average tax rate of 20 percent would give an annual deduction of $1,198.80, or $99.90 monthly. Total tax deductions, based on deductible expenses of $5,994, for income tax rates from 20 percent to 50 percent are shown below:

Average Tax Rate	Annual Deduction	Monthly Deduction
50%	$2,997.00	$249.75
40%	2,397.60	199.80
30%	1,798.20	149.85
20%	1,198.80	99.90

If the monthly mortgage payment is $437.00, the effective monthly payment may be calculated from these income tax deductions. For the average rates selected, the *effective monthly payment,* after income tax deductions, ranges from $187.25 to $337.10.

The income tax advantage increases as the average income tax rate increases. Further, the higher the interest rate and the longer the mortgage term, the greater the deduction. In other words, the prospect purchases a home partly at the expense of the federal government.

Average Income Tax Rate	Effective Monthly Payment
50% ($437.00 — $249.75)	$187.25
40% ($437.00 — $199.80)	237.20
30% ($437.00 — $149.85)	287.15
20% ($437.00 — $ 99.90)	337.10

Furthermore, although homeownership requires payment of annual property taxes, the expense is partly offset by its income tax deductibility. Again, the advantage increases as the average tax rate increases. Therefore, when adding property taxes and escrow payments to the mortgage, you should advise the prospect about the *effective property taxes,* not only the dollar amount.

If property taxes on the house you are showing approximate $1,000, multiply the (estimated) average income tax rate by the annual property tax to calculate the deduction. Thus, for this example, a family paying average federal income taxes of 30 percent would have an effective property tax of $700 after taxes. Both the mortgage interest deductibility and the property tax deduction are advantages of home ownership not extended to renters.

Capital Gain Tax Deferment

Under present legislation, homeowners may build up their equity and later sell without paying capital gain taxes. This feature should appeal to the young married couple who replace their modest first home with a larger house as the size of the family and the income increases. A property owner who buys a house for $62,500, holds it for four years, and then sells it for $80,000 would have a taxable capital gain of $17,500.

If the dwelling is the principal residence and the gain is reinvested in a new residence 18 months before or after the sale (or for new construction 24 months after the sale), the capital gain tax is deferred. Further if the seller is over 65 years of age, the capital gain tax may be avoided without buying another home. Currently, $35,000 of the gain is exempt if the net sales price (after sale expenses) is $35,000 or less. If the selling price is greater than $35,000, the capital gain tax is reduced by the ratio of $35,000 to the actual sales price.

Furthermore under the Revenue Act of 1978, persons over 55 are granted a once in a lifetime capital gain exemption of up to $100,000 on the sale of a residence. The exemption is allowed without having to buy another residence. The residence must have been used as the principal residence during three of the last five years.

There is still another advantage realized by deducting expenses of the sale. The capital gain tax is based on the *adjusted basis.* The seller is allowed to deduct real estate commissions, legal fees, and the cost of permanent improvements that may have been made in anticipation of the sale. The capital gain is based on the net sale proceeds (after expenses) and the adjusted cost basis.

To illustrate, suppose the property was sold for $80,000. Suppose the seller realizes $74,175 after deducting allowable expenses actually incurred in selling the property. If the house was originally purchased for $62,500, the owner is allowed to add costs incurred in selling the property plus any permanent improvements made during ownership. Suppose that in addition to paying closing expenses of $1,300 the owner invested $2,100 in landscaping and a garden shed. The figures are summarized below:

Sales price		$80,000
Less selling expenses:		
Real estate commission	$ 4,000	
Legal fees	600	
Recording fees	25	
Repainting	1,200	− 5,825
Adjusted sales price		$74,175
Cost of house and lot:		
Original price	$62,500	
Closing costs (buyer)	1,300	
Landscaping	1,200	
Garden shed	900	−65,900
Capital gain on sale		$ 8,275

In this instance, although the difference between the purchase price and the sales price totals $17,500, the capital gain reported would be $8,275.

The seller is allowed to deduct painting and repair costs for the purpose of preparing the house for sale. Costs of fixing up the house to make it more saleable are permitted if the work is done *within 90 days* before signing the sales contract and if all bills are paid *within 30 days* after the sale.

POINTS TO REMEMBER

Home ownership advantages depend on amenities, economic advantages, and certain income tax advantages. In describing home ownership amenities, you should stress the community amenities, neighborhood amenities, and amenities centering around the house. Remember that amenities are those factors that create pleasant satisfactions.

Recognize amenities associated with the older house: its architectural style, unique owner improvements, and special advantages typically not found in a new house.

On the other hand, new houses generally have the best construction features, primarily, modern color schemes, the latest materials, and the most modern equipment.

Search for the hidden amenities, for example, compatible neighbors, children, and the activities and organizations in the neighborhood and community.

Home ownership gives certain economic advantages not realized by those who rent. These advantages are in the form of (1) imputed income, (2) a hedge against inflation, (3) ownership leverage, and (4) equity build-up. The imputed income represents income in kind received in the form of housing shelter, regarded by many as income earned on invested capital—the down payment. Past experience shows that home ownership usually represents a hedge against inflation. Generally speaking, dwelling prices move upward with the general price level. It is true that owners gain from leverage with projected price increases. The leverage increases as the equity interest decreases. By the same token, amortized mortgages give owners the benefit of mortgage principal payments.

Housing prospects should consider the after income tax advantages of a housing purchase. Advantages accrue to owners who deduct mortgage interest and property tax payments from their taxable income. Therefore, the advantage increases with the increase in the average income tax rate. The effect is to *reduce the effective monthly payment* and to *reduce the impact of property taxes.*

The prospect subject to a 30 percent average income tax and a mortgage payment of $437.00 has an effective monthly payment of $305.90. Similarly, under the same assumption, an effective property tax of $1,000 is reduced to an effective tax of $700 per year.

It should be added that capital gain deferments are available to homeowners who reinvest their equity within 18 months of the sale (24 months for new construction). Persons over 55 years of age have a one-time capital gain exemption of $100,000 on the sale of a residence. Even with capital gain taxes, homeowners are allowed to deduct (1) selling expenses and (2) the cost of preparing the property for sale from the realized sale price. Moreover, the cost of acquisition is reduced by closing costs and permanent investments made during ownership.

REVIEW QUESTIONS

1. What are home ownership amenities?
2. Give examples of the amenities associated with the community, the neighborhood, and houses.

3. What special amenities are found in an older house?
4. What amenities are usually found in a new house?
5. Explain the meaning of imputed income earned by homeowners.
6. Explain how home ownership represents a hedge against inflation. Give examples.
7. Explain the importance of equity build-up.
8. Give examples of home ownership leverage under housing appreciation.
9. Explain the income tax advantages of home ownership. Give an example.
10. Explain how homeowners may defer capital gains.
11. Give an example of how you would calculate capital gains on the sale of a house used as a residence.

17

Condominium Sales

As condominiums become more popular, it is increasingly difficult not to list and sell condominiums. By April, 1975 condominium units totaled 1.25 million units—85 percent have been constructed since 1970. Their growing popularity arises partly because of income tax advantages over renting apartments and because of economic advantages of condominium ownership. At the same time, condominiums have many of the amenities of single-family ownership in addition to the convenience of multiple-family housing. For the salesperson, condominiums, their listing and sale, require specialized marketing procedures not encountered in the sale of detached houses.

SELLING OPPORTUNITIES

Typically, new condominiums are sold by developers. The developers have their own salespersons who show model units to prospects. But since this form of housing is becoming more popular, buyers and sellers dealing with "resales" increasingly turn to real estate agents because the developer is not available to sell to second owners. Moreover, owners are poorly equipped to transfer their ownership to new buyers. For this reason, salespersons experience unique sales advantages.

For instance, condominium listings are more readily obtained than are listings of the more scattered houses. Since condominium units are concentrated in projects, a listing farm may be more easily worked. An additional advantage is that there is a greater community of interest in condominiums that provides the benefits of word-of-mouth advertising and a favorable reputation.

In fact, some real estate brokers work closely with the condominium association, the governing body of the condominium unit, which provides a relationship difficult to duplicate among most neighborhood subdivisions.

Usually, condominium projects provide units that have three or four different floor plans. Since owners are restricted in remodeling individual units, it is easier to form judgments on the recommended listing price. A review of resales indicates the value of different floor plans, view, and better locations throughout the condominium unit. Resale prices do not necessarily agree with the builder's original offer. For example, condominiums on the tenth floor with a waterfront view may show greater appreciation than ground floor units.

There is the added advantage of managing condominium units as part of the sales operation, especially for second-home condominiums or the recreational unit occupied by the owner only part of the year. A combined management-broker operation constitutes an important source of listings, resales, and commissions not realized in home sales.

The Condominium Vocabulary

A condominium is defined as the *ownership of a single unit in a multiple unit structure with an undivided ownership in the land and structures held in common with other unit owners.* This kind of ownership gives rise to certain common terms describing property rights of condominium owners. The salesperson who specializes in condominiums must learn these terms:

1. *Condominium unit.* That part of the condominium subject to private ownership and exclusive use, such as an apartment unit.
2. *Common elements.* That portion of a condominium not included in a single unit.
3. *Limited common elements.* Common elements reserved for the use of unit owners to the exclusion of other unit owners, e.g. an exterior balcony.
4. *Common expenses.* Expenses of operation that are shared by unit owners.
5. *Condominium association.* The legal entity responsible for operation of the condominium.
6. *Undivided share in common elements.* The share of ownership held by unit owners that determines the prorated share of operating expenses borne by unit owners.
7. *Management agreement.* The contract between the condominium association and the managing agent.
8. *Condominium bylaws.* Rules of the condominium association specified in corporate bylaws covering rights, powers, and duties of condominium owners.

9. *The declaration.* [Also known as the *declaration of restrictions or covenants, conditions, and restrictions* (CC and R's).] A document that is recorded and that commits the property to condominium ownership.

Condominium ownership required changes in property laws to provide for the allocation of property taxes to cover units and the prorated share of undivided common elements held by unit owners. Also, the legal description of a condominium must refer to a cubic-foot area in contrast to the flat plane described by noncondominium property: All states have enacted legislation providing for these changes. Figure 17-1 illustrates a condominium developed in five phases. Unit owners share an undivided interest in the clubhouse, pool, land, and other facilities used in common.

FIGURE 17-1.   A Condominium Project Developed in Five Phases with an Undivided Interest in Common Elements.

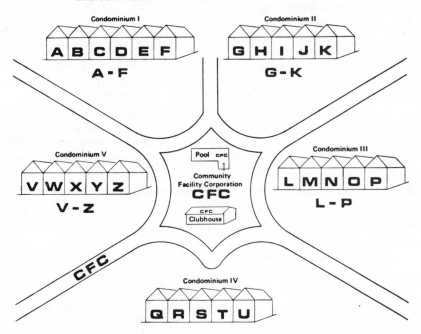

Source: *HUD Condominium Cooperative Study,* Vol. III (Washington, D.C.: Government Printing Office, 1975), p. G-12.

Sales Restrictions

The purchase of a condominium is subject to fairly restrictive state laws requiring that buyers be given certain documents. As a consequence, salespersons must not only demonstrate all the selling techniques associated with the listing and sale of homes but they must also observe the legal requirements covering rights of buyers and sellers who transfer condominium ownership. Some lenders require these documents and reserve financing of condominiums only for projects in which they have appraised the condominium as a whole. Depending on state law, the listing of a condominium and its sale are considerably more complex than the listing and selling of houses.

CONDOMINIUM ADVANTAGES

Selling benefits of condominium ownership is a matter of stressing certain financial advantages and condominium amenities. In both instances, condominiums show superiorities over apartment house rental, single-family ownership, and even cooperative apartments.

Financial Advantages

In the main, condominium ownership provides the income tax advantages of home ownership, primarily mortgage interest and property tax deductions from personal net income taxes. These deductions especially appeal to high- and middle-income families since the advantage increases with higher progressive income rates and higher mortgage and tax payments.

If the condominium is financed under a long-term mortgage, the condominium owner (like the homeowner) benefits from equity build-up, an advantage not realized by apartment occupants. Although operating expenses tend to increase with the rising price level, it may be anticipated that the cost of condominium ownership will not increase as rapidly as other prices, thus giving the condominium owner a financial advantage over the apartment occupant. Further, under rising prices and housing values, the condominium owner's equity will tend to increase in contrast to the rising rents faced by the apartment dweller.

Condominiums, because of their high land use density, tend to lower the cost of recreational facilities such as the clubhouse, swimming pool, sauna, tennis courts, and even golf courses. Because the proportion of land per unit is less than for the land of detached houses, condominium owners gain from the lower per unit land costs. In brief, condominium owners benefit from lower cost recreational facilities, superior locations, and other conveniences of an apartment house.

Add to these factors the benefit of a nonprofit operation. For not only is the condominium operated at cost (under control of the membership through an elected board of directors) but a successful condominium will also show lower vacancies, making for a more efficient operation. In contrast, apartment projects by their nature have higher rates of tenant turnover and higher vacancy rates.

Condominium Amenities

Condominium amenities have a wide appeal. This appeal lies partly in ownership of a multiple family unit under direct control of members. The members control the level and quality of service. Control over services such as maids, doormen, central switchboard, security, and janitorial allows owners to participate in management decisions important to their welfare.

In the view of some observers, condominium owners generally demand a higher level of operation and amenities than do apartment occupants. Developers, in order to sell condominiums, provide more recreational space, superior club rooms, quality swimming facilities, and a broad range of extra features not always found in apartments operated for investment purposes.

Condominiums also appeal to those who prefer to have a centralized management relieve them of maintenance chores. Condominium management provides for the daily maintenance of grounds, the structure, and common areas. As a result, condominiums appeal to persons who want the financial advantages of home ownership and the convenience of multiple family living and services.

Condominium Disadvantages

To be sure, there are certain disadvantages, at least to some families, that might offset these benefits. It is abundantly clear, for example, that multiple family ownership calls for group living. Condominium occupants must observe house rules, covenants, and conditions that ensure the operation of the condominium for the benefit of the group. In this respect, the condominium owner gives up certain property rights associated with fee simple ownership of a house.

For example, the condominium owner does not have the *unrestricted* use of condominium land and other common areas. Further, parking for guests and recreational vehicles may be very limited. And as are apartment occupants, condominium owners are subject to noise and other disturbances, which, however, are largely controlled by fairly restrictive condominium rules.

Condominium Ownership Compared to Cooperative Ownership

Before condominiums were authorized by state legislatures, the alternative to apartment living was the cooperative. Cooperatives are popular in the metropolitan and resort areas of California, in metropolitan Chicago, and in luxury units in New York City. Some cooperatives were organized under the Rochdale plan (one vote, one member) by labor unions in New York City during the late 1920's for lower- and middle-income ownership. Cooperatives share some of the benefits of condominiums, but their legal entity creates an ownership unlike that of condominium ownership.

Condominium Ownership	Cooperative Ownership
1. Condominium owners acquire title to a unit and an undivided interest in the common elements.	1. Cooperative owners purchase cooperative shares and gain possession under a proprietary lease.
2. Condominium owners finance a purchase with a mortgage on their units.	2. Cooperative owners pay a prorated proportion of a mortgage on the cooperative project.
3. The liability of condominium owners for operating expenses is limited to the prorated share of their ownership interest.	3. Cooperative owners are liable for an unlimited share of operating expenses.
4. Generally, condominium owners may buy and sell as do homeowners.	4. Cooperative owners may have restricted resale rights.

The limited liability of the condominium owner and individual financing of a condominium unit favor condominium ownership over cooperative ownership. Indeed, on resale, the cooperative shareholder, financing under FHA subsidized plans, may be entitled only to the original down payment plus equity build-up and cost of living price increases. Cooperatives financed under a conventional mortgage usually allow sales at the market price.

LEGAL ASPECTS

Salespersons may be asked about condominium ownership. In some instances, the requirements of state law advise a review by an attorney before purchase. Knowing the main features of legal instruments associated with condominium ownerships helps salespersons understand condominium ownership features.

The Declaration

The declaration, master deed, or covenants, conditions, and restrictions establish condominium property rights. The declaration is a formal contract that is recorded the same way that a deed and other conveyance instruments are. In Florida the contents of the declaration, which must be furnished to buyers in the sale of new condominiums of more than 20 units, must include the following:

1. A statement committing the property to condominium ownership.
2. The name by which condominium properties are identified.
3. The legal description.
4. Identification of each unit.
5. A survey of the land and a description of improvements.
6. The share of common elements pertinent to each unit stated as a percentage or fraction which must equal the whole.

7. The proportion, percentages, or manner of incurring common expenses.
8. The name of the condominium association.
9. Membership and voting rights.
10. Incorporation documents.
11. A copy of the bylaws.
12. A copy of easements.
13. Covenants and restrictions.
14. Use occupancy and provision for transfer of units.[1]

Although the declaration grants the right of exclusive use for a unit and the right to use common elements, these rights are limited by the bylaws, covenants, and restrictions. Figure 17-2 illustrates how the declaration con-

FIGURE 17-2. Condominium Ownership Showing the Creation of the Condominium Unit and Undivided Share in Common Elements

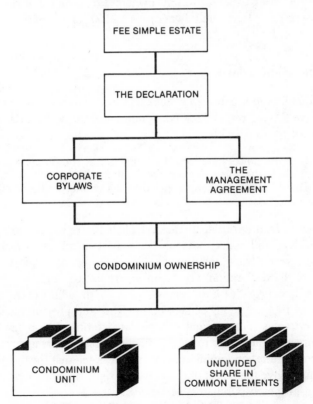

Source: William M. Shenkel, *Modern Real Estate Appraisal* (New York: McGraw-Hill Book Company, 1978), p. 445.

[1]Chapter 718, *Condominium Act,* Florida Statutes Annotated, April, 1978.

verts fee simple ownership to condominium use. Owner rights are largely defined by corporate bylaws and the management agreement. The owner of a
condominium unit acquires two interests: title to the unit and title to an
undivided share in the common elements.

The legal description of the condominium includes the unit designation
identified by a letter, name, or number sufficient to identify the unit, its
placement, and the legally described land area representing part of the undivided share in common elements. State legislation may require that an exhibit
be given each unit owner which describes the land and shows the location of
each unit on a plot plan.

The undivided share in the common elements controls the allocation of
operating expenses and property taxes shared individually by unit owners.
Ordinarily, the undivided share is based on the proportionate square-foot area
of a condominium unit. The undivided share, stated in the declaration, is used
to allocate operating expenses to unit owners. For instance, if the undivided
share is 1.9500 percent, the unit owner pays 1.9500 percent of the total operating expenses and property taxes.

Corporation Bylaws

Condominiums are formed under a nonprofit corporation that is empow-
ered to serve the interests of the condominium unit owners. Known as the
association, it is vested with

> . . . all of the powers and privileges granted to corporations not for profit
> except where the same are in conflict with the declaration of condominium
> and exhibits attached thereto, including the charter and the bylaws of the
> association.

The articles of incorporation further establish the right to make rules and
regulations, levy and collect assessments against members to maintain, improve, repair, reconstruct, and manage the condominiums, and to enforce the
provisions of the declaration, articles of incorporation, and bylaws.

The bylaws provide for the administration of the affairs of the condominium. Most of the provisions define voting rights and provide for a board of
directors, meetings, notices, and other related terms. The bylaws give the
board of directors the power to levy and collect assessments against members
to defray costs of the condominium. It should be noted that the bylaws of some
condominiums give the board of directors the right to approve or disapprove
owners and proposed purchasers or lessees.

Some condominiums (Florida) give the board of directors the right to
ratify a long-term lease on recreational facilities such as the swimming pool,

clubhouse, tennis court, and so on. Originally, some Florida leases provided for an adjustment of rent on recreational facilities based on changes in the consumer price index. Under current Florida law, such leases are subject to considerable restriction. The 1977 Florida statute defines leases as *presumptively unconscionable* if certain conditions exist including, in illustration, a lease that requires the unit owners to pay rents for a period of 21 years or more or a lease that provides for a periodic rent increase based on a price index. The law states further that

> . . . such leases often contain numerous obligations on the part of either or both the condominium association and condominium unit owners with relatively few obligations in any given case.[2]

Because of the legal interpretation required to define rights of the parties, salespersons should advise prospective purchasers to seek legal counsel before purchasing a condominium interest. The length and detail of the articles of incorporation, bylaws, and leases go beyond a reading of the warranty deed, title insurance policy, and mortgage of a home purchase.

The Management Agreement

Equally important is the management agreement, which is a contract between the association and the management firm. Typically, the management agreement provides for employment of a professional management firm. Usually, the management agreement

> . . . delegates to the management firm, to the exclusion of all persons including the association and its members, all the powers and duties of the association set forth in the declaration and exhibits attached thereto . . . supervision of employees, their payment, and repairs to the common elements to some maximum amount without approval of the board of directors, and to enter into contracts for insurance and other services.

The management fee for this service is based on a percentage of monthly charges or a flat sum per month per condominium unit.

Purchasing a condominium is like moving to a new community. Members must observe the rights of their neighbors who are entitled to the use of common facilities and who have an interest in maintaining the highest level of amenities. Because of these relationships, condominiums provide restrictions that govern landscaping and outside storage; they restrict the use of condominiums for residential occupancy only and prohibit signs, billboards, outside storage, and property use so as to avoid offensive noises, odors, and unsightly conditions.

[2]*Florida Laws,* 1977, Chapter 77-221, Section 3.

SELLING PROCEDURES

Although your prospective buyer may have been briefed by an attorney on the rights and duties of condominium owners, prospects will make inquiries about purchase details. Even if the inquiries are not made, salespersons are advised to make certain that buyers new to condominiums understand the nature of condominium ownership. For example, a garden-type condominium project may have restrictions that prohibit the owner from changing the outside landscaping. Misunderstanding on this point may create problems with purchasers who want to plant their favorite hanging baskets. A satisfied buyer who is aware of his or her rights will be an important source of referrals and repeat business.

Sales Preparation

To prepare for the condominium sale, agents should review the main points of (1) the declaration, (2) the corporate charter and bylaws, (3) the operating budget, (4) the management agreement, and (5) conveyance documents. For older condominiums, ask for the last annual operating budget and the proration of monthly assessments. For new projects, explain that monthly assessments may be increased to cover maintenance and related expenses, especially if the project operation will be transferred from the sponsor to the condominium association. Review how the interest in common ownership is calculated, the determination of voting rights, the appointment of the board of directors, and the financial terms of recreational leases and their rental cost.

Be prepared to explain how the management firm has been selected and the main terms of the management agreement, which preferably covers from one to three years. The rules of operation, restrictions on the use of individual units, other house rules, and the right of resale should also be explained to prospects.

If the condominium association must approve purchases, explain how the board of directors exercises this right. Insurance is another sensitive issue. Individual units should be insured against loss from fire and other perils. Condominium projects should have sufficient liability coverage and the board of directors in each individual unit should be named as co-owner.

Because in some states, such as Virginia, real estate license law officials enforce the provisions of the state condominium act, salespersons may be subject to license suspension or revocation unless they observe the state law in the purchase and sale of condominiums.

Securing New Listings

Listings should be solicited among the most saleable condominiums. In your market area you will observe that condominiums cater to specialized markets. Condominiums of Fort Lauderdale, Florida, or Palm Springs, California, serve the resort and second home market. In metropolitan areas, unit owners may represent the professional occupations, including large numbers of singles. Still others appeal to the retiree. In each instance, the services of the condominium, its location, its appearance, and its facilities must be adapted to the prospect's requirements.

Even if condominiums are designed for specialized markets, they must all provide a minimum level of services, including adequate parking, a well-maintained swimming pool, superior landscaping, and exterior maintenance. The recreational facilities, including the clubhouse, the sauna, and the tennis courts, must be suitable for prospects. Avoid a listing campaign among condominiums that show deficiencies in these important areas.

One way to judge condominium acceptance is to review past sales. If the original sales were drawn out over several months, the project probably suffers from some important lack, for example, a poor location, inadequate facilities, or inefficient operation. Your listing prospects are more favorable if resales show condominium appreciation—not depreciation. If the conditions are favorable, you should organize a condominium listing farm as you would a listing program for the more conventional residential neighborhoods.

Begin by forming a working relationship with the condominium associations. Most of the large units have regular meetings with guest speakers. If you present a real estate topic before the group, you build good will for your firm. Some real estate firms sponsor a brunch, a tea, or Sunday morning coffee and donuts in the clubhouse or sponsor recreational programs through the board of directors.

Supplementing these more indirect procedures are direct mail facilities, telephone solicitation, and personal visits. Where permitted, salespersons approach the condominium listing as they would a neighborhood listing farm by making door-to-door visits. Yet, because condominiums are concentrated in a relatively small area and because unit owners congregate in clubhouse meetings, owners have more of a common interest. Some salespersons believe that it is much easier to establish a reputation among these groups than among the more scattered houses of less homogeneous neighborhoods.

Selling Techniques

There is more to selling condominiums than to selling detached houses. It has already been pointed out that salespersons must be aware of the legal differences, property rights, controls, and financing complications of the condominium. But there is more. First-time buyers of condominiums are likely to question the maintenance charge.

Maintenance Charges.   If your prospects are former renters or home-owners, they will probably view the maintenance charge as an additional cost which they have not previously encountered. In reality, the same operating and maintenance charges are experienced in other types of ownership. But in the condominium these charges are specified and allocated to unit owners as a fixed sum payable monthly.

To make the proper comparison, you should reduce the per unit mainte-nance charges to separate items and make a comparison with similar home ownership operating costs. Although it is difficult to compare condominium ownership costs with home ownership costs (strictly speaking, they are not comparable), you should make the comparison and show the homeowner that he or she pays virtually the same charges. Such a comparison is shown in Figure 17-3.

The data in Figure 17-3 are for illustration only. These costs vary over time, by type of condominium, and by region. For example, in the North indoor swimming pool charges would be different from those in Palm Springs, California. In Palm Springs air conditioning costs would be higher than in the

FIGURE 17-3.   A Monthly Budget Comparison of Condominium Ownership with Home Ownership

Expense Item	Budget for Common Area	Comparable Budget for Single-Family Home
Utilities		
Water	$ 2.53	$ 6.95
Electrical	7.53	27.00
Heating	3.50	10.00
Maintenance		
Pool	2.65	20.00
Recreation building	1.54	—
Landscaping	12.90	25.00
Private streets	1.05	—
Trash removal	3.00	—
Administration		
Audit and legal	.50	—
Postage	1.25	—
Insurance	3.50	—
Management fee	7.50	—
Miscellaneous	2.00	—
Reserves		
Painting	5.00	—
Replacement of equipment	3.25	—
Total	$57.70	$88.95

North. Note that these costs refer to common area charges which cover services and recreation. If you prepare a form similar to the one in Figure 17-3 for local use, drawn from actual common area expenses of the condominium, your prospect will be able to compare condominium ownership costs with the costs of owning a comparable home.

Ordinarily, utility, maintenance, and insurance costs will be lower for the condominium because of the smaller floor area and economies of scale experienced by sharing these services with other unit owners. It probably follows that the condominium has certain amenities not found in previous housing, namely, a more luxurious pool, a clubhouse, and recreational facilities such as a golf course or tennis courts—besides a better location.

In addition, the maintenance costs for operating a condominium unit would probably be lower than the costs for operating a single-family dwelling.

Financing Details. To sell a condominium, you must determine in advance the available financing. Some lenders may charge higher appraisal fees. Others may lend only under relatively unfavorable terms because of the uncertainties of the local condominium market and the higher costs of administering and servicing the condominium loan. Remember that a default on a condominium loan requires that the lender pay for monthly maintenance expenses.

Normally, foreclosure expenses are higher in condominiums because of the added legal expenses encountered in foreclosing on the condominium unit. Special state statutes may be such that lenders face added costs of appraisal, inspection, and compliance. At any rate, you must be prepared to advise the prospects on likely financing terms and closing costs common to condominium ownership.

SELLING CONDOMINIUM CONVERSIONS

Converting former rental apartments to condominiums is a special marketing challenge. Under favorable circumstances, conversion appeals to tenants, some of whom become new owners. The challenge stems from working with tenants who must be shown the financial advantage of ownership. And, too, the challenge lies in apartment conversions that require modernization and a careful public relations program. Developers report that if these conditions are met, conversion of apartments to condominiums is less risky, and often less costly, than construction of new projects.

Conditions Favoring Conversion

The older apartment districts dominated by tenant occupancy are usually poor candidates for conversion. The better locations that have a view, recreational facilities, convenient transportation and shopping, and other amenities seem to be preferred.

Physical Facilities.   By the same token, an apartment building requiring substantial renovation or rehabilitation is not advised for condominium conversion. The cost of replacing elevators and heating equipment, such as steam boilers, and making other major improvements introduces expenses unlikely to result in a feasible project. On the other hand, the repair and modernization of common areas (exterior and interior walls, the lobby, halls, and stairways), laying new carpets, and landscaping seem common to most conversions.

The architecture of the building affects the feasibility of the conversion. Balconies, private patios, and adequate parking make condominium conversion less risky. Older buildings in the shape of alphabetical letters do not give sufficient light, air, or view, all of which seem to be preferred by purchasers of condominiums.

Economics of Conversion.   The economics of conversion are encouraged by rising residential land prices, rising construction costs, and various environmental restrictions and growth policies that restrict new housing construction. As rents move upward under growing housing shortages, tenants tend to favor condominium ownership. With favorable financing, condominium ownership (after taxes) may be less costly than rental occupancy.

To illustrate this point, consider the conversion of a two-bedroom apartment unit that rented for $350 per month. A parking space and utilities (except electricity) were included. After being renovated, the apartment sold for $60,000 with a 75 percent mortgage, 25 years, 9 percent. The monthly condominium costs after taxes approximated $327.50.[3]

Mortgage payment		
Principal	$ 40.50	
Interest (first month)	337.50	$378.00
Maintenance charge		65.00
Property taxes		50.00
Insurance		30.00
Total monthly outlay		$523.00
Less equity build-up		−40.50
Less tax savings		$482.50
(40% tax bracket)		
Mortgage interest	$337.50	
Property taxes	50.00	
($387.50 × 0.40)	$387.50	−155.00
Condominium payments		
comparable to rent		$327.50

[3]For additional detail, see William M. Shenkel, *Modern Real Estate Appraisal* (New York: McGraw-Hill Book Company, 1978), p. 450.

Under the assumption of a 40 percent federal income tax rate and even after allowing for a maintenance charge of $65 per month, owner occupancy costs $22.50 per month less than the monthly rent. Add to this advantage, the possibility of property appreciation and protection from added rent increases.

In addition to this economic advantage, rent control and unfavorable tenant–landlord legislation give owners further incentive to convert to condominium occupancy. Hence, it is necessary to have the right location and apartment units that are adaptable to condominiums and that do not require extensive renovation. Provided the housing market favors condominiums and provided that owners have an incentive to convert to condominiums, successful conversion depends on the marketing plan.

Sales Techniques.   Developers report that from 25 percent to 50 percent of the tenants purchase units. The more profitable projects have tenants who have savings for the down payment and incomes that qualify for long-term mortgages. Tenants who do not purchase units represent an important source of income to the developer while the apartments are undergoing conversion, modernization; and sale.

The marketing plan develops from (1) a feasibility study to analyze the rental and potential ownership market and (2) a physical survey showing the condition of the building equipment. The engineering survey is used to make estimates of the cost of modernizing individual units prior to sale.

Real estate firms that sell converted units usually accept smaller commissions on sales to existing tenants and charge higher commissions on sales to the public or through cooperating brokers. And to expedite sales, existing tenants who purchase their own units may be given credits if they purchase in an "as is" condition. Discounts of from $1,500 to $3,000 are not unusual. Discounts are regarded as a "decorating credit" which saves the developer the cost of recarpeting and redecorating the interior.

Brokers use newspaper display advertising to announce the availability of condominiums and their advantage over renting. A model apartment usually doubles as a temporary office. All prospects are given brochures that explain the benefits of condominium ownership and that describe the project. The more serious prospects are given copies of the declaration, use restrictions, deeds, and engineering reports.

The Marketing Plan.   The marketing plan starts with a projection of the monthly sales quota. The preliminary market survey provides an estimate of the number of probable units that can be sold to existing tenants. The best plan is to give tenants an exclusive advance period to buy, say, 30 days before the public sale. After 30 days the project is widely advertised in newspapers emphasizing amenities of the project, primarily, recreational facilities such as the pool and tennis courts, new appliances, air conditioning, and energy conservation construction.

Sales may be increased by providing a reserve account, paid by the developer, equal to so many dollars per condominium unit for maintenance and repairs. Sales are further encouraged by an agreement that operating charges per unit will be limited to a stated dollar amount until a certain percentage of the units are sold and final control is transferred to unit owners. Salespersons are advised to make maximum use of owner and tenant referrals among friends and relatives.

Common Sales Problems

The main handicap to selling conversion units is that prospects sign agreements without understanding condominium documents. In the past, salespersons have not had enough information to advise the prospect-purchaser or they have failed to recommend legal counsel. Some have not prepared the required disclosure documents. Salespersons should adopt a rule that contracts for sales and deposit agreements should be signed only after prospects have been given the required explanations and documents.

Sales agents who promise unusually low monthly condominium maintenance fees create misunderstandings and ill will. Your reputation will increase if you provide the prospect with a realistic monthly budget or an explanation of how the existing budget is calculated and how it might vary later.

Undoubtedly, the leading difficulty in condominium sales relates to legal complexities. It is unusual for prospects to understand the lengthy documents: the declaration, the corporate charter and bylaws, the management agreement, and lengthy leases. It is not unusual for these documents to range in length from 50 to 250 pages. In these cases, prospective purchasers should obtain legal counsel and a summary statement of their legal rights and occupancy privileges.

A related issue concerns the management of the condominium, which preferably should be delegated to experienced, competent real estate managers. It is unlikely that laypersons operating as a board of directors could professionally operate a condominium with all its regulations, rules, and legal constraints. Condominiums must be operated as a business like other large-scale apartments.

POINTS TO REMEMBER

More than ever, the real estate market favors condominium ownership. The income tax advantages and other economic benefits of condominium ownership create unusual selling opportunities: selling opportunities in the form of more efficient listing programs and selling opportunities created by the complexity of transferring ownership which usually advises against a "for sale by owner."

Before starting an active sales campaign for condominiums, salespersons must be versed in state law controlling condominium ownership. It is essential that they learn the vocabulary and explain the legal meanings to their prospects in nonjargon terms.

Salespersons market condominium benefits in the form of *financial advantages* and *condominium amenities.* The financial advantages include the income tax deductibility of mortgage interest and property taxes. With rising housing costs and rents, condominium owners buy free of future rent increases and they benefit from the possibility of capital appreciation. The amenities are in the form of superior conveniences of multiple family ownership without sacrificing the equity interest of a home buyer. The amenities center around the location, view, and central facilities of a multiple unit project, e.g., swimming pool, recreation, clubhouse, tennis courts, and like features.

Offsetting these advantages are the restrictions of group living and the lack of privacy provided by single-family ownership. In weighing the relative merits of condominiums, salespersons recognize that condominium ownership varies markedly from cooperative ownership: an ownership represented by a cooperative share with possession acquired under a proprietary lease. The cooperative owner has unlimited liability for the expenses of the cooperative, but he or she is not personally liable for the mortgage which is assumed by the nonprofit cooperative corporation.

Condominium prospects acquire ownership rights under the *declaration* or other instrument which is recorded and dedicates the property to a condominium. The charter provides for *bylaws* that control condominium operations. Voting rights, membership rules, and regulations are found in the bylaws. The bylaws give the board of directors the right to delegate day-to-day operations to a professional management firm. Under this agreement, called the *management agreement,* the manager has all rights delegated by the board of directors necessary for condominium operation.

In selling condominiums, salespersons must be familiar with the legal documents which, in some cases, by law, must be given to condominium buyers. Usually, the complexity of these documents advises that prospects refer to legal counsel before making a condominium purchase. The salesperson should be prepared to discuss property rights, economic advantages, and other operating details of the condominium.

Although new listings are acquired the same way that new listings are acquired for homes, the condominium association gives salespersons ready access to owners. By acting through the association, for example, sponsoring some of the condominium association's projects and programs, salespersons realize listings by developing a close relationship with an organized group.

In selling, it is important that salespersons acquaint buyer-prospects with the details of the maintenance charges. The salespersons should compare the monthly operating budget of a condominium ownership with the monthly operating budget of a home ownership. Usually, condominium ownership shows lower operating costs. Before presenting a condominium for sale, salespersons must review the possibilities of financing a condominium among local lenders.

Apartment conversions constitute a special challenge, for here salespersons concentrate first on tenants who are likely to buy converted units—usually at a discount—and then on the outside public. Special care should be taken to explain how ownership of a converted unit compares to straight rental. After an initial period in which tenants are given preference in sales, conversions are widely advertised by direct mail and in newspapers. In comparison to selling original condominiums, selling conversions calls for a special public relations campaign, primarily to gain tenant cooperation.

REVIEW QUESTIONS

1. Compare the selling opportunities associated with condominiums with the selling opportunities associated with detached houses.
2. Define the vocabulary terms common to condominium ownership.
3. Review the financial advantages associated with condominium purchase.
4. What condominium amenities should be emphasized?
5. Cite the disadvantages of condominium ownership.
6. Contrast condominium ownership with cooperative ownership.
7. Describe the main purpose of the declaration and describe its contents.
8. What main points are covered by condominium bylaws?
9. What is the importance of the management agreement?
10. What special preparation must you make if you are to sell condominiums?
11. Describe how you would secure new listings for condominium resales.
12. What special selling techniques would you apply to condominiums?
13. What are the factors that favor conversion of apartments to condominiums?
14. Explain the economics of condominium conversion. Give examples.
15. Describe recommended sale techniques and marketing plans for selling condominium conversions.

18

Selling

Residential Land

There is always an active market in residential land—and there probably always will be. Consequently, most communities have salespersons who specialize in marketing residential land. Such land sales appeal to investors and builders who buy acreage potentially suitable for subdivision and to others who buy residential lots for their own use. In some areas, potential residential land may show a rate of turnover comparable to houses.

To explain these points, it seems worthwhile to evaluate land as an investment, turning next to methods of selling potential subdivision land, and then to covering the special selling requirements developed for the sale of residential lots. The chapter concludes on land sales financing.

LAND INVESTMENTS EVALUATED

Do not be deluded into assuming that residential land will necessarily increase in price. Do not be misled into thinking that all land is adapted to residential use. Local zoning, environmental restrictions, and limited growth policies make much of the land—at least for residential use—unsaleable. And, further, do not be misled into thinking that land represents a suitable investment for all your prospects. The evaluation of land investment indicates that you should concentrate your selling efforts on selected buyers.

Land Investment Advantages

1. *Land Investments Give Prospects Unusual "Leverage" Advantages.* Leverage refers to the use of credit to increase the rate of return on invested capital. If prospects buy under long-term installment land contracts, say 10 years or more, they gain from seller financing. If you negotiate a 10 percent down payment on a $100,000 parcel, a 10 percent increase in value during the first year *doubles* the prospect's equity from $10,000 to $20,000. Exercising "leverage" in this way varies by the projected annual rate of land value appreciation and the amount of the down payment. Recall that an annual 7 percent compound rate of increase doubles the value in ten years. In the preceding example an average annual gain of 7 percent in value over ten years would result in a market value of almost $200,000, increasing the equity interest of your prospect tenfold—in addition to the gain realized by equity build-up.

Owners who exercise leverage advantages have incentives to resell in the shortest period of time. In the preceding example a $10,000 equity, though initially controlling land worth $200,000, in ten years would show a declining rate of return on equity since at the end of ten years the purchaser would have a 100 percent equity on cost. Therefore, the specialist in land investments works with the investor to market the investment at the appropriate time in order to maximize leverage advantages.

2. *Federal Income Tax Laws Favor Land Investors.* If the land is purchased under an installment plan, mortgage interest deductibility lowers the effective rate of interest. Suppose, for example, that land may be purchased with payments that include 10 percent interest on the remaining balance. To a taxpayer in the 49 percent marginal income tax bracket, this would be an effective interest rate of 5.1 percent. This advantage grows as the taxpayer's marginal income tax rate increases (to 70 percent) and as the proportion of monthly payments going to interest increases.

Investors in the upper income tax bracket have an added incentive because *land appreciation at resale* is subject to a 60 percent exemption. Presently, individuals pay income taxes on only 40 percent of the gain, which is considerably lower than progressive income tax rates that range upward to 70 percent. Therefore, land that shows promise of probable appreciation appeals to upper income groups that convert ordinary income to capital gains.

3. *Land Value Tends to Increase as the General Price Level Increases.* Though subject to considerable qualification, historically, as prices increase, individuals convert money in intangible assets (for example, deposits) to tangible assets (for example, land). Land is popularly viewed as a hedge against inflation.

This view is subject to qualification. Changes in public preference, in public facilities such as transportation, or in public policy on local land use controls, environmental restrictions, and limited growth make generalizations on this point hazardous. Although land may increase in value as confidence in the dollar decreases, each parcel of land may be subject to other forces that decrease land values.

Nevertheless, land values on the average have tended to rise, in some cases much greater than the rise in the consumer price index. The salesperson who correctly interprets land value trends as influenced by population growth and local market forces encourages land investment. The land investor avoids unpredictable variations in financial markets.

4. *Land Investments Require a Minimum of Management Time or Expense.* An investor in stocks and bonds must keep abreast of daily market changes. Similarly, income property requires daily self-management or a monthly review of financial statements. Management policies on investment real estate must be continually revised to meet market requirements. Land ownership is relatively free of decision making during the investment period.

5. *An Installment Land Purchase Adds to Personal Savings.* Time payments add to the equity interest, and at the same time the investor benefits from possible capital appreciation. Although land does not have the liquidity of a savings deposit, the installment payments appeal to investors who want to add to their investments regularly.

Land Investment Disadvantages

It is fairly obvious that land investments are suitable for a restricted list of prospects. Because much of the potential residential land is unproductive and does not earn income, prospects must have sufficient (and certain) income to maintain payments. Other disadvantages of investing in land narrow the number of potential buyer-prospects still further. These disadvantages are discussed below.

1. *Land Investments Lack Liquidity.* In this context, liquidity is defined as the ability to convert an investment to dollars at no loss. The uncertainty associated with land investment means that extra time must be taken to search for qualified buyers. Moreover, the risk associated with land investment may require advertising for out-of-town buyers. Therefore, for the most part, many buyers are not attracted to land investments because they do not have the liquidity to meet personal emergencies.

2. *Future Land Value Is Uncertain.* Experience reveals that land values are affected not only by variations in supply and demand but also by local, state, and federal policy. Public improvements, new highways, new government buildings, and new drainage facilities are among the many major government programs that bear on local land values.

Add to this list land use controls in the form of zoning and environmental restrictions on new sewer, water, and drainage systems, among others, that largely control the location of residential property, its development, planning, land use and, consequently, value. Limited growth policies are subject to unpredictable change which lowers the value of vacant land and increases the value of improved land. These changes in government policy complicate orderly market forces.

3.   *Land Investments Are Relatively Expensive.* Vacant land that is held for future residential use requires substantial investments for the original purchase and for meeting periodic payments with interest. The potential investor must anticipate capital appreciation that compensates for lack of income, mortgage interest, property taxes, and other holding costs over the projected investment period. The number of purchasers who would be willing to assume these fixed obligations, in the face of virtually no annual income, reduces the number of qualified prospects.

POTENTIAL SUBDIVISION LAND

Your ability to market potential subdivision land depends on your critical analysis of the land use potential. The analysis includes not only judgments on the demand and supply for residential sites but also critical judgments on land use controls, government policy, utility availability, and on-site and off-site cost.

Before considering these factors, you should bear in mind that land purchased for residential purposes is subject to unpredictable factors that affect value. The marketability of land may be influenced by the following:

1. General economic conditions (local, regional and national) that affect employment, population growth, and new housing starts.
2. The local supply of residential land, the unsold inventory of houses, and competitive land suitable for residential development.
3. Environmental laws and regulations that require environmental impact statements.
4. Limited growth policies.
5. The attitude of local officials in processing land development projects through many government offices.
6. The availability of utilities and their cost.
7. The administration of the local property tax.
8. The availability of financing from local lenders or federal and state agencies.

Because of these uncertainties, the marketing of potential subdivision land is undertaken with more than the usual facts itemized on the listing form. Because the risks in purchasing land may seem formidable, your marketing plan must be prepared so that the land value and your marketing service show how these risks may be offset or minimized.

Preliminary Market Analysis

Although a detailed appraisal report would not normally be required, the listing should incorporate statements on the *direction of population growth.* Communities that have master plans probably have these reports available for the public. Some acreage purchasers would consider *per capita income, trends in retail sales,* and *sources of employment* as part of their preliminary review of a proposed land purchase. Highway departments publish 24-hour *traffic counts* along main highways which may be significant to a land purchase. Present and proposed *highway construction* and the *extension of utility lines* (water and sewer) are factors important to the land use potential. Be prepared to supply data on *topography, soil characteristics, drainage problems, present vegetation,* i.e., trees and their type, and the *cost of land leveling and grading.* The number of *unsold houses* and the *price range of nearby subdivisions* are equally relevant.

The Listing Checklist. Land purchasers judge the residential potential according to the requirements of (1) local zoning and building ordinances, (2) environmental controls, (3) physical characteristics, (4) neighborhood analysis, and (5) financing terms. The listing information will not be exhaustive, but your buyer should know the general requirements in each of these areas if he or she is to judge the land use potential and value.

1. *Local zoning and building ordinances.* The listing checklist should indicate the present zoning and the probabilities of rezoning the property for residential use. The recommended building standards, minimum lot size, set-back lines, street width, and other requirements to develop residential property should be incorporated in this review. A review of published subdivision regulations provides helpful information to judge the residential potential. The main objective is to discover if there is some compelling reason why residential use would not be permitted, for example, because of limited growth policies, open space requirements, or other factors.

2. *Environmental controls.* If land development requires low-density development or open space dedication, subdividing will be more costly. Prospects will want to know what reports or investigations must be made before final development. Determine from FHA or HUD sources their requirements for project approval if you think government-assisted financing seems recommended.

3. *Physical characteristics.* If you are marketing the land for residential use, determine the availability of sewage disposal. Some communities will restrict additional hookups until the local system is improved. If septic tanks are approved, a soil percolation test would determine their suitability for residential purposes. Usually, topographic maps (and even

area maps) may be obtained from local sources and used to determine whether or not there may be drainage problems. Title records should be searched to indicate power line easements, cables, or pipelines that might bear on the final site plan.

4. *Neighborhood analysis.* First, there are the local community facilities that are important to residential land use—the schools, transportation, shopping, garbage removal, police, and fire protection. There are local assessment policies, property tax levies, and the possibility of a tax revaluation. There are the locally available recreational facilities in the form of parks and playgrounds. And there are the churches. All of these are included in the neighborhood analysis. The neighborhood analysis is completed by identifying the land use of adjoining sites. If they are residential sites, the price range of the adjoining houses should be reported.

5. *Financing terms.* Although the listing owner will specify acceptable terms of sale, alternative terms for negotiation should be prepared. Balloon payments, second mortgage financing, and interest payments only over the initial years should be considered. The availability of mortgage money for purchase of house and lots should also be explored. Lenders should be interviewed to determine if mortgage money would be available to potential house buyers for the neighborhood in question.

6. *Environmental impact statements.* Environmental impact statements prepared for numerous agencies and for special purposes tend to lower the value of potential subdivision land.

Environmental Controls.   As residential land becomes scarce, developers shift environmental costs to purchasers by increasing prices. The analysis of the potential demand for residential sites indicates whether or not these costs may be shifted to buyers. As an illustration of the complexity of the reports that precede project approval, listed below are the reports that the Irvine Company of California needs to process projects.

1. Environmental impact reports (required by the California Environmental Quality Act).
2. Zoning conformity (California Planning Law).
3. General plan of local agencies.
4. Tentative maps (required by the state subdivision map act).
5. The Clean Air Act, including indirect pollution sources and parking approval.
6. Water Quality Act (Section 208).
7. Land use legislation, open space/agricultural legislation.
8. Environmental management regulation required by local government.
9. Noise controls.
10. Housing ordinances.

11. Archaeological and historical preservation requirements.
12. Coastal Zone Management Act.

Processing a development involves public hearings, filing of property notices, and numerous consultations between government agencies. Detailed checklists are required to ensure that the project procedures conform to these new legal requirements. Therefore, in listing acreage the salesperson should be aware of the environmental controls administered in his or her local area.

Subdivision Value

Inexperienced salespersons would estimate subdivision land value by multiplying the number of lots times their price less the cost of development. If 100 acres could be divided into 3 lots per acre, producing 300 lots, retail value would be indicated by the price per lot, $10,000 times 300, or $3 million. Land having a retail value of $3 million and an estimated cost of development of $1,500,000 would have an indicated market value of $1,500,000.

Experienced salespersons would not estimate subdivision land value this way. Subdivisions are a means of producing deferred income. In fact, lots would not be available until several months after the project has started because of the time required to seek approval and to make necessary improvements. Even then the subdivision typically would not be sold out for several months or even years after development starts. For this reason, experienced salespersons value subdivisions according to the annual estimated cash flow.

Cash Flow Estimates. The cash flow estimate starts with a survey of competitive lot prices. A current market value is placed on each lot of the proposed subdivision according to comparable market evidence. Although lot prices vary according to location, an average lot value is calculated for this purpose. In a subdivision of 100 acres the average lot values would be established by weighing the characteristics of each lot and block assuming that the project will be fully developed.

Next, an estimate of development expenses would be made. These expenses would be put into four categories: (1) property taxes, (2) development costs, (3) selling expenses, and (4) profit and overhead. The development costs would include on-site and off-site utility expenses. Off-site utility expenses are the costs for extending utility lines to the sites.

Three other estimates are necessary at this point: (1) an estimate of development costs by time periods, (2) a projection of lot sales per year, and (3) a discount rate to convert future cash flow to present value. In normal practice, development costs occur early in the project, usually in phases as the subdivision develops. Selling expenses would be prorated according to the projection of sales volume. Table 18-1 projects these costs over a series of six-month periods.

TABLE 18-1. Calculation of Subdivision Market Value

					Six-month Periods						
	1	2	3	4	5	6	7	8	9	10	11
Retail price per lot		$20,800	$20,800	$20,800	$20,800	$20,800	$26,720	$28,800	$28,800	$23,300	$23,300
Number of sales		4	4	5	5	5	5	5	5	5	3
Gross revenue		$83,200	$83,200	$104,000	$104,000	$104,000	$133,600	$144,000	$144,000	$116,500	$69,900
Less expenses											
Development costs	$133,000	$0	$0	$0	$0	$61,500	$61,500	$42,000	$42,000	0	0
10% selling expense	0	8,320	8,320	10,400	10,400	10,400	13,360	14,400	14,400	11,650	6,990
Taxes*	0	7,275	0	5,703	0	4,514	0	3,569	0	1,796	0
10% profit	0	8,320	8,320	10,400	10,400	10,400	13,360	14,400	14,400	11,650	6,990
Estimated cash flow	($133,000)	$59,285	$66,560	$77,497	$83,200	$17,186	$45,380	$69,631	$73,200	$91,404	$55,920
PW factor @ 12%	.943396	.889996	.839619	.792094	.747258	.704961	.665057	.627412	.591898	.558395	.526788
Present value	($125,472)	$52,763	$55,885	$61,385	$62,172	$12,115	$30,180	$43,687	$43,327	$51,040	$29,458

Total present value	$316,540
Per acre	$ 4,820

*Taxes are based on $74.39 per acre of undeveloped land and $225 per unsold lot plus a pro rata seller carry of lots closed on that year.

Source: Data contributed by Stewart Wight, MAI, Landauer Associates, Inc., Atlanta, Georgia.

Note that in the first six months the project indicates a substantial negative cash flow. As phase 2 starts at the end of the sixth period, calling for additional development expenses, cash flow again turns negative for the next two years.

The discount factors in each instance indicate the present worth of postponed income. The present worth of one dollar six months later, discounted at 12 percent, is $.943396. This means that one dollar postponed for six months has a present worth of 94 cents. If you paid 94 cents today for the right to one dollar six months later you would recover your 94-cent investment and would earn 12 percent on your capital investment of 94 cents. Similarly, in subdivisions, the present worth of one dollar for each period is multiplied by the estimated cash flow of each period to convert future income to present value.[1] Thus, the $316,540 represents the present worth of future income generated by the subdivision. This value estimate would be supplemented by the comparable price per acre of subdivision land showing the feasibility of the proposed subdivision.

Leverage

Leverage, in this case, refers to buying land under favorable credit terms. Here, the rate of return on invested capital increases with the amount of credit. The alternatives range from a cash purchase, giving the smallest annual rate of return and the least risk, to 100 percent financing requiring no minimum investment but substantial payments. Ideally, land is purchased under the most favorable terms, held for relatively short periods (three to five years), and sold at a substantial capital gain. Unfortunately, it does not always happen this way.

Prospects gain the maximum advantage by purchasing land which is nearing the "ideal" time of development. Preferably, land would be undergoing a change from pasture, timber, or crop use to urban use. If the change in use is projected to 15 or more years, returns are less certain.

Another requirement is that prospects have the resources to make the annual payments. Knowing that land represents a nonliquid investment, and dealing with an investment giving a low annual return (or no annual return), the land investor must look to independent sources to make the installment payments. Such investors should not be under pressure to liquidate during periods of slow economic development. They should have sufficient personal resources to continue making payments and hold the land until capital gains are realized. Given these circumstances, projections should be prepared show-

---

[1] For present worth of one factors and other capitalization rates, consult standard capitalization tables. For additional explanation, see William M. Shenkel, *Modern Real Estate Appraisal* (New York: McGraw-Hill Book Company, 1978), pp. 230–54.

ing the rate of return under different land appreciation and financing assumptions.

Cash Investment.   Assume that your prospect anticipates an annual increase in land value of 10 percent per year. At the end of seven years an annual compound increase of 10 percent would produce a land value of $194,871 (for this illustration rounded upward to $200,000). Since the annual rate of increase applies to the value at the end of each year, the 10 percent increase is compounded. An initial investment of $100,000 cash showing land appreciation of 10 percent per year for seven years would appreciate annually from $10,000 to $17,716 according to the following schedule:

Value of a $100,000 Land Purchase Assuming a 10 Percent Annual Increase in Value
Seven-Year Investment

End of Year	Value	Annual Increase
1	$110,000	$10,000
2	121,000	11,000
3	133,100	12,100
4	146,410	13,310
5	161,051	14,641
6	177,156	16,105
7	194,872	17,716

Figure 18-1 shows the percent of value increase for selected interest rates over a ten year term. The figure indicates that the annual dollar increment accelerates rapidly, after the fifth year of ownership. Conversely, during the early years of an investment, even with relatively high compound rates of increase, the greatest advantage of capital appreciation is gained in the later years of the ten-year holding period.

As an additional illustration, assume (1) a $200,000 value at the end of seven years and (2) a selling cost of 10 percent, or $20,000. The total land appreciation over seven years amounts to $80,000, or an average annual increase of $11,429 ($80,000 divided by 7). Or, to put it differently, an $80,000 appreciation is equal to 80 percent of the original investment, or an average annual rate of profit of 11.41 percent. These data are summarized in Case 1.

Ordinary Leverage.   To indicate how financing increases the rate of return, let us say that the land is purchased for 29 percent down, the balance is paid over 15 years, and the interest is 10 percent. A loan of $71,000 paid monthly under these terms would require monthly payments of $763.25. Let

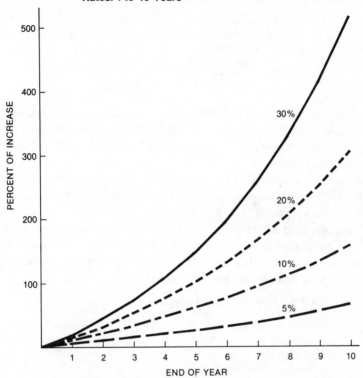

FIGURE 18-1. Percent of Value Increase for Selected Compound Interest Rates: 1 to 10 Years

us assume further that your prospect is in the 50 percent federal income tax bracket (which presently could range upward to 70 percent).

Over the first year the prospect would pay $9,159 on the mortgage, including principal and interest. Of this sum, $7,029 represents mortgage interest, which is deductible from taxable income. This amounts to $585.75 per

CASE 1. Rate of Return Analysis: Cash Investment

Sales price, 7 years		$200,000
Less original cost		− 100,000
Land appreciation		$100,000
Less selling costs		
(10%)		− 20,000
Capital gain		$ 80,000
Annual appreciation $80,000/7	=	$ 11,429
Average annual rate of profit:		
$80,000 ÷ $100,000	=	80%
80% ÷ 7	=	11.4%

month. With a 50 percent income tax bracket, the effective monthly payments are reduced by 50 percent of this amount, or $292.88 as shown below.

Monthly payment	$763.50
Less 12 months	
average interest	
deduction (first year)	−292.88
Effective monthly	
payment	$470.62

These figures indicate that the monthly payment after income taxes has been reduced to $470.62 over the first year. This calculation is based on total mortgage payments over the 12 months of $9,159, of which $2,130 applies to the reduction of principal.

Now let us suppose that the investor sells a property at the end of seven years for $200,000. After paying the 10 percent selling cost, the prospect owes $50,268 on the original $71,000 mortgage.

Note that after allowing for selling costs and repayment of the outstanding mortgage balance, the investor realizes a capital gain of $29,730. With a $29,000 down payment, this represents a 102.5 percent gain, or an average annual rate of return of *14.6 percent* as indicated in Case 2.

CASE 2. Rate of Return Analysis: Ordinary Leverage

Sales price, 7 years		$200,000
Original price		−100,000
Land appreciation		$100,000
Less selling costs (10%)		
	$20,000	
Less mortgage		
balance	50,268	−70,268
Capital gain		$ 29,732
Return on invested		
capital $29,732 ÷ $29,000		= 102.5%
Average annual rate		
of return 102.5 ÷ 7		= 14.6%

The example shows that credit increased the annual rate of return over a cash purchase. Observe, however, that the example is based on a capital gain equal to a 10 percent annual compound rate of increase and a 29 percent down payment. The rate of return would increase with a higher proportion of credit.

Note further that this example is selected only to show the effect of leverage. The land owner would also pay property taxes and perhaps other operating expenses which would tend to lower the actual rate of return.

Maximum Leverage.   Some sellers list their land at inflated prices, selling under a land contract with little or no down payment. Alternatively, installment credit may be arranged through financial institutions with the owner accepting a second lien subordinate to the first loan. The additional credit risk assumed by the owner is secured by the land contract which keeps title in the name of the seller until the contract is satisfied. The higher than market price helps offset the added risk. This arrangement gives the buyer-prospect maximum leverage.

To simplify the illustration, let us assume that the first seller accepts a purchase money mortgage for the amount of the listing price. Again, a 15-year mortgage, 10 percent interest is assumed. The same assumptions apply to this illustration to allow comparison with the preceding cases. Mortgage payments are based on amortization of $100,000, the original purchase price. The mortgage interest deduction would show an effective monthly payment as follows:

Monthly payment	$1,075
Less 12 months	
Average interest deduction, 50% tax rate (first year)	− 413
Effective monthly payment	$ 662

The monthly payment of $1,075 provides for total mortgage payments, interest and principal, of $12,900 of which $3,000 represents repayment of principal with a balance of $9,900 going to interest. The $825 monthly average interest cost over the first year provides for an average interest deduction of $413 (50 percent income tax rate) or an effective monthly payment of $662. Because of the mortgage interest deduction, effective monthly payments are reduced to approximately 62 percent of total mortgage payments of $1,075.

The capital gain under the same assumptions shows a land appreciation of $100,000. Deducting the selling costs and the remaining mortgage balance, which total $90,800, gives an appreciation of $9,200 at the end of seven years, or an average annual dollar gain of $1,314. See Case 3.

CASE 3. Rate of Return Analysis: Maximum Leverage

Sales price, 7 years		$200,000
Less original price		−100,000
Land appreciation		$100,000
Less selling costs (10%)	$20,000	
Less mortgage balance	70,800	
		− 90,800
Capital gain		$ 9,200
Average annual gain ($9,200 ÷ 7)		$ 1,314

Since the mortgage interest equals the assumed annual rate of appreciation (10 percent), the dollar appreciation is considerably reduced. Maximum leverage and the annual rate of return increase substantially as the rate of land appreciation rises above the installment interest rate. However, even here the annual average gain of $1,314 is earned with no capital investment. Figure 18-2 illustrates the effect of leverage in the three cases.

FIGURE 18-2.   Leverage for Three Selected Cases*

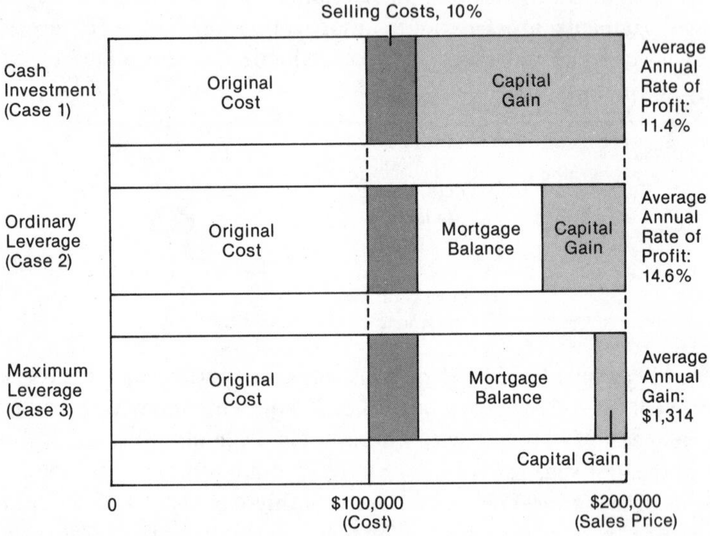

*For assumptions, see text.

It will be appreciated that maximum leverage results in considerable risk. After allowing for property taxes and other holding costs, most investors would view the latter as a nominal return in view of the risks assumed. Moreover, with little or no capital investment, reverse leverage exposes the buyer-prospect to a possible loss of capital and contract default with consequent personal losses.

RESIDENTIAL LOTS

Residential lots are priced according to dollars per front foot, dollars per square foot, or their site value. Site values follow from the difficulty of assigning a per unit price on irregularly shaped lots of varying square-foot area. For instance, an inside lot on a culdesac—a fan-shaped lot—may have less than the standard frontage but more than the usual square-foot area. Here virtually the only recourse is to establish site values from sales comparisons of similar lots showing equal residential site utility.

Furthermore, for each neighborhood there tends to be a normal relationship between the land and building value. A subdivision of $75,000 to $100,000 dwellings (house and lot) would show a range of lot values, say, from $20,000 to $40,000.

Residential Lot Checklist

You will find it helpful to prepare a checklist that lists the main benefits of the lots you have listed for sale. The checklist will make it easier for you to answer most prospect inquiries and to explain and support the listed price. Your checklist should include details on physical, social, political, and other features, for example:

Physical Features
  Topography/slope
  Streets
  Storm drains
  Natural vegetation
  Dimensions/area
  Soil characteristics

Social Features
  Age level
  Size of family
  Main occupations
  Average family income
  Education

Political Features
  Land use controls
  Police protection
  Fire protection
  Garbage service
  Property tax
  Crime rates
  Quality of schools

Other Features
  Surrounding land use
  Location (parks, recreation, shopping, churches, schools, access to freeway)
  Age of subdivision
  Typical housing values
  Proportion of unsold lots
  Protection from noise
  Neighborhood vacancy rate
  Air quality
  Energy conservation: exposure to wind, solar energy

The topography and slope affect construction costs and the type of dwelling for which the lot is adapted. Most families prefer a site above the street grade. Downward sloping lots requiring construction below the street grade are usually discounted. A slope favoring sun radiation and protecting the house from cold winds reduces energy costs. The quality of curbs, storm drains, and streets must be suitable for the neighborhood.

Natural vegetation adds value, but the location of the vegetation is important. Recall that evergreen trees protect the house from winter winds and that deciduous trees provide cooling shade during the summer months and give maximum solar exposure in the winter. Other things being equal, a wooded lot in most communities has greater value than a cleared lot.

Lot dimensions must be appropriate for the neighborhood. An unusually large lot of one acre would probably be discounted in a neighborhood of one-half acre lots. The additional area may contribute little value; it depends on the neighborhood and neighborhood prices. Soil characteristics concern water runoff, drainage, and construction costs.

Social features concern occupant age level, typical family size, occupations, and family income. Though subject to qualification, a homogeneous neighborhood of compatible families generally seems to add value and increase lot saleability.

Political features concern local government services: their quality, frequency of service, and cost. The main question is do political features conform to local resident requirements? A high crime rate may discourage residential lot sales.

For newly developed subdivisions, *other features* control the rate of land absorption: The more surrounding land conforms to subdivision use, the more likely the subdivision will attract new lot buyers.

Similarly, the ideal location would be convenient to parks, playgrounds, recreational facilities, convenience shopping, churches, schools, and even access to the freeway, all of which should be within reasonable driving times— 15 minutes to 30 minutes at the most. The importance of locational factors may be expected to vary widely and depends on local preferences.

Increasingly, residents expect protection from neighborhood nuisances, for example, disturbing noises. Residents want sites free from smog and smoke or smells created by local industry. You may expect lot buyers to pay more attention to the exposure of the lot to the wind and sun, especially where rights to solar energy assume greater importance.

Land Value Trends

Usually, developers list lots at the competitive level with other subdivisions having similar features. As the subdivision becomes more popular, land prices increase. Therefore, in listing land, your prospects of sale increase if you can explain a favorable trend in local land values. Consequently, it is advisable to compare the current listing price of lots with lot prices of say three to five years ago. Although locations vary, these data show how the prospect gains from buying property which in the past has undergone rising values.

The rising land value trends may be expected to continue with the growth in the local economic base and with added public improvements such as highways, mass transportation, new public construction, and population growth. Population growth relates not only to regional growth but also to shifts in population from less favored neighborhoods to the new subdivisions. Your analysis of local land value trends should be an important part of your presentation.

FIGURE 18-3. Residential Lot Prices, Lake Tahoe, Nevada, for Selected Years

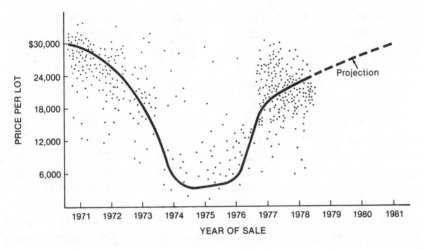

Source: Address by Robert F. Soma, Systems Analyst, Washoe County, Nevada, before a Colloquium on Land Valuation Methods sponsored by the Lincoln Institute of Land Policy, Cambridge, Mass., June 2, 1978.

The unpredictable variation in residential lot prices is illustrated by an eight-year record of residential sites sold in Lake Tahoe, Nevada, between 1971 and 1978. These sales are shown by year of sale in Figure 18-3. This diagram plots 628 residential sales, mostly sold by a major developer who subdivided land and provided for streets and underground utilities. Two years after construction the developer filed for bankruptcy. Many lots were sold for taxes and some lots were sold at public auction, which explains why real estate sales were depressed from 1974 to 1976. With a change in the economic base in Reno, Nevada, sales prices rose steeply to the level shown in 1978.

Prices shown in Figure 18-3, though varying widely because of site differences, show substantial change over the eight-year term. Your review of past sales in this manner gives prospects added information for making buying decisions.

FINANCING PLANS

Sellers must consider the tax consequences of selling their property. The danger is that the capital gain tax may exceed the down payment, thus requiring that the seller pay taxes from personal funds. To avoid this impasse sellers may elect to sell under the *installment plan* or *deferred payment plan.* Even though you advise your clients to consult a tax attorney, your awareness of these plans will help in listing and in closing sales.

The Installment Plan

Suppose you list land priced at $100,000 which originally cost the seller $20,000. If the seller agrees to accept an installment land contract, he or she may report the capital gain from an installment sale as if *a pro rata portion of the total gain were realized with each payment.* Provided certain qualifications are met, the seller allocates the gain proportionately over the life of the installment contract.

Economic Advantages. There are certain economic advantages realized by the installment sale: (1) Only a share of the down payment will be needed to pay capital gain taxes during the year of the sale. The seller will need no additional funds from other sources to pay capital gain taxes. The greater proportion of the down payment will be available for personal use. (2) There is an advantage in postponing capital gain taxes until the time capital gains are realized, namely, at the time of installment payments. (3) Some taxpayers may be taxed at ordinary income tax rates on the gain. Federal income tax rates are progressive. Hence, the installment sale spreads the gain over several years, thus giving the seller the advantage of lower progressive tax rates.

If the seller is subject to capital gain taxes, there is the risk that Congress may increase (or decrease) capital gain tax rates. The capital gain tax rate applies to the year in which the payment is received.

Installment Sale Requirements. To qualify for the installment method, the seller must meet two requirements: (1) Not more than 30 percent of the total sales price may be received by the seller in the year of sale. Custom dictates that sellers accept not more than 29 percent of the purchase price under the installment sale as a down payment. (2) The seller must elect the installment method on a tax return for the year of sale. The personal income tax return will show the total price paid, the capital gain realized over the life of the contract, and the pro rata portion of the gain taxable in the year of sale.

Application. Assume that land is sold for $100,000 and the selling expenses are $10,000. If the land originally cost $40,000, the seller has a taxable gain of $50,000 or 50 percent. See Case 4.

CASE 4. An Illustration of an Installment Sale

Sales price	$100,000	
Less selling expenses		
(10%)	−10,000	$90,000
Less cost of land		−40,000
Taxable gain (50% of price)		$50,000
Payments received in		
year of sale		
Down payment	$ 20,000	
Payment on principal	10,000	$30,000
Capital gain taxable		
in year of sale (50%)		$15,000

If the sales agreement calls for a down payment of $20,000 and a first payment of $10,000 during the year of sale, the sale qualifies as an installment sale because the amount of payment received in the year of sale is not more than 30 percent. During the first year the seller reports a taxable gain of $15,000. The taxable gain of 50 percent is prorated on payments received each year. If in the succeeding year a $10,000 payment is received, the capital gain tax is based on a gain of $5,000.

Note that in arranging an installment sale the amount received during the first year in the form of a first payment and the down payment together must not exceed 30 percent of the sales price. There are many qualifications to the treatment of an installment sale, but space does not allow more detailed treatment. Advise clients and prospects to seek tax counsel.

Deferred Payment Plan

The seller may elect to report capital gains only when total payments received equal the original land cost.

Under the deferred payment plan, the seller reports no capital gain until total payments, including the down payment and installments, equal the original land price plus selling costs. When these costs have been recovered in payments received, all remaining payments are subject to capital gain taxes.

Economic Advantages. This method of arranging contract payments gives the seller the advantage of postponing capital gains until original costs have been recovered. (1) Initially, the down payment and installment payments are available to the seller for reinvestment without deducting capital gain taxes. (2) Moreover, the seller avoids the risk of reporting gains realized before monies have been received. In effect, this method shifts capital gains to the later years of the installment contract. In contrast, the installment method spreads capital gain taxes evenly over the life of the contract. (3) Under the deferred payment plan, there is no restriction on the amount of the total payment received in the year of sale. As would the seller who elects to use the installment plan, the seller who elects to use the deferred payment plan runs the risk of changes in the capital gain tax rate in future years.

Application. Using the former illustration, suppose that the seller provides for ten installments of $10,000 over ten years and an initial down payment of $20,000. Assume an original land cost of $40,000 and selling costs of 10 percent. This illustration is summarized in Case 5.

At the end of the first year the payments received total $30,000, which is less than the adjusted basis of $50,000. No capital gains are reported. At the end of year 2 no capital gains result because the seller still has not recovered

CASE 5. An Illustration of a Deferred Payment Sale

Year 1		
Adjusted basis		
Original land cost	$40,000	
Selling costs (10%)	10,000	
Total adjusted basis		$50,000
Less recovered amount		
Down payment	$20,000	
First installment	10,000	−30,000
Unrecovered amount		$20,000
Capital gain		0
Year 2		
Adjusted basis		$50,000
Less recovered amount		
Recovered first year	$30,000	
Second installment	10,000	−40,000
Unrecovered amount		$10,000
Capital gain		0
Year 3		
Adjusted basis		$50,000
Less recovered amount		
Recovered second year	$40,000	
Third installment	10,000	−50,000
Unrecovered amount		0
Capital gain		0
Year 4		
Adjusted basis		$50,000
Less recovered amount		
third year		50,000
Unrecovered amount		0
Fourth installment		$10,000
Capital gain		$10,000

payments equal to the recoverable cost of $50,000. At the end of year 4 the entire payment of $10,000 is subject to a capital gain tax because recoverable costs have been received.

Common Financing Methods

The installment and deferred payment plans assume financing by the seller. If the seller wants cash, the buyer has the option of forming a joint venture. If the land is suitable for subdivision development, buyers experienced in developing subdivision land turn to private sources of capital (typically those in the higher income brackets) who wish to convert ordinary and progressive income tax rates to the lower capital gain rate. In return for purchase capital, they normally expect 50 percent of the profits.

Joint Venture with Seller. Another plan is to joint venture with the seller. Here, the landowner commits vacant land to the project at its cost and agrees to subordinate the land to a first mortgage or construction loan for development purposes. The landowner and developer then arrange for financing and development jointly through conventional institutions. Profits realized are divided equally as the subdivided land is sold, a selling period which may extend over several years. The willingness of the seller to subordinate the land to a development loan allows the joint venture partners to pledge the land as security for the development loan.

Blanket Mortgages. Builders have frequently used the blanket mortgage as a financing device. Under this plan, the landowner pledges land to a developer who proceeds with subdivision development. The seller normally accepts a nominal down payment in return for substantial capital gains. The seller accepts a blanket mortgage which pledges subdivided lots to the seller. As each lot is sold, a mortgage release is executed by the seller that frees the lot from the blanket mortgage. A part of the lot price is paid to the seller against the original sales price.

In other words, the seller helps the developer finance the project in return for earning a substantial capital gain. This device usually works best for agricultural land that is converted to residential purposes.

Options to Purchase. Developers also finance land under options. For example, a 100-acre tract property is to be developed in units of 25 acres. The initial sale applies to the first phase, or 25 acres. At the same time, the buyer exercises an option to buy additional 25-acre increments within a given time limit at a stated price. The developer is able to arrange for a 100-acre subdivision because he or she knows in advance that additional land will be available at a fixed price. The seller gains from option payments which, however, are credited against the purchase price as options are exercised.

In other instances, the credit for the option payment decreases as the time extended for exercising the option increases. For example, if the developing company elects to purchase an additional 25 acres in three years, the company secures the full $5,000 option credit. The option credit may be reduced $1,000 for each additional year after three years.

Land Contracts.   Land contracts are subject to considerable flexibility. Buyers negotiate financing using installment contracts and partially amortized mortgages with balloon payments made at the end of five or ten years. Other variations require interest payments only during the initial years. Because of the tax consequences to both parties, these installment variations should be reviewed by tax attorneys.

POINTS TO REMEMBER

The main advantages of land investment arise from opportunities to increase the rate of return by *leveraging* investments. In this context, leveraging refers to increasing the annual rate of return by maximizing credit. The *tax deductibility* of mortgage interest and relatively *low capital gain* tax rates give land investments an added advantage. Buyers purchase land as a *hedge against inflation;* moreover, land requires a *minimum of management time* and if purchased under an installment plan, it represents a form of *annual personal savings.*

Against these advantages is the fact that future land value is highly uncertain, it is relatively expensive, and it lacks liquidity.

Potential subdivision land values are influenced by general economic conditions. Land values are further influenced by the local supply of residential land and its projected demand, the administration of environmental laws, and various local land use regulations, including limited growth policies, available utilities and their costs, property taxes, and development financing. These factors recommend a preliminary market analysis that includes an analysis of forces significant to potential residential land use.

In listing land that is believed potentially valuable for residential use, you should prepare a minimum listing checklist for your prospects. This checklist should include local zoning and building ordinances, the impact of environmental controls, physical characteristics, neighborhood analysis, proposed financing terms, and the requirement for environmental impact statements. In the final analysis, subdivision values arise from the present worth of the estimated cash flow.

The annual rate of return tends to increase as the loan to value ratio increases, especially if the projected rate of land value increase is greater than mortgage or installment interest rates. The data indicate that an average annual value increase of 10 percent, compounded, almost doubles land values in seven years.

Selling residential lots, which includes listing and sales, requires preparation of a residential lot checklist adapted to the neighborhood. The checklist incorporates the main physical, social, political, and other features associated with residential site value. Your prospects for marketing residential lots are enhanced if you critically review local land value trends, which may be fairly unpredictable.

Although the tax complications of installment or deferred payment plans suggest that clients and prospects should obtain competent legal advice, you should be able to explain to your clients and prospects the basics of these plans. The installment sale requires a down payment and first year payment which together total not more than 30 percent of the sales price. The installment sale allows the seller to prorate capital gains proportionately over installment payments.

The deferred payment plan allows the deferment of capital gain taxes until the seller recovers original land and selling costs. At this point, the total remaining installment payments are subject to capital gain taxes as they occur.

A review of the more popular financing plans shows that buyers and sellers, and the selling agent, have considerable financing flexibility. The variations include buyers who secure capital by joint venturing with partners who take 50 percent of the profit in return for financing the land purchase. Sellers may also joint venture by dedicating land at their cost and dividing profits equally with the developer. Blanket mortgages, options to purchase, and land contracts are other popular methods of financing land purchases.

REVIEW QUESTIONS

1. What are the advantages in investing in land?
2. What are the disadvantages in investing in land?
3. What are the factors that largely determine the marketability of subdivision land?
4. What would you include in a preliminary market analysis of potential subdivision land?
5. What information would you include in the listing checklist to judge residential potential?
6. Explain how you would value subdivision land.
7. Give an example of leverage realized in a land investment. Explain fully.
8. What factors would you include in a checklist that covers physical, social, political, and other features of residential lots?
9. What are the economic advantages associated with an installment sale?
10. What are the requirements for an installment sale?
11. What are the economic advantages of arranging a deferred payment plan?
12. What common financing methods would you recommend for land purchases?

19

Selling the Financing Plan

Ordinarily, your sale is not assured unless the buyer can finance the purchase. Frequently, you must sell a financing plan that satisfies the buyer, the seller, and the mortgage lender. Because of the many sources of mortgage credit and the different ways of buying a house, you do not necessarily abandon the sale because the buyer cannot qualify for a first mortgage.

Consider, for example, the buyer who tendered an offer of $55,000 which was accepted. The savings and loan association would approve a mortgage of only $42,000. Therefore, the prospect, who had only $8,000 in savings, required an additional $5,000. The salesperson arranged a second mortgage from a private party who agreed to advance $5,000 on a second mortgage, 10 percent interest, repayable in monthly payments over five years. The income of the husband and wife was more than adequate to meet the additional second mortgage payments of $106.23 per month.

Special financing may be arranged for buyers who have insufficient income to make first mortgage payments. The knowledgeable salesperson directs these buyers to lenders who provide *flexible payment mortgages*—mortgages having unusually low monthly payments during the early years. These mortgages are adapted to buyers who expect increasing income over the next few years, for example, a medical doctor beginning a new practice.

In sum, if you have an offer and acceptance, the final step may require that you direct the buyer and seller to a financing plan that meets their mutual requirements. You should first consider the more common financing arrangements, then review second mortgage financing, and next be prepared for more specialized mortgages, a topic that will be discussed at the end of the chapter.

Before covering these topics, it is worthwhile to explain the standard procedures to determine borrower mortgage credit. A knowledge of the probable credit status of the buyer saves time because the buyer is shown the right house and, more importantly, it helps guide the buyer to the best financing plan.

DETERMINING BORROWER CREDIT

The property placed as security for a loan must meet the minimum standards of the lending agency. If the property being sold qualifies, your prospect will be judged according to his or her credit-paying ability. In judging credit, three items are significant: *the anticipated income, assets and liabilities,* and *estimated housing expenses.* Given these favorable relationships, approval of borrower credit depends on judgments over the *borrower's willingness* to satisfy debts, which is indicated by the borrower's record of past payments.

Anticipated Income

Lenders are mainly concerned about the amount of income that can be reliably expected over the early years of the loan—and the relative stability of the income. Anticipated income is intrepreted as *effective income:* that income which is reasonably certain less nonrecurring income earned on an infrequent basis. Lenders tend to discount Christmas bonuses, overtime pay, and other nonrepetitive income of infrequent payment, for example, royalties, profits, commissions, extra dividends, and the like. Lenders who process loans for FHA financing are guided by *net effective income:* effective income less federal income tax withholding. Net effective income is comparable to take-home pay.

Current law requires that income from an employed spouse be included for mortgage credit purposes. To verify income, lenders usually require verification of employment and income or even ask for personal income tax statements over the preceding years.

Stability of income is subject to a similiar review. More stable incomes are made by middle-income groups employed in junior management, the professions (lawyers, accountants, architects), the white-collar trades, skilled workers, government employees, and utility personnel. At the other extreme, musicians, entertainers, salesmen, actors, and writers are often subject to varying, uncertain income. Lenders ask these people for a record of past income to establish some reasonable estimate of expected income.

Assets and Liabilities

Available assets are relevant to the minimum cash required at closing. Before a loan is approved, assets must be verified. Most lenders use deposit verification forms for this. Expect the property of your prospect in the form of other real estate (especially vacant land), household furniture, and other personal items to be discounted for mortgage loan purposes because these are typically nonliquid assets and may give a false indication of the borrower's ability to pay.

Special care is taken in judging liabilities, namely, installment debts and other fixed obligations of the borrower, for example, retirement plans, child support, alimony payments, insurance, and other unusual family expenses.

Housing Expenses

Since consumers are unlikely to change their spending habits, lenders review past housing expenses in the light of the new mortgage application. Current practice requires not only consideration of the mortgage payments, insurance, and property taxes on a monthly prorated basis but also a review of anticipated utility expenses. That is, a borrower may be eligible to finance an energy-efficient house, but the utility costs would prevent the borrower from qualifying for an energy-inefficient house. Housing expenses would normally include the following:

Mortgage principal.
Mortgage insurance premium.
Hazard insurance.
Taxes and special assessment payments.
Maintenance and repair expenses.
Heating and other utility charges.
Association assessments in the case of cooperatives, condominiums, and planned unit developments.

Finally, lenders evaluate the mortgage risk. The Department of Housing and Urban Development (HUD) rates six elements of the borrower (see Figure 19-1).

FIGURE 19-1. Evaluation of Mortgagor Risk Report

Mortgagor Features	*Rating*
1. Credit characteristics of mortgagor	_____
2. Motivating interest in ownership of the property	_____
3. Importance of monetary interest to mortgagor	_____
4. Adequacy of available assets for transaction	_____
5. Stability of effective income	_____
6. Adequacy of effective income for total obligations	_____
Mortgagor rating	_____

Source: *Mortgage Credit Analysis Handbook* 4155.5 (Washington, D.C.: Department of Housing and Urban Development, July, 1972, as amended), pp. 2–3.

Although these rules are not controlling for all lenders, they do show the common factors that most lenders consider. Motivating interest in ownership, according to the judgment of HUD, is demonstrated by whether or not the house is suitable for the family. Monetary interest is judged by the amount of cash the borrower pays down.

Final approval rests on a favorable credit report. The report gives information on employment, past credit deficiencies, and judgments that may have been filed against the borrower.

The salesperson does not have to qualify as a loan officer, but he or she does have to learn the credit standards of local lenders. For example, in the Atlanta, Georgia area, borrowers qualify for conventional mortgages if their monthly payments including principal, interest, taxes, and insurance are not more than *one-fourth of the gross monthly income,* provided their total recurring monthly *debt payments do not exceed one-third of the gross monthly income.* As a general rule, FHA considers effective income as adequate if the borrower's total obligations are not more than *50 percent of net effective income.*

These rules are relaxed under unusual circumstances. A borrower who has good prospects of rising income, for example, a young professional starting private practice, persons accepting new jobs who have excellent opportunities for advancement, and borrowers who have an unusually large amount of assets.

THE FINANCING PROCEDURE

Most houses are sold under one of four financing plans: (1) a new first mortgage, (2) the assumption of an existing mortgage, (3) a new first mortgage and a second mortgage accepted by the seller, and (4) the assumption of an existing first mortgage and the acceptance of a second mortgage by the seller. These financing plans and the typical language found in the contract for sale or deposit receipt are discussed below. A $75,000 sales price and a lender who is willing to grant an 80 percent loan, $9\frac{1}{2}$ percent interest, 25 years are assumed.

First Mortgage Financing: New Loan

In this first case, typical language in the contract for sale or binder would read:

Case 1

Purchaser to apply for and to accept if approved a new first loan in the principal amount of $60,000 secured by said property bearing interest at the rate of $9\frac{1}{2}$ percent per annum and amortized over 300 equal monthly payments of $524.40 each, including principal and interest. Purchaser to pay balance to seller in cash at closing.

Under this arrangement, the sale depends on the approval of the buyer's credit and the appraisal which must be sufficient to support the requested mortgage. The initial qualification of the prospect minimizes the chance that the occupant's credit will not be approved for the house selected.

FHA Loans.   If the house is to be financed by a Federal Housing Administration insured loan, most sales contracts include a special stipulation stating: "Purchaser agrees to accept the above described loan at the current interest rate as set by the Federal Housing Administration as of date of closing." Under current legislation, housing purchased under FHA terms must meet the following minimum down payment schedule:

Loan Amount		Percent of of Down Payment	Total Down Payment
1st $25,000	×	3.0	$ 750
Next 25,000	×	5.0	1,250
Total $50,000			$2,000

This schedule requires a total down payment of $2,000 for a $50,000 loan or $2,500 for a $60,000 loan.

VA Loans.   Assume the house is purchased by a veteran who is eligible for a VA guaranteed loan. The prospect may apply for a maximum guaranteed loan of $25,000 or 60 percent of the appraised value, whichever is less. The effect of this guarantee changes the effective loan-to-value ratio. For example, a veteran who is entitled to the full guarantee may obtain a $50,000 loan with no down payment. The lender who grants this loan, in effect, secures a 50 percent loan-to-value mortgage since the lender risks only $25,000 ($50,000 minus $25,000). In practice, the maximum guarantee of 60 percent only applies to loans of $41,667 or less ($25,000 ÷ $41,667 = 60.0 percent).

Under VA loans, loan origination fees are limited to one percent of the loan; veterans are prohibited from paying discounts and the loan must not include prepayment penalties for payment before loan maturity.

First Mortgage Financing: Loan Assumption

Frequently, it is to the advantage of the buyer to pay the seller an agreed sum and assume the seller's first mortgage or trust deed. Such an arrangement gives the buyer the advantage of a lower interest rate mortgage and permits the buyer to avoid certain closing costs associated with a new mortgage. Suppose, for example, the buyer agrees to assume the payments of the first mortgage of Case 1. At the date of closing the mortgage has 20 years remaining and a balance of $56,220. Under these circumstances, the contract for sale would read:

Case 2

Purchaser to assume and agrees to pay the first loan now against said property in the original principal amount of $60,000 dated March 15, 19___ in favor of John Jones and wife, bearing interest at the rate of $9\frac{1}{2}$ percent per annum and amortized over 300 equal monthly payments of $524.40 each, including principal and interest. Principal balance of said loan, which is to be assumed by a purchaser as of June 1, 19___, is $56,220. Purchaser to pay balance of purchase price to seller in cash at closing.

The cash paid the seller depends on the amount of the equity, which, in turn, depends on the original equity, mortgage principal repayments, and the degree to which prices have increased or decreased since the seller's purchase.

It should be noted that if the buyer *assumes* the seller's loan, both the buyer and seller can be held liable for the debt. Only if the buyer, the seller, and the lender agree to release the seller from the debt would the seller limit his or her further liability. Legally, the release of liability requires a *novation* executed by the lender. Novation is a term describing the instrument under which the lender releases the seller from an existing mortgage and substitutes the buyer.

Ordinarily, to recover the cost of changing records, the lender may ask for an *assumption fee*. The assumption fee may be provided by an assumption statement furnished by the lender showing the balance of the mortgage. The statement may include an agreement that the assumption fee will be paid to allow the buyer to assume the loan.

Assumption fees range from a flat fee of $25 to one percent of the loan. Generally, assumption fees are provided for in new mortgages and trust deeds so that the loan may not be assumed without consent of the lender. The lender may require a change in the interest rate or an assumption fee before approving the loan assignment. Several real estate brokers anticipate the assumption fee by stating in the contract for sale that the purchaser will pay the assumption fee.

Second Mortgage Financing: New First Mortgage

First mortgages or trust deeds may be combined with a second loan. A common arrangement is to negotiate a first mortgage loan and obtain a new second mortgage, which is assumed by the seller, with the buyer paying the balance in cash. A real estate agent would arrange this sale by incorporating in the contract for sale or deposit receipt provision for anticipating the financing plan:

Case 3

Purchaser to apply for and to accept if approved a new first loan in the principal amount of $60,000 secured by said property, bearing interest at the rate of $9\frac{1}{2}$ percent per annum and amortized over 300 equal monthly payments of $524.40 each, including principal and interest.

Seller will accept from purchaser a note secured by a purchase money mortgage, secured by said property, and subject to first loan described herein, in the principal amount of $10,000 bearing interest at the rate of 10 percent per annum and amortized over 60 equal monthly payments of $212.50 each, including principal and interest. First payment of said purchased money note shall become due the tenth day of the month after the closing period. Purchaser to pay balance of purchase price to seller in cash at closing.

In this instance, the seller sells for $75,000 and realizes (1) $5,000 cash paid by the buyer and (2) the buyer's promise to repay $10,000 with 10 percent interest over the next five years. The outstanding balance of an existing mortgage is repaid from proceeds of the new mortgage. It will be appreciated that the more conservative lenders would hesitate to accept a first lien from a borrower who has, say, less than a 10 percent equity in the property.

Second Mortgage Financing:
First Mortgage Assumption

An alternative would be for the buyer to assume the existing loan and to execute a second loan to the seller and pay the balance of the price in cash. The contract for sale would state the facts in these general terms. Assume again the original $60,000 loan, 20 years remaining, and a selling price of $75,000. In this case, the seller accepts a second mortgage or trust deed.

Case 4

Purchaser to assume and agrees to pay the first loan now against said property in the original principal amount, dated March 15, 19__, in favor of John Jones, bearing interest at the rate of $9\frac{1}{2}$ percent per annum and amortized over 300 equal payments of $524.40 each, including principal and interest. Principal balance of said loan, which is to be assumed by purchaser as of June 1, 19__, is $56,220. Seller will accept from purchaser one note secured by a loan described herein in the principal amount of $10,000 bearing interest at the rate of 10 percent per annum and amortized over 60 equal monthly payments of $212.50 each, including principal and interest. Purchaser to pay balance of purchased price to seller in cash at closing.

This is frequently advantageous to both buyer and seller. The buyer gains from the relatively low interest rate of the first loan. The seller, who agrees to take a second lien, gains from the higher sales price negotiated by the broker. By agreeing to a second loan, the seller increases the number of potential prospects, for here the buyer does not need to qualify for a higher first mortgage loan. Moreover, the buyer avoids loan origination fees and higher interest rates on new loans.

First Mortgage Default. The status of the second lien holder should be understood by both buyer and seller. Second priority loans such as second trust deeds, purchase money mortgages, or second mortgages held by the seller, usually include a statement that the mortgage is subordinate to a prior mortgage which is then described according to the amount of indebtedness, date of recording, names of the parties, a legal description, and other details.

The holder of the second mortgage usually requires an agreement providing for the right to pay the first mortgage if the borrower defaults on the first priority loan. Such an agreement protects the holder of the second priority loan from foreclosure by the holder of the first mortgage.

The borrower, in turn, would be advised to include a waiver in the second mortgage stating that the borrower may refinance the first mortgage providing that the refinanced mortgage does not exceed the remaining balance of the first mortgage. This permits the borrower to refinance the first mortgage with another first mortgage without affecting the priority of the first mortgage loan. Later the borrower may elect to refinance in order to obtain cash or secure more favorable mortgage terms.

Second Mortgage Default. If the borrower defaults on the second mortgage, the rights of the first mortgage lender prevail over the rights holder of the second mortgage lender. If the property is foreclosed and sold at a foreclosure sale, proceeds of this sale first satisfy the holder of the first loan. Any balance remaining after the foreclosure goes to the owner of the second priority loan.

Flexible Financing. Figure 19-2 indicates the flexibility in the four common ways to finance a dwelling. The four cases illustrated provide for down payments ranging from $5,000 to $18,180. In each case, the example assumes an 80 percent, first mortgage loan.

The new mortgage financing of Case 1 is recommended if the seller is unwilling to finance part of the purchase or if the original loan has a relatively small remaining balance that makes the required down payment prohibitive. The cases showing loan assumption are recommended (1) if the existing loan is relatively new, requiring a reasonable down payment, or (2) if the seller is willing to accept a second mortgage as part of the purchase price.

Moreover, the monthly payments range from $524.40 per month for Cases 1 and 2 to $736.90 for Cases 3 and 4. Although the payments are equal for Cases 1 and 2, in Case 2, because of the larger equity, the borrower has only 20 years remaining on the original 25-year mortgage. Similarly, although the payments are equal in Cases 3 and 4, the larger equity (Case 4) limits remaining monthly payments on the first mortgage to 20 years on the original 25-year mortgage.

FIGURE 19-2. Typical Purchase and Mortgage Plans, $75,000 Sale

New First Mortgage		Assume Existing Mortgage	
CASE 1		CASE 2	
1. New first mortgage	$60,000	1. Assume existing first mortgage	$60,000 (original) $56,220 (remaining balance
2. Down payment	$15,000	2. Down payment	$18,180
CASE 3		CASE 4	
1. New first mortgage	$60,000	1. Assume existing mortgage	$60,000 (original) $56,220 (remaining balance
2. Second mortgage to seller	$10,000	2. Second mortgage to seller	$10,000
3. Down payment	$ 5,000	3. Down payment	$ 8,180

SPECIALIZED MORTGAGES

Certain other mortgages may be adapted to requirements of the seller and the buyer-prospect. One group of mortgages provides for variations in payment plans. A second group of mortgages is adapted to meeting more specialized types of financing. Both groups are adapted to the sale of houses and condominiums.

Variations in Payment Plans

In the first place, mortgages more commonly provide for constant level monthly payments. Another repayment plan provides for a constant level of payments only on the *principal.* Since interest is paid on the remaining balance, interest payments tend to decline with each payment in proportion to the declining outstanding principal. Under this latter plan, monthly payments decrease each period.

Level Payment Mortgages. Here, the monthly payment must be greater than the interest owed; each monthly payment provides for payment of the mortgage interest on the remaining balance; the balance of the payment is used to retire or amortize the principal. The allocation of principal and interest for a $40,000, 8 percent mortgage of 25 years (300 payments) for the first year is shown in Table 19-1. Note that with the level payment of $308.80, interest is deducted first with the balance of the payment allocated to the principal. Under this plan, interest decreases with each payment and the amount to principal increases.

TABLE 19-1. Allocation of Monthly Mortgage Payments for $40,000 Loan, 8% Interest, 25 Years: First Year
Constant Level Payments

	Monthly Payment	Interest Payment	Principal Payment	Mortgage Balance
1	$308.80	$266.80	$42.00	$39,958.00
2	308.80	266.80	42.00	39,915.60
3	308.80	266.00	42.80	39,872.80
4	308.80	266.00	42.80	39,830.00
5	308.80	265.40	43.20	39,786.80
6	308.80	265.20	43.60	39,743.20
7	308.80	264.80	44.00	39,699.20
8	308.80	264.80	44.00	39,655.20
9	308.80	264.40	44.40	39,610.80
10	308.80	263.60	45.20	39,566.00
11	308.80	263.60	45.20	39,520.80
12	308.80	263.59	45.21	39,475.59

The percent of interest paid over selected years is shown in Table 19-2 for 20-, 25-, and 30-year mortgages assuming interest rates of 5 to 10 percent. Note that under a 25-year mortgage, 9 percent interest, over the first year the borrower has repaid 11 percent of the principal. Note that during the fifth year the total principal payments equal 16 percent of mortgage payments; during the tenth year 25 percent of mortgage payments go to the principal.

Another way of reviewing the level payment mortgage is to calculate the monthly and total cost to finance a loan of $1,000. These figures are shown for 20-, 25-, and 30-year mortgages for interest rates ranging from $5\frac{1}{2}$ percent to 10 percent in Table 19-3. Under a $9\frac{1}{2}$ percent mortgage, 30 years, the borrower pays $8.41 monthly per $1,000 of debt, or $336.40 monthly for a $40,000 mortgage.

Constant Principal Payment. Under this plan, which is fairly common in financing land purchases, equal amounts are applied to principal reduction plus interest for the current period. Here, the principal is paid off faster during the earlier years of the loan than would be the case under the constant level payment plan. Over the life of the loan the amortization of the principal is not as accelerated over later years as it would under the constant level payment plan. An example of a short-term second mortgage repaid under this plan is shown in Table 19-4.

TABLE 19-2. Principal Repayment as a Percent of Annual Mortgage Payments in Selected Years

Interest Rate	1st Year	5th Year	10th Year	15th Year	20th Year	25th Year	30th Year
Life of mortgage—30 years							
7	13	17	24	34	48	68	96
7½	11	14	21	32	45	66	96
8	9	12	19	29	43	64	96
9	7	10	16	25	39	61	95
10	5	8	13	21	35	58	95
Life of mortgage—25 years							
7	18	24	34	48	68	96	
7½	16	21	32	45	66	96	
8	14	19	29	43	64	96	
9	11	16	25	39	61	95	
10	8	13	21	35	58	95	
Life of Mortgage—20 years							
7	26	34	48	68	96		
7½	23	32	45	66	96		
8	21	29	43	64	96		
9	18	25	39	61	95		
10	15	21	35	58	95		

TABLE 19-3. Monthly and Total Costs to Finance $1,000 for Selected Interest Rates and Years

Rate of Interest	Years Financed					
	20 Years		25 Years		30 Years	
	Monthly Cost	Total Cost	Monthly Cost	Total Cost	Monthly Cost	Total Cost
5½%	$6.88	$1,651	$6.15	$1,845	$5.68	$2,045
6	7.17	1,721	6.45	1,935	6.00	2,160
6½	7.46	1,790	6.76	2,028	6.33	2,279
7	7.76	1,862	7.07	2,121	6.66	2,398
7½	8.06	1,934	7.39	2,217	7.00	2,520
8	8.37	2,009	7.72	2,316	7.34	2,642
8½	8.68	2,083	8.06	2,418	7.69	2,768
9	9.00	2,160	8.40	2,520	8.05	2,898
9½	9.32	2,237	8.74	2,622	8.41	3,027
10	9.66	2,318	9.09	2,727	8.78	3,161

Source: William M. Shenkel, *Modern Real Estate Principles* (Dallas, Texas: Business Publications, Inc., 1977), p. 537.

Five-Year Loan, 10% Interest

Month	Principal Repayment	Interest	Total Payment
1	$100	$49.80	$149.80
2	100	48.47	148.47
3	100	48.14	148.14
4	100	47.31	147.31
5	100	46.48	146.48
6	100	45.65	145.65
7	100	44.82	144.82
8	100	43.99	143.99
9	100	43.16	143.16
10	100	42.33	142.33
11	100	41.50	141.50
12	100	40.67	140.67

*A 10 percent interest is equivalent to
.83 percent monthly (.10 ÷ 12 = .0083).

This plan satisfies the seller taking a second mortgage who wants a constant reduction of principal with a greater proportion of early payments made on principal rather than on interest. Under this schedule, the equity builds up more rapidly in the early years of the loan than it would under the constant level payment plan. Given these two repayment plans, the next task is to consider other variations in repayment schedules.

Variations in Repayment Schedules

Among the more popular financing plans are the flexible payment mortgages (FPM); variable rate mortgages (VRM), and mortgages providing for balloon payments.

Flexible Payment Mortgage (FPM)   Suppose that your prospect requires a $50,000, 30-year mortgage available at the current market interest rate of $9\frac{3}{4}$ percent. This results in a monthly mortgage payment of $344. In addition, suppose that local lenders will not approve a conventional loan if the total monthly debt payments exceed one-third of gross monthly income. After calculating mortgage payments, property taxes, and insurance, you estimate that the maximum monthly mortgage payment that the prospect could make would be approximately $280.

In these circumstances, search for a lender like the Washington Mutual Savings Bank of Seattle, Washington, that has issued mortgages with mortgage payments graduated upward over the first six years. At the seventh year the mortgage payments are based on the market rate. For instance, the lender might agree during the initial two years to begin payments with a $7\frac{1}{2}$ percent interest rate. The graduated payment schedule on a $50,000 loan might follow this schedule:

Years	Interest Rate	Monthly Payments
1 and 2	$7\frac{1}{2}$	$280.00
3 and 4	$8\frac{1}{4}$	300.80
5 and 6	9	322.00
7 to 30	$9\frac{3}{4}$	344.00

Under this plan, your prospect (who has expectations of higher income) may buy with payments tailored to his or her ability to make the payments.

Alternatively, flexible payment mortgages vary the amortization period in the initial years, thus effectively increasing or decreasing the monthly payments. Frequently, prospects facing early retirement may be granted a 25-year loan based on a 15-year amortization schedule for the first five or ten years. This plan increases their equity before retirement and decreases payments when the borrowers must depend on lower retirement income. Variations of this plan allow prospects to make principal payments only over the initial years.

In short, if you face a prospect whose earnings are likely to vary in the early years of the mortgage, turn to a lender who will adapt the payment schedule to your prospect's needs.

Variable Rate Mortgage (VRM).   Variable rate mortgages refer to payment plans in which mortgage interest varies by a stated price index. In fact, some institutions require variable rate mortgages: Wells Fargo of California requires a VRM on a loan over $40,000; the Bank of America specifies a VRM on a loan over $50,000. A state-chartered savings and loan association in California holds 90 percent of its loans in VRMs. Some 19 states have approved VRMs for state supervised lenders.

In California most plans vary interest rates every six months according to changes in the money index published twice a year by the Federal Home Loan Bank of San Francisco. Under other plans, interest rates are changed as the consumer price index or wholesale index varies. Under changing interest rates, the lender may increase the maturity date of the mortgage, renegotiate the annual mortgage balance, change monthly payments, or renegotiate the annual mortgage balance; monthly payments do not necessarily vary.

Borrowers are given certain inducements to accept variable interest rates. Generally, the initial interest rate is slightly lower than the rate on a conventional fixed rate mortgage. Prepayment penalty clauses should be reduced or virtually disappear as VRMs are more widely used. In addition, VRMs encourage open-end mortgages because they allow the borrower to increase his or her loan as additional capital is needed.

Other restrictions imposed by state law give your prospects additional advantages. For example, under California law,

Variable rate mortgages must be flexible downward in the same way they are flexible upward.

Increased interest rates are restricted to one-quarter of 1 percent semiannually.

The borrower has the right to prepay the mortgage within 90 days of a notice in the change of interest rates without penalty.

The interest rate cannot be changed more than 2.5 percentage points over the life of the loan.

Amortization may be increased to 40 years at the option of the buyer without increasing existing monthly payments.

Suppose that the initial loan of 20 years, $8\frac{1}{2}$ percent, and $40,000 provides for a variable interest rate. Payments would be $338 per month. If the variable interest rate increased to $9\frac{1}{2}$ percent, the $338 payment could be maintained by increasing the original loan to 29 years and 3 months.

In sum, your prospect may not have access to a loan under conventional mortgage terms. In this case, the property and the borrower may secure needed financing with a VRM. Again, this is a case in which your knowledge of mortgage credit may help close the sale.

Balloon Mortgages. These mortgages provide for lower monthly payments than do conventional mortgages. Only part of the mortgage principal is amortized. At the end of a stated time the balance of the unamortized mortgage is due. In effect, the lender grants relatively short-term credit and, facing expectations of rising interest rates, terminates the loan with the balloon payment. At the same time, the borrower increases the equity under the amortized loan schedule to the point that the property may be refinanced to meet the balloon payment.

Thus, a $40,000 loan may be granted with monthly payments based on a 30-year repayment schedule. But suppose that the lender is unwilling to make a loan for more than 15 years. In this case, the mortgage would require payment of the unpaid balance at the end of 15 years. With a $40,-000 loan, 9 percent interest, the balloon payment at the end of 15 years would be $31,720. If a rising or stable market value and an eligible borrower are assumed, the house could be refinanced to pay the balloon payment. Consider this plan for a borrower who must reduce monthly payments on a house but the lender is unwilling to make the loan for more than 15 or 20 years.

Special-Purpose Mortgages

Mortgages are further adapted to the requirements of borrowers facing unique situations. Buyers and sellers frequently include personal property in their housing mortgages. These are referred to as *package mort-gages*. Other mortgages in common use include the open-end mortgage, the blanket mortgage, and the purchase money mortgage. Real estate contracts may be combined with long-term mortgages and deeds. A brief discussion of these instruments suggests how they adapt to buyer and seller requirements.

Package Mortgage.   A young couple buying their first home may wish to minimize the cash needed for the down payment, closing costs, furniture, and appliances. It is to their advantage to include appliances such as washers, dryers, and even refrigerators in the long-term mortgage. Not only does this procedure reduce the cash required to establish a new household, but it also enables the borrower to buy appliances at relatively low mortgage interest rates which are paid on the remaining balance. Consumer installment credit is usually much more costly. A mortgage that includes real and personal property is called a package mortgage.

For example, a $400 appliance might be included in a 30-year, $9\frac{1}{2}$ percent mortgage and would increase monthly payments by $3.36. In other words, the purchaser would acquire a $400 appliance at the annual cost of $40.32. To be sure, payments on the appliance would continue beyond the life of the appliance (over the 30-year term), but the probabilities are that the borrower would not hold the mortgage to maturity. The average life of a mortgage is approximately seven years. The package mortgage allows the borrower to maximize the available cash in acquiring household appliances.

Open-End Mortgage.   The open-end mortgage allows the borrower to gain additional funds under the original mortgage at the same terms. Suppose during the seventh year of a mortgage with 23 years remaining, the borrower wants to build an additional bedroom, add a swimming pool, or make other expensive alterations. The open-end mortgage permits the borrower to acquire additional money and avoid the refinancing charges of a new mortgage. The monthly payments are increased by a relatively small additional amount.

The open-end mortgage substitutes for a home improvement loan granted for a shorter term at a higher interest rate. It also avoids the higher financing charges of a second mortgage. In other words, the open-end mortgage provides the borrower with an inexpensive source of funds to make housing improvements or to meet other family needs.

Blanket Mortgage.   There may be an occasion when the lender might be reluctant to finance the proposed sale. If the prospect has other real estate, suggest a blanket mortgage: A blanket mortgage covers more than one parcel of real estate. Thus, to provide additional loan security, the borrower pledges other real estate as security for the proposed loan.

A blanket mortgage would ordinarily include a clause that releases the property from the mortgage if the borrower repays a certain propor-tion of the mortgage. If the blanket mortgage includes vacant land, have the borrower secure counsel of an attorney who will structure the agree-ment so that the borrower may sell portions of the land that are subject to the blanket mortgage.

Purchase Money Mortgage. The purchase money mortgage is usu-ally granted by a seller who is willing to accept all or part of the price in the form of a mortgage. Purchase money mortgages are accepted as substi-tutes for cash.

In some states the purchase money mortgage does not include a promis-sory note. It is secured by the real estate and not the personal promise of the buyer. For houses financed with a first mortgage from a savings and loan association and a purchase money mortgage from the seller, the purchase money mortgage represents a second lien. That is, the interest of the seller who holds the purchase money mortgage is subordinate to the claim of the first mortgage. In effect, the purchase money mortgage is a means of financing the sale by the seller.

Real Estate Contract. A real estate contract may substitute for a mort-gage until the contract payments give the buyer sufficient equity to finance under conventional mortgage terms. This is a device frequently used by build-ers, but it could also be used by sellers dealing with buyers who cannot meet the down payment.

For example, the seller might agree to sell the property under a contract providing for monthly payments with interest and with an agreement that at the end of five years the buyer will apply for a first mortgage. This arrangement has certain advantages for the seller:

1. The seller retains title until the first mortgage is issued and the seller is paid the full price.
2. In the event of default the seller may recover the property without the delays associated with mortgage and trust deeds.

These advantages serve the interest of the seller, but the borrower also gains because he or she is able to purchase a house with a minimum down payment —whatever satisfies the immediate requirements of the seller, which is below conventional first mortgage financing. One disadvantage is that the seller may not be able to deliver a marketable title. Before the buyer acquires title, liens and judgments may be placed against the seller and his or her property, thus endangering the interest of the buyer.

Even with these disadvantages, the plan serves a buyer who has limited assets but who has sufficient income to make monthly contract payments. The contract is entered into in anticipation of first mortgage financing as the equity increases over the life of the contract.

POINTS TO REMEMBER

It pays to know the lending practices in your community. You will save your time, your employer's time, and your prospect's time and money by matching your prospect's financial resources to a house suited to your prospect's individual preferences. Learn the main sources of mortgage credit and how these sources judge houses, neighborhoods, and the borrower. In particular, you are advised to

1. Learn how lenders judge the borrower's credit. Know the common ratios used in your area. Learn when lenders make exceptions to lending rules.

2. Have a general idea of the borrower's assets, anticipated income, housing expenses, and credit status, i.e., the willingness of the borrower to repay debts.

3. First mortgage financing includes *new loans* and the *assumption of existing loans*. Know the relative advantages of both plans for your prospect.

4. First mortgages may be combined with *second mortgages* either advanced by the seller or by a third party. Be prepared to show how second mortgage financing may meet your prospect's needs. Be prepared to offer various financing alternatives.

5. Learn the differences between level payment mortgages and constant principal payment mortgages. If the seller is willing to accept a second mortgage, he or she might prefer constant principal payments instead of level payments.

6. Explore the willingness of local lenders to advance flexible payment mortgages. Know the main features of the more prevalent plans in your area.

7. Learn the details of local variable rate mortgage law. The index used for these mortgages varies geographically.

8. Consider balloon mortgages as a means of lowering monthly payments.

9. Be aware of special-purpose mortgages that may secure your sale. The *package mortgage* reduces the cash required, which is especially important to the first home buyer. The *open-end mortgage* benefits the borrower who wants additional credit over the life of the mortgage. The *blanket mortgage* may be used if your prospect has other real estate. The *purchase money mortgage* can be a first lien or a second lien, depending on your seller. If your buyer does not qualify or if local lenders are not willing to advance the necessary loan on the property listed, the seller may execute a purchase money mortgage and assume the role of a lender.

10. Develop a real estate contract plan as a substitute for a first mortgage.

The point is fairly plain: Since most houses are sold on credit, your prospects for completing the sale partly hinge on matching the best financial plan for the borrower with the cash requirements of the seller. In truth, a conventional first mortgage is only one of many alternative lending practices available to you, your principal (the seller), and your prospect (the buyer).

REVIEW QUESTIONS

1. Define effective income for mortgage credit purposes.

2. What factors would you consider in judging the assets and liabilities of a buyer-prospect?

3. For mortgage loan purposes, what housing expenses are relevant to judging credit?

4. What features does the FHA use to evaluate mortgagor risk?

5. In your own words, explain the terms of the four major financing plans.

6. Compare a level payment mortgage to a constant principal payment mortgage.

7. What are the main features of a flexible payment mortgage?

8. Explain what a variable rate mortgage is.

9. Explain and give examples of a balloon mortgage.

10. What are the relative advantages of a package mortgage, an open-end mortgage, and a blanket mortgage? Explain thoroughly.

11. How would you adapt a purchase money mortgage for a prospective buyer?

12. Explain how you would combine a real estate contract with first mortgage financing.

Home Warranties
and
Trade-in Plans

Home warranties for both new and occupied homes and trade-in plans reduce the risks of the home buyer. First, the National Association of Home Builders sponsors a Home Owners Warranty Program (HOW) for new homes and the National Association of Realtors ® approves various home protection programs offered by private companies on existing homes. Second, the risks faced by a buyer in selling his or her present home in order to purchase a new dwelling are reduced by different types of trade-in plans.

Members of the National Association of Home Builders in Atlanta, Georgia, built 5,000 houses by the end of 1977 under the HOW plan. In the first two and one-half years of operation, defects in some 16 houses were repaired under HOW at costs ranging from $300 to $10,000. Defects repaired included leaky basements, sagging ceilings, popping nails, buckling floors, crooked door jambs, and defective paint. The most expensive repairs were for a buckled floor and a fireplace chimney that pulled away from a house that sold for $90,000. Total repairs costing $10,000 were covered by the HOW plan without cost to the owner.

ADVANTAGES OF WARRANTY PLANS

Simply stated, warranty plans serve real estate brokers in three ways: (1) They protect brokers and salespersons from possible liability from misrepresentations and nondisclosure by third parties. (2) They allow the Realtor® to better serve clients. (3) They minimize conflicts of interest between Realtors® and customers. Indeed, the importance of warranty plans has led the National Association of Realtors® to state:

> The Home Protection Program conceived by the National Association of Realtors® promises a new professionalism for the Realtors® of America. It is a manifestation of the Realtors® traditional concern with the protection of his [or her] clients and his [or her] customers and service to the public.[1]

The National Association of Realtors® has further observed that protected properties are more valuable to buyers than are unprotected properties. They advise that protected properties be identified in classified advertising, on signs, and on listing forms. Warranties make the property more marketable; protected properties are more likely to result in a confirmed sale and prices are established with more knowledge of the property condition. This plan allows the seller to obtain the best price and the Realtor® to sell the property free from fears of misrepresentation, thus building confidence in the seller and adding to the credibility of Realtors® among prospective buyers.

Protection Against Misrepresentation

Historically, the rule of *caveat emptor* (let the buyer beware) applied to sales of real and personal property. It was presumed that the buyer and seller dealt with one another at arm's length and that the buyer had the opportunity to discover facts about the property sold.

Consider the buyer who purchased a dwelling on a site that was improperly filled before construction. While still occupied by the original buyers, the house settled, thus causing the floors to sag and the concrete basement floor to crack. The damage was repaired by the builder. When the house was resold, the brokers disclosed to the prospect-buyer that the foundation had previously settled but the situation had been remedied.

Within a year after the second buyer took possession, additional settling caused damages amounting to $20,000. The second buyer sued the developer. The court ruled that the developer sold an improperly compacted lot as suitable for residential purposes and was liable for damages suffered by the second buyer. The developer was responsible to the original buyer, but if the rule of caveat emptor were to govern, the developer would not ordinarily be liable to a remote second buyer. On this issue, the court stated:

> Through the years the pendelum has swung circle and now the *Rule of Caveat Emptor* has fast become obsolete.[2]

[1]*Home Protection Program,* 2nd ed. (Chicago: National Association of Realtors®, 1978), p. 34.

[2]485 S.W2nd 261 (Tenn. App. 1971).

Similar cases have led the courts to extend further protection to buyers under implied warranties of fitness and marketability.

Implied Warranties

Legal cases on this point have implied the doctrine of warranty and fitness only for houses sold under construction at the time of sale. The reasoning was that the agreement covered a completed house that would be reasonably fit for its intended use and that the work would be done in a reasonably efficient and workmanlike manner. Some early cases held that there can be no implied warranty on the quality of construction in a completed house because there was no further construction to be done; the liability of the seller ended with the sale.[3]

Later decisions extended the meaning of implied warranties. One of the first cases held that the builder was liable to the son of a tenant of a purchaser who was burned by hot water from a defective faucet.

In another landmark case the court ruled against a builder who constructed a house over a filled-in, spring-fed pond. After the purchase, water seeped into the basement of the house. The buyer sued the builder. The court ruled that even if the builder did not know of the existence of the spring, "where a person holds himself out and is especially qualified to perform work of a particular character there is an implied warranty that the work shall be done in a reasonable, good, and workmanlike manner and the completed product or structure shall be reasonably fit for its intended purpose."[4]

In this case, there was nothing in the physical appearance of the house or lot that would have alerted a reasonably competent person to the damaging spring-fed water. In this case, however, the court stated there would be no implied warranty or reasonable workmanship against inhabitability in the "resale of used housing. . . ."

Later decisions that extended benefits to subsequent purchasers who are not parties to the original agreement make sellers and brokers equally liable. Consider the house that was built with a steel tube radiant heating system in a concrete slab floor house. The house in question was built in 1950 and resold in 1957. In 1959 the corroded steel tubing damaged the house. The second buyer was allowed to collect damages from the original builder. The court stated that purchaser relied on the skill of the builder in producing the home with a heating system that was reasonably fit for its intended purpose. The statute of limitations has been enacted in California to limit recovery for defects occuring within ten years after completion.

[3]140 NE 2nd 819.
[4]154 NW 2nd 807.

Statutory Provisions

Some municipalities require inspection of residential dwellings before sale. The purpose of the inspection is to improve housing conditions and prevent neighborhood deterioration. Local inspection also protects inexperienced home buyers from purchasing unsound dwellings. Municipalities that have enacted home inspection programs are Cincinnati, Ohio; Detroit, Michigan; Flint, Michigan; Madison Heights, Michigan; Minneapolis, Minnesota; Wilmington, Delaware; and University City, Missouri.[5]

Generally speaking, the inspection in these cities covers electrical and mechanical systems and major structural components. Appliances are not usually inspected. For example, the electrical system must have adequate outlets, average service, and lighting fixtures. Loose or exposed heating wires are not permitted. The inspection covers the roof, wall, ceilings, floors, foundation, and basements.

Operation of Warranty Programs

Home owners warranty plans are available to sellers from the participating members of the National Association of Home Builders and from private firms. Private firms offer warranties with and without inspections.

Home Owners Warranty Program (HOW). Over 7,000 builders participate in the Home Owners Warranty Program. At the end of 1977, more than 170,000 homes were covered by the ten-year protection plan. The National Association of Home Builders reports that more than 10,000 new homes are added to the plan each month. Builders pay $2.00 per $1,000 of the selling price. For a $50,000 house, the one-time fee totals $100.

Under the Home Owners Warranty Policy, given to home buyers, participating builders subscribe to a Code of Ethics which states in part:

American homes should be well-designed, well-constructed, and well-located in an attractive community with educational, recreational, religious, and shopping facilities accessible to all.

High standards of health, safety, and sanitation shall be built into every home. Members shall deal fairly with the respective employees, contractors, and suppliers.

Buyers of new homes subject to this warranty are given a ten-year policy that provides the following:

1. Warranty of construction covering all phases of construction for a period of *one year* subject to the manufacturer's warranty on individual equipment.

[5]*A Study of Home Inspection and Warranty Programs,* Vol. I (Washington, D.C.: U.S. Department of Housing and Urban Development, 1977), p. 33.

2. Warranty covering major structural defects for *two years* which includes piping, wiring, and duct work. For the remaining *eight years* the warranty continues to protect the home against major structural defects.

Note that the warranty applies only to new houses constructed by participating members of the National Association of Home Builders. Programs approved by the National Association of Realtors® may cover existing homes.

The coverage provided by the Home Owners Warranty Policy is shown in Figure 20-1. The policy further provides for a one-time $50 deductible limit and provides for actual, reasonable shelter expenses during repairs. The exclusions cover such items as defects in out buildings and damage to the extent that it is caused or made worse by:

1. Negligence, improper maintenance, or improper operation by anyone other than the builder or his employees, agents, or subcontractors; or
2. Failure of anyone other than the Builder or his employees, agents, or subcontractors to comply with the warranty requirements of manufacturers of appliances, equipment, or fixtures; or
3. Failure to give notice to the Builder of any defect within a reasonable time; or
4. Changes of the grading of the ground by anyone other than the Builder, or his employees, agents, or subcontractors.

In addition, the policy excludes normal wear and tear, accidental loss or damage from fire, explosion, smoke, water escape, glass breakage, storms, aircraft, floods, and earthquake. Insect damage and losses arising while the home is used for nonresidential purposes are also excluded.

The National Association of Realtors® (NAR).   The National Association of Realtors® approves home protection programs offered by private firms if these programs meet certain standards. The three objectives of the NAR-approved warranty programs are:

1. To disclose material defects in the basic structure and functional components of the property.
2. To minimize, through insurance or warranty, the loss to the home buyer resulting from undisclosed material defects in such components.
3. To protect the Realtor® and protect his (or her) clients from liability for misrepresentation, fraud, or breach of warranty, express or implied.[6]

Companies approved by the organization must meet rigid requirements: (1) They must operate on a national basis. (2) They must be financially responsible. (3) They must have facilities and staff to properly process orders, inspect properties, and receive, review, and adjust claims expeditiously.[7]

1. *Scope of Coverage.* The scope of coverage varies according to whether or not an inspection is provided. For companies offering a program

---

[6]See *Home Protection Program,* p. 7.

[7]*Ibid.,* p. 12.

FIGURE 20-1. Warranty Coverage Provided by Home Owners Warranty Policy (National Association of Home Builders)

Identity of Warrantor. The Builder named on page 1 is the warrantor under this warranty.

To Whom Given. This warranty is extended to you as Purchaser (the first owner to occupy the home as a residence for yourself or your family) and automatically to any subsequent owners of the home and any mortgage lender who takes possession of the home (see exclusion during non-residential use, page 5).

Coverage During First Year. For one year, beginning on the commencement date filled in on page 1, the Builder warrants that the home will be free from defects due to noncompliance with the Approved Standards and from major construction defects.

A "major construction defect" is actual damage to the load-bearing portion of the home (including damage due to subsidence, expansion or lateral movement of soil from causes other than flood or earthquake) which affects its load-bearing function and which vitally affects (or is imminently likely to produce a vital effect on) the use of the home for residential purposes.

Coverage For Up to One Year. The Builder warrants that all appliances, fixtures and items of equipment will be free from defects due to noncompliance with the Approved Standards for one year or for the term of the manufacturer's written warranty (if a manufacturer's written warranty is assigned to you by the Builder), whichever is less.

Coverage During Second Year. During the second year after the commencement date, the Builder continues to warrant that the home will be free from major construction defects and that the plumbing, electrical, heating, and cooling systems will perform according to the Approved Standards, unless their failure is the result of a defect in an appliance, fixture, or item of equipment. (See the Approved Standards for definitions).

Coverage of Common Elements in Condominiums. Common elements serving condominium units are also covered by this warranty. "Common elements" mean any structural portion of a condominium structure (including, but not limited to, any passageways, rooms or other spaces) which are provided for the common use of the residents of the structure. It also means part of a mechanical, electrical, heating, cooling or plumbing system serving two or more condominium units and outbuildings containing parts of such a system.

Common elements are covered for the same length of time as similar items which are part of an individual unit, but the beginning date of the warranty period on common elements is determined by the common elements commencement date on page 1.

Builder's Performance. If a defect occurs in an item which is covered by this warranty, the Builder will repair, replace, or pay you the reasonable cost of repairing or replacing the defective item. The Builder's total liability under this warranty is limited to the purchase price of the home filled in on page 1. The choice among repair, replacement or payment is the Builder's. Steps taken by the Builder to correct defects shall not act to extend the terms of this warranty.

Other Insurance. In the event the Builder repairs or replaces, or pays the cost of repairing or replacing, any defect covered by this warranty for which you are covered by other insurance, you must, upon request by the Builder, assign the proceeds of such insurance to the Builder to the extent of the cost to the Builder of such repair or replacement.

Other Rights. This warranty gives you specific legal rights. You may also have other legal rights which vary from state to state. This agreement does not affect any rights of you or the Builder under any other express or implied warranty.

that requires an inspection, coverage usually extends to the following structural and mechanical components:

1. The central heating system.
2. The interior plumbing system, including the hot water heater.
3. The electrical system.
4. The structural soundness of the exterior and interior walls, including floors and ceilings.

5. The structural soundness of the foundation and basement.
6. The structural soundness of the roof and the absence of water penetration.
7. The central air conditioning system.

For noninspection programs (not approved by NAR), the coverage generally covers the following:

1. The central heating system.
2. The interior plumbing system, including the hot water heater.
3. The electrical system.
4. The central air conditioning system.

Some companies provide for certain optional programs for an additional fee. To insure the financial soundness of the program, NAR approval requires a deductible allowance of not less than $25 and not more than $100 per occurrence. This deductible feature eliminates excessive and unwarranted claims. Programs must specify the limits of liability.

Table 20-1 summarizes the main features of the private warranty plans that are currently available. The National Association of Realtors® at this writing has approved the following (but the list will be expanded as more firms enter the market):

Certified Home Inspection Program
First American Home Protection Insurance Program
Homestead Inspection Warranty Program
Sound Homes Assurance Program
St. Paul Home Protection Program

2. *Program Cost.* Note that the private warranty programs listed in Table 20-1 show costs that vary from $100 for a $30,000 house to over $500 for a $150,000 house. These fees are generally paid by the seller and provide protection for one year; some plans are renewable for additional periods. Presumably, the seller recoups the fee in the asking price. Even if the fee may not be recoverable, a "protected" house ordinarily may be sold within a shorter time.

The National Association of Realtors® estimates that eventually at least 35 percent of all real estate transactions on existing loans will carry a warranty; some even estimate that warranties will cover 70 percent of all house sales within the next few years. An example of the general nature of protection afforded buyers is the plan covered by the Homestead Inspection Warranty Program approved by the National Association of Realtors®.

Started in 1977, the program was first available in New Jersey, Pennsylvania, Delaware, and Virginia. The Company projects coverage of 9,000 houses over the next several years. The protection plan is marketed through real estate agents who offer the program to buyers and sellers. Condominiums are covered with respect to the components that may be repaired inside the unit. The warranty may be renewed.

The cost of the warranty is based on the selling price of the house: $200 for houses selling for under $35,000; $275 for houses selling for $70,000 or less, and $425 for houses selling for more than $140,000. The coverage is for two years and provides for a $100 deductible charge for each repair item. The deductible is waived for repairs that cost over $500. The plan covers basic mechanical systems such as the heating system, central air conditioning, hot water heater, humidifiers, electrical systems, plumbing fixtures, and laundry ducts. The plan also covers structural components such as the basement, foundation, garages, carports, and the roof with respect to structural soundness and protection from water penetration.

3. *Administration.* Houses covered by the warranty are given a one- to two-hour inspection. Items found to be in unsatisfactory condition are either repaired or excluded from warranty coverage. The inspection report includes a photograph of the dwelling and photographs of each major defect. The buyer and seller may decline warranty protection and purchase only the inspection for a fee of $100 to $125. Claims are made directly to the company representative, but the home owner selects a contractor to perform any repair costing less than $200. If repairs are over $200, the company assigns an adjuster for inspection and repair authorization. The total claims are limited to a maximum of $100,000.

TRADE-IN PLANS

Warranty programs help make houses more marketable and protect salespersons from misrepresenting the houses. They promote long-run reputations. Trade-in plans may be viewed in the same light. They overcome the buyer's reluctance to commit on a new home before the existing home is sold. Trade-in plans also make listings more marketable.

With a trade-in plan, the buyer avoids the risk of owning two homes. In addition, the buyer pays only the fair market value of a new home and at the same time receives the fair market price of the former home. In this way, the buyer acquires a new home without selling the present home first. Under these arrangements, financing is planned in advance before the buyer makes a commitment on the new home; family moves can be planned in an orderly manner, an especially important factor in arranging for new schools. Builders and Realtors® using this plan advertise that the buyer is under no obligation to make a purchase unless he or she is satisfied with the trade-in plan.

TABLE 20-1. A Comparison of Existing Private Warranty Programs

Program	Premium Cost for			Deductible or Service Charge	Coverage[b]	Period of Coverage; Renewable[c]	Inspection Level[d]	Source of Repair[e]	Insurance or Warranty[f]	Principal Purchasers	Warranty Contracts In Effect (Annual Inspections)[8]
	$30,000 House	$70,000 House	$150,000 House[a]								
American Home Guard	$195	$245	$285	$65–135	BA BMS + central air and plumbing fixtures BST + roof water penetration	1 yr.; NR	O-R	Owner	Warranty	Sellers	1,800
American Home Shield	$220–240	$220–240	$220–240	$20–50	BA BMS + central air and/or plumbing fixtures in some locations	1 yr.; R	O-R	SC	Warranty	Sellers	30,000
AMC Home Protection	$180	$210	$275	$250	BMS + central air BST + roof water penetration	1 yr.; R	D-Ins	Owner	Warranty	Buyers	60 (1,200)
Certified Home Inspection (CHIP)	$195	$215	$285	$100	BMS + central air, bathroom fixtures, kitchen sinks BST + roof water penetration, attached garages	1 yr.; R	D-Ins	Owner	Warranty	Buyers	720 (2,700)
Electronic Realty Associates Low Med. High	$180 220 260	$180 220 260	$270 330 390	$100 50 25	BA + slide-ins, counter-top blenders, central vacuum BMS + plumbing fixtures, door bells, central air and built-in wall units, water softeners	1 yr.; NR	O-R	SC	Warranty	Sellers	16,000
First American Home Protection Service	$217	$293	$527	$100	BA BMS + central air, plumbing fixtures BST	1 yr.; NR	S-Ins	SC	Insurance	Sellers	1 (NA)

Program				Coverage	Term	Inspection	Arranger	Type	Covers	Volume
Homestead Inspection Warranty Program	$200	$275	$425	$100	BMS + bathroom fixtures, laundry tubs; BST + roof water penetration, attached garages and breeze ways	2 yr.; R	D-Ins	Owner	Warranty	Buyers	3 (30)
Pacific Cal-West	$210	$210	$210	$15–20	BA + bathroom and kitchen fans BMS	1 yr.; R	O-R	SC	Warranty	Sellers	6,000
Rollins Home Care	$230	$230	$230	$100 (cumulative)	BMS + central air, plumbing fixtures, sump pump	1 yr.; NR	O-R	SC	Warranty	Sellers	1,000
Saint Paul Home Protection	$100	$140–210	$300–450	$25–50	Optional: BA, water softeners; BMS + central air, bathroom fixtures BST	1 yr.; R	S-Ins	SC	Insurance	Buyers	300 (1,000)
Soundhome Assurance Program	$200	$270	$430	$100	BMS + central air BST + water penetration due to structural defects	2 yr.; NR	D-Ins	Owner	Insurance	Buyers	5 (24)

[a] The average price is listed for Rollins Home Care.

[b] Basic appliance (BA) = built-in garbage disposal, dishwasher, range, and oven. Basic mechanical systems (BMS) = central heating, interior plumbing, interior electrical. Basic structural (BST) = roof, wall, ceiling, and floor structure, foundations, basements.

[c] R = renewable. NR = nonrenewable.

[d] O-R = cursory inspection by owner or Realtor. S-Ins = short inspection by independent inspector. D-Ins = detailed inspection by independent inspector. Owner = owner arranges repair and is reimbursed.

[e] SC = warranty firm provides a subcontractor. Owner = owner arranges a subcontractor.

[f] insurance companies are currently subject to regulation by insurance commissions; warranty programs are not.

[g] Approximate volume in year ending April, 1977. Estimates are not available for First American (NA).

Source: A Study of Home Inspection and Warranty Programs, Vol. 1 (Washington, D.C.: U.S. Department of Housing and Urban Development, 1977), pp. 15–16.

Eligible Homes

Not all properties are eligible for a trade. First, the prospective seller and buyer of a new home must have *sufficient* equity in the old home to warrant a trade. Second, the trade will not be consummated unless the prospect *financially qualifies* for the purchase of the new home.

Added Precautions

Salespersons take added precautions when they arrange for a sale and trade-in. A preliminary review of these precautions helps in reviewing the different types of trade-in plans.

1. Salespersons should not discuss the method of establishing the guaranteed price.
2. Salespersons should not be involved in discussing with the homeowner the value of what his or her present home should be (a third party should be called in).
3. Trade-in procedures require that other staff members compare the listed price with recently sold comparable properties in the neighborhood.
4. All costs associated with the trade-in should be explained to the seller. The seller should be informed of the equity that he or she would have after all costs are deducted.

Usually, the trade-in plan calls for the cooperation of the salesperson and the firm's trade-in specialists. The trader has the responsibility of discussing fees, commissions, and financing costs and explaining the trade-in plan. For this reason, communities having a population of less than 30,000 people—rural or outlying communities—are not suitable for trade-in plans. Salespersons are cautioned not to guarantee or trade in houses that are difficult to sell: primarily, houses in poor condition, in a poor location, in a declining neighborhood, or of substandard construction.

Types of Trade-In Plans

A trade-in plan assumes one of three forms: the direct trade, equity loan, and guaranteed sale. These are substitutes for the conditional sale sometimes referred to as a *conditional trade-in plan* that parallels a conditional option or time-limit sale.

Conditional Sale. A conditional sale requires that the seller (usually the builder) agrees to sell the prospective buyer a new house *providing* the prospect's existing home is sold within a stated time. If the prospect does not sell the home within the stated time, no sale results; neither party is under obligation to perform further.

While the agreement is in force, the seller must hold the house off the market until the stated time expires. This plan is practical for a subdivision developer who has other homes to sell, but it is not always satisfactory for the average seller because it provides no assurance that the sale will be completed. However, the plan is recommended if the builder (seller) is hesitant about trade-ins and has no capital for their financing. This plan might be advised if the prospect has little equity in the existing home that must be sold.

Direct Trade.   The direct trade is a sale agreement executed at the time of the original transaction. In essence, the buyer-prospect agrees to buy a new home for a specified amount if the seller or his or her agent takes title to the buyer's existing property for a stated amount. Under this plan, the seller takes direct title to the buyer's home and holds it for resale.

This plan has certain disadvantages for both the real estate firm and the prospect. It requires more capital and it is more difficult to negotiate with the buyer who may not be realistic about the price of the old home. Further, the buyer has no opportunity to sell the house at the highest price on the open market.

Despite these limitations, the direct trade solves three problems: (1) Brokers and builders turn to this plan if the property is in poor condition or if it must be repainted, repaired, and cleaned (including yard work). (2) The plan is recommended if circumstances require an immediate closing on the new home. If either the seller of the new home or the buyer with his or her old home has an urgent need to close, the direct trade-in is the most feasible plan. (3) It may provide a good long-term investment for the agent or party taking title to the old property. If the property is rentable or saleable after renovation, it might be profitable to take immediate title.

Equity Loan.   Under this variation, the salesperson or real estate firm guarantees that if the owner's home does not sell within the time limit of the listing, the salesperson or firm guarantees to lend the client sufficient money for the down payment of the new home being purchased. Typically, the loan is made on a short-term basis, i.e., 90 days, and is secured by a mortgage on one or both properties. The prospect pays interest on the loan and usually a loan fee to the trader.

For example, suppose the prospect buys a new home for $90,000, $30,000 down, and a $60,000 first mortgage and lists the old home under a 90-day exclusive agreement. If the house does not sell within 90 days, the prospect is loaned $30,000 for 90 days secured by a mortgage on his or her old home. Thus, the prospect is given an additional 90 days to sell the home or pay off the loan from other sources.

Typically, during the next 90 days the seller reduces the price and makes other arrangements to repay the loan. As a result, this plan creates less risk for the trader because the trader has no unsecured funds committed to the property. It also gives the trader a chance to convert the equity loan to a guaranteed sale.

A variation of this plan provides the client with funds borrowed under a personal loan from the bank. The broker co-signs the note at the bank. The broker secures the risk by accepting a note and second mortgage or trust deed against one or both of the properties. When the client repays the bank loan, the broker is relieved of the contingent obligation to the bank and collects a fee for the guarantee.

Guaranteed Trade-In.   Because this plan combines features of the conditional sale and direct trade, it is the most popular trade-in plan. It allows the buyer to obtain the maximum price for his or her house on the open market. The guaranteed plan is based on the concept of underwriting the customer's equity with a guarantee of performance if the property is not sold within a specified period.

Although there are many variations, usually the broker guarantees the prospect a minimum guaranteed equity which is the least the prospect will receive for the old home. Under a typical listing period, say 90 days, the home is offered on the market under local listing arrangements. If the sale is made during the listing, it is unnecessary for the trader to exercise the guarantee agreement. If the property does not sell within the listing period, the prospect receives a predetermined guaranteed price and title passes to the broker.

On review, it is evident that the prospect has the opportunity to get the market price for his or her house. Usually, the guaranteed price ranges from 80 percent to 90 percent of the fair market value less the brokerage fee. In most cases, the house is sold within the listing time and no guaranteed assistance is used.

1.   *Guaranteed Purchase Agreement.* The guaranteed purchase agreement is based on a published guaranteed sales policy. The McLennan Company of Park Ridge, Illinois, advises customers that its guaranteed sales policy includes four steps:

1. Select the home you want to buy and reserve it for yourself, subject to McLennan Company's issuing a satisfactory trade-in guarantee on your present home.
2. The McLennan Company will then promptly inspect your present home and recommend a fair selling price as well as a guaranteed net price.
3. Your present home will be placed on the market with McLennan Company and every effort will be made to sell your home at the recommended price.
4. In the event your home is not sold within the guaranteed period, McLennan Company will promptly purchase your property so you can complete the purchase of your new home.

Clearly, this plan overcomes the dilemma facing the buyer: "Do I buy now and sell later, or do I sell now and buy later?" In a sense, this technique frees equity and makes older homes more marketable. If it is necessary to purchase a house, the McLennan Company returns any profit made to the original owner.

FIGURE 20-2. Guaranteed Purchase Price Agreement

Guaranteed Purchase Price Agreement

*Dated:*_____

*Owner:*_____

Realtor: McLennan Company

*Real Property commonly known as:*_____

_____

_____

Personal Property included are the following, if any, now on premises: heating, central cooling, ventilating, plumbing, and electrical fixtures; screens and storms for windows and doors; shades; awnings; blinds; drapery rods; curtain rods; radio and TV aerials; attached mirrors, shelving, cabinets and book cases; and all planted vegetation; also,

_____

_____

_____

_____

_____

_____

_____

*Personal Property excluded:*_____

_____

_____

_____

_____

*Guaranteed Purchase Price: $*_____

Lot approximately _____ X _____

I. PRE-CONDITION

This Agreement is contingent upon:

    A. Either Owner has already contracted to purchase another residence through McLennan Company, or

    B. Owner shall contract within _____ days after the date of this Agreement to purchase a residence through McLennan Company.

If this contingency is not satisfied, this agreement shall, at Realtor's option, be null and void.

FIGURE 20-2 (cont.)

II. LISTING PERIOD

A. The listing period shall begin on _____, 1975.

B. Realtor shall have sole authority to advertise, display signs, and sell the property for a period of _____ days thereafter.

C. The listing price shall be:

First _____ days of listing period................$ _____

Next _____ days of listing period................$ _____

Next _____ days of listing period................$ _____

D. Realtor agrees to list the property with the Northwest Suburban Board Multiple Listing Service and to cooperate with all members in effecting a sale; to make a continued and earnest effort to sell the property; to advertise the property as he deems it advisable to obtain prospective purchasers.

E. Seller agrees to cooperate fully with Realtor and refer all inquiries to him; to conduct all negotiations through Realtor; to pay a real estate brokerage commission of 6% of the sale price if this property is sold by Realtor, by Seller, or by or through any other person during the period of this agreement.

F. Seller agrees to furnish:
1. A survey by a licensed land surveyor showing the location of the buildings and improvements to be within the lot lines and no encroachments of buildings or other improvements from adjoining properties;
2. Either a commitment for title insurance in the amount of the sale price or a Torrens Certificate and Torrens Tax and Special Assessment Search as evidence of marketable title;
3. A Revenue Stamped Warranty Deed to the purchaser of the property;
4. A Bill of Sale to the purchaser for the personal property included;

G. This listing agreement shall take precedence over any listing agreement (whether exclusive or not) which is prior in time and which has expired in accordance with its terms and conditions.

H. Realtor's sole duty is to effect a sale of the property and he is not charged with the custody of the property, its management, maintenance, upkeep, or repair.

I. It is mutually understood and agreed that, by law, a Realtor is only permitted to prepare a contract of sale. Seller agrees to furnish or have his attorney furnish all legal documents necessary to close the transaction.

III. GUARANTEED PURCHASE BY REALTOR

If the Listing Period has ended and the property has not been sold, the parties agree as follows:

A. Realtor agrees to purchase the real property and included personal property for the Guaranteed Purchase Price.

B. Closing shall be 15 days after the end of the Listing Period. Possession shall be delivered at closing. Closing shall be at Realtor's office.

C. Owner agrees to furnish the instruments specified in Paragraph II (F) above.

D. Title shall be conveyed subject only to:

1. General Taxes for 19____ and subsequent years.
2. Building and Zoning Ordinances.
3. Easements, covenants, and Restrictions as to use and occupancy.

E. If the evidence of title discloses defects, Owner shall have 30 additional days from date evidence of title is furnished to cure such defects and notify Realtor. If Owner is unable to cure such defects Realtor may, at his election, terminate this contract, or Realtor may take the title as it then is (with the right to deduct from the purchase price liens or encumbrances of a definite or ascertainable amount) by notifying Owner and tendering performance.

F. If prior to closing, improvements on said premises shall be destroyed or materially damaged by fire or any other casualty, this contract at option of Realtor shall become null and void.

G. Real Estate Taxes (based on most recent bill) and other proratable items (except insurance) shall be prorated to the date of closing.

H. Existing mortgage and other lien indebtedness may be paid at closing out of sale proceeds.

I. Realtor may place a mortgage on this property and apply proceeds on purchase.

REALTOR: OWNER(S):

McLennan Company

By: _____   _____

_____

FIGURE 20-2 (cont.)

Guaranteed Purchase Price Agreement Addendum

IV. RETURN OF REALTOR PROFIT

A. *Definitions:*

1. *"Gross Profit" is the difference between the resale price and the Guaranteed Purchase Price.*

2. *"Actual Expenses" are all expenses which Realtor incurs in the purchase, holding, and resale of the property guaranteed.*

3. *"Net Profit" is the "Gross Profit" less a commission of 6% of the resale purchase price and less "Actual Expenses". (These expenses have been estimated on the Guaranteed Valuation Analysis.)*

B. *If Realtor purchases the property in accordance with this agreement and upon resale a "Net Profit" results, this "Net Profit" shall be paid to the Owner.*

GUARANTEED VALUATION ANALYSIS

Appraisers_____Date_____

Property Address_____

Occupant's Address_____

Original Listing Price _____

Guaranteed Sales Price _____

MINUS ESTIMATED HOLDING COSTS

Interest On Purchase Money	_____*Annual Amount*_____	*Months*_____	
Taxes on Property	_____*Annual Amount*_____	*Months*_____	
Insurance on Property	_____*Annual Amount*_____	*Months*_____	
*Maintenance Services: Lawn/Misc.*_____	*Annual Amount*_____	*Months*_____	
Utilities: Gas, Water, Electric	_____*Annual Amount*_____	*Months*_____	

Transfer Fees: (Note: A constant cost no   *Total*_____
matter who sells property)

*Deed,*_____*Revenue Stamps*_____

*Title,*_____*Legal Fee*_____

                 *Total*_____

                         *Total*_____

Reconditioning:

Interior Walls _____		*Exterior Painting* _____	
Woodwork _____		*Gutters* _____	
Ceilings _____		*Windows*_____	
Floors _____		*Roof* _____	
Windows _____		*General—Heating Equipment* _____	
Cabinets—Doors _____		*Cooling Equipment*_____	
Misc. _____		*Electrical Fixtures*_____	
Advertising _____		*Plumbing Fixtures*_____	
Other _____		*Total*_____	

           BROKERAGE COMMISSION _____

           NET TO SELLER _____

REALTOR: *OWNER(S):*

McLennan Company

*By:*_____   _____

_____   _____

FIGURE 20-3. Benefits of Guaranteed Trade-in Plan

TELEPHONES: Suburban 825-0011 · Chicago 831-6400

TWENTY-FIVE NORTH NORTHWEST HIGHWAY, PARK RIDGE, ILLINOIS 60068

THE BEST PRICE FOR YOUR HOME -- GUARANTEED!

This plan offers many benefits to you. Listed below are some of the benefits you could realize should you decide to avail yourself of our plan:

1. You are guaranteed in writing a net purchase price in the event we do not sell your house within the listing period.

   You are under no obligation to accept any offers and also you do not have to sell your house to us if you wish not to.

   Simply, if you want us to exercise our guarantee to purchase, we will do so.

2. It avoids the high costs of double moving expenses.

3. It allows the buyer to secure firm, favorable financing commitments at the best interest rates and costs. Over a few years, that can represent a substantial difference.

4. It avoids double ownership costs of interest, taxes, insurance, maintenance and repairs.

5. The buyer can purchase the property at today's prices... avoiding inflationary or appreciated increases because he does not have to wait to sell his old home before he buys.

6. Since he has definite moving dates in advance he can make moving arrangements when convenient... and not disrupt other income producing occupations.

7. He will never be forced into accepting a "distress price" for his property which could cost him thousands of dollars.

8. He has "purchased" the time to find the right buyer who will pay more and that fact alone may yield him an increased return for his ownership interests.

9. He is able to select the time in which to market the old home... picking the most favorable season of the year and the best marketing approach. The control over this factor can make a substantial difference in the net results.

In sum, I think it of sufficient import to suggest that you listen to our proposition, since it can afford you substantial benefits in terms of convenience and maximum equity.

Warmest regards,

Roger J. Karvel
Residential Sales Manager
McLennan Company

RJK/dsp

RESIDENTIAL-COMMERCIAL-INDUSTRIAL SALES · CONSTRUCTION · MANAGEMENT · INSURANCE
REALTOR®

The guaranteed purchase price agreement is illustrated in Figure 20-2. Note that the first page makes the agreement contingent on the owner's willingness to purchase another residence through the company. If the owner does not contract to purchase through the McLennan Company, the guaranteed purchase price agreement is null and void. The second part of the form describes listing terms and commits the Realtor® to the guaranteed purchase: If the listing period has ended and the house has not been sold, the parties agree as follows: "Realtor® agrees to purchase the real property and included personal property for the guaranteed purchase price."

2. *Valuation Analysis.* Attention is especially invited to the Addendum to the Guaranteed Purchase Price Agreement. Here, the broker provides a valuation analysis giving the original listing price and the guaranteed sales price, less estimated holding costs, namely, interest, taxes, insurance, maintenance service, utilities, and transfer fees. All reconditioning costs are listed showing the net price to the seller.

Similarly, the Heritage Group of West Hartford, Connecticut, provides a trade-in assurance policy that advises prospects:

> There is no substitute for experience! Every member of the trade-in plan staff has been thoroughly trained in the specialized business of home trade-ins. He will transfer the worrisome details from your shoulders to his and make trading your home an easy step for you.

The policy explains that there is no possibility of owning two homes and making two mortgage payments: "Your equity is guarded from bargain-hunting speculators." The company also states in its policy: "You get the new home that you want, guaranteed sale of your present home, elimination of reconditioning, duplicate moving costs, high rents, and other problems of uncertainty." Figure 20-3 summarizes other advantages of the trade-in plan. The advantages of these plans, as explained by experienced Realtors®, call for careful staff organizing.

Organizing a Trade-In Policy

Realtors® exercising this sales technique have a plan that attracts additional buyers and sellers to the office. The Heritage Group of West Hartford, Connecticut, finds that its trade-in assurance policy "converts lookers into buyers" and it helps in gaining additional listings. Successful trade-in programs raise the prestige of the office in the local community. It could also provide a good relationship with builders who need a trading service.

The plan has been widely used in selling intercity listings from cooperating brokers in other areas who sponsor professionally administered trade-ins. Further, the trade-in plan appeals to corporations that underwrite homeownership transfer costs of their employees. There are certain steps that should be followed in administering the program: arranging for capital, presenting the plan, and developing procedures. These steps are discussed below.

Arranging for Capital.   Salespersons and brokers often invest personal funds in a trust to finance operation of a trade-in purchase. Typically, the fund earns more than regular bank deposits and provides a method of financing additional real estate commissions. The syndicate agreement may provide that employee-investors share profits and losses in proportion to their invested capital.

The larger firms agree to guarantee a minimum return for the capital invested with management making up for possible losses. Employee-financed trade-in plans give salespersons incentives to promote and sell trade-in properties. Management maintains control of the capital, thus avoiding the inconvenience of dealing with financial institutions. Salespersons, however, should not neglect the sales task in their interest to make money on trade-in funds.

Experts report success with local savings and loan associations that finance a special trust account for trade-ins by pledging individual savings accounts. Individual depositors (salespersons) pledge their deposits as security for real estate loans needed to finance trade-in programs. If loans are outstanding, the individual account is frozen against withdrawals. Meanwhile, interest payments on the savings account continue. Real estate companies managing the fund agree to protect the fund from any losses and agree to release deposits pledged as security once a 30-day notice has been given.

This latter plan provides working capital without loss of interest in savings accounts. Individuals are not risking funds since the company agrees to make good on losses. The money is used only as security to make loans on real estate trade-ins.

Outside investors are sometimes used to gain additional funds. Funds are also gained from (1) corporate ventures, builders, and subdividers or (2) a line of credit with a local bank or lender.

Presenting the Plan.   Work sheets are essential in presenting the plan. The salesperson introduces the basic outline of the trade-in plan and if the prospect seems interested, the inquiry is turned over to a trade-in specialist. After making the investigation, the trade-in specialist goes over the work sheet with the prospect and shows the prospect how the guaranteed price was estimated. Note that in Figure 20-2 costs incurred in holding the property are itemized because most buyers would neglect these expenses. If the house needs redecorating, the trade-in specialist can defend these estimates. The competitive market analysis enables the trade-in specialist to explain why the guaranteed price represents a realistic value.

Developing Procedures.   There are compelling arguments for separating the functions of the salesperson, who deals directly with the prospect, and the trade-in specialist. Many buyers tend to be emotional about the value of their homes. By turning this trade-in procedure over to a specialist, the salesperson avoids disagreements and delegates the final arrangements for the trade-in to a more experienced person.

In this regard, it is assumed that the trade-in specialist knows the current market. He or she continually reviews local offerings and recently sold houses in the same neighborhood. Not only does the trade-in person have to have a knowledge of appraisal methods, but he or she must also know financing, real estate taxation, and construction costs.

It should be noted that salespersons must avoid discussing the trade-sell plan until the prospect shows a keen interest in a new house. If the prospect's circumstances recommend a trade-sell, a salesperson initiates the request and presents the trade-in brochure. No mention is made of the price of the older home.

After the appraiser for the trade-in makes the inspection, the trade-in plan form is completed and the type of trade that best meets the buyer's needs is recommended. In some cases, it may be desirable to combine a conditional sale with a follow-up using the guaranteed sales plan. If the local housing market is dominated by persons already owning their own homes, developing procedures for trade-in plans becomes a necessary part of the office operation.

POINTS TO REMEMBER

Your selling techniques are incomplete if you do not consider warranty and trade-in plans. Indeed, as the rule of caveat emptor undergoes change, warranty plans may be advised as a means of protecting you from misrepresentations and implied warranties of third parties not under your control.

More importantly, the growing acceptance of warranty plans on new homes increases your prospects for sales. You should learn about the home owner warranty plans approved in your area and the number of cases in which builders have made good on their warranties. This information creates confidence in your buyer-prospect and it certainly increases the marketability of houses listed with a home owners warranty.

The National Association of Realtors® has strongly approved and recommends warranty programs covering material defects in the basic structure and housing components. They protect the Realtor® and clients from liabilities for breach of warranty and misrepresentation. Explain to clients that organizations approved by the National Association of Realtors® operate on a national basis, maintain sufficient financial reserves, and have facilities and staff to properly process orders and inspections and adjust claims.

Even the inspection without a warranty gives your prospect invaluable information on the listed house. By reviewing the main features of the plan, you show how the prospect reduces risk in buying a house in which he or she has little knowledge about the basic structure and its components.

Similarly, trade-in plans make houses more marketable. These plans may be used if the buyer of the new home has *sufficient equity* in an old home to warrant a trade. The prospect must also have the *financial ability* to qualify for a new home. Trade-ins that are *difficult to sell* (the obsolete house in a poor location and in a declining neighborhood) must be avoided.

The available trade-in plans adapt to virtually all qualified prospects. The *conditional sale* is more likely to be approved by the developer of a subdivision who is willing to keep a house off the market while the seller tries to sell his or her old home. There is the advantage that the conditional sale requires no capital for financing and is adapted to the buyer who has little or no equity in his or her existing house.

The *direct trade* is used if the house is in poor condition and clients require an immediate closing. If your valuation analysis is accurate, a direct trade may provide a good long-term investment.

An *equity loan* expedites the sale because it guarantees that the prospect will have funds to purchase the new house. Usually, a loan is secured by placing a lien on the old, the new, or both houses for a short term, say 90 days. The seller is required to repay the loan, usually through reducing the price of the old home, to meet the due date. Variations of this plan provide for a personal loan from the bank, co-signed by the broker who is secured by a lien on the old or new house (or both).

A *guaranteed plan* is the most frequently used trade-in plan. Under this arrangement, the buyer-prospect gains from listing the house under normal listing arrangements. If the house does not sell within the listing period, the prospect receives a predetermined guaranteed price and title passes to the participating broker.

Considerable care must be taken in executing the guaranteed purchase agreement: Holding costs, selling costs, and repair expenses necessary to the sale must be explained. Some brokers rely on the guaranteed sale because they feel that the technique frees equity and makes older homes more marketable; other brokers view the guaranteed sale as a means of gaining more listings.

In organizing a trade-in policy, you must arrange for capital, (frequently through an employee-syndicate), a line of credit, or a pledge of employee savings deposits. Successful administration requires that special forms be used to help explain the details of the plan to the prospect.

Most brokers recommend that the functions of the salesperson and the trade-in specialist be separated. The person responsible for a trade-in must have a background in appraising, construction, financing, and sales. By delegating these tasks to the trade-in specialists, the salesperson avoids technical discussions with the buyer and concentrates on marketing the listed property.

REVIEW QUESTIONS

1. Summarize the main advantages of warranty plans.

2. Explain the meaning of implied warranties.

3. Explain the main features of the Home Owners Warranty Policy.

4. What requirements must a warranty company meet if it is to be approved by the National Association of Realtors®?

5. For companies offering a warranty program that requires an inspection, what items are usually covered in the inspection?

6. What precautions would you recommend in arranging a sale and trade-in plan?

7. What is a conditional sale?

8. Contrast the three major trade-in plans. Explain the advantages of each plan.

9. What are the main provisions of the guaranteed purchase agreement?

10. What sources of capital are available for financing trade-in plans?

21

Rental Housing Sales

Rental housing sales refer to houses sold for income purposes, not for owner-occupancy. Almost every community has a supply of rental housing that serves both low- and middle-income groups. Almost every community has buyers for houses suitable for rental occupancy. Although owner-occupancy dominates the housing market, a certain proportion of houses satisfi es renters who prefer houses to apartments or mobile homes. And almost every real estate broker has listings of rental houses that require more specialized selling techniques.

THE MARKET FOR RENTAL HOUSING

To be sure, there is a specialized market for rental housing in resort and vacation areas. Houses in this category are more comparable to commercial property subject to professional management and operation. For the present purpose, attention is directed to urban houses operated for year-around occupancy and which are usually in neighborhoods dominated by owner-occupants.

Demand for Rental Housing

To some degree, the market for rental housing is similar to the market served by apartments. But rental housing appeals to a group having more unique requirements. Renters tend to be in one of the following groups:

1. Single persons who appreciate the privacy of a house.
2. Families with children that prefer single-family dwellings to apartments.
3. Families that would not qualify for comparable apartment units because they have pets.
4. Families that prefer temporary rental occupancy pending a housing purchase.
5. Families that do not have the funds or credit for a home purchase.
6. Families that follow the "mobile" occupations (for example, executives, entertainers, salespersons, and construction employees) and families that change jobs.

In fact, because of the unique market for rental housing—both its supply and demand—salespersons who deal with rental housing create new prospects among renters who later elect to purchase. In fact, to encourage house sales in slowly moving new subdivisions, developers often rent with an option to purchase for a stated period. Generally, if the renter elects to buy, a portion of the rent applies toward the down payment.

Supply of Rental Housing

New neighborhoods are unlikely to have many houses to rent. New houses that qualify for liberal mortgage terms are more saleable compared to older homes. But as neighborhoods mature, some owners facing an estate settlement, a job transfer, or other compelling circumstances find it prudent to rent instead of sell. For instance, if a buyer purchases a house for $50,000 under 95 percent financing, at the end of the year the equity is only slightly above $2,500, which is less than the selling cost if the property is sold through a real estate broker. If in the meantime the housing market has declined, the owner would be unable to sell for the amount of the present mortgage.

Assume, therefore, that the home could not be sold for more than $40,000. Here it probably would be advisable for the seller to rent for a year and deduct property taxes, mortgage interest, and depreciation over the year. After the rental lease expires, the house could be listed and sold. If a loss results, it would be income tax deductible. Therefore, for some owners, renting rather than an immediate sale might be recommended.

Consider, however, the more established neighborhoods which are in a stage of stable values. Further, other houses may occupy key potential business corners that may be converted to commercial purposes over the next few years. These are the houses that are typically purchased for investment purposes. Most investors would reject houses that require extensive repairs in plumbing, heating, and air conditioning or correction of major structural faults in the foundation, basement, or frame. Houses that require minimum landscaping and nominal interior redecorating would be more likely to justify investment for rental purposes. These houses are usually purchased for tax shelter and capital gain opportunities.

HOUSING PURCHASES FOR TAX SHELTER

The investor purchasing a home for rental purposes has certain tax advantages over the owner-occupant: The investor may deduct depreciation allowances on the dwelling and annual operating expenses. In addition, the investor benefits from other economic advantages of home ownership. To market these homes, it is believed helpful to concentrate on certain income tax advantages of rental housing.

Tax Advantages

The owner of a rental home is allowed to deduct the following from gross rentals:

Operating expenses.
Depreciation.
Mortgage interest.
Property taxes.

Normally, single-family dwellings purchased for income purposes would be uneconomic if it were not for the present income tax deductions. The small-scale operation appeals to owners who are willing to undertake repairs and, frequently, secure tenants, collect rents, and complete other management chores.

It should be added that repairs such as painting, floor resurfacing, and the like are expenses of operation that are deductible from gross income, but they also add to the value of the property. Therefore, while the property is operated for income purposes and tax shelter, annual repairs (1) reduce net income tax liability and (2) add to property appreciation.

The depreciation allowance is based on the estimated life of the building. IRS guidelines suggest 45 years for dwellings, but a shorter life may be allowed for older buildings. For example, if the house is purchased for $40,000 and the land has an estimated value of $5,000, the amount depreciated would be $35,000.

If there is a 40-year life, the property owner has the option of depreciating an existing house on a *straight-line* basis over the building life of 40 years or *125 percent* of straight-line rates. A 40-year life would result in a straight-line depreciation deduction of $2\frac{1}{2}$ percent of the building value per year (40 divided into 1—1/40, the reciprocal of the building life).[1]

If 125 percent of straight-line rates apply to the undepreciated balance

---

[1]Straight-line rates are calculated by dividing estimated building life into 1.0. For example, a building that has an estimated life of 25 years would be depreciated at 4 percent per year, straight-line rates ($1 \div 25 = 4.0\%$).

each year, the first-year deduction would be 3.125 percent of the depreciable building value. For a $35,000 building, these annual depreciation allowances would amount to $875 (straight-line) or, for the first year, $1,093.75 (a declining balance depreciation equal to 125 percent of straight-line rates).

Calculation of Tax Shelter

As an illustration of how an investor would benefit from tax shelter, assume that you have a house listed for $40,000 available under a 75 percent mortgage, repayable with $9\frac{1}{2}$ percent interest over 25 years. Suppose the property may be rented for $350 a month and you consider $175 as a reasonable annual vacancy (two weeks). Suppose further that your first year estimate of net income is $3,165 as indicated below:

Annual gross income, ($350 month)		$4,200
Less vacancy		−175
Effective gross income		$4,025
Less operating expenses		
Property taxes	$600	
Insurance	200	
Water	60	−860
Net operating income		$3,165

The housing purchase would appear feasible under these circumstances because the owner would have enough net income to satisfy the mortgage payments. The annual net income, though small, would be sufficient to cover the mortgage payments. Before tax cash flow would be positive: It is defined here as the net operating income after mortgage payments, including principal and interest.

Net operating income	$3,165.00
Less mortgage payments	−3,146.60
Before tax cash flow	$18.40

Assume next that the building has an estimated value of $35,000 which may be depreciated over 40 years. The tax shelter for the first year may be calculated as follows:

Net operating income		$3,165.00
Less		
Mortgage interest	$2,846.60	
Depreciation	1,093.75	
		−3,940.35
125%, 40-year life,		
$35,000		
Tax shelter		($ 775.35)

Because interest and depreciation are deducted from net operating income to give taxable income, this example shows greater than net operating income or tax shelter.

Other Advantages.   After depreciation has been deducted, the prospect has an estimated tax shelter of $775.35 during the first year of operation which may be subtracted from other taxable income. If the prospect is subject to a 50 percent income tax rate, this amounts to an additional saving of $387.67.

The tax shelter in succeeding years would decrease because of the gradual decline in mortgage interest and depreciation. In estimating the tax shelter for succeeding years, you might want to adjust net income upward to account for rental income that increases at a greater rate than expenses increase.

It should be pointed out that the prospect will have the use of the $1,093.75 depreciation allowance and if the house resells for $40,000 or more, the owner will recover the $300.00 principal repayments accumulated over the first year—and additional principal repayments made over the ownership.

Tax Shelter Qualifications.   In this example no allowance has been made for annual maintenance and repair expenses. In addition, the calculation makes no provision for replacement of refrigerators, ranges, air conditioning units, washing machines, dryers, and other equipment. Although these are proper expenses of operation for other income properties, the relation between mortgage payments, monthly rent, and expenses usually does not allow for

FIGURE 21-1:   Calculation of Tax Shelter Summarized

1. Estimate the annual gross income from your estimate of the monthly market rent.

2. Reduce the annual rent by an allowance for vacancy. A vacancy of more than four weeks would probably reduce the value of the property or make the purchase uneconomic.

3. Estimate annual operating expenses. As a minimum, include annual property taxes, utility costs assumed by the owner, and insurance.

4. Deduct the monthly mortgage payments from the annual net operating income, and multiply by 12 to get the annual before tax cash flow.

5. Calculate (from mortgage tables) the total amount paid on mortgage interest over the first year. Deduct this sum from the before tax cash flow.

6. Determine the depreciable basis of the building (selling price less land value) and calculate the depreciation based on the remaining depreciable life. To maximize cash flow, use 125 percent of straight-line rates—the declining balance method of the depreciation.

7. After subtracting the mortgage interest and depreciation from before cash flow, multiply the result by the estimated income tax rate. Subtract this sum from income after depreciation and mortgage interest to give (1) after tax cash flow or (2) a negative sum indicating the tax shelter.

profitable operation if these economic costs are included. If operating expenses for these are recorded, they decrease the profitability and increase the tax shelter.

The point has been made, however, that some owners contribute "sweat equity" (their own labor) to the enterprise. Even if repair, replacement, and redecorating expenses are contracted (resulting in an unprofitable operation), the owner-investor benefits by the probable appreciation in value. The extent to which repairs, replacement, and redecorating expenses may be recovered in capital appreciation is determined by the local real estate market and the amount of expenses incurred. If, in fact, repairs and like expenses add to property appreciation, the owner converts ordinary income to capital gains, which may be deferred or which may benefit the owner because he or she may substitute lower capital gain taxes for higher ordinary income taxes.

Because of the critical importance of the tax shelter calculation, the main steps in its calculation are summarized in Figure 21-1, which is relatively easy to follow. In the last analysis, tax shelter estimates are based on published mortgage tables, current financing terms, the building depreciable base and estimated life, and the prospect's income tax rate.

CAPITAL GAIN OPPORTUNITIES

If housing prices increase as the general price level increases, investment in rental housing will provide not only tax shelter but it will also create opportunities for capital appreciation subject to favorable capital gain tax rates. Currently, individuals pay income taxes only on 40 percent of the gain. If a rental house sells for more than its original price, capital appreciation arises from (1) equity build-up and (2) capital appreciation.

Consider the preceding example of a house purchased for $40,000 which increases in value at an annual compound rate of 10 percent. If the property were to be held for five years, increasing in value at an annual 10 percent compound rate, the property would sell for $64,400 (rounded). Allowing a 7 percent cost of sale ($4,509) would result in a net sales price of $59,892. To estimate the capital gain tax, it is necessary (1) to calculate the original cost less depreciation and (2) to estimate recaptured depreciation in excess of straight-line depreciation.

Income property held for less than 100 months is subject to a tax recapture if other than straight-line depreciation is used. The amount that accelerated depreciation exceeds straight-line rates will be taxed at ordinary income tax rates, assumed to be 40 percent in this example. The 125 percent declining balance depreciation in this case adds to $5,137.47 over the five years.

Year	Annual Depreciation (125%) Declining Balance: Five Years
1	$1,093.75
2	1,059.57
3	1,026.46
4	994.38
5	963.31
Total	$5,137.47
Less straightline depreciation	−4,375.00
Depreciation subject to recapture	$ 762.47

Straight-line depreciation is based on a 2.5 percent annual allowance. On a depreciable basis of $35,000, depreciation equals $875 a year, and over five years depreciation subject to recapture totals $762.47.

These figures provide the basis for calculating the adjusted tax basis:

Original cost	$40,000.00
Less accumulated depreciation	−5,137.47
Adjusted tax basis	$34,862.53

With an original cost of $40,000 and a 125 percent depreciation deduction of $5,137.47, capital gain taxes are based on the adjusted tax basis of $34,862.53. The capital gain would then be equal to:

Net sales price	$59,892.00
Less adjusted tax basis	−34,862.53
Taxable amount	$25,029.47
Less depreciation recapture	−762.47
Capital gain	$24,267.00
Less 60% exemption	−14,560.20
Gain subject to tax	$9,706.80

The taxable amount totals $25,029.47—the difference between the net sales price and the adjusted tax basis. The depreciation recapture is deducted because this is taxed at the higher ordinary tax rates. Under the present assumptions, the total tax payable would amount to $4,187.70.

Taxable capital gain $9,706.80 × .40 (ordinary tax rate)	$3,882.72
Recapture (40% ordinary tax rate)	304.98
Total tax payable	$4,187.70

Table 21-1 shows the net result of these transactions. Starting with the net sales price of $59,892 and after paying the remaining mortgage balance, the investor has $31,782. Deducting the taxes payable on the total transaction gives sales proceeds after taxes of $27,594.30, or an average annual gain of $3,518.86. The data reveal after taxes, an average annual rate of return of 35.18 percent on an original investment of $10,000—the down payment.

TABLE 21-1. Calculation of Sales Proceeds after Capital Gain Taxes.

Net sales price		$59,892.00
Less mortgage balance		−28,110.00
		$31,782.00
Less tax payable		−4,187.70
Sales proceeds		
after taxes		27,594.30
Less Equity		−10,000.00
Net profit, after taxes		$17,594.30
Average annual profit		
$17,594.30 ÷ 5	=	$3,518.86
Average annual rate of return		
$3,518.66 ÷ $10,000.00	=	.3518 or 35.18%

Clearly, these results depend on the assumption of property appreciation. The relatively high rate of return is largely the result of the assumed property appreciation at an annual 10 percent compound rate. You are prohibited from making false promises or misrepresentations, but you can reveal the present analysis that emphasizes (1) tax shelter and (2) the tax treatment of property appreciation. Let the prospect make the assumptions; you only provide counsel on the analytical procedure common to knowledgeable investors.

TAX-DEFERRED EXCHANGES

It has been pointed out that one of the main reasons for buying rental houses is the opportunity to realize capital appreciation. If appreciation is realized, the investor is subject to capital gains; yet, under certain circumstances, capital gain taxes may be temporarily avoided by arranging a tax-deferred exchange.

To qualify for tax-deferred treatment, the owner must hold the property for investment or for use in trade or business. Tax-deferred exchanges are not allowed for real estate held for sale to customers, for example, houses sold by a developer. Similarly, the benefits of a tax-deferred exchange are not extended to owner-occupants who do not own the home as an investment. The tax-deferred privilege applies only to exchanges of property "of a like kind."

Property of Like Kind

Property of like kind refers to the *nature* or *character* of the property, not to its grade or quality. Section 1031 of the Internal Revenue Code states in part:

> . . . the words "like kind" have reference to the nature or character of the property and not to its grade or quality. One kind or class of property may not under (Section 1031) be exchanged for property of a different kind or class. The fact that any real estate involved is improved or unimproved is not material, for the fact relates only to the grade or quality of the property and not to its kind or class. Unproductive real estate held by one other than a dealer for future use or future realization of the increment in value is held for investment and not primarily for sale.

Generally speaking, real estate has been interpreted as property of like kind. Property approved for a tax exchange under Section 1031 has included exchanges of:

A rented commercial building for unimproved city lots.
Mineral rights for hotel property.
An oil or gas lease for a ranch.
Timberland held for trade for timberland held for investment.

Certain other exchanges that include real estate have been denied treatment as a tax-deferred exchange. Property transfers disapproved as a tax-deferred exchange have included:

Real estate exchanged for personal property.
Real estate exchanged for stocks and bonds.
Vacant land exchanged for a building.

In questionable cases, the legal interpretation given tax-deferred exchanges would call for a review by tax counsel. There is a further requirement that prospects must hold the exchanged property for business or for investment. If your prospect immediately resells the property acquired in a tax-deferred exchange, the Internal Revenue Service may treat the property as acquired for purposes of resale and taxable as a capital gain. Hence, both the property exchanged and the property received must be held for investment or for use in trade or business.[2]

Tax Treatment of Real Estate Exchanges

In the simplest case, if property of like kind and value is exchanged, both properties benefit by deferred gain taxes. Property acquired in a tax-deferred exchange includes the transfer of the *depreciable basis* of the old property.

[2]Paul E. Anderson, *Tax Factors and Real Estate Operations,* 4th ed. (Englewood Cliffs, N.J.: Prentice-Hall, Inc. 1976), pp. 122–23.

Depreciable basis refers to the amount remaining subject to future depreciation
—the undepreciated amount. In other words, the depreciable base of property
exchanged transfers to the new property.

For example, if your prospect exchanges a rental house for a duplex, the
depreciable basis of the house carries over to the duplex. If it is assumed that
the properties exchanged have the same value, the transfer would be exempt
from capital gain taxes.

Depreciable basis of	
rental house	$35,000
Market value of duplex	$60,000
Less depreciable basis	
of rental house	−35,000
Gain realized	$25,000
Taxable gain	0
Depreciable basis of	
duplex	$35,000

In this instance, A exchanges a rental house that has a market value of
$60,000 for a duplex of equal market value. Since this is a straight trade,
neither party transfers other cash or assets; there is no taxable gain. Note that
A, in exchanging the house for the duplex, must base future depreciation on
the duplex according to the depreciable basis remaining on the rental house.

Real Estate Exchanges with Boot.   It is unlikely that a real estate
exchange will cover two properties having the same market value. Usually, one
party or the other must make up the difference in market value with a cash
payment. Such cash payments are referred to as *boot.* Boot, which could be
money or other assets, changes the tax treatment of the exchange. However,
the payment of boot does not make the total transaction taxable; boot makes
only a proportion of the transaction subject to tax.

The taxation of property that includes boot requires that two types of
gain be defined: realized gain and recognized gain. The exchanger's improved
financial position defines *realized gain.* It is equal to the market value of the
property received less the depreciable basis of the property given up. *Recognized gain* is gain reported for capital gain taxes.

Consider Seller A who exchanges a $50,000 building that has a depreciable basis of $25,000 for a $40,000 building and $10,000 cash. If a seller sold
the $50,000 building, he or she would pay capital gain taxes on $25,000
($50,000 − $25,000). Under the exchange, Seller A pays only capital gains on
the boot: $10,000.

Assume that Buyer B, who has a $40,000 building, has a depreciable
basis of $10,000. The new basis of the $50,000 building is the depreciable basis
of the old building traded ($10,000) and the $10,000 cash given in boot, which
totals $20,000. By trading, Buyer B defers the capital gain tax and adds to the
depreciable base. These arrangements are illustrated in Figure 21-2.

FIGURE 21-2. An Example of a Two-Party, Tax-deferred Exchange

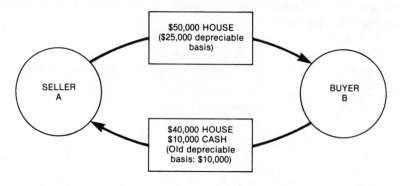

The amount of recognized gain applying to Seller A is summarized below:

Amount of gain realized by Seller A	$40,000 house	
	$10,000 cash	
		$50,000
Less basis of house given up		−25,000
Realized gain		$25,000
Recognized gain (boot received)		$10,000

There are occasions when the boot received exceeds the realized gain. In this case, the gain realized is taxed in full. The excess amount of boot is considered tax-free because it represents part of the owner's basis of the former property. For instance, assume that Seller A exchanges a house worth $60,000 (the depreciable basis is $40,000) for an apartment house site worth $30,000 plus cash of $10,000 and promissory notes worth $20,000. Seller A's total gain of $20,000 would be fully taxed.

Value of apartment site	$30,000	
Cash	10,000	
Promissory notes	20,000	
		$60,000
Less depreciable basis of house traded		−40,000
Realized gain		$20,000
Boot received		30,000
Gain taxed to extent of boot		$20,000
Remainder of boot applied to new basis		$10,000

In this instance, the realized gain of $20,000 is taxable and the remaining $10,000 of the boot received is added to the new basis of the property traded.

Trading Mortgaged Property. Property traded subject to a mortgage may result in a capital gain tax even though *no cash boot* is paid because the law treats being relieved or giving up a mortgage indebtedness as equal to receiving cash in a like amount.

1. *Mortgage on one property.* Suppose that the trader exchanges property that has a market value of $60,000 and a depreciable basis of $50,000. Assume further that the property is subject to a mortgage of $30,000. If the property is traded for an unencumbered house that has a fair market value of $40,000, the total recognized gain would be $20,000.

Value of house received	$40,000
Plus mortgage given up	+30,000
Total	$70,000
Less depreciable basis	
of property traded	−50,000
Realized gain	$20,000
Boot received	30,000
Gain recognized	
(the lesser of realized	
gain or boot received)	$20,000

If the boot received is $20,000, the gain would be the lesser of realized gain or boot received, or $20,000 for capital gain treatment.

2. *Mortgage on Both Properties.* Normally, both properties traded would have mortgages. In this case, traders *receive* boot in mortgages and *give* boot by accepting mortgages. Usually, a cash payment is made to equalize the differences in mortgages and market value. Suppose, for example, that property having a fair market value of $60,000 is subject to an outstanding mortgage of $30,000 and a depreciable basis of $50,000. In return, the property is exchanged for real estate having a market value of $50,000 subject to a mortgage of $15,000. To equalize the equities, the trader must pay $10,000 in cash to result in the following realized gain:

Value of house received		$55,000
Plus mortgage given up		+30,000
Total received		$85,000
Basis of real estate given		
up ($60,000 value)		
Depreciable basis	$50,000	
Assumed mortgage	15,000	
Cash given	10,000	
Total given		$75,000
Realized gain		$10,000

The figures show that the trader has received $85,000: $55,000 for the value of the house received and $30,000 for the mortgage given up on the traded property. The depreciable basis of the real estate given up consists of the

$50,000 depreciable basis of the property traded, the $15,000 assumed mortgage, and the cash total ($10,000), which total $75,000, or a realized gain of $10,000.

To estimate whether or not boot has been received, the boot given must be compared to the boot received. The following calculations show that the trader has received a net boot of $5,000:

	Boot Given	Boot Received
Mortgage given up		$30,000
Assumed mortgage	$15,000	
Cash given in trade	10,000	
Net boot received (capital gain)	$ 5,000	
	$30,000	$30,000

Since cash or other boot is paid to compensate for a large mortgage, a trader may receive net boot because cash is not offset by the excess of the mortgage on the property received over the mortgage on the property transferred. A better solution in trading property that has a low mortgage where cash is received—and not offset by a larger mortgage—is to increase the mortgage before the property is traded so that the mortgages are equalized on both properties. Alternatively, the property that has a large mortgage traded may be paid off or paid down before the exchange in order to equalize the mortgages on both sides.

Multiple Exchanges

Multiple exchanges help buyers and sellers gain tax-deferred treatment. The more common three-party trade may even use a cash sale to expedite the trade between two parties. Suppose that Owner A owns a $40,000 rental house and wants to trade the property for a $65,000 duplex owned by Seller B under a tax-deferred exchange. But Seller B does not want to acquire a $40,000 rental house.

The solution is to have *Buyer C* purchase the rental house and trade with Owner A. Owner A, in these circumstances, qualifies for a tax-deferred exchange. This three-party device is used under the following circumstances:

1. Owner A wants to trade a $40,000 rental house for Seller B's duplex.
2. Seller B owns a $65,000 duplex but does not want the $40,000 rental house.
3. Buyer C wants Owner A's rental house.
4. Solution: Buyer C purchases Seller B's duplex and exchanges the duplex for Owner A's rental house.
5. The result: Owner A makes a tax-deferred exchange of a $40,000 rental house for the $65,000 duplex. Figure 21-3 summarizes this three-party exchange.

FIGURE 21-3. Three-party Exchange with a Cash Sale.

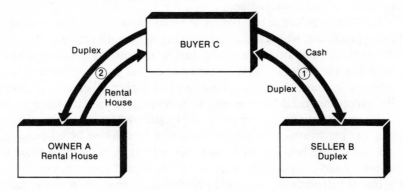

In this transaction, Buyer C must not have been under any other obligation to buy the rental house from Owner A before the purchase of the duplex was arranged. Here, the court might consider Buyer C as an agent of Owner A, using Owner A's money to buy the duplex. Therefore, clients should obtain competent tax advice before closing any multiple exchange sales.

POINTS TO REMEMBER

Clearly, there are opportunities in specializing in rental housing sales because in most communities there are some who, because of their special circumstances, actively seek rental housing. Similarly, in established neighborhoods the economic position of the seller may recommend renting, not sale. There are others who prefer to acquire qualified rental housing for investment purposes.

For the most part, the buyers of rental housing are individuals who capitalize on the tax shelter provided by housing investments. If you are presenting a house to a prospect who has these buying motives, show the tax advantages by deducting from the gross rent the operating expenses, depreciation allowances, mortgage interest, and property taxes.

Show the tax advantages in reporting accelerated depreciation over straight-line depreciation—for existing houses, 125 percent depreciation based on straight-line rates and declining balance depreciation. If the property indicates a tax shelter, show how the benefits increase as the income tax rate of the buyer increases.

Few houses available for rent under present mortgage terms provide much allowance for annual maintenance, repair, and replacement expenses as operating expenses. If these expenditures must be made, they reduce the profitability (or increase tax shelter) or, to make the investment economic, they must add to capital appreciation.

It will be appreciated that buyers of rental housing may be motivated by capital appreciation, which is taxed at ordinary income tax rates on 40 percent of the realized gain. Investors in the higher income tax brackets may be motivated by the more favorable treatment of capital gains compared to taxes on ordinary income, which are progressive and higher. Therefore, prospects in the market for rental housing may be motivated by the tax shelter or the favorable tax treatment of property appreciation. Under certain circumstances, the tax treatment of capital gains may be deferred by an exchange.

If houses are held for investment, the seller may exchange a house for like property and defer the capital gain tax. The capital gain is deferred in the sense that the depreciable basis of the old property transfers to the acquired property. The depreciation basis is defined as the amount remaining subject to future depreciation. In the simplest case, property exchanged for the same market value, where neither party realizes a gain, would qualify as a tax-deferred exchange.

Usually, real estate exchanges cover two properties having different market values. Usually, one party or the other must make up the difference in market value or equities with a cash payment. Cash payments are referred to as boot. Boot, however, may be represented by money or other assets transferred as part of the exchange. Realtors® must distinguish between the *realized gain,* which is the market value of the property received less the depreciable basis of the property given up, and *recognized gain,* which is the gain reported for capital gain taxes. As a general rule, when an exchange on mortgaged property is made, the law treats the mortgage given up in exchange as equal to receiving cash in like amount. Similarly, traders who accept a mortgage on an acquired property are considered to give boot equal to the amount of the mortgage assumed and cash paid.

Multiple exchanges include the exchange of two properties involving a cash sale. If a cash buyer is available to purchase one of the properties to be exchanged, a sale may be arranged so that a three-party exchange takes place. In the end, the cash buyer acquires the desired property and the parties to the exchange complete the purchase and sale through a tax-deferred exchange.

REVIEW QUESTIONS

1. What factors determine the demand for rental housing?
2. What market forces affect the supply of rental housing?
3. What tax advantages are enjoyed by an investor who purchases a home for rental purposes?
4. Show by an example how you would calculate tax shelter.

5. Give an example showing how accelerated depreciation would be taxed under recapture provisions.

6. Show by an example how you would calculate total tax payable for a rental house subject to capital gain taxes and depreciation recapture.

7. What are the requirements for a tax-deferred exchange?

8. What is meant by property of "like kind?"

9. Explain the difference between realized gain and recognized gain.

10. Give an example of capital gain tax calculations where a boot is received.

11. How is mortgaged property treated under a tax-deferred exchange?

12. Show how you would arrange a three-party exchange involving a cash sale.

Index